Making Foreign Investment Safe

Making Foreign Investment Safe

Property Rights and National Sovereignty

Louis T. Wells
Rafiq Ahmed

OXFORD
UNIVERSITY PRESS

2007

OXFORD
UNIVERSITY PRESS

Oxford University Press, Inc., publishes works that further
Oxford University's objective of excellence
in research, scholarship, and education.

Oxford   New York
Auckland   Cape Town   Dar es Salaam   Hong Kong   Karachi
Kuala Lumpur   Madrid   Melbourne   Mexico City   Nairobi
New Delhi   Shanghai   Taipei   Toronto

With offices in
Argentina   Austria   Brazil   Chile   Czech Republic   France   Greece
Guatemala   Hungary   Italy   Japan   Poland   Portugal   Singapore
South Korea   Switzerland   Thailand   Turkey   Ukraine   Vietnam

Copyright © 2007 by Oxford University Press

Published by Oxford University Press, Inc.
198 Madison Avenue, New York, New York 10016

www.oup.com

Oxford is a registered trademark of Oxford University Press

Library of Congress Cataloging-in-Publication Data
Wells, Louis T.
Making foreign investment safe : property rights and national
sovereignty / Louis T. Wells and Rafiq Ahmed.
p.   cm.
Includes index.
ISBN-13 978-0-19-531062-7
ISBN 0-19-531062-4
1. Investments, Foreign—Indonesia—Case studies.   2. Infrastructure (Economics)—
Indonesia.   3. Government ownership—Indonesia.   4. Right of property—Indonesia.
5. Arbitration, International.   I. Ahmad, Rafiq.   II. Title.
HG5752.W45 2006
332.67'309598—dc22   2006003813

9   8   7   6   5   4   3   2   1

Printed in the United States of America
on acid-free paper

To our wives, Ellen and Soraya,
whose patience with our project held to the end,
which they sometimes doubted would ever come.

Acknowledgments

We benefited greatly from discussions with or comments from Rawi E. Abdelal, Constance E. Bagley, Benjamin C. Esty, David Hawes, José A. Gómez-Ibáñez, Stephen J. Kobrin, Donald J. Lecraw, Henry Lee, Jeffrey Meller, Theodore H. Moran, David A. Moss, David N. Smith, Gerald T. West, participants in James K. Sebenius's negotiations seminar at Harvard Business School, and anonymous reviewers who responded to Oxford University Press's call. We were helped by the back-and-forth on Thomas Wälde's Internet mailing lists (ENATRES and OGEMID), especially by the well-argued points of Mark Kantor. We were deeply influenced by Raymond Vernon's ideas, although he can no longer make corrections. As an intern, Jessica Leight did superb Web-based research at the beginning of the study of electric power. Another intern, Jeff Shiozaki, and research associate Barbara Zepp later checked sources and followed up with further Web-based research. Mary Helen Spooner provided very useful editorial help mid-project. To be sure, some of those we thank disagree with us; they nevertheless sharpened our arguments.

We thank all those advisors, government officials, managers of private and state-owned firms, professionals at multilateral organizations, journalists, and others involved in the events who agreed to be interviewed in connection with our research. A number of those individuals are mentioned in the text. In other cases, they preferred to remain anonymous. Two of those anonymous sources were especially helpful not only in providing information but also in reading and correcting drafts. They will be able to identify themselves.

Finally, Rafiq Ahmed expresses deep gratitude to the Freeman School of Business, particularly Professor John M. Trapani, for encouragement to keep the book project alive. Of the Freeman School's staff, Clara Holmes merits special mention for her help with transcripts of recorded interviews. Louis Wells thanks the Harvard Institute for International Development for his experience over a 30-year period in Indonesia, the Harvard Business School for research support, and the Centre for Strategic and International Studies in Jakarta for space and administrative assistance while he was conducting interviews.

Contents

Making Foreign Investment Safe

Introduction

The New York mail carrier brought a disturbing letter to a division president of International Telephone & Telegraph (ITT): "Indonesia proposes to enter into negotiations for the purchase of PT Indosat. . . ." Until the Indonesian minister's letter arrived, management at ITT had spotted nothing to suggest that another of the powerful conglomerate's overseas subsidiaries was about to be nationalized. But this was in 1980. Over the next decade, the world community tried to construct a new system that would end unilateral revisions of countries' commitments to foreign investors and the nationalization of their projects. The assurances included a greatly expanded role for arbitration of disputes, broader coverage under official political risk insurance, and more home government support for investors. Nevertheless, in January 1998 managers at U.S.-based CalEnergy discovered that a presidential decree had "suspended" agreements for its geothermal power plants in Indonesia. These two events, separated by 18 years, ought to make managers wonder whether foreign investment is really any more secure now than it was in the past.

The 1998 collapse of CalEnergy's costly investment in Indonesia was not an isolated event. With almost unbridled enthusiasm for the emerging markets, in the 1990s inexperienced firms from rich countries had jumped directly into huge projects for infrastructure in some of the world's least developed countries.[1] This time managers trusted that new guarantees—as well as new forms of corruption—would protect them from the waves of conflicts and nationalizations that had overtaken similar investments in the past. Yet within only a few years, business pages of the world press were reporting an exploding number of disputes between foreign investors and governments in Argentina, Bolivia, the Czech Republic, India, Turkey, Indonesia, the Philippines, Pakistan, and elsewhere. As many as two-thirds of the private power projects that had been negotiated in the 1990s were renegotiated by 2005.[2] As the bonanzas forecast by investors proved elusive and the guarantees turned out to be weaker than managers had anticipated, many foreign investors became disenchanted with emerging markets. So bad were the outcomes of several investments that a few notable infrastructure firms came close to bankruptcy. Several others hurriedly fled poor countries as projects soured. Our stories of some of these investments explain the failures and offer lessons to managers about how to make their foreign investments more secure.

In some of the emerging markets themselves, disenchantment with foreign investment was even greater than on the investor side. Private investors were expected to earn reasonable returns for assuming various risks. Yet in many cases the agreements promised investors huge returns while, it seemed, governments assumed most of the risks. A foreign lawyer familiar with Indonesia described private investment in electric power: "As Indonesia sees it, they have been robbed blind by the system at the hands of those who are highly adept at manipulating it" (pers. comm.). In many countries, public opinion of private investment in infrastructure turned hostile as the calendar of the International Centre for the Settlement of Investment Disputes became clogged with claims. A few governments attempted to frustrate the new international assurances, issuing bold statements that they would not honor international arbitration awards. In one of our stories, a disillusioned government is alleged to have kidnapped an arbitrator. In the strife, non-government organizations (NGOs)[3] have attacked the official insurance agencies of the rich countries for supporting commerce—and sometimes corruption—over the needs of the poor. The stories we relate explore big-power politics, corruption and political influence, poor organization, and, on occasion, perhaps incompetence that led to some rather one-sided deals. By learning from these cases, officials can avoid repeating their mistakes.

The World Bank and other development-oriented institutions had counted on foreign private funds to pay for the power, clean water, transport, and telecommunications projects that are so essential for development and the relief of poverty. Turning to markets to serve the poor sounded good, but proponents had not reckoned with the destruction that bad deals would yield. Privatization was oversold, as development institutions paid little attention to what was needed to make it work. In the end, the World Bank would wonder where investment for infrastructure and other needs would come from for the twenty-first century. The institutions encouraged new assurances to investors, but those assurances incorporated the seeds of their own destruction. The assurances can and should be reformed in the interest of development, but also that of business.

In this nonfiction account of business, government, and development, our stories draw on law, economics, and politics. Some readers might consider these to be dry subjects, but some of the events we describe—an extramarital affair, an alleged kidnapping, a murder threat, bribery, and conflicts of interest—as well as some of the parties involved, including the U.S. Central Intelligence Agency and shadowy and powerful companies run by ex-soldiers and dentists, might seem like the stuff of pulp fiction. These are not irrelevant anecdotes to jazz up the stories. Rather, all of them are essential to an understanding of the high-stake negotiations and disputes.

The New International Property Rights

Running through the book is concern about a fundamental issue: property rights, including enforcement of contract.[4] Developing countries alone cannot make credible commitments to foreign investors. As sovereign nations, they can always renege on promises, and have often done so by insisting that investment terms be renegotiated or by nationalizing projects. To overcome the inability of a sovereign to provide binding guarantees, in recent decades external parties have stepped in with assurances to foreign investors. It seems, however, that efforts to protect investors' property rights have gone astray. As governments have challenged new assurances for not being responsive to their legitimate interests, investors have found them less useful and reliable than they expected. The resulting tensions threaten not only business and development but also healthy relations between nations.

Arbitration

One very important and expanding part of the new assurances for investors has been a system of state-authorized private justice: international arbitration. Before the mid-1980s, arbitration had been available to only a few foreign investors, and awards were difficult to collect. This had changed by the 1990s. Access, rules, and enforcement are now covered by a network of international treaties among nations. As a result, arbitration is becoming available to almost any foreign investor who believes it has been mistreated by a host government. And the number of cases "on trial" has shot up accordingly.

Official Political Risk Insurance

Investors' new rights are also supported by expanded political risk insurance from home governments and multilateral organizations. Official political risk insurance has been offered at least since the Marshall Plan of the post–World War II period, but at the outset it provided little protection against "creeping expropriation," the modern risk of gradual changes to the terms under which investors commit their funds. In practice, this has changed over the past two decades.

Home Government Support

The 1990s also saw an increased willingness on the part of home governments—especially that of the United States—to intervene abroad to protect their investors. Although the U.S. government had rarely hesitated to intervene in the late nineteenth and early twentieth centuries,[5] between World War II and the 1990s it did fairly little to defend its overseas investors. Reticence ended when victory in the Cold War erased fears that intervention would push host countries to the communist side. As we will show, official insurance or government export credit has added to pressures on home governments to support investors.

Future of the System

The new international protections for foreign investment are quite unlike the rules of the World Trade Organization (WTO) that govern international trade. The system for investment is not the result of a broad multilateral accord. Moreover, it includes neither the trade organization's rich legislation nor its dispute settlement tools. As a result, global investment rules lack mechanisms to generate a socially and politically responsive body of international civil or common law.

Still, the new international property rights supported the general investor euphoria of the 1990s. Looking to the new assurances, and with a herd mentality, firms from the industrialized countries leapt on the much-touted golden opportunities in infrastructure across Asia, Latin America, and to a lesser extent Africa. Enthusiasm for foreign investment seized many capital-starved Third-World governments as well; it seemed an easy solution not only to a shortage of capital but also to the problems of poorly run state-owned companies. The period was one of great excitement, accompanied by some rather odd behavior: competitive struggles among Third-World countries to attract foreign capital, wildly optimistic profit projections by managers, and unquestioned devotion to private investment by multilateral financial institutions.

In such conditions, mistakes of judgment were almost inevitable, and so were some eventual disputes. The scale, the frequency, and the geographic spread of the disputes that emerged, however, have been much greater than the inevitable collapse of euphoria would suggest. In a number of developing countries, private investment in infrastructure, once touted as salvation for these capital-short nations, turned into catastrophe.

The disputes exposed the weaknesses in the new property rights for foreign investors. By 2005, the system was faltering. The new rights had proved far too rigid in the face of dramatic economic events such as the Argentine and the Asian currency crises, and they were too politically charged for governments concerned about sovereignty. As external parties tried to hold Indonesia to strict views of its electric power contracts, one foreign lawyer asked us, "The injustice screams out. Is a contract more sacred than the well being of the fourth largest populace on the planet?" (pers. comm.). If external guarantees try to override legitimate national interests, they will fail.

We will argue that not only were rights interpreted inflexibly, but outcomes proved unpredictable, access to protections was asymmetric, and the assurances were fraught with the kinds of destructive "moral hazards" that are so often associated with insurance.

Even in the United States, perhaps the leading proponent of new investor protections, politicians were having second thoughts as foreign investors in the United States used the new rights to challenge decisions made within America's own borders.

The new international system has become so different from property rights in the industrialized countries that, we suggest, it will collapse unless it is revised. Collapse will make foreign investors hesitate to invest in useful projects in the developing world.

The Broader Issue of Property Rights

Property rights lie at the heart of a capitalist system, as the popular writings of Hernando De Soto have pointed out.[6] De Soto is most often cited for his work on the poor, especially in urban areas of developing countries. Without clear title, the poor cannot use their land or housing as security to raise funds for business investment. Concern about property rights is much broader, of course, and it is not misplaced.[7] As many writers have said, capitalism cannot succeed unless firms have reasonable confidence that their physical property and contracts will be safe.

To be sure, as long as development is slow and outsiders are not involved, some entrepreneurs have always found ways to protect their contracts and investments even in countries without legal guarantees similar to those of the West. For example, domestic entrepreneurs co-opt politically powerful figures into their businesses. Similarly, ethnic and family ties may provide protection. In Indonesia, a symbiotic relationship between officials and ethnic Chinese businessmen supported unwritten assurances and years of rapid economic growth. When foreign investors arrive, however, they struggle for protection within systems that differ from what they know at home. Some form joint ventures with influential local partners for protection, but such traditional approaches turn out to be unhelpful to both foreign and local investors if there are shifts in political power. Eventually, economic growth can falter as old and less widely understood methods of protection discourage new kinds of investors, such as those from abroad.

We agree with De Soto that clearer property rights can enable urban dwellers of the Third World to raise capital. But most proposals for reform of property rights in emerging markets implicitly assume that stronger rights are always better. We will argue that workable and lasting property rights are more complicated. Meaningful rights are essential, but rights cannot be treated as absolute. The problems with the system to protect foreign investors suggest caution when it comes to more general recommendations for property rights in developing countries. If the construction of broader property rights aims to establish absolute rights, it will fail for domestic investors, as it is failing for foreign investment.

In fact, in some cases the problem with traditional property rights is not that they are too weak but exactly the opposite: They are too inflexible for the needs of a modern economy. Thus, where small communities hold clear rights to land they have farmed for generations, the issue may not be their lack of rights, but the rigidity of those rights. Banks are unwilling to lend when borrowers' rights keep lenders from foreclosing on pledged property. Similarly, owners of property may not be willing to surrender their rights for national development ends such as mining, roads, or other infrastructure.[8] The rigidity sometimes emerges from deep-rooted traditions and beliefs connected with ownership,[9] but often the problem is simpler. In many places, the judicial process inspires little confidence that property will be taken only when there is a genuine national interest and that compensation will be fair. Fearing takings designed only to enrich foreign firms or local elites, traditional owners fight to hold onto property, even when the national good is truly at stake. If some flexibility in rights is to be accepted for development goals, property owners must have confidence that the property rights system will protect them from unreasonable seizure and compensate them adequately when seizure is justified. Property rights—for both foreign and domestic investors—need to be interpreted in the context of broader national interests; at the same time, investors must believe that they will be treated fairly in the process.

Privatization, Business Strategy, and Negotiations

Our case histories offer more than lessons on property rights and contractual relationships. Although our research is not structured to provide a thorough evaluation of privatization, the stories raise questions about the enthusiasm with which certain kinds of privatization were embraced by governments and multilateral institutions in the late twentieth century. By the end of the book, the reader should be convinced that ITT's investment in Indonesia's telecommunications was beneficial, but that same reader may doubt whether Indonesia gained at all by turning to private investors to expand its capacity to generate electricity.

The different ways our investors handled similar crises point out the importance of managers' experience, overall corporate strategy, and even a company's nationality when investors face problems in the Third World. Host governments have paid far too little attention to these factors when they deal with investors. Moreover, business managers themselves may not always understand thoroughly their own interests and limitations. A better grasp of the relationship between corporate behavior and management of crises can make for better decisions overall.

Our stories will also help the reader learn how major negotiations and renegotiations between big businesses and Third-World governments are conducted. Managers of both multinationals and development institutions have frequently failed to understand government decision making. Adding to the usual complexity of government organizations, we will show, are the varied roles that foreign advisors and (with increasing democratization) political opposition, labor, the press, NGOs, and even regional governments play in Third-World business negotiations.

The Choice of Events

Changing Views

The period that separates the investments we describe witnessed dramatic changes in attitudes toward the roles of private investment in the Third World. The 1980 takeover of ITT in Indonesia marked the end of an era. In the early part of the twentieth century, a large part of the infrastructure in the developing world had been built and owned by private, usually foreign, investors. From the 1960s until 1980, however, private investors had seen most of their infrastructure projects transferred into state hands. Between 1950 and 1975, for example, the share of electricity generated by privately owned utilities had declined from 67% to 10%.[10] A fate no better awaited many foreign-owned mines in the developing world.

But new attitudes toward the market and foreign investment began to spread in the late 1980s and early 1990s. Emerging countries eagerly marketed themselves as sites for foreign investment. The sharp change in attitude led to the return of private investment to infrastructure and other large projects. History may repeat itself: By the end of our analysis, this cycle of private investment in infrastructure seemed to be on the wane.

Our first story is of the investment made by very experienced ITT in Indonesia to build the country's new satellite link for international telecommunications. The investment, negotiated in 1967, proved very profitable until its 1980 nationalization. This is a classic story of an investor entering a politically sensitive industry in a risky country. The company had little protection beyond the very important fact that the host government recognized that a foreign owner was offering technology that the country lacked and few other investors could bring. ITT's profitable 13-year run for its money brought benefits to Indonesia, but Indonesia finally nationalized the project. By carefully handling the nationalization, the government acquitted itself well, losing no respect in the international business community. In fact, almost no one but those directly involved has heard of this story. Indosat's profitable survival for almost a decade and a half illustrates a traditional way of protecting foreign investment—and the one that still offers investors the most security. Further, the company's graceful exit from the project provides lessons for today's managers who wish to continue to profit in emerging markets.

The second set of cases is selected from the 27 electricity-generating facilities that Indonesia negotiated almost three decades later, in the mid-1990s. These investors brought no special technology that might offer protection. Unlike ITT, the power projects relied on external assurances—the new international property rights—for security against host-government actions. Investors also hoped that a more modern form of co-opting political influence might add protection. Yet the power plants were not even up and running by the time disaster struck. The Asian Currency Crisis of 1997 led to the collapse of all the agreements, and a staggering number of powerful outsiders—the U.S. government and its agencies, the Japanese government, the Multilateral Investment Guarantee Agency of the World Bank Group, international arbitrators in Switzerland and The Hague, and courts of at least seven countries—were drawn into the conflict. The Indonesian government struggled internally to determine who should straighten out what became a colossal mess, but a united home front turned out to be almost impossible to build during the country's simultaneous transition to democracy.

During the strife, Indonesia feared that the investors in the 27 projects would unite against the government. In fact, they did nothing of the sort: Different investors went their own ways. In the first case we report, Paiton I, although foreign investors drew on U.S. government support to negotiate the original deal and to protect them when things turned sour, they did not use their right to arbitration or their political risk insurance. In the second case, however, the investors in Karaha Bodas carried their case to arbitration. In the third and fourth cases, CalEnergy and Enron collected on their political risk insurance from a U.S. government agency and from a member of the World Bank Group.

In the end, it seems that the investors who were committed to the power business in developing countries or to other businesses in Indonesia drew only cautiously from the new safeguards. Arbitration or insurance claims would have left so much bitterness that the investors' futures would be in jeopardy. In contrast, some other power investors appeared to have decided that their ventures into the Third World had been mistakes; they turned to the new assurances to collect what they could and run. The results of some of these bitter disputes not only have left Indonesians angry and disenchanted with the investors but also have raised questions about the fairness of the new property rights themselves.

Other changes had, of course, occurred over the 30-year period covered in our stories. The United States had passed the Foreign Corrupt Practices Act to make illegal the kind of payments that had helped ITT to obtain its agreement. Yet in some ways this was less of a change than it might seem. Rather than putting an end to private deals with government officials, the

Foreign Corrupt Practices Act led investors to new kinds of arrangements that were not covered under the Act but were at least as destructive to capitalism as the old bribes. In the cases we examine, the shady deals failed to protect foreign investors.

We will also argue that the decade or so of U.S. support for its foreign investors may well be drawing to a close. Today, the safest foreign investors in large sensitive projects appear to be those who have special assets—technology or access to markets—just like the old ITT.

Case Approach

Detailed descriptions of a few investments allow us to explore important factors that we would lose with a larger data set. The reader will see that the personalities and backgrounds of both individuals—including some rather colorful characters—and companies affect high-stake negotiations. The cases convince us that it matters whether advisors have worked together in the past, whether someone renegotiating a contract was involved in striking the original deal, whether a company's managers look down on nationals where they have invested, and whether a company has other investments in the country and rich experience in the Third World. It also matters whether a manager comes from headquarters or a product division, and whether a local partner is the son of the country's president. And it might even matter that a company manager has fallen in love with an Indonesian woman.

Focusing on one nation, Indonesia, offers some control over country variables. Further, Indonesia is an instructive example. The average incomes of this populous developing country fell in the "lower middle" category. Corruption was widespread, and law did not rule. In this environment, we explore how officials' personal interests and rivalries influenced investment outcomes, but we remember that economic growth was nevertheless rapid over most of the period. Very important, the nation underwent radical political change during the late 1990s. It struggled to replace an authoritarian government with democracy while trying to restructure its arrangements with foreign investors. In contrast to the quiet Indosat conflict, the disputes with foreign investors in the 1990s were as intense and public as those anywhere in the developing world. Democracy brought a freer press, more outspoken labor unions, more critical NGOs, and political opposition, all of which proved eager to take on what they saw as exploitive terms granted foreign investors. Democracy offers many advantages, but a restful life for investors may not be among them.

In short, although we look in detail at the events in only one country, the stories were very similar to those that occurred across the developing world in the 1990s and early 2000s. Each situation had its own twists, of course, but any reader of the business press will recognize in our stories the conflicts that erupted in Asia, Latin America, and Africa.

Heroes and Villains

It is tempting to see heroes and villains in our cases. Some readers will view the business managers as willing to bribe anyone to increase profits and unsympathetic toward a poor country caught up in an economic crisis not of its own making. In fact, in 2005 U.S. investors in one unfinished project were still trying to collect from Indonesians a sum that was more than twice the annual U.S. government aid to the country.[11] Others will see corrupt Indonesian officials as the villains, eager to make themselves rich without regard to the interests of their populace. Some will view international law firms as money grabbing while they ignored possibly intractable conflicts of interest. The same observers may see international arbitrators as unresponsive to the development interests of poor countries. Others will see multilateral institutions, such as the World Bank, as caught up in an ideological stance in favor of privatization and markets without regard to the realities in the countries they were charged with helping. Still others will see investors' home countries—in particular, the United States—as interested in ensuring the profits of their companies regardless of the cost to poor countries or even to their own broader national interests.

There is some truth in all these views. We hope that the reader will also understand that complex pressures pushed each of these actors into positions that may in the end have been damaging, but that does not necessarily mean that the actors were evil. In most cases, the actions of business managers are not difficult to explain. Faced with pressures to accelerate their firms' growth and incentive systems that downplayed risk, they did what they could to respond. Although some probably did act cynically, many of them believed that they offered better management than the Indonesian state could provide. In this, they were probably right. On the other hand, few had been trained or faced corporate incentives to think deeply about the economic consequences of their projects or their behavior. None of the managers seemed to consider the damage wrought by their decisions—especially with respect to corruption—on the capitalist system that they claimed so ardently to support.

Arbitrators did what was expected of them under precedents and rules that governed them, perhaps without a great deal of thought as to whether their technical decisions were really fair and just, or were even what they would have ruled if they had been judging similar cases inside their own countries. As foreigners to Indonesia, they were not subject to the political and social concerns that might have led them to more appropriate and development-oriented decisions.

In supporting American investors abroad in the 1990s, the U.S. government was willing to overlook corruption by its companies and to push for deals that were hardly good for development. The demands of campaign finance and budget pressures may have played a role in some rather perverse and unattractive government behavior that was contrary to broader U.S. interests.

On the other side, pervasive corruption in Indonesia can be partially explained—although not in any way forgiven—by looking to the role that the resulting funds played in propping up a political system that was stable and produced rapid economic growth for 30 years. Even then, a number of Indonesian officials, political figures, and their relatives seemed to consider their personal interests and "entitlements" to be far more important than the country's development. We offer no excuses for their self-interested behavior. It came at a great cost to the Indonesian people, and most of the guilty have never been held accountable for what they did.

We do, however, want to recognize the numerous dedicated Indonesian officials who worked long hours with a strong sense of ethics, for very little pay, and with a view to advancing the interests of their country. This was the case with a select group of professionals within the Indonesian state-owned electricity company and with certain ministers and members of their staffs. But their effectiveness was always constrained by the greedy and by a political system that depended heavily on corruption and cronyism for survival.

Similarly, several individuals in multilateral organizations spoke out for positions that they thought right, even if their voices were not always heard within their own bureaucracies. Foreign embassies also had those who tried to solve problems fairly while their official lines sometimes blatantly favored foreign investors.

In the end, investigating what drove individuals to act as they did is more helpful than are value judgments. Better understanding might lead to changes in incentives and to more constructive behavior.

Disclosure and a Note on Sources

Wells, one of the authors of this book, is a professor at Harvard Business School and served for 30 years as an advisor to the Indonesian government, mainly through the Harvard Institute for International Development (HIID),[12] but on occasion, he was hired directly by that government. He was an advisor to the 1980 Indonesian renegotiating team for the ITT agreement. Although he was a resident advisor in the Ministry of Finance in 1994 and 1995, he was only peripherally involved in electric power issues. He wrote or co-authored one or two of the very general HIID memos referred to in Chapters 8 and 11, but he was not involved in any of the individual cases.

Ahmed, the other author, worked for Exxon Corporation for some 20 years. Stationed in Indonesia from 1981 to 1986, he was first a member of a project team and then country manager for the chemical business. Afterward, he spent 18 months as a visiting scholar at Harvard Business School, at which time he wrote the original drafts of the chapters on ITT/Indosat. Later he taught and managed international programs at Tulane University's Freeman School.

In gathering material for this book, we interviewed (personally, on the phone, or occasionally by e-mail) more than 70 individuals. Indonesian officials and their advisors and the professionals from multilateral development organizations, in particular, the World Bank and the Multilateral Investment Guarantee Agency, were eager to tell their sides of the stories. However, U.S. government officials responded guardedly or sometimes not at all to invitations for interviews and to requests under the Freedom of Information Act. The responses of company managers to our efforts to collect information were, at best, mixed.

We have attempted to tell the stories as accurately as we could. We regret any errors, including those that resulted from the unwillingness of some parties to discuss the events. We believe, however, that the lessons would have differed little if we had obtained full cooperation from everyone involved.

Next, we provide two guides, one to unravel the puzzles of Indonesian names and spelling, and one as a reference for who held what position at what time.

Names and Spelling

The spelling of the Indonesian language changed in 1972. Some proper names use the earlier spelling, some use the later. Sometimes both are used by different writers to refer to the same person. Thus, Suharto and Soeharto and Ginanjar and Ginandjar are alternative spellings of the same two names. A few conversion rules can help the reader:

Old Spelling	New Spelling
Oe	U
Dj	J
J	Y (or I)
Tj	C

Westerners' confusion with Indonesian names extends beyond spelling. Some ethnic groups use family (or even clan or *marga*) names, but many others do not. Some Indonesians have only one name. Many have more than one but generally use only one, which is not easy for a foreigner to guess. For example, Professor Widjojo Nitisastro is usually known as Professor Widjojo, not as Professor Nitisastro. On the other hand, Minister Ali Wardhana is commonly reported in the press as Professor Wardhana. Moreover, many Indonesians of Chinese extraction have both Indonesian and Chinese names. A few commonly use only their Chinese name: Kwik Kian Gie, for example. Others use the Chinese name much of the time but the Indonesian name on occasion: Liem Sioe Liong and Sudono Salim. Although we have tried for consistency and what we believe to be common usage, we may have erred in some cases.

Unsurprisingly, the names of ministries and other government offices are occasionally translated differently. Moreover, some names changed slightly over the period we cover. To reduce confusion, we have tried to stick with one name throughout the book. Thus, the exact name at a particular time may differ slightly from the translation we use.

Officials of Frequently Mentioned Government Entities

Information about ministers came primarily from "Indonesian Cabinet 1945–2001" and "Profile of the Cabinet."[13] We made some corrections to these documents from the embassy in London.

Heads of State

Sukarno: Independence–1967

Suharto: Effectively took over power in 1965; president from 1968–May 1998

B. J. Habibie: May 1998–October 1999

Abdurrahman Wahid (Gus Dur): October 1999–July 22, 2001

Megawati Sukarnoputri: July 23, 2001–October 2004

Sisilo Bambang Yudhoyono: October 2004–

Ministers of Finance

Ali Wardhana: March 10, 1968–March 16, 1983

Radius Prawiro: March 17, 1983–March 20, 1988

J. B. Sumarlin: March 21, 1988–March 16, 1993

Mar'ie Muhammad: March 17, 1993–March 13, 1998

Fuad Bawazier: March 14, 1998–May 21, 1998

Bambang Subianto: May 22, 1998–October 25, 1999

Bambang Sudibyo: October 26, 1999–August 22, 2000

Prijadi Praptosuhardjo: August 23, 2000–June 11, 2001

Rizal Ramli: June 12, 2001–August 8, 2001

Boediono: August 9, 2001–October 20, 2004

Jusuf Anwar: October 21, 2004–

State Ministers of Research and Technology

B. J. Habibie: March 29, 1978–March 13, 1998

Rahardi Ramelan: March 14, 1998–May 21, 1998

Zuhal: May 22, 1998–October 25, 1999

A. S. Hikam: October 26, 1999–August 8, 2001

M. Hatta Rajasa: August 9, 2001–

Ministers of Mines and Energy

Moh. Sadli: March 27, 1973–March 28, 1978

Subroto: March 29, 1978–March 20, 1988

Ginandjar Kartasasmita: March 21, 1988–March 16, 1993

I. B. Sudjana: March 17, 1993–March 13, 1998

Kuntoro Mangkusubroto: March 14, 1998–October 25, 1999

Susilo Bambang Yudhoyono: October 26, 1999–August 22, 2000

Purnomo Yusgiantoro: August 23, 2000–

Ministers with State Enterprise Portfolios

Tanri Abeng: March 14, 1998–October 25, 1999

Rozy Munir: October 26, 1999–August 22, 2000

Laksamana Sukardi: October 26, 1999–June 2000

Rozy Munir: June 2000–August 8, 2001

Laksamana Sukardi: August 9, 2001–October 20, 2004

Soegiarto: October 21, 2004–

Heads of the National Planning Board (BAPPENAS)

Widjojo Nitisastro: 1967–March 15, 1983

J. B. Sumarlin: March 16, 1983–March 20, 1988

Saleh Afiff: March 21, 1988–March 16, 1993

Ginandjar Kartasasmita: March 17, 1993–May 21, 1998

Boediono: May 22, 1998–August 8, 2001

Kwik Gian Gie: August 9, 2001–October 20, 2004

Sri Mulyani Indrawati: October 21, 2004–

Coordinating Ministers with Economic Portfolios

Ali Wardhana: March 16, 1983–March 20, 1988

Radius Prawiro: March 21, 1988–March 16, 1993

Saleh Afiff: March 17, 1993–March 13, 1998

Ginandjar Kartasasmita: March 14, 1998–October 25, 1999

Kwik Kian Gie: October 26, 1999–August 22, 2000

Rizal Ramli: August 23, 2000–June 11, 2001

Burhanaddin Abdullah: June 12, 2001–August 8, 2001

Dorodjatun Kuntjoro-Jakti: August 9, 2001–October 20, 2004

Aburizal Bakrie: October 21, 2004–

Coordinating Minister for Industry and Trade

Hartarto Sastrosoenarto: March 17, 1993–March 13, 1998 (Minister of Industry, March 16, 1983–March 16, 1993)

Coordinating Minister for Development Supervision and State Administrative Reforms

Hartarto Sastrosoenarto: March 14, 1998–October 25, 1999

CEOs of the State-Owned Electric Power Company (PLN)

Ermansyah Jamin: 1988–April 1992

Zuhal: April 1992–1995–January 1995

Djiteng Marsudi: January 1995–July 1998

Adhi Satrya (Satriya): July 1998–January 2000

Kuntoro Mangkusubroto: January 2000–March 2001

Eddie Widiono: March 2001–

U.S. Ambassadors to Indonesia

Marshall Green: 1965–1969

Francis J. Galbraith: 1969–1974

David D. Newsom: 1974–1977

Edward E. Masters: 1977–1981

John H. Holdridge: 1982–1986

Paul D. Wolfowitz: 1986–1989

John C. Monjo: 1990–1992

Robert L. Barry: 1992–1995

J. Stapleton Roy: 1996–1999

Robert S. Gelbard: 1999–2001

Ralph Leo Boyce: 2001–2004

Part I

State Takeover of Infrastructure, 1967–1980

1

Indosat: Foreign Investment in a Risky Environment

It is an immutable law in business that words are words, explanations are explanations, promises are promises—but only performance is reality.
—Harold S. Geneen, former Chairman, International
   Telephone and Telegraph[1]

O ur first story opens in 1967. At the time, International Telephone and Telegraph (ITT) belonged to a small group of pioneer firms that were negotiating their way into "New Order" Indonesia—the world's fifth most populous country.[2] How this company profited from its project, even without modern external investment guarantees, offers lessons for investors that are especially valid today, when managers are discovering that new assurances from multilateral institutions and home governments offer less safety than they promised.

To ITT's managers, the risk must have seemed stupendous. Under General Sukarno, the previous regime had expropriated foreign investments. The nation had just undergone a violent upheaval, with perhaps hundreds of thousands dead from the political turmoil. That the legal system and the courts were underdeveloped and corrupt is a dramatic understatement.[3] In sum, Indonesia itself offered very little assurance of property rights for an incoming foreign investor. Nevertheless, ITT dared to invest and profited handsomely, and for a substantial period.

Indonesia in the 1960s

Indonesia proclaimed independence from its Dutch colonial rulers on August 17, 1945. Subsequent armed struggle and eloquent appeals to the United Nations finally led to international recognition of Indonesia's statehood in December 1949.

During the first two decades of self-rule, the government worked to build a nation out of some 13,000 islands and at least 300 ethnic groups, bound together by little more than common colonial rule. The country's first president, Sukarno, turned ever more inward, with an import-substitution strategy, state-ownership of industry, nationalization of foreign-owned firms, and withdrawal from the United Nations, the World Bank, and the International Monetary Fund. Sukarno declared a state of "confrontation" against Malaysia, Indonesia's neighbor, and eventually most foreigners were, as a practical matter, expelled. Indonesia was being called "an economist's nightmare"[4] and "the number one failure among the underdeveloped countries."[5] In terms of normal economic indices, these pronouncements were hardly exaggerations. By 1965, the annual inflation rate stood at 500% to 1,000%,[6] per-capita income was probably lower than that of 1938, and arrears on the country's foreign debt were growing. Exports in 1966 were perhaps half of those of 1951.[7] Industry operated at some 20% of capacity, 80% of the textile mills in parts of Java had completely closed down, and even production of rice—Indonesia's staple—had dropped below the 1935 to 1939 average.[8]

Foreign capital was frightened away by a wave of nationalizations and the maltreatment of foreign businessmen. A foreigner's property, be it business or personal, had been subject to seizure at any time.[9]

Out of the deadly upheaval in 1965 that ended Sukarno's reign,[10] General Suharto eventually emerged as the dominant authority, with Sukarno formally yielding power to him in March 1966. A year later, Suharto officially took the title of President.

Repairing the economy and regaining the confidence and support of the international community were the top priorities of the new government. Unlike some other Third World leaders, Suharto was not the product of the socialist philosophies of European academic institutions in the 1920s and 1930s. There were no ideological imperatives, just a job to be done—pulling Indonesia out of the economic quagmire—and Suharto went about it with the determination of a soldier as he embraced the pragmatic market orientation espoused by his economic advisors. (See Box 1.1.)

"The basic objective of Indonesia's current economic policy," explained Professor Widjojo Nitisastro, chairman of the National Development Planning Board (BAPPENAS), "is to secure a breathing space of a few years.... It is essential that during this period Indonesia should receive sufficient assistance from abroad and that it should be spared the burden of excessive foreign debt servicing."[11] The heavy emphasis on economic development and foreign participation marked the beginning of the "New Order" in Indonesia.

In quick succession, Indonesia rejoined the United Nations, the World Bank, and the International Monetary Fund (IMF), and promptly became a member of the newly formed Asian Development Bank (ADB). Hostilities with Malaysia were ended. With some assistance from foreign

---

Box 1.1 The Berkeley Mafia

Rather quickly, Suharto turned to the economics faculty of the University of Indonesia. Starting in 1956, the Ford Foundation had invested heavily in the department to train future professors, sponsoring overseas graduate work in cooperation with the University of California at Berkeley for the most promising students. It was from these professors that Suharto chose his key economic ministers.

Sumitro Djojohadikkusumo, a one-time minister of finance, had become dean of the economics faculty early on, but he had fled the country as a result of his involvement in an abortive revolt of outer islands in the mid-1950s. By the time Suharto ascended to power, Widjojo Nitisastro headed the faculty group. The new president quickly brought Sumitro back from exile to head the trade ministry and appointed Widjojo to lead a new planning agency.

These and the other economic technocrats eventually became known as the "Berkeley Mafia,"[a] and they will appear frequently in subsequent chapters. However, their influence would not remain unchallenged, as we shall see.

[a]Named by David Ramson in *Ramparts* [magazine] in October 1970 after the California university where Widjojo had received his Ph.D. The story of the Ford Foundation's program and biographical sketches of some of the principal technocrats appear in the very readable Goenawan Mohamad et al., *Celebrating Indonesia: Fifty Years with the Ford Foundation 1953–2003* (New York: The Ford Foundation, 2003).

---

advisors, the economic technocrats successfully rescheduled the country's debt and received fresh credits totaling some $1 billion. At the same time, the new government took steps to settle claims of past foreign investors, reaching an overall settlement in the case of Dutch investors and returning other properties to their former owners. With the socialist-leaning Sukarno gone, the United States and the World Bank embraced the Suharto government as a steady "domino" in a region shaking from war that threatened to spill over the borders of Vietnam.

Suharto invited new foreign investors to the country. Professor M. Sadli, chairman of the Indonesian investment board, reported that "The country needs not only capital but also a fresh infusion of managerial skills and up-to-date technology."[12] Indonesia was not an easy place for foreign business people, however (see Box 1.2). In an effort to attract investors, in January 1967 the government promulgated a foreign investment law.[13] Among other attractions, it provided for as much as a five-year holiday from corporate income taxes; allowed employment of

---

Box 1.2 Jakarta of the 1960s

In the 1960s, American investors would arrive in Jakarta—once called Batavia—at an airport that was almost in the city itself. Its dark, paneled terminal housed hungry customs officials who would look for a small gift from arriving passengers. A jar or two of jam would get an American through, but ethnic Chinese arrivals were "taxed" more. Exiting the terminal, the visitor faced a number of decrepit 1950s cars, mostly American or Australian, with no indication that they were taxis. Without meters, drivers negotiated, and the executive could expect his taxi to break down a couple of times before it reached its likely destination, the Hotel Indonesia.

Built in 1962, the Hotel Indonesia, managed by Intercontinental and featured in the 1982 movie *The Year of Living Dangerously* (although that movie was not actually filmed in Indonesia), was, by today's standards, rather sparse and boring. Yet, with the exception of one hotel that catered to Japanese businessmen, there simply was no other international-standard hotel in Jakarta. Reservations at HI, as it was nicknamed, had to be made a month or two in advance because business (and aid) people were flocking to the newly opened country. The big event for foreigners was HI's Sunday evening buffets, which offered Western food—scarce at the time in Indonesia—that had just (the eater hoped) arrived by air from Europe.

Exiting HI, a visitor would be surrounded by pedicab (*becak*) operators shouting "Hey Mister, where are you going?", a literal translation of the common Indonesian greeting *ke mana*. Traffic was unheard of, except for occasional jams in the dense old part of the city where pedicabs could block the narrow streets—luckily, because sending a car and driver with a message provided the visiting executive with an alternative to local telephones, which rarely worked. Development would change all this.

---

foreign personnel; exempted machinery, equipment, and initial plant supplies from import duties; guaranteed transfer of profits, depreciation of fixed assets, and compensation in case of nationalization; and spelled out procedures for arbitration of certain disputes. The law closed some fields of activities to the full control of foreigners: "those of importance to the country and in which the lives of a great many people are involved."[14] Although the new law sounded good, any potential investor must have recognized that laws can be changed again by the same or a subsequent government. Moreover, laws have little power when courts are corrupt. In other words, the new promises of property rights were not very credible, and they could not be made so by the Indonesian government alone.

Nevertheless, within 18 months of the law's enactment, some 70 foreign companies signed up, with combined potential investment estimated at $300 to $400 million.[15] At the top of the list, negotiating before the law was even passed, was ITT[16]—and it got more than the law seemed to permit, as we shall see.

The Indosat Project

For an archipelago nation stretching some 3,200 miles from east to west and about 1,100 miles from north to south, some kind of communications network is essential. Unfortunately, the economic misrule of the Sukarno regime had left rail, road, and sea systems in complete disarray, and "the state of telecommunications left much to be desired. . . . High frequency radio equipment was still in use, and 24-hour service was not yet available; communications between cities were difficult and with isolated areas virtually impossible."[17] Telephone calls to the United States were booked a day or two in advance in the hopes of getting a line.

Satellite systems could solve the problem for international communications, but Indonesia had neither the capabilities nor the funds to organize and run the equipment required by the International Telecommunications Satellite Union (INTELSAT).[18] It would have to turn to a foreign firm. And there were few candidates. ITT and Siemens were possibilities.

The Indonesian government sent representatives to INTELSAT's periodic meetings. In an Australian round, George Mausch, a representative of ITT World Communications, met Indonesia's director general of posts and telecommunications, General Soehardjono, who mentioned the idea of a satellite communications facility in Indonesia and sought ITT's help. He proposed that ITT pay for the facility and turn it over to the Indonesian government, which would then lease it back to ITT to operate and manage.

ITT was interested. "We did some internal studies based on whatever sketchy data were available and came to the conclusion that investment in Indonesia was justified—because we thought the country was going to boom," Derrick W. Samuelson, assistant general counsel of ITT Corporation, told us. The ensuing discussions led to the signing of a "Memorandum of Understanding" on September 12, 1966. ITT would become a subcontractor under lease from the government, and the government would "designate this satellite terminal as *the sole facility* [italics added] to participate in the INTELSAT system," provide "protection for the ITT investment," and allow "adequate return on investment."

As the future would show, however, the protection of ITT's property rights would lie more in its "unique capability," as the letter described ITT's input, than in any contract or the soon to be passed foreign investment law.

ITT

ITT's recent policies had been shaped by its extraordinary and controversial chief executive, Harold S. Geneen.[19] Its extensive experience in the developing world and the fact that it diversified into a wide range of industries and services differentiated ITT from most of the investors in our later stories.

In the late nineteenth and early twentieth centuries, a major portion of Latin American, African, and developing Asian telephone networks, electric power systems, and tramways had been built by foreign private investors. This boom period had created some huge and powerful companies such as ITT, American & Foreign Power (GE-related), and Societé Financiére de Transportes et d'Entreprises Industrielles (Sofina).

In the 1930s, government regulations led to several cases of "creeping expropriation." As rates were not allowed to increase with costs, many foreign owners of utilities were eager to sell their investments to governments even without an overt act of expropriation.[20] Then a growing wave of resentment against foreign direct investment in the 1960s and 1970s ended in outright nationalization of most of the remaining foreign-owned utilities.

ITT had been a part of this history. The company had been founded by Sosthenese Behn and his brother. Born in the Danish Virgin Islands, of a Danish father and a French mother, Behn was educated in Corsica and then in Paris, and began his career by brokering sugar in Puerto Rico. In settlement of a debt, he and his brother picked up a local telephone firm. They incorporated International Telephone and Telegraph Corporation in 1920, a high-sounding name for a tiny enterprise.[21]

The first big step for the company came in 1923 and 1924 when it accepted an invitation from the Spanish to run their telephone system. The result was Compañía Telefónica de España. Then, in 1925, the brothers bought the international operations of Western Electric, on the market in response to antitrust action. The young American ITT was on its way to becoming the most important multinational firm in telecommunications. It would protect its overseas operations by an arrangement with AT&T, reserving the U.S. market for AT&T in exchange for the commitment of AT&T not to compete abroad.

ITT acquired facilities in the United Kingdom and then entered Germany in 1930. In a series of cartel agreements, ITT, Siemens, Ericsson, and General Electric divided up Europe and Latin America. Soon, Behn was working with the Nazi government and collaborating with the pro-German government of Argentina. In 1943, the U.S. Federal Communications Commission concluded that ITT subsidiaries were maintaining contact with the enemy and monitoring communications by the state department.

Like many other foreign investors in infrastructure, ITT suffered setbacks in its telecommunications business after World War II. For example,

Franco nationalized the Spanish company in 1945, and Peron's Argentina took over ITT's subsidiary in 1946. ITT's Hungarian subsidiary became involved in U.S. espionage, although the full details have never been revealed.[22] The company's ties to U.S. intelligence were to continue, and to make the company into a lightning rod for protests later when it appeared to collaborate with the U.S. Central Intelligence Agency (CIA) in Chile.[23]

Behn left the company and in 1959 and was followed by Harold Geneen, who built the diversified company that was to enter Indonesia. Geneen would rule ITT tightly.

The year in which ITT signed its agreement with the government of Indonesia—1967—was the most successful in the company's 47-year history.[24] By this point, ITT was acknowledged as one of the most prominent multinational conglomerates, with such varied business interests as international communications, electronics, manufacturing, car leasing, mutual funds, and hotels. It operated in more than 50 countries and had a workforce of 204,000. In fact, ITT was poised to go on an explosive acquisition binge in the next few years and to take its place among the top 10 in the *Fortune* 500 list of companies.[25] Already by 1967, barely seven years after Geneen had become chief executive, ITT's net income had quadrupled, from $30.5 million in 1960 to $122 million in 1967.[26] Geneen himself was for many the apotheosis of professional management.

In pursuing profits, however, the company and its managers had also acquired an unusual degree of notoriety, having been accused of interference in politics abroad, possible conflicts of interest at home, insider trading, and efforts to shape U.S. foreign policy.[27] ITT's propensity to mix politics with economics led to criticism that it was growing by means of corruption, both at home and abroad. In fact, Behn once promised to pay only "a little graft" in Cuba.[28] By the time of the Indonesia negotiations, ITT's policy had not noticeably changed.

The most blatant and publicized instance of ITT's involvement in host country politics—and U.S. foreign policy—came a bit later. In 1970, the company tried to enlist the help of the CIA by offering a contribution of $1 million in a plot to prevent the election of the avowed Marxist Salvador Allende to Chile's presidency. ITT had recognized a common goal: ITT's ultimate objective was to avert expropriation of the company's Chilean investments,[29] and the United States was intent on blocking the installation of another Marxist regime in Latin America. As it turned out, the CIA probably funneled some $8 million through ITT to anti-Allende groups.[30]

In sum, ITT knew how to handle its international business. Having dealt with tough environments in the past, its management must have known what they were likely to encounter in Indonesia. But the U.S. government would not help ITT get the terms it wanted on entry nor would it help the company when it faced trouble. Later American investors would have a more cooperative home government.

Entering Indonesia

The violent events of 1965 to 1966 attracted world attention to Indonesia. The former head of ITT's Asia Pacific operations, Robert Piccus, told us that at a management meeting Geneen singled out Indonesia as a country worth paying a great deal of attention to, even though he had shown little past interest in Asia.

Other U.S. companies, such as Freeport Sulphur and Kennecott, were also optimistic and rather quickly negotiated access to Indonesian minerals. And the principal Japanese conglomerates began to arrive ready to secure local markets.

Using Gold

Although the nation was opening its doors to foreign capital, it was not easy for a foreign investor to cut through the thick bureaucratic undergrowth to obtain the scores of approvals required for new projects. Companies found "friends" and "facilitators" useful in this climate of turmoil and corruption.[31] The slightly (or more) shadowy middleman will be a familiar type to those who have done business in developing countries.[32] In some cases, they even negotiate contracts with corrupt governments and then peddle them to potential foreign investors.

One such middleman was Vladimir Gold (see Box 1.3). Because Gold had access to important officials, he could help ITT at a time when Siemens was also wooing the government. One of Gold's first assignments as a general representative was to assist with the satellite ground station project.

With no Foreign Corrupt Practices Act (FCPA) in place, payoffs were common and rarely carefully hidden.[33] Gold would handle this task for ITT. The power investors that we describe later would be subject to the FCPA, but they would also find ways to ensure that officials grew richer in exchange for favorable contracts. But in 1967 giving straight bribes to Indonesian officials did not violate U.S. laws.

According to an ITT manager, one target for payment was none other than Indonesia's respected foreign minister, Adam Malik (see Box 1.4), who seems already to have been taking payments from the U.S. embassy.[34] Author Theodore Friend expressed surprise that Malik engaged in such practices, noting that "[his] image and his eminence are hard to reconcile with his accepting a 'black bag' of money from the U.S. Embassy for the purpose of wiping out communists. But he did it."[35]

As the story was told to us,[36] ITT transferred money to Gold. Soon, however, CIA headquarters in Washington received word from an agent in Jakarta that an Indonesian VIP was very unhappy about not receiving his share of the ITT bribes.[37] To express his displeasure, Malik was quoted as threatening to "shut out ITT from all future opportunities in Indonesia." The CIA was concerned because this particular VIP had been

Box 1.3 Vladimir Gold

Vladimir Gold was a hefty, tall, blond ("fiery red hair," according to John G. Christy, former head of Far East Group, ITT) who hailed originally from Czechoslovakia. As he told it, his uncle was head of the country's central bank after World War II. In one account, he escaped to Canada in 1948 where he worked for a social club and learned to cook. From Canada he came to the United States and eventually acquired American citizenship, of which he was very proud. By his account, he was employed by the Essex Club in New York for a period before becoming the chief chef at the Waldorf Astoria hotel. In another version, his family owned a bottled water company near Prague. Having come under a P-47 machine gun attack while he was driving one of the company trucks, he fled, disguised as a nun, to Paris, where he took a job in a restaurant. Seeing an ad in the *International Herald Tribune* for a chef for the Waldorf Astoria, he applied and got the job, knowing little to nothing about "chef-ing."

Gold went to Indonesia during the turbulent 1960s. In one account, he took a job protecting the physical assets of a Dutch-owned paper plant that had been closed. In another version, he went as the agent of an American wigmaker to buy human hair. Maybe both stories are true. He also claimed to have served as a procurer for Sukarno, equally plausible.

Gold was variously described to us as sharp, very perceptive ("understood the Javanese mind"), entrepreneurial, energetic, a hustler with a touch of cunning, "one who would never come into a house from the front door if he could enter from a back window." One former ITT executive told us he had no morals at all. Gold was said to have bragged that he kept his household effects in a semi-packed state in case he had to leave in a hurry. He drank a lot ("nipped at a brandy bottle from waking to sleeping"[a]), becoming unpleasant at times.

Yet he and his wife Melata Gold were very popular hosts. The parties at their residence were well attended by the elite of Jakarta. Melata was, according to some who knew the couple, on very friendly terms with a wife (Dewi) of the first president, the wife of Foreign Minister Adam Malik, and the wife of Soehardjono, the director general of posts and telecommunications. According to one interviewee, "Melata used to bring suitcases full of goodies, not excluding hard currencies, from abroad for her friends."

[a]Theodore Friend, *Indonesian Destinies* (Cambridge: Belknap Press for Harvard University Press, 2003), p. 138.

Box 1.4 Adam Malik

Adam Malik, born in North Sumatra in 1917, became politically active early on, chairing a political party in his home region by 1934. He soon founded a press bureau, which eventually became the official state news organization, Antara. During Indonesia's struggle for independence, Malik created two new political parties. Under Sukarno, he served as a member of parliament, as minister, as ambassador to the Soviet Union and Poland, and as delegate to the United Nations Conference on Trade and Development (UNCTAD). He joined with Suharto and Sultan Hamengko Buvono IX in late 1965 to form what has been called a "ruling triumvirate." The next year he became minister of foreign Affairs, negotiating Indonesia's return to the United Nations and peace with Malaysia. He was vice president of Indonesia from 1978 to 1983 and died in 1984.

During his career, he built a highly regarded collection of Chinese porcelain, which now resides in the Jakarta Fine Arts Museum, and his former home in Jakarta has become the Museum Adam Malik, with various personal items and a small collection of artifacts from his native Batak culture. He was officially declared an Indonesian national hero in 1998.[a]

---

[a]"Adam Malik, 3 Freedom Fighters Declared Heroes," *Jakarta Post,* November 10, 1998.

---

helping the American cause in Indonesia generally. The agency therefore brought the matter to the attention of John McCone, an ex-CIA director who was on the board of ITT. The issue was finally resolved by an additional payment of half a million dollars directly, despite strong protests by Gold who persisted in his claim that he had faithfully dispensed all required payments.[38]

John (Jack) G. Christy, an ITT manager who arrived in Indonesia soon after the contract had been concluded, told us he knew nothing about this event.[39] Rather, he offered an additional story: Gold approached him on his arrival to ask for $1 million for Soehardjono, to be paid through the Singapore agent who was bringing in ITT's equipment. Surprised and offended, Christy refused, and set up a meeting with Soehardjono to tell him directly that he could not make such a payment. Christy reported that Soehardjono issued a "soft threat" of retaliation.

These events marked the beginning of the end of Gold's career with ITT. The ITT official involved in the alleged payment to Adam Malik suspected that Gold had helped himself to some of the gratuities meant for others. Offended, Gold claimed that the company had jeopardized "his effectiveness by questioning his integrity" and by resolving the issue of gratuities over his head. When Gold's contract came up for renewal, he asked that the terms be improved. ITT turned him down. Christy, by then ITT's Far East communications head, told us that he fired him. When asked about Gold, our source for the first story explained to us. "Vladimir was a great fellow, but he was, frankly, losing his mental balance because of heavy drinking. Besides, he had really outlived his utility for ITT. His type of personality was no longer helpful in Indonesia." But the manager also admitted that he was not absolutely sure that Gold had pocketed the money.

Gold left, but had a legal notice sent to ITT by Herbert Brownell, a former U.S. attorney general. Brownell had once visited Indonesia with George Brown, an ITT director, and had been lavishly entertained by Gold. The American ambassador to Jakarta,[40] career foreign service officer Francis (Frank) Galbraith, also wrote to ITT in support of Gold, commending his services and complaining that ITT had not treated him fairly. The dispute was in the end settled with Geneen's personal intervention on what were said to be very generous terms. Then Gold promptly went over to ITT competitor General Telephone and Electronics Corporation, and began to represent its interests from its Singapore offices. Not very successful for GTE, Gold went on to make some money in Sumatran timber, according to Christy, but he died fairly soon thereafter of a stroke, having just turned 40.[41]

The 40 Million Dollar Man

General Soehardjono, who had dealt with telecommunications for most of his career (see Box 1.5), provided a willing target for promoters.[42]

For a long time Soehardjono had resisted attempts to upgrade the country's domestic telephone network, which only Siemens supplied, arguing that that Indonesia should first develop an indigenous switching system to break the country's dependence on foreign systems. In reality, Soehardjono appeared to be disinclined to deal with institutions such as the World Bank for funds because their loan programs had too many monitoring devices. He was known to have frustrated World Bank negotiating teams by openly talking about his desire to buy additional thoroughbred horses. He relented only when export credit facilities were made available by donor nations for Indonesia's telecommunications expansion program, for Soehardjono could then deal directly with private businesses, which were more "flexible" than World Bank personnel.[43]

Bribes could buy a contract at that time in Indonesia. Once paid (and actually received), they might clinch the deal, but there was no guarantee whatsoever that the bribed official would continue to support the project. We will see that, by the 1990s, investors had found new tools that would avoid problems under the U.S. Foreign Corrupt Practices Act and also connect Indonesian officials more firmly to a company's longer term interests. For ITT, getting the deal was enough.

Box 1.5 General Soehardjono

General Soehardjono, born in 1913 on Java, joined the army during the Japanese occupation and built his career in signals. His daring exploits during the war of independence from the Dutch won him permanent scars in the twisted fingers of his right hand and the respect of his compatriots, including General Suharto. He was in time to rise to be a major general. He is reported to have been personally so close to President Suharto that he claimed the privilege of intervening in the First Family's domestic affairs.

In contrast to the modest and self-effacing nature of most Javanese, General Soehardjono was given to ostentation. Somewhere along the line he had also developed an expensive hobby, horse breeding. His ranch at Pamulang, outside Jakarta, bore testimony to his discerning taste for carefully collected race horses and to his wealth.

It was said that the land for the ranch was presented to him by Siemens. Whatever the truth of the allegation, Siemens did a great deal for him—and he reciprocated generously. Consider, for instance, the following anecdote: He was once with Vladimir Gold in the latter's suite at a hotel in Singapore when the telephone rang and the hotel operator put through a call from Germany. Having completed the call, Soehardjono rather casually remarked that Siemens had wanted to inform him of his student son's desire to have a Mercedes car in Germany. He added, "I told them a BMW will do."[a]

Later, in 1977, the *New York Times* published an investigative report concerning a bribery scandal for Indonesia's domestic satellite communications,[b] claiming that Soehardjono had asked General Telephone and Electronics Corporation (GTE) for a $40 million kickback on a $330 million contract. A manager reportedly asserted that, if Soehardjono had scaled down to the usual $3 million or $4 million demand, "we might have gone along."

Pertamina, the state oil company, would have a 10% interest in this contract. The GTE sales agent who met with Pertamina's director for communications was none other than Vladamir Gold. The *New York Times* added that Gold told GTE that Pertamina demanded that he, Gold, be appointed agent for this set of transactions, and that the usual money that Pertamina would receive was 30%. In the end, the contract winners were Hughes Aircraft, Philco-Ford,[c] Phillips, and Federal Electric and Bell Telephone Manufacturing of Belgium, both ITT affiliates.

---

[a]Related by William Bell.
[b]Seymour M. Hersh, "Hughes Aircraft Faces Allegation That It Used Bribery in Indonesia," *New York Times,* January 25, 1977, pp. A1, A14.
[c]This deal also created a crisis within the Ford Motor Company. As stated by Lee Iacocca in his autobiography, Ford was promised a U.S. $29 million contract by an Indonesian general to build satellite ground stations in return for a commission of $1 million. One of Iacocca's assistants was sacked—quite unfairly, in his view—because of a premature leak and the resulting adverse publicity in the American press. See Lee Iacocca, *Iacocca: An Autobiography* (New York: Bantam Books, 1984), pp. 113–114.

Agreement Reached

President Suharto himself authorized a formal agreement, signed on June 9, 1967, "with the understanding that some changes should be made in the structure of [its] contents...."[44] ITT would receive a 20-year monopoly over international telecommunications and face no effective control over the prices it could charge. The company agreed to put up about $6 million[45] for the project.

ITT felt sufficiently secure to invest, but it found a way not to put up too many dollars. According to Christy, ITT bought blocked and heavily discounted rupiah from U.S. publishers who had supplied school books to Indonesians.[46]

Lenders to the project purchased insurance for political risk from the U.S. Agency for International Development (USAID).[47] ITT's equity, however, was not protected by any carefully constructed legal system or insurance coverage. ITT's investment was safe as long as Indonesians saw the foreign firm as essential for the skills that it brought and Indonesians lacked.

2

The Indosat Deal

My advice to you is not to inquire why or whither, but just enjoy your ice cream while it's on your plate.
—Thornton Wilder, *The Skin of Our Teeth* (1942)

The 1967 agreement between ITT and Indonesia stated that Indonesia would own the satellite facility from the outset. At the same time, ITT would build and operate it for 20 years. Instead of taxes ITT would make lease payments to the Indonesian government. As such documents now go, the agreement was extremely brief, only 11 pages. In contrast, one power purchase agreement signed almost 30 years later in Indonesia contained more than 300 pages, with its appendixes. Neither brevity nor length, it turned out, would guarantee the promises made.

One reason for the brevity of the 1967 agreement: It was almost completely silent on perhaps the most contentious and complex issue in infrastructure arrangements. On the issues that were covered, the agreement could hardly be viewed as balanced, and some terms would later be seen as affronts to national sovereignty. Moreover, serious questions would eventually arise about the basic legality of the agreement. Although later on we will argue that these were not the only—or even the principal—reasons for problems, they did play a role in the agreement's eventual downfall.

Prices and Costs

Price turns out to be the most difficult issue in infrastructure agreements. Investors usually end up in a monopoly position, because the project itself is inherently a natural monopoly or the agreement creates monopoly rights. Governments thus worry that investors might exploit their positions to charge high prices. On the other hand, investors fear that submission of price to government regulation will not allow them to charge enough to earn an adequate return on investment. Both worries are completely justified.

Price is generally handled in one of two ways. In the first, the investor relies on the decisions of a government regulatory body, but the investor in turn obtains some assurances on regulatory standards. Guidelines might, for example, ensure investors a specified rate of return. In the second approach, the investment agreement sets out formulas to determine price under various circumstances, rather than specifying a single number. Neither route was followed in the agreement for Indosat. To be sure, ITT did not completely ignore the matter of price, obtaining a guarantee that it could charge certain minimum rates for its services: U.S. $4.00 per minute to points in Europe, Africa, and the Americas, $3.00 per minute to Asia and Southeast Asia. Rate changes would be by mutual agreement, but the contract spelled out no standards nor who had the authority to represent the government in any future rate discussions.

By assuring minimum rates, in dollars, the pricing provisions sharply reduced ITT's exposure to what might be considered normal commercial risk for foreign direct investment. One must assume that the minimum rates had been calculated to permit at least an acceptable return on investment, but the provision left open the possibility that the foreign investor could exploit its monopoly. In practice, there was to be no control over ITT's rates.

Protected on the pricing side, ITT had sought and won some assurances on the cost side as well. In particular, the venture was guaranteed free services from P.N. Telekom, the new name for the domestic phone company,[1] which would link to domestic phones and bill customers.

The agreement went a step further: ITT was promised monopoly rights over any future facilities of similar kind. This was interpreted as monopoly rights over international telecommunications.

Of course, revenue depends on demand as well as prices. The principal commercial uncertainty was whether Indonesia would generate a sufficient volume of international telephone traffic to make the venture profitable. From where it was in 1967, one might forecast that the country had no way to go but up. In contrast to our later stories, however, at least in theory ITT remained vulnerable on the demand side.

Foreign Exchange

With minimum prices set in dollars, ITT did not face risks of a depreciating exchange rate. Nevertheless, because Indonesia was emerging from a regime of tight controls on the purchase of foreign exchange, ITT sought assurances that foreign currencies would actually be available when needed. In some cases, a foreign investor might ask the government for promises that it will provide convertible currencies in exchange for local currency receipts for necessary imports, foreign debt service, and earnings remissions. ITT, however, took the substantial step of reserving the ability to demand that ITT's one customer, the domestic telecommunications company, would have to pay Indosat in foreign exchange, if ITT so demanded.[2]

ITT asked for and received still more. And, in so doing, it created the potential for a judicial nightmare. The agreement set criteria for the rate at which local currency would be exchanged for foreign currency, calling for

> a realistic exchange rate representing a fair approximation of equivalent purchasing power of the respective currencies involved; provided, however, that such exchange rate . . . shall not be less favorable to the Company than any exchange rate . . . applicable to any other substantial foreign enterprise engaged in business in Indonesia. . . .[3]

The likelihood for disagreement among reasonable parties should be quite obvious. It is rare to find two economists who will agree on the calculation required. If the company had ever invoked this clause, the debate would likely have lasted for years. It is unclear whether the two parties fully saw the implications of this paragraph, but we suspect not. In fact, the provision hardly seems necessary as the investor faced no serious constraints on the rates it could charge for its services.

Taxes and Duties

ITT's obligations to the government were determined according to a formula that was unique to the project, and which promised only a limited burden for the company. Labeled as "lease payments," they were calculated as a percentage of profits (50%). In turn, the project was exempted from corporate income tax and all other taxes for the entire 20-year duration of the agreement.[4] In addition, in plain language, the agreement[5] gave two very significant benefits: (1) unlimited loss carry-forward, and (2) no taxes—or their equivalent in the form of lease payments—until ITT had obtained an 8% after-tax return on its average equity investment.

Further, and important, the agreement did not spell out rules for calculating the profits that would determine the lease payments. Normally, tax codes lay out tedious rules on calculating taxable income, covering such matters as depreciation, transfer pricing among affiliates, and the handling of training and research expenditures. In addition, tax authorities have experience in auditing taxpayers to determine compliance. By exempting Indosat from the corporate income tax, the agreement also exempted the company from all these rules and procedures, and provided no substitute.

The document also ensured that the company would be entitled to unrestricted import of all equipment, materials, and other goods for its activities and that the "Company shall be exempt from *all present and future* customs and consular duties, sales and other taxes and royalties on all such goods [emphasis added]."[6] This went beyond the incentives offered by the Indonesian investment law, which limited tax holidays and concessionary tax rates to short time periods and restricted duty exemptions in time and to an approved list of necessary equipment and materials.

Most Favored Company

Another paragraph, if ever invoked, also promised a serious dispute:

> The Company shall enjoy the most favorable conditions granted by the government to any international telecommunications company or agency, whether public, governmental or private. If any such company or administration shall enjoy rights or privileges not accorded to the Company, then said rights and privileges shall *automatically* be extended to the Company [emphasis added].[7]

ITT undertook no reciprocal obligation to concede the most favorable terms to Indonesia that it might grant elsewhere or even to match what another firm might offer in Indonesia. Moreover, presumably the company could demand that it receive one favorable provision granted another investor in Indonesia without taking on more burdensome obligations that might have accompanied the concession. In the words of one critic, it could "cherry pick" the provisions it liked from any arrangement.

"Most favored company" provisions were not so unusual in investment agreements of the 1960s and early 1970s, particularly for mining, but they have only rarely been called on. Presumably, they were so patently unfair and the odds of dispute so great that investors were reluctant to turn to them.[8]

End of the Term

The Indosat agreement contained a surprising gap: the ultimate fate of the assets at the conclusion of the lease period, or earlier if the agreement were to end. In principle, the assets were the property of the government of Indonesia all along, so one might simply assume that they would go to the government. Yet the assets appeared on the balance sheet of Indosat, a wholly owned subsidiary of ITT. Because the ground station and other facilities ought to outlive the agreement, one might have expected that ITT would be entitled to some form of parting compensation, if for no other reason than to encourage upkeep of equipment. Or the Indonesian government, being the owner, might at least have required that ITT hand over the facilities in good running condition. Both parties, presumably for their own reasons, chose not to tackle this issue at all.

Sovereignty

Several terms of the Indosat agreement would have been considered affronts to national sovereignty in countries in a more nationalistic mood, even if their practical consequences were minimal.

First, the agreement made English the ruling language.[9] Although one could view this as an innocuous attempt to avoid future misunderstandings, this choice would have proved deeply offensive to most nations in Latin America at the time.

Second, fearing that Indonesian courts would do little to protect the rights of a foreigner, ITT had inserted a provision into the agreement for international arbitration in the event of a dispute. This kind of provision would also have been viewed as inflammatory in most Latin American countries, where the Calvo Doctrine reigned, calling for foreigners to settle disputes in local courts. In reality, at the time arbitration was very rarely used to settle disputes between foreign investors and host governments. This would change in the 1980s, even in Latin America.

Third, a paragraph made a mockery of national immigration laws, allowing employment of as many foreign personnel as the company "may deem appropriate until qualified Indonesian personnel are trained and available."[10] This open-ended right conflicted with the Indonesian investment law,[11] which provided for *government supervision* where "foreign capital enterprises are allowed to bring and employ foreign managerial and expert personnel in positions which cannot yet be filled by Indonesian nationals."[12]

Fourth, ITT retained the right to deal directly with overseas telecommunications administrations to influence the terms of payments and obligations, normally the task of the national telecommunications company. ITT's reasons for seeking the rights are clear enough. Even its financial backers, led by Bank of America, had expressed serious concern over the international rates and collections issue. But Samuelson, ITT's counsel, later said that these rights were definitely resented later by Perumtel (Indonesia's state-owned telephone company) and also Soehardjono, director general of posts and telecommunications.

One may dismiss a critique of these noneconomic issues as "emotional." But in the real world, these very issues can cause discontent and conflict, particularly in countries that believe they have been subjected to long periods of colonial suppression and exploitation—a feeling that was alive in Indonesia at the time. Although it found little voice in the tightly controlled press, that feeling would erupt in riots targeting Japanese investments in 1974.

Conformity with the Law

There were serious questions—at the outset and later—about whether the agreement conformed to Indonesian law and its constitution. The new investment law, in place when the final agreement was signed, had specifically banned foreign investors from "exercising full control" in certain activities,[13] one of which was telecommunications. This only reiterated two earlier laws,[14] both of which required telecommunications activities to be undertaken and controlled by the state. The limitation was in complete harmony with provisions of the country's constitution and legal system.[15] But the preamble of ITT's 1967 agreement stated, "Whereas the Government has determined that such joint undertaking with ITT is consistent with the purposes and terms of the Act on Investment of Foreign Capital ... and the benefits provided for therein, as well as other benefits hereinafter set forth, shall be made available in connection with such undertaking. ..."

ITT, of course, knew of the problem. The agreement, Samuelson argued, did not conflict with the investment law because the government of Indonesia would be the owner of all physical facilities, while ITT only operated them on the government's behalf. The arrangement called for ITT to "transfer title to the Station to the Government."[16] Nonetheless, Indosat was to be wholly financed, built, operated, and managed by ITT or its designated affiliate.[17]

The transfer of assets to Indonesia was something of a fiction, even from an economic point of view. In its own accounts, the project was to be treated as an asset owned by ITT[18] and the capital costs amortized as "an expense ... for purposes of computing its net profit."[19] In other words, the company was allowed to take depreciation on assets that it did not technically own. Denying that the project was a foreign direct investment was convenient for some purposes and inconvenient for others. The label depended on the issue at hand.[20]

When asked further about the issue of legality, Samuelson admitted that "there were hardly any legal skills available in Indonesia in the late sixties—the country was in dire straits." Samuelson had drafted the agreement virtually by himself. But, he said,

> I took pains to explain every aspect of the agreement to my Indonesian counterparts, going over clauses repeatedly to be sure that they were understood and accepted. We had developed so much trust in each other that people from the Communications Department would in the end come to me and ask me to draft, and insert in the agreement, items of concern to them. I do not believe in taking advantage—I approach negotiations with conscience.

Evaluation

The 1967 agreement owed much to Indonesia's weak bargaining position at that rather difficult time in its history. The country desperately needed capital and technology, even if some foreign investors got their own way. ITT's Samuelson described the attitude: "Whenever a problem arose, we would remind our Indonesian colleagues of our pioneer status—and they would acknowledge and respond positively. We did receive some privileges on account of that." Indeed, ITT might not have invested without the special concessions. There is even some evidence on this point: At about the same time (1966), ITT is reported to have opposed a proposal from the government of Argentina to set up satellite communications there under state control because the project would have adversely affected ITT's radio and cable business in the country. There, ITT's "obstruction" to the country's satellite plans generated enough resentment in the country eventually to cause expropriation of the company's assets.

Reflections from the Indonesian government side were consistent with this view of relative bargaining power. Professor Sadli, chairman of the Indonesian board of investment at the time of the investment, and one of the Berkeley Mafia, described their attitude:[21]

> When we started out attracting foreign investment in 1967, everything and everyone was welcome. We did not dare to refuse; we did not even dare to ask for bonafidity of credentials. We needed a list of names and dollar figures of intended investments, to give credence to our drive. The first mining company virtually wrote its own ticket. Since we had no conception about a mining contract, we accepted the draft written by the company as basis for negotiation, and common sense and the desire to bag the first contract were our guidelines. We still do not regret it.

Sadli's specific reference was to mining contracts for Irian Jaya, but the conclusions are equally applicable to the ITT agreement.

In the mid-1980s, Professor Sadli's memory of the original ITT negotiations was remarkably fresh, even after almost 20 years. Here is what he had to say specifically about the investment in retrospect:

> There was high controversy surrounding ITT's Jatiluhur station right from the beginning. For one thing, we were not sure whether Indonesia could afford such sophistication at the expense of other, more pressing projects. What decided the issue was that ITT would finance and operate the station and the country would get a "costless" high-tech toy. But evidently we had to pay a stiff price for that toy over time. [But we] were advised that the international telephone rates proposed by ITT—$4 or $5 per minute—were competitive at that time. . . .

It took some entrepreneurial daring in 1967 for ITT to go to Indonesia, with its stormy past, record of erratic international behavior and impetuous takeovers of foreign businesses, and a politico-economic future that, at that time, could only be regarded as uncertain. One would understandably be tempted, in such circumstances, to lock up all facets of business. "It was a tough agreement," reflected George Hunter, former head of ITT's telecommunications facility in Indonesia. "The ITT negotiators," he added, "were probably trying to get the most for their company as a good sales job, having given away nothing."

Little did the ITT negotiators know that the extraordinary strength of the agreement would in turn add to its ultimate weakness. They had unwittingly fertilized the seeds of discontent by demanding major concessions from a host country direly in need of assistance. Bribes surely played some role in inducing Indonesians to accept the terms; but Indonesia was in any event in a weak bargaining position because only a few companies could provide what it so needed. If a company shifts most risks to the government, gains monopoly control of a politically sensitive sector, and exploits that monopoly, it is likely eventually to reap what it has sown. The resulting harvest was in the end bountiful, but not lasting. That harvest is the subject of the next chapter.

3

Nationalization of Indosat

This act is as an ancient tale new told.
—William Shakespeare, *King John,*
  Act IV, Scene ii

No question, ITT's Indosat developed into a very successful
enterprise. After a slower than expected start, it provided
handsome returns to its parent. At the same time, it yielded significant
benefits to Indonesia by introducing modern telecommunications technology into a country where making international phone calls had been a
huge chore. And there is no indication that Indonesia could have done this
alone. The improvement came at a critical time, when the country was
trying to attract foreign investors, for whom telecommunications really
mattered. Moreover, and very important, Indosat set the stage for the
subsequent development of the country's domestic satellite communications network by training Indonesians in technical and managerial skills.
Finally, ITT was a "name brand" company; its decision to go to Indonesia
probably signaled other potential investors that the time was right.

But by late 1979, almost 13 years after the original deal was struck, ITT's
expatriate manager in Indosat, George Hunter, began to hear rumors of
trouble. It would turn out that ITT's unwillingness to respond favorably to
a politically attractive proposal triggered a chain reaction of unexpected
magnitude. The trigger was similar to ones that have set off reactions to
investors elsewhere. The trouble, however, reflected much deeper causes
that affect relations between foreign investors and the governments of
developing countries.

In the subsequent events, ITT executives managed the crisis well, receiving reasonable compensation and protecting the company's other
business interests. Lacking ITT's experience and having little other

business to protect, several investors in our later stories reacted differently when they faced rather similar problems. In the ITT case, the Indonesian government also handled its side of the renegotiations effectively. But the lessons from this experience were not passed down to later negotiators. Both government officials and investors can learn from the events.

A Successful Project

Clear Skies

Within a few months of signing its agreement, ITT set up a wholly owned subsidiary, P.T. Indonesian Satellite Corporation (Indosat),[1] assigning formal ownership to American Radio and Cable Corporation (ACR), a subsidiary responsible for the conglomerate's worldwide communications business. Financing arrangements followed quickly.[2] ACR was to put up $2.8 million in equity, and $5.46 million was to be borrowed.[3] ACR guaranteed $1.365 million of the debt; the balance was covered by a USAID extended risk guarantee to Bank of America, serving as agent for the lenders.

Construction began in February 1968. The prime contractor, selected without bids, was an ITT affiliate. Construction incurred a 50% cost overrun, due mainly to local "environmental factors," as an ITT executive vaguely put it. To cover additional costs, ACR made advances of $1.888 million to the subsidiary. In our later stories, similar arrangements with affiliates raised suspicions that transfer prices ran up costs, to the benefit of equity investors. In this case, the ground station was completed three months behind schedule, in September 1969.

Expanding Business

Managing the facility was not easy. Samuelson, ITT's counsel who had led the negotiations, told us: "Frankly, Indonesians made life very difficult for ITT operating people initially—a couple actually went over the bend." On top of that, when profits failed to materialize immediately, headquarters' complaints created another problem for those on the ground.

But the bad days were soon over. Indonesia's gross domestic product (GDP) grew at an average annual rate of 9% from 1969 to 1974 while inflation dropped to under 19% in 1974; industrial output tripled, and food production grew at roughly 3% annually. International telephone traffic outpaced it all. Traffic in 1971 was almost double that of 1970, reaching 1,930,974 minutes, and the year following it went up by another 50%.[4] In this environment, the telecommunications subsidiary thrived with its unregulated monopoly. Success led other ITT product divisions to enter Indonesia, granting a Sheraton hotel franchise, licensing local assembly of TV sets, and participating in assembly of telephones.

Changing Relations

Ironically, the more international telephone traffic grew, the greater the negative impact on state-owned Perumtel,[5] which had to provide all local services such as switching facilities, extension service to customers' terminal devices, and collection of tolls from subscribers. Perumtel had not been enthusiastic about the ground station from the start, viewing it as "an encroachment on its territory and livelihood." In 1972, Perumtel decided to take up "this unfair situation" with Indosat.[6] Two years of negotiations concluded with a concession: Indosat would pay Perumtel a fee of 15% of tolls for inbound and outbound calls.

This was just the beginning of a new and very different phase in Indosat's life. A revived spirit of nationalism was starting to manifest itself in Indonesia. The country's confidence had been boosted by the 1973 boom in oil prices and its membership in the Organization of Petroleum Exporting Countries (OPEC). Unlike the events of decades past, however, the national awakening this time around was aimed more at economics and less overtly at politics.

The new climate was evident when, in November 1973, the Dutch chair of the organization of governments providing aid to Indonesia was met at the Jakarta airport with signs reading "Foreign Investment Creates Domestic Colonialism" and "Indonesia for Indonesians." Two months later, on January 15, 1974, riots erupted when Japanese Prime Minister Tanaka visited the country. Some 50,000 Indonesians took to the streets, burning Japanese cars, motorcycles, and other products, and setting fire to a shopping mall and a Japanese car dealership. The deeper political struggles that might have been behind the riot are still debated, but the rioters themselves were clearly expressing frustration at the control over the economy seemingly exercised by foreign investors and ethnic Chinese, as well as the new consumer society from which most of the rioters were excluded.[7] (See Box 3.1.)

Perumtel responded to the growing nationalism by formulating its own ambitious program to reinforce the unity of the 13,000-island nation. It would build an integrated domestic telecommunications system based on satellites.

The new assertiveness of Indonesians led to another round of negotiations between Perumtel and Indosat, at the end of which the companies agreed to a formula that allocated more revenue to Perumtel. One should note that in each negotiation with Perumtel, Indosat asked for, but failed to receive, an extension to the original 1967 agreement.

Still, Indosat thrived, with its operating revenue rising at an average annual rate of 33% for 10 years running. Its annual rate of return on equity rose from 58% in 1973, to 248% in 1978, before coming down to an immodest 85% in 1979 on account of some fresh capital investments, including participation in a $17-million Indonesia–Singapore submarine

Box 3.1 Indonesian Business People

Many successful Indonesian business people were ethnic Chinese, a small group of whom had done very well indeed in obtaining licenses and permits. Liem Sioe Liong, the leading example, had come from Fujian, at age 21, to Central Java, where he peddled goods on the street. Having garnered Suharto's trust at a time when Suharto was a supply and finance officer, Liem's career took off. In 1969, he started his climb to become one of Indonesia's richest people when Suharto granted him a monopoly license for flour mills.[a]

Chinese Indonesians could pay necessary bribes from the money earned from trading. More important, allowing Chinese to become wealthy posed little threat to the political system because this generally disliked minority was in practice excluded from government.[b] In addition, the income from their licenses could be "taxed" informally to support the president's interests.[c] For example, when Bank Duta ran into trouble in the late 1980s, two Chinese businessmen were called on by Suharto to bail out the bank. Similarly, they could be counted on for other political ends, when needed. In March 1990, for example, 30 business leaders were summoned by Suharto and told that they should sell up to 25% of the equity in their businesses to "cooperatives."[d]

Ambitious Chinese business people understood that they must, in exchange for privileges, regularly reward individual officials. A revealing report quoted a childhood friend of Suharto's second son: "I remember when we were younger, me and Bambang and his other friends would go over to Uncle Liem's house. Uncle Liem would always give us a package of money wrapped in newspaper." The package, he recalled, would contain at least a $1,000 in cash.[e] Another compensation for the powerful was appointment as director ("commissioner") on the supervisory board of a Chinese-controlled company. Directors were paid well by Indonesian standards. Although directors might help the firm on occasion to get licenses and permits, and to block outsiders from obtaining them, they had no real role in supervising the company.

The ethnic Chinese were complemented by a small group of non-Chinese Indonesians (*pribumi*), who emerged as successful business people primarily in the 1980s. Maybe 40 of the top 140 business groups were non-Chinese.[f] Their success was a result of explicit government policy. The banking system was ordered to direct more credit to them, and the "Team 10" program (described later) was meant to send business their way. Many of the successful *pribumi* were closely related to the president, ministers, or Golkar party officials, directly or by marriage. Of the 40 mentioned above, 16 were actually "First Family," direct members of the Suharto clan.[g]

(continued)

Box 3.1 (continued)

Wealth in relatives' hands also did not threaten existing political arrangements.

There was a third successful group in the domestic business sector, the military. Businesses run by military units allowed off-budget financing of the armed services, and businesses for retired officers brought their interests in line with the status quo. Who would support a coup if he could earn plenty under the current government?

Unlike some other countries, Indonesia seemed to ensure that the payments extracted from business people were never so large as to leave them without an incentive to earn more. In fact, the system generated a rather secure, if non-Western style, set of property rights for well-connected local business people.[h]

[a]Liem took in Sudwikatmono, variously described as a cousin or a foster brother of President Suharto, as well as two other Chinese, Djuhar Sutanto and Ibrahim Risyad (Risjad). Risyad was to go on to build another group of companies. Sudwikatmono, Liem Sioe Liong, Djuhar Sutanto, and Ibrahim Risyad were to become the business tycoons known as the "Gang of Four." For more, see Adam Schwarz, "Indonesian Patriarch Prepares to Hand over Reins of Salim Group: Empire of the Son," *Far Eastern Economic Review*, March 14, 1991, p. 46; for a biography of Liem, see Willie Hsu, "Liem Sioe Liong (Indonesia), Chairman of Salim Group, Economic Advisor to The Indonesian Government," available at http://www.huayinet.org/biography/biography_liemsioeliong.htm (accessed April 2006).

[b]Adam Schwarz recognizes this important factor in *A Nation in Waiting: Indonesia in the 1990s* (St. Leonards, Australia: Allen & Unwin, 1994), p. 127.

[c]Some were taxed more formally. Liem's flour mill group, for example, was required by its original articles of association to pay a part of its profits into social foundations controlled by the president's wife and by the Army Strategic Reserve Unit (Kostrad). See George J. Aditjondro, "The Myth of Chinese Domination," *Jakarta Post*, August 14, 1998.

[d]See, for example, "Sejarah Indonesia: An Online Timeline of Indonesian History. Orde Baru—The Suharto Years: 1965–1998," available at http://www.gimonca.com/sejarah/sejarah10.shtml (accessed April 2006).

[e]"Suharto Inc. Special Report: Children of Fortune," *Time Asia*, May 24, 1999, available at http://www.time.com/time/asia/asia/magazine/1999/990524/cover4.html (accessed April 2006).

[f]The data come from Jim Castle, "Road Map to Indonesian Business Groups" (1997), cited by Theodore Friend, *Indonesian Destinies* (Cambridge: Belknap Press for Harvard University Press, 2003), p. 233.

[g]For a calculation of the value of ties to Suharto, see Raymond Fisman, "Estimating the Value of Political Connections," *American Economic Review*, 2001, 91(4), pp. 1095–1102.

[h]For analogies in early Latin America, see Cyrus Veeser, "In Pursuit of Capital: Concessions as a Modernizing Strategy in the Dominican Republic, 1876–1916" (unpublished paper, 2006), and Stephen Haber, Armando Razo, and Noel Maurer, *The Politics of Property Rights* (Cambridge, England: Cambridge University Press, 2003).

cable, an ambitious project agreed to by the Association of South East Asian Nations economic ministers. In spite of the impressive rate of return, the total figures—dividends of $25.16 million, advisory fees of $1.13 million, and potential tax credits of $28.25 million for the first 10 years[8]—accounted for only a small part of overall ITT corporate income.

Overcast

A dark cloud began to form one day in early March 1979. At a summit meeting in Yogyakarta, in Central Java, President Suharto and the prime minister of Malaysia decided that the North Sumatran city of Medan should be connected by submarine cable with Penang across the Strait of Malacca on Malaysia's west coast. Speaking on the occasion, the Indonesian minister for transport, communications, and tourism stressed: "The agreement concerning this submarine cable . . . [will] strengthen ties between Indonesia and Malaysia."[9]

Although the two Asian neighbors saw the cable as one way to reinforce their new-found friendship, Indosat saw it only as a poor investment. ITT would have to absorb the $12 million cost, while the potential revenue would amount to barely $250,000 per year. Hence, when the company was asked, as the 1967 agreement required, for its views on the subject, it balked, responding by letter[10] that the cable was "not economically viable" and that a cheaper alternative existed; but if the cable proposal were to go ahead, Indosat's contract should be extended, the revenue agreement with Perumtel should be revisited, or the government might become a joint venture partner in the expansion.

There was no formal response from Indonesians. But the tone of the ITT letter suggested that ITT had seriously misread the political sensitivity of the cable project. Moreover, these nationalistic times were hardly propitious for a reminder of Indosat's inviolable right to perform "the function for Overseas Telephone for all Indonesia until September 29, 1989." Although no one quite recognized it at the time, ITT's objections to this politically important project had violated the kind of social contract that is implicit in so many infrastructure investments. Private monopolists are expected to respond positively to unstated social and political goals, not to limit themselves to making money out of their activities.

Reevaluating the Deal

Cable as Trigger

President Suharto was "unhappy," according to one insider, when his communications minister informed him that ITT's cooperation had to be secured before the cable project could proceed. He turned to J. B. Sumarlin, minister of state for administrative reform and deputy chairman of the planning board (BAPPENAS), to look at the issue and, in the words of one

---

Box 3.2 J. B. Sumarlin

With a master's degree from Berkeley and a Ph.D. from the University of Pittsburgh and as one of the Berkeley Mafia technocrats, Sumarlin was widely respected. He had distinguished himself by his handling of the 1970s Pertamina debt crisis. Pertamina, the state-owned oil company, had been close to collapse, with debts of over $10 billion that it was unable to service due to unbridled expansion and inept management. Among the many tasks he had to perform, Sumarlin led delicate renegotiations with the large German firms that had signed multimillion dollar supply contracts for the Krakatau Steel project, one of the many ill-considered ventures Pertamina had taken on. The diminutive Sumarlin had stood up to foreigners on behalf of Indonesia. As a result of his leadership, Pertamina was soon on its way to recovery, and the minister had firmly established a reputation for astute problem solving and clear thinking.

---

official, "remove the obstacle." Sumarlin was a natural choice for the task (see Box 3.2).

Sumarlin had earlier considered reviewing the Indosat arrangements in light of the need to integrate Indonesia's rapidly expanding telecommunications facilities. But he had been counseled by a "senior minister"—a reference to General Soehardjono—to proceed cautiously lest he run afoul of the powerful Indosat lobby in the government. By the time the cable issue arose, however, the general was no longer in power, having been replaced by Suryadi in July 1978.

This time Sumarlin moved swiftly and resolutely, addressing a memorandum to the communications minister, the finance minister, and the governor of Indonesia's central bank about the need to revise Indosat's contract.[11] Perumtel would require some $925 million over the next decade to expand the country's telecommunications network. Borrowing by the state-owned company could be reduced if it did not have to pass on as much as 85% of its international revenues to foreign-owned Indosat. Over the period, projected payments to Indosat amounted to more than 20% of Perumtel's total earnings. In Sumarlin's view, "this kind of arrangement obviously not only curtails Perumtel's management rights and its income...but it also conflicts with the economic policy outlined in the GBHN [Broad State Policy Guidelines] inasmuch as it has created a monopoly." Huge government investments in domestic telecommunications, consequently, had not "yielded a fair return compared with what Indosat enjoys."

Now was the time to act on the problem. ITT's refusal to lay the politically sensitive cable had triggered a new visit to the old agreement.

Box 3.3 William C. Hollinger

William "Bill" Hollinger, with a Ph.D. in economics from the Massachusetts Institute of Technology, had first taught at the University of Indonesia in 1954 as a graduate student. Many of the technocrats who became ministers after the fall of Sukarno had been his students or colleagues. Included among them was Sumitro. Like other foreigners, Hollinger had left Indonesia during Sukarno's most xenophobic days. Having remained in contact with Sumitro during his exile, Hollinger was invited to return in 1968; he took up the leadership of the new Harvard advisory team[a] in the planning agency.

When the time came for the Harvard Group to rotate Hollinger out of Indonesia, he chose to remain as an independent consultant, usually directly to Sumarlin. He settled into a comfortable, but not exorbitant, colonial house in the close-in old Dutch suburb of Menteng, and built a reputation with the foreign community for his excellent French cooking and fine wines.

[a]The team came from the Harvard Development Advisory Service, later the Harvard Institute for International Development (HIID), and would remain in Indonesia in an advisory capacity until 1999.

Building a Team

Sumarlin assembled a team to review the agreement and "to arrive at more just and reasonable arrangements." With nine members, it would be chaired by a director general from the Ministry of Finance, Oskar Surjaatmaja. The responsible director general from posts and telecommunications, and chairman of Indosat, Suryadi, would serve as vice-chairman. The team would be guided by Sumarlin himself, as a member of a ministerial steering committee that included the communications minister, the finance minister, and the governor of the central bank. The latter two were closely allied economic technocrats, members of the Berkeley Mafia.

The steering committee decided to enlist the help of international consultants, but their approach differed significantly from what was to come in later stories. This time the advisors had previously worked together, they had a clear leader who had Sumarlin's confidence, and they all reported solely to Sumarlin. Later advisors would be strikingly less effective, but not because of any shortage of skills on their part.

The first advisor was Sumarlin's long-time American economic consultant, William C. Hollinger (see Box 3.3). Hollinger belongs to that category of Western experts who capture the confidence of important

Third World government officials not so much with their narrow expertise, but with their versatility, relationships, and ability to call on specialists elsewhere.

Hollinger suggested Professor Wells, from the Harvard Business School, as an additional consultant. Wells had worked with Hollinger on mining agreements in Liberia in 1967, and Hollinger had subsequently brought him to Indonesia as a consultant for the Harvard Group. Because Wells had recently drafted a memo on the Indosat agreement for the finance minister, his view was known: A simple revision of the agreement would probably not satisfy the government's objectives. A state take-over had better prospects, if Indonesians now had the skills to run the facility.

Hollinger soon signed on outside legal help, a trusted Australian lawyer, Ezekiel Solomon,[12] who had earlier assisted Sumarlin with Krakatau Steel negotiations. His preliminary view was that *prima facie* grounds for renegotiating the 1967 agreement existed. Agreeing that documenting the high returns earned thus far by Indosat would be useful, the advisors brought Price Waterhouse and Company into the picture. Price Waterhouse was again a known entity: Hollinger and Sumarlin had worked with the company to straighten out the Pertamina tangle.

By the time the core advisory team had been assembled, the new year, 1980, had already rolled in.

An Approach Develops

The team's report concluded that Indosat's incentives were exceptional and out of line with those given to other investors. The agreement should be revised, and Perumtel should run the ground station or at least gain a majority shareholding in Indosat.

But the ministerial steering committee hesitated, worrying about possible disruption of services or expansion projects. Moreover, it harbored some fear in challenging a multinational with a history of defying host governments in the Third World. Allegations of ITT's intervention in Chilean politics were by this time well known and especially frightening.

ITT Unaware

It was Sumarlin's September 1979 memorandum that had led to the rumors reaching George Hunter. In retrospect, he told us, he suspected that his senior Indonesian managers in Indosat, including Jonathan Parapak, were not only aware of the memo's contents but might have even obtained a copy of it. As we will later see, little remained confidential for long in Jakarta, where loyalties among a small elite and a little money would buy a great deal. As Hunter later reflected on events, he said he could understand why Parapak might hide the information because he was slated for promotion to managing director of Indosat very soon.

Parapak was indeed promoted to managing director at Indosat, and business continued as normal, with the Singapore submarine cable and expansion of international telephone switching moving forward. The 1981–1985 business plan identified investment programs for participation in additional submarine cables in Southeast Asia, which Indosat was expected to finance. As a result, capital in the venture would be increased.

In preparing his business plan, Parapak was clearly limited by the fact that the original agreement would expire in eight years. In his report, however, Parapak revealed no suspicions that government plans for the short run might make the end date a moot issue.

Advisors' Work

The government ministers and their advisors had been busy investigating all aspects of Indosat business, marshaling evidence for the brief to confront ITT.

The Wells Report

Wells argued that ITT's monopoly over a public utility without any effective control over the rates had led to excessive profits for an investment that faced little commercial risk. Moreover, the reported profits did not even capture additional income to ITT from purchases of equipment, supplies, and construction from affiliates, interest on loans from the parent, fees on these and other loans, and the regular "advisory fee" to the parent. This last fee was based not on cost of services but on a fixed percentage of revenue. Even in the absence of these interaffiliate transactions, Wells concluded, "the rate of return to ITT has been enormous, given the nature of the project." The problem was not one of taxes or lease payments, but one of unrestrained monopoly. Under the circumstances, Wells concluded, the government had two basic alternatives: It could allow ITT to continue to operate the public utility as a regulated monopoly, or the government could acquire and run the enterprise under state ownership.

If the choice was state ownership, the government, in Wells's opinion, should provide compensation to ITT for its investment and assume the project's debt. The alternative of no compensation would be politically costly. Determining the amount of compensation would be the most difficult issue, with ITT likely demanding the present value of the projected stream of earnings that would accrue to them under the existing agreement. Wells argued that this was unacceptable because that stream of earnings included monopoly profits. He recommended compensation based on book value of the entity, net of depreciation taken by the company in calculating its lease payments.

Wells expected ITT to complain bitterly if the government were to go for state ownership. Other investors might raise questions "about the security of contracts in Indonesia" at a time when Indonesia was trying to build a reputation of respecting investors' property rights. But there had been many a nationalization of foreign-owned entities, including some ITT subsidiaries, throughout Latin America and elsewhere, without any lasting impact on foreign investment flows.

Wells proposed that the government prepare a legal brief to argue the illegality of the original agreements, develop an economic brief to demonstrate the unreasonableness of ITT's monopoly profits, and examine the company's Overseas Private Investment Corporation (OPIC)[13] insurance to reduce the chance of U.S. government intervention. The next steps would be to inform the U.S. ambassador of the reasons for renegotiating the ITT arrangements; announce a firm timetable to ITT, including an effective date of settlement to prevent any delaying tactics on the part of the company; simultaneously assure lenders that the government would honor Indosat's liabilities; and immediately after the first meeting with investors, initiate an audit of Indosat's books.

Legal Work

The justice minister prepared the legal brief, concluding that the agreement was contrary to the 1945 constitution, which states that sectors of productive activity with dominant influence on public life "will be controlled and carried out by the state."[14] The brief added that it was inconsistent with the investment law, which "explicitly states that foreign capital investment in telecommunications is not permitted." Finally, he observed, "After making a careful assessment, it has become evident that the said agreements are not reasonably balanced as between the parties but are detrimental to the interests of the Government."

His unequivocal conclusion was ready in May 1980:

> I am of the opinion that the said agreements are in contravention of the laws and contrary to public order and good morals . . . and, accordingly, based on the provisions of the Civil Code of Law, null and void.

This provided negotiators with a handy threat should ITT resist renegotiation.

Doing the Numbers

Price Waterhouse also presented its preliminary financial findings in May. As expected, they confirmed the high returns earned by Indosat's owner. For instance, the average annual rate of return on equity, measured as income after tax, was more than 83% over the period of 1969 to 1978, and almost 63% when measured in terms of dividends received by ACR. The average annual return on total plant, property, and equipment was 26% for the early period and 46% during the 1973 to 1978 period. These were in

Table 3.1 Present Value of Projected Earnings ($000s)

	Discount Rate		
	8%	10%	15%
Case I	103,200	92,100	70,200
Case II	127,400	113,300	85,700
Case III	136,300	122,900	95,900

addition to foreign tax credits that the parent could use (some $20 million to 1978), interest paid on loans from affiliates (totaling close to $1.4 million), and advisory fees paid to affiliates (more than $800 thousand over 10 years).

Lacking Indosat projections for the period of 1980 to 1989, the accountants made their own forecasts on the basis of three sets of assumptions. The present values (on August 1, 1980) of these streams of projected earnings to the end of the lease period were then calculated at the discount rates of 8%, 10%, and 15% with the results in Table 3.1.

Indosat's net book value at the end of 1979 amounted to $11 million, according to one simple calculation. A number of adjustments, however, could be made as warranted by the company's accounting practices.

The accountants' report included a comparison of Indosat's performance with that of the consolidated ITT and other companies. Finally, the report listed all the known outstanding debt agreements and financial commitments, and all the company's construction programs, completed or in progress.

Technical Advisors

The economic and legal advisors recommended an evaluation to determine whether Indonesian technical and managerial staff could operate and maintain Indosat facilities if foreigners were to leave quickly. In the end, two independent consultants, both former ITT employees, were hired. Quick, but careful, investigation indicated that Indonesian skills were indeed adequate, and in fact strikingly so in comparison to what the consultants had encountered in other developing countries.

Keeping the U.S. Government Out

To preempt the possibility that ITT might invoke the "expropriatory action" clause of insurance contracts with OPIC, Wells sought a copy of the policy. OPIC responded that the agreements were considered confidential. Meanwhile, ITT got wind of the request—an OPIC official told us recently that OPIC notifies the company involved about any request—and authorized OPIC to release the documents.[15]

The insurance contract excluded from the definition of expropriatory action any steps that occurred as a result of:

> any law, decree, regulation, or administrative action of the Government of the Project country, which is not by its express terms for the purpose of nationalization, confiscation, or expropriation . . . is reasonably related to constitutionally sanctioned governmental objectives, is not arbitrary . . . and does not violate generally accepted international law principles; or any action that occurred in accordance with any agreement voluntarily made.

This complicated statement provided much less protection to investors than would later OPIC insurance contracts.

The terms of the policy increased advisors' confidence. First, insurance did not cover equity, only debt, which Indonesians planned anyway to honor. Second, the total coverage was small (the maximum was $4,095,000). Payments to ITT would clearly exceed this amount. Third, the action being contemplated was consistent with the country's constitution.

The team's legal advisor, Solomon, recommended that any formal decree issued by the government simply authorize renegotiation of all ITT agreements so as to adjust them to the laws of the country, to reduce the likelihood that the language itself might be interpreted as indicating expropriatory action. Similarly, communication to be addressed to ITT should state its intent to enter into bona fide negotiations. Because ITT would probably notify OPIC of any action by the Indonesian government, it was doubly important that the government inform the U.S. ambassador of the upcoming negotiations in advance and make it clear to lenders that their debts were secure. Both the lenders and the ambassador should hear the government's case before ITT could argue its side.

The advisors' work resulted in an official position paper of August 7 that summarized for the benefit of the steering committee the "weaknesses" of the existing arrangements, confirmed the makeup of the negotiating team, and repeated that the objective was to renegotiate the agreements "to eliminate Indosat's monopoly in the area of international telephone [services]."

The decision was made: ITT's 13-year control over Indosat would end.

Company Management

Two days later, Indosat directors gathered for a board meeting in Jakarta. Guests from ITT headquarters included John C. Reynolds, president of U.S. Telephone & Telegraph, William M. Brown, vice president and executive director for Asia-European Operations, and Ranjit Khosla, assistant comptroller. They had come especially to participate in ceremonies marking the inauguration of the Indonesia–Singapore submarine cable and a switch that had made possible international direct dialing facilities in Indonesia for the first time. Parapak responded to Reynolds's congratulations by saying that his "achievement was only possible because of the excellent cooperation he received from the director general of posts and telecommunications and Perumtel."[16] Parapak may have known that his butter was about to slip to the other side of the toast.

After a review of normal business, Parapak raised the issue of the Medan–Penang submarine cable as the government had gone silent on the issue. The chairman, Suryadi, who as a member of the government's review team knew exactly what was going on behind the scenes, turned the query over to the alternate director from Perumtel. According to the minutes of the meeting, this director correctly reported "no new progress had been made on the Medan–Penang cable." After the meeting, the guests returned to their hotels, oblivious to the pending threat.

Indonesian Goals and Negotiating Strategy

Advisors and consultants to the Indonesian Steering Committee were busy finalizing negotiation strategies. The advisors wanted the negotiating team to have a clear mandate but also a full set of arguments. Data were assembled, including all recent ITT filings with the U.S. Securities and Exchange Commission. Communications were drafted and approved for (1) ITT, informing the company of the government's intent to renegotiate the arrangements; (2) Indosat creditors and contractors, reassuring them that obligations would be honored; and (3) the international press, in the event ITT decided to take its case public. A timetable for the negotiations was also formulated, with specific tasks, deadlines, and responsibilities.

An offer also had to be ready. The advisors had warned that ITT would ask something like $110 million for the subsidiary, reflecting the net present value of future earnings. The government should start with an offer of around $11 million, one interpretation of book value. The gap between offer and likely counteroffer warned of the size of the struggle ahead.

Even with the advantage of surprise, no Indonesian ever thought that, to quote a consultant, "ITT would be easily overpowered." In fact, Perumtel's managing director, Willy Moenandir, was sure that ITT would make things very difficult. Advisors anticipated that the company would try to draw out the negotiations as it had in other countries. In fact, why not, given the profits that would accrue to the company while it was stalling? In that case, the government must be prepared to take harsh measures. As a last resort, Perumtel could stop paying international telephone revenues to Indosat and instead put those funds in a special account, releasing only enough to enable Indosat to meet its operating costs and debt obligations. And the government might interrupt ITT's other businesses in Indonesia if delays continued.

Without doubt, the most important step to speed negotiations would be a firm announcement by the government team at the outset of an effective date for any eventual agreement. The company could delay, but the outcome would be effective on the announced date, even if that date had passed. The government must stick by this date, no matter what.

Notifying the Company

President Suharto issued a decree on August 30, 1980,[17] authorizing Sumarlin to renegotiate all agreements involving Indosat. In fulfilling his assignment, the minister was, according to the decree, responsible directly to the president.

Subsequently, by a decree of his own issued on September 18, 1980, Sumarlin confirmed a "steering team" and an "implementation team." Sumarlin himself would head the steering team, with members comprising Achmad Tahir, the secretary general of the Department of Communications; Suryadi, the director general of posts and telecommunications; and Muchtarudin Siregar, an assistant to Minister Sumarlin. The implementation team would comprise Oskar Surjaatmadja from the Ministry of Finance as chairman and six other members including Willy Moenandir, the managing director of Perumtel; Sukarno Abdurachman, the chief of planning of the Department of Communications; and Sumantri Sumadirono, the director of government finance supervision. The implementation team would report directly to Sumarlin.

Events were now moving so fast that the very next day, September 19, Sumarlin issued a carefully worded letter to the president of American Cable and Radio Corporation summoning company officials to negotiations. On the same day, Sumarlin invited U.S. Ambassador Edward E. Masters to his office to apprise him of the entire ITT situation. Messages were also dispatched to Indosat's creditors: Bank of America, European Asian Bank, and Société Générale de Banque.

A Bewildered Management

At ITT headquarters, the minister's letter left everyone bewildered. Hunter told us, "There was a scramble at the last minute because the head office people did not have exact prior information about what was coming."

This was an understatement. Under Geneen, field managers were expected to keep headquarters informed even of far less important matters, but no warnings had come from Reynolds and Brown, two men who had attended the recent board meeting in Jakarta. Receiving the news, ITT chairman Rand Araskog asked Brown whether he and the staff knew anything in advance about the matter. "Not specifically," Brown replied, "but we had been getting disturbing vibes for some time. . . ." This apparent slip-up on the part of the managers might be blamed on the change in top leadership in the second half of 1979—from Geneen to Lyman C. Hamilton to Araskog. Tending to bigger issues, managers may have let Indosat simply fall through a crack.

Opinion within ITT management was soon divided on what might be an acceptable settlement. One school favored a quick, "reasonable" settlement, while the other wanted to stretch the process of negotiations so as not to "throw away" an ongoing concern with growing profits.

Contrary to Indonesia's expectations, ITT's top management reached a decision to avoid confrontation. The corporation's new leadership in the post-Geneen era was simply not interested in taking on host governments and thereby risking a fresh round of negative publicity. Chile had been enough. As Brown put it, "Considering the size and scope of Indosat in the overall corporate context, it was really a minor contributor and therefore not worth picking a fight with a sovereign government." Also, under Araskog a program of "deconglomorization" and consolidation had been set in motion,[18] so one more divestiture would hardly matter.

On the other side, Indonesia also wanted to reach a settlement, in the words of Oskar Surjaatmadja, head of his country's negotiating team, "in a friendly and amicable way":

> We did not want them to think that we were going to nationalize their company because the principle of open economy [practiced by Indonesia] demands that there will be no nationalization. So there were no threats, just simple negotiations.

But regardless of the words chosen to describe the events, nationalization was the goal. ITT would receive compensation, but in the end the Indonesians insisted on owning Indosat.

Negotiations

The two sides met on October 13 in Minister Sumarlin's spacious office in the national planning agency. Representing Indonesia with Sumarlin were the secretary general of the Department of Communications, the director general of posts and telecommunications, Oskar Surjaatmadja, and a number of other officials. Also present were four advisors to the government: Hollinger, Wells, Solomon, and Jonathan Harris of Price Waterhouse. The advisors' presence was a source of surprise, and it seems of some discomfort, to ITT managers, who had expected a contingent of only Indonesians, and rather unprepared ones at that.

ITT was represented by James J. Gillrane, senior vice president/treasurer of ITT World Communications; William M. Brown, vice president/executive director of U.S. Telephone and Telegraph Corporation; Hunter, resident director of Indosat; and Jonathan L. Parapak, Indonesian managing director at Indosat.

Sumarlin opened the meeting with a statement[19] that Indonesia wanted to complete the purchase of Indosat by no later than December 31, 1980. This was "non-negotiable." The purchase price would be determined on the basis of "adjusted net book value," a figure that was "negotiable." The government was satisfied with and appreciated the services provided by ITT, and the purchase of Indosat by the government would "not affect other ITT business" in Indonesia. Hunter suspected that the reference to ITT's other business was a veiled threat, as it indeed was. Sumarlin also announced that the government was going ahead on the Medan–Penang cable. In other words, ITT's monopoly was over.

After the Indonesian negotiating team had been introduced, ITT was told that team chairman Oskar would be the company's sole contact during the negotiations. The team was empowered to complete all aspects of negotiations. The Indonesians added that the ITT team should be similarly empowered and that the two teams would meet every morning at 9:00 AM for the week, and for the next week, if necessary. Some of the other points made were:

- Profits up to December 31, 1980, would belong to ITT, and all profit accruing thereafter would be Indonesia's.
- Between October 13, 1980, and December 31, 1980, all commitments and agreements by Indosat would have to be approved by the government.
- The Indonesian negotiating team "has full access to books, records, and employees of Indosat."

Then it was ITT's turn. Indosat director Brown said that both sides wanted to settle on an amicable basis, but that ITT had made "major new investments and our intent was to earn on [the] said investments through 1989," the end of the lease period. "Net book value," he added, "was not a fair basis of settlement." Surprising no one, he said that in ITT's view the fair basis for compensation was the net present value of future earnings.

ITT's team seemed selected to reduce tensions. John Reynolds, the addressee of Sumarlin's September 19 letter, could not come to the meeting for what were described as "unavoidable reasons." Hunter later surmised to us, however, that "headquarters probably kept him away because he tended to be brash and abrupt." Hunter did not appear in subsequent meetings. In a later conversation he told us, "I felt very strongly that the integrity of the [1967] agreement had to be respected and I started to say so in the meeting, but was cut off by Oskar. The result was that I was dropped from the [ITT] team after the first meeting. My colleagues were afraid that I might rock the boat."

Hunter's own interests had to be tied up with obtaining as much as possible in the sale of the subsidiary that he had so carefully built and run. It is not unusual to find that those who had negotiated a deal or long operated a subsidiary could stubbornly support what had become outdated arrangements. By dropping Hunter from the team, however, his colleagues betrayed their eagerness to accommodate Indonesia's desires, a stance that hardly went unnoticed on the government side.

Offers and Counteroffers

Negotiations began in earnest on the next day. ITT conceded that ownership of Indosat would be transferred to the Indonesian government. But the company continued to insist on receiving the net present value of future earnings, while Indonesia was equally adamant that adjusted net book value would establish the price.

ITT vice president Brown soon challenged Indonesia's offer by asserting that ITT had never sold a subsidiary for book value anywhere in the world. This turned out to be a costly misstatement. Just six years earlier ITT had accepted a settlement on that very basis when Puerto Rico purchased an ITT telephone company. Moreover, the Indonesian government knew it from the 10-K reports ITT had filed with the U.S. Securities and Exchange Commission. A consultant passed a note to team leader Oskar, who countered Brown by reading aloud from the company's own report. Brown's assertion had managed to create the impression that either he was not high enough in the ITT hierarchy to have accurate knowledge of company dealings or he was deliberately trying to bluff. Either way, his personal effectiveness as a negotiator fell. More importantly, ITT's negotiators belatedly realized just how well-prepared the Indonesians were.

Quickly the two sides began a struggle for control of the agenda. After an ITT negotiator was allowed to make the opening speech in an early meeting, the consultants were determined to regain control for the Indonesians. To accomplish this, Wells wrote opening speeches for Oskar to start each subsequent meeting. At one point, while delivering one of the speeches, Oskar apologized for his poor English. An ITT team member responded that he thought it "eloquent," while staring fixedly at Wells. Solomon similarly managed to retain the drafting initiative throughout, "thus virtually setting the tone and pace of negotiations."[20] This was in stark contrast to the events of 1967 when ITT practically "wrote its own ticket."[21]

The ITT team soon tabled a proposal to sell Indosat for a reduced $93 million, still based on a calculation of the net present value of future cash flow. The Indonesian side responded by upping its formal offer to $30 million, a figure that approximated an evaluation of property, plant, and equipment (cost less depreciation), including about $20.5 million for which long-term debt had been incurred. Thus began the bargaining, which is what it really was.

Around this time, the Indonesian team began to realize that the contents of its preparatory discussions were being leaked to ITT's negotiators. Because the government team had grown quite large as interested agencies insisted on seats in the discussions, it was difficult to determine sources of leaks. As a result, a small core of trusted people began to meet separately to make real decisions about the negotiations. The full team also gathered, but no serious discussions transpired in those meetings.

This was a harbinger of things to come in later stories, as Indonesians regularly found it difficult to maintain confidentiality.

The government now made new use of its two former ITT technical experts, bringing them into the negotiations. The move was meant to send a clear message to ITT about the government's resolve: They could even muster support from former ITT employees. However, the experts' presence also contributed to an unexpected and unwanted side effect: Employees of Indosat began to grow alarmed. Only now did they grasp that ITT would really be gone and that they would be working for a state-owned company. This prompted Minister Sumarlin to send a letter on November 3, 1980, to assure all employees that "It is not the Government's intention to abolish PT Indosat or that its acquisition of PT Indosat should adversely affect the employment status, and terms of existing employees. . . ." In later years, the employees of state-owned companies would have strong reactions to privatization, but that was because they feared it would mean layoffs and tougher work standards.

ITT had brought in its own experts as well: One was James Needham of White Weld, a capital markets group associated with Merrill Lynch. Needham was to coach the Indonesian side on the "intricate" technique of discounted cash flow analysis. He might also play on the concerns of the Indonesian government that foreign investors, or more particularly U.S. investors, would be watching these negotiations with alarm.

In the end, Needham's intervention would provide a face-saving way of reducing the offer price. After a forceful presentation, he concluded that the project was worth $72,685,000, leading the ITT negotiating team to propose this as the price. In response, the Indonesian side again rejected the discounted cash flow argument, saying that it was a "non-issue," repeating that the projected earnings stream was possible only because of the illegal monopoly.

When they discovered advisors from Harvard Business School and Price Waterhouse, ITT had realized that Needham's coaching on financial techniques was unnecessary. With his presentation completed, Needham, according to a consultant, "thereupon retreated to the fabled Indonesian island of Bali for personal recreation."

Seeking U.S. Government Help

Frustrated, ITT turned to the U.S. embassy in Jakarta for help. Hunter reported to us,

> Ambassador Masters and his economic counselor advised us against taking a tough stand, quoting the Weyerhaeuser logging case,[22] which had not produced any positive results despite a bitter fight waged by the owners. Weyerhaeuser investments had also been taken over by the Indonesians. The U.S. embassy did, however, pass on the information regarding our case to the Indonesian foreign ministry—at least, that's what they told us. . . . Their [the embassy's] attitude was, "Keep us informed."

The U.S. government was not going to defend this American investor's property at possible costs to its strategic interests in Indonesia. The U.S. embassy did not want to upset relations with a strongly anti-communist government and a major oil supplier over a simple commercial issue. A little more than a decade later, U.S. ambassadors reacted very differently to requests from American firms for help. By the time of our next stories, U.S. foreign policy had undergone a major change with the end of the Cold War.

Challenging the ITT Team

Negotiations over Indosat were deadlocked, with a large gap between offers. Meetings between large teams are not conducive to great breakthroughs, but informal conversations between principals can be just the ticket to get things moving. At one stage, during a friendly conversation away from the negotiating table, Oskar asked Brown informally what amount might really be acceptable to ITT. "I told him," Brown recalled, "$55 million, plus or minus adjustments."

Brown went on to tell us that the $55 million figure had been arrived at through analysis of earnings up to 1989, adjusted by the cost of potential future investments as well as possible increases in revenue sharing with Perumtel. He said, "I could foresee Indonesia continuing to make demands on us until we got out. Also, I had obtained a copy of the Indonesian constitution and I knew it was a matter of time before somebody invoked the 'public interest' clause." The informally offered figure was very helpful but not quite enough to get discussions moving.

Meanwhile, the Indonesian side was becoming irritated with the ITT negotiating team, which was more or less reduced to Indosat director William Brown. The government wanted someone from corporate headquarters who represented a wider view of ITT's business interests in the country. Indonesians suspected that managers from the product division were concerned only with the price obtained for this project, not with the benefits and costs of a settlement to other parts of the conglomerate. The goal was a new, high-level person who might consider the broader interests of the company and have the authority to break the deadlock.

To make its point, the government began to apply subtle pressure in other areas of the company's operations in Indonesia. ITT's color TV assembly plant had won a contract to supply Hotel Borobudur Intercontinental, in which the state had the majority shareholding. The hotel abruptly suspended the supply contract in a signal to ITT of the consequences of stubbornness and procrastination. Indonesians also explicitly expressed their desires for a representative from corporate headquarters.

The message was heard. Soon, two more executives arrived on the scene, namely, James T. Woolf, corporate vice president in charge of acquisitions and divestitures, and Derrick W. Samuelson, assistant general counsel of the corporation who had all but drafted the original agreement.

Although such managers often inflexibly defend what they have done, Samuelson must have seen himself as representing the corporate view. Most likely, the fact that the original negotiations had occurred thirteen years earlier helped him to avoid the usual trap of defending old and outdated terms.

Wrapping It Up

The right moves had been made. Negotiations began to edge forward again as broader company concerns replaced the narrower interests of the product division. To encourage progress, the government made a proposal that ITT accepted: While the price issue was still being discussed, all other aspects that had been agreed would be spelled out in a sale/purchase agreement. The maneuver was useful because major points of agreement were being neglected and lost rather than being used as stepping stones for progress. Still, the new ITT team was not throwing away anything. Negotiations between the two teams involved, in the words of one consultant, "No shouting, no tantrums, but tough and hard bargaining."

The final session to draw up the sales agreement stretched well into the early hours of the morning. The Indonesians' consultants, suffering from jet lag, were relatively wide awake at odd hours and were delighted to push on. To accelerate progress, sometime around midnight each side nominated three representatives to negotiate in a separate room. When they had questions, the representatives would return to the full teams and their chairmen for authorization. Exhausted from the lengthy negotiations and without the advantage of jet lag, more and more Indonesians in the anteroom would lay their heads on the table to doze off.

At one point, the head of the Indonesian team, Oskar, asked his advisors whether he could be excused to go home. The three representatives on the Indonesian side (by this time, an Indonesian lawyer, Solomon, and Wells) said "sure," and Oskar left. But no one told the company side of his departure. Several times in the early morning hours representatives of the Indonesian side pleaded that they needed authority before they could yield to company demands. They proceeded to the Indonesian anteroom, and soon returned to report that the exhausted Oskar had said "no." The ploy worked, and drafts of two interim agreements were finally hammered out before daybreak. It had taken four days and nights from November 17 to November 20, 1980, to create a Share Sale Agreement and a Release and Indemnity Agreement.

The documents were surprisingly difficult and complicated, even in the absence of the actual price figure. The Share Sale Agreement set out the date of share transfer; the payment schedule; the rights of government auditors, consultants, and officials to company books; and the required warranties with respect to ownership, accuracy of information, lists of property, directors' remuneration, pending law suits, potential claims and liabilities, and all agreements to which Indosat was a party. The government committed to producing any needed approvals, no taxes on settlement payments, and permission for dividends to be remitted for 1980. Further, it promised to assume financial obligations and to cover claims under "letters of comfort" issued by the company in connection with finance. The Release and Indemnity Agreement provided for the termination of all existing agreements between ITT/ACR/Indosat and all other ITT affiliates as well as those between ITT/ACR/Indosat and the government and its agencies upon payment of the sale price to ACR and the transfer of shares to the government. The parties also indemnified each other in respect of "all claims, demands, actions or proceedings of any kind" after the sale and purchase of shares.

Even at dawn, a couple of items remained under dispute. With the signing scheduled for mid-day, the Indonesians set up a signing room. Flags of both nations were placed on the formal table setup where ministers were to sign. The idea was to make failure to reach agreement embarrassing to company managers. Sometime in the morning, the company conceded on the remaining items. There was one hitch: At the last moment, the only copying machine available broke down, holding up the copies to be signed. The problem was overcome in the nick of time, and the suspicious ITT team was able to compare the photocopies line by line with the original to make sure that nothing had been surreptitiously inserted during the reproduction process. The formal signing of the two documents went ahead, with the government represented by Minister Sumarlin and American Cable and Radio Corporation by Woolf.

The price still had to be settled. The most recent proposal from ITT had been $72.6 million; the government's formal offer on the table was $30 million. Principles had been shoved aside. ITT was no longer persisting seriously in its demand for the present value of future earnings, nor was the government insisting on the old measure of book value. The Indonesians had, meanwhile, managed to convince themselves that the net value of Indosat's property, plant, and equipment as of the end of November 1980 was over $40 million. Hence, there was still room for compromise and face saving on both sides.

"There was a large gap between their position and ours," Oskar told us afterward. "Although we did not by any means want ITT to leave without compensation—this was not a case of revocation or nationalization—but it had to be reasonable compensation." Then he added an aside: "On one occasion, someone from the ITT side asked me whether there would be a commission involved in settling the final price." This confirmed Oskar's fears that he might later be accused of taking a bribe. In response, he requested Sumarlin to assign two additional officials to be present during price negotiations, including a director from the state audit department.

During our years of research, we have yet to come across any evidence of bribes in the purchase of Indosat. But Minister Sumarlin was sufficiently concerned about the possibility of subsequent allegations that he decided to step into the negotiations himself to resolve the price issue. Consequently, the ITT executives from here on began to meet with both Sumarlin and Oskar in private sessions.

What exactly transpired between the parties is known only to the participants, but the approach finally produced a sale price of $45 million, almost matching one evaluation of Indosat's net property, plant, and equipment as of the end of November 1980. Some adjustments reduced the amount to $43,616,000.[23]

A Supplemental Agreement incorporating this price was signed on December 16, 1980, and was made a part of the earlier Share Sale Agreement. Within a week, ACR was to receive $10,400,000 and the balance by the "closing date" of January 15, 1981. In the end, payment was accelerated, and all pieces of the jigsaw puzzle fell into place on December 30, 1980. Accounts were settled, payments made, and share certificates handed over to the new owner of Indosat. The Indonesian flag flew over Indosat on January 1.[24]

At the ceremony marking the transfer of ownership, the two sides expressed the public versions of their sentiments. Speaking on behalf of ITT's corporate headquarters, Woolf said,

> We understand the reasoning behind the Government's desire to acquire ownership of Indosat. . . . We feel that the outcome in terms of price and manner of payment has been fair to both sides.
>
> In view of the Government's treatment of ITT in this transaction as well as in other matters, we will be ready, if you should wish, to act as a reference for other foreign companies who may be contemplating investments in Indonesia, to state that, based on our experience, one can expect fair treatment here.
>
> We expect to continue to be active in Indonesia in the future in business areas where we have expertise [referring explicitly to sales of telecommunications equipment to Perumtel, local assembly of telephones and color televisions, and franchises for Sheraton hotels]. . . . We will look favorably on other future investment opportunities here where we feel we have something to contribute.

Protected in its business interests in Indonesia, ITT had done what was expected of it: It did not complain about how it was treated. Suharto's government controlled the local press and could ensure no coverage at home. ITT must have decided that international coverage would not help its position in Indonesia. In fact, to this day most foreign investors in Indonesia know nothing of this nationalization by the Suharto government.

Minister Sumarlin reciprocated on behalf of Indonesia. After thanking Woolf for his words and ITT for its cooperation, he reiterated the reasons why the government had purchased Indosat and concluded that "PT Indosat is legally and effectively owned by the Government of Indonesia as of today. . . ."

In the middle of rejoicing and farewells, though, there was one final touch of irony: The man who had led Indosat for a decade and helped to build it into a thriving and lucrative enterprise for ITT, George Hunter, was excluded from the last act and was not permitted to attend the concluding ceremony. Presumably because of fear of what he might say, Hunter was advised by his colleagues "you are not needed."

With this piece of commercial diplomacy, the curtain came down on a very eventful era in the history of one foreign-owned project, and one might also say, on an era in the history of foreign investment in Third World infrastructure. The end of ITT's ownership was one of the very last in a long wave of nationalizations of similar projects around the world that had begun more than two decades earlier. For the next decade or longer, almost all infrastructure in the Third World would be state owned.

4

The Power of Being Needed

The conception of two people living together for twenty-five years without having a cross word suggests a lack of spirit only to be admired in sheep.
—Alan Patrick Herbert[1]

Viewed in isolation, the Indosat affair might be seen as a case of a Third World host country that capriciously and opportunistically took over a financially attractive foreign-owned enterprise. But an examination of other foreign investment disputes in developing countries during the previous two decades indicates that Indonesians and others acted with more reason than caprice. The overall pattern suggests that there was probably little that ITT could have done to protect its investment once its hold on technology had slipped.

The Obsolescing Bargain

Large projects, particularly in infrastructure or mining, have certain characteristics that have made them frequent subjects of conflict with host governments. One powerful explanation of the disputes and nationalizations has been called the "obsolescing bargain," and it helps greatly in understanding the ITT story.[2]

The obsolescing bargain begins with the assumption that developing countries are uneasy with foreign ownership of politically sensitive assets. This includes particularly businesses such as minerals or petroleum, public utilities, and defense. A telecommunications facility, like ITT's, was certainly sensitive. Discomfort may result from simple nationalism, but it also may be a reaction to the obvious costs of foreign investment, in terms of dividends and external control. Nevertheless, even in the days when antiforeign sentiments were especially strong in the Third World, countries accepted foreign ownership in sensitive sectors when it brought undisputed benefits. That is, when the foreigner had assets of some kind that were not available locally or that could be obtained from foreign investors at a substantially lower cost than from alternative sources. ITT's contribution to Indonesia, of course, was critical technology.

When very desirable investors arrive for negotiations, governments view almost any deal as better than no deal. The investor, on the other hand, often hesitates, seeing risks in spite of officials' frequently reiterated promises. The tone is set for an outcome that favors the investor, or that will likely eventually be seen that way.

Agreements favorable to the investor are even more probable when governments lack information about terms signed elsewhere for similar projects. In Indonesia in the late 1960s, government officials knew little; we doubt that they had any information at all on what ITT had agreed to in other projects, for example. On the other hand, the private side has access to both its own agreements and, often, agreements of other investors. The asymmetry in information weakens host countries in negotiations.

Once the foreign investor sinks his funds into excavations, attitudes easily change. First, when commercial risk has been resolved, it is more or less forgotten by both sides. With the economy booming and Indosat raking in money, it was very easy for Indonesian officials, and ITT managers for that matter, to forget the earlier perceptions of risk. And of course, all overlook the investments that failed. Why, someone will ask, should the country allow the foreigner a huge return when the capital could have been borrowed for much, much less?

Safe Havens

To be sure, not all large and profitable projects are slated for renegotiation or nationalization. If the host government sees the continued presence of the foreign investor as essential, it is likely to consider challenges to arrangements as far too dangerous to national interests. This kind of protection for the foreign investors can come from various sources.

Technology

Especially safe is the investor who maintains control over essential technology. For decades, IBM relied on its continuing input of new know-how to demand 100% ownership of its subsidiaries around the world. If a potential host government pressed hard for a joint venture, IBM would refuse to invest; if IBM was already in the country, it would leave rather than submit to demands. As a result, the company retained its wholly owned operations, while lesser firms succumbed to nationalistic pressures for joint ventures. Of course, IBM eventually lost its huge technological lead and was, not surprisingly, forced to retreat from its policy of total control.

ITT came to Indonesia with technology that Indonesians did not have and only a few foreign companies could provide. By transferring technology to Indonesians, the investment had accomplished exactly what the country wanted. By 1980, Indonesians had mastered the skills; the continued presence of ITT was unnecessary. Consequently, ITT's bargaining power declined accordingly.

Control over Export Markets

Foreign investors also find security when they control export markets. Fearful of losing those markets, governments hesitate to tangle with such investors.

Minerals industries offer important illustrations. Nationalism in the 1970s led to the renegotiation or nationalization of many copper investments. Foreign firms lost control over their mines in Chile, Zambia, and Zaire, for example, while agreements in Papua New Guinea and Indonesia were revised.

In contrast, in the same decade and in spite of nationalism, most foreign investment in bauxite remained secure. Unlike the copper industry, aluminum was dominated by a small number of vertically integrated firms that owned not only bauxite mines but also the alumina plants, smelters, and often even the fabricating facilities through which bauxite had to pass. Because these multinational enterprises carefully avoided locating mines, alumna plants, and smelters in the same countries, a country with mines did not have access to the chain without the foreign investor. A country that took its cues from copper and pressed too hard for revision of a mining agreement would find itself without a market.[3] Jamaica learned the power of the multinational firms the hard way, as pressure on investors accelerated its decline to an insignificant supplier to the world market. The lesson, of course, was not lost on other host governments.

But even in bauxite, there were instructive exceptions. A few mines in Guyana, for example, produced calcine bauxite, a variety sold outside the vertically integrated industry. Guyana could take over its bauxite mines with little risk to its export sales. and it did so.

The structure of the aluminum industry changed in the late 1970s and the 1980s as Japanese and Eastern Bloc technology led to smelters outside the control of the major multinationals. The new smelters showed no hesitancy in buying bauxite from the cheapest source, regardless of ownership. The result was that foreign investors in bauxite mining saw their bargaining power erode, and they had to strike new and less favorable deals with several host governments.[4]

Continuing Inflow of Capital

In a few cases, foreign investors have found protection in industries where they were the only reasonable source of risk capital. While governments in the Middle East were reshaping arrangements with oil investors in the

1970s, Indonesia's petroleum investors remained relatively secure. Unlike in the Middle East, maintaining or expanding production in Indonesia required large and regular investments in risky exploration projects. At one point in the 1970s, without much analysis Indonesia sought to force its oil producers to pay shares of profits similar to those being taken by Middle East governments. Squeezed, the companies slowed their drilling, and Indonesia's reserves began to fall. Quickly learning the lesson, Indonesians backed off and new investment flowed in again.

How Special Are Mining and Infrastructure?

Although the obsolescing bargain model was first used to explain events in petroleum, mining, and infrastructure, it was extended to other sectors, as our IBM story illustrates. But conflicts over manufacturing and service investments have declined in recent years as governments have allowed foreign investors to enter without ad hoc agreements. General legislation may change with time, but usually slowly and not in ways that discriminate among investors.

Yet infrastructure and mining remain especially subject to the obsolescing bargain because private investors almost inevitably require some kind of special agreement with the host government or government-authorized entity. If mineral rights belong to the state, as they do in most of the world, at the minimum the state has to allocate deposits to individual firms. In exchange, it typically demands some kind of compensation, often based on the value of the individual deposit. The government does not have the option of saying that mining is open to any and everyone and then remain aside.

Neither is simply opening markets for most infrastructure investments a practical proposition. Rights to build roads, string up electric wires, dam rivers, and use airwaves must be allocated. If the investor is to obtain the necessary property, it requires government support. Moreover, because competitors cannot efficiently build parallel roads or power lines, an element of monopoly is almost certain. The results are long-term contracts or regulation, again involving the government. Even when the investor might be in a potentially competitive segment of an industry, the customer may be a monopoly. Electricity generators usually sell to monopoly distributors, for example. In these cases, fearing opportunistic behavior, investors will make large investments to serve single buyers only under long-term contracts or under a trustworthy regulatory framework. Those contracts are often with government or government-owned entities, as was Indosat's. Thus, ad hoc agreements with government or government-owned entities are essential, along with their inevitable risks.

The immobility of infrastructure and mining projects adds to their vulnerability. Although demands for renegotiation might lead IBM simply to depart the country with its know-how, telephone lines, underwater cables, roads, water pipes, satellite stations, open pits, and underground shafts cannot, as a practical matter, be moved. Some investors in infrastructure have increased mobility by, for example, building power plants on barges that are linked up by wire to the shore, but genuine mobility is quite rare.

Finally, infrastructure and mining projects are almost always politically sensitive. Infrastructure is basic to the economy and mines involve the national "patrimony." As Indonesians recognized, good telecommunications systems lie at the heart of attracting foreign investment. Electric power is absolutely essential to modern industry. Much infrastructure is important, and in a very direct way, to consumers as well. Even the poorest citizens quickly begin to rely on lights, clean water, and telephones. As a result, foreign investors face a broad constituency ready to attack arrangements, especially if prices rise after private investors arrive. Mining is similarly sensitive because it depletes the national patrimony.

Trigger

Failure to honor an unwritten social contract has often served as a trigger to renegotiation, as it did when ITT hesitated to build the Medan–Penang cable. When the request is for facilities that may not be profitable but serve domestic or foreign policy objectives, investors who ignore political objectives do so at their own risk. Similarly, reluctance to expand capacity or to provide low-priced service to high-cost customers has often brought unwanted attention to investment arrangements.[5] Already by the 1870s, British-owned Argentine railroads found themselves engaged in a dispute over expansions, for example.[6]

If an investor's bargaining power is weak, a change in the host country's government can trigger renegotiation. In the frequently studied Enron/ Dabhol power project in India, for example, immediately upon coming into office in 1995 the BJP government of Maharashtra State repudiated the Enron agreement, blaming unfavorable terms on the corruption of the previous government. Even a gradual change in officials can replace those with commitments to an old deal. One important player in constructing the original Indosat deal, Professor M. Sadli, commented to us on the nationalization that "it was a new breed of decision makers who conducted negotiations with ITT. I would not have canceled the agreement." Sadli, who no longer chaired the investment board, was in no position to argue strongly against nationalization of ITT.

As we shall see later, the 1990s produced a new kind of trigger for renegotiation: the currency crisis.

Other Defenses for Investors

Investment Climate

In spite of the predictions of the obsolescing bargain, foreign investors without special technologies, access to markets, or regular inputs of risk capital have not been completely at the mercy of host governments. Like Indonesia, host governments have to worry about how their actions might be viewed by lenders and other investors. Borrowing abroad for its development needs[7] and eager to attract foreign direct investment, Indonesia feared that nationalization of Indosat might reducing future inflows. Thus, the government went to great lengths to ensure that the outcome of the ITT negotiations would be perceived by the outside world as fair—or better that the outside world would never hear of the nationalization. That concern was reflected in Woolf's mention, in his parting speech, of ITT's willingness "to act as a reference for other foreign companies who may be contemplating investments in Indonesia, to state that, based on our experience, one can expect fair treatment here." The statement was, of course, not gratuitous at all. Sumarlin had won something very important in the negotiations: a promise that the company would not spoil Indonesia's improving reputation among foreign investors. The cost to the country was reasonable compensation to ITT for its subsidiary.

Although national governments feel the constraint of reputation, local governments and government-owned enterprises are often less concerned. Not surprisingly, disputes with investors are therefore frequently initiated by independent units of the central government or by regional authorities. The Dabhol conflict mentioned above originated with an Indian state government, and the Bangkok toll road dispute of 1993 was initiated by the state-owned Expressway and Rapid Transit Authority of Thailand.[8] Neither unit focused sharply on the impact of its actions on other foreign investors. Some years after the ITT story, government decentralization in several Third World countries would give more voice to sub-federal bodies; the result was increasing dangers for foreign investors.

Home Governments

In another line of defense, foreign investors sometimes ask their home governments to intervene on their behalf. Although the days of U.S. Marine intervention had long passed, by 1980 the United States could invoke the Hickenlooper Amendment to cut off aid to a country taking U.S. property, or the Gonzalez Amendment to instruct its directors in multilateral finance organizations to vote against loans to an offending country.[9] In fact, Harold Geneen, ITT's dramatic head, had been personally involved in promoting the Hickenlooper legislation.[10]

In spite of ITT's close ties with the U.S. government, the American embassy remained aloof from the nationalization. Not a peep was heard from OPIC, which had insured some Indosat debt and therefore stood to lose if the lenders were not adequately compensated. In fact, the lack of intervention by the U.S. government was in marked contrast to what was to happen in the later electricity stories.

Ambassador Masters' hands-off attitude toward ITT's problem may have been influenced by his awareness of much bigger American business interests at stake in the Indonesian telecommunications sector during that period: The expansion of Indonesia's domestic satellite communications was attracting private U.S. firms. Further, since mid-1979 NASA had been in discussions with the Indonesian Department of Posts and Telecommunications over the launching of Indonesia's second-generation communications satellites.[11] But certainly more important was that the U.S. government had become hesitant to fight for the interests of U.S. companies against a strongly anti-communist regime. In 1980, the Cold War dominated U.S. foreign policy, and a major goal was to keep developing countries from falling into the communist camp. Words might be exchanged to satisfy the U.S. treasury, the commerce department, and Congress, but the local embassy and the state department usually resisted aggressive action. In Indonesia in particular, the U.S. government did not hide its enthusiasm for the anti-communist government of Suharto. It had intervened covertly earlier, in the 1950s, to support the civil war to topple the left-leaning Sukarno.[12] Happy to be rid of the leftist regime and not eager to cross horns with this now friendly regime, the United States would not provide meaningful support to an American company engaged in a struggle with the government.

Arbitration

ITT had another line of defense: Its agreement called for international arbitration in the event of dispute. But ITT chose not to turn to arbitration. There are at least three possible explanations for ITT's decision, and probably all played some role.

First, in 1980 international arbitration between a private investor and its host government was not yet a common way to settle disputes. The International Centre for the Settlement of Investment Disputes (ICSID), the forum under which an ITT case would have been heard, had been established just before the Indosat agreement was signed. By the time of the dispute in 1980, ICSID had registered only nine cases, more than half of which had involved natural resources, two thirds in Africa. The procedures remained somewhat uncertain. Even less clear was whether a winner could collect an arbitration award. Only later would the so-called New York Convention gather enough members to convince investors that other countries would enforce awards. At the time of Indosat, turning to little-tested arbitration must have seemed like a large gamble.[13]

Second, ITT managers must have wondered how their case would be viewed by arbitrators. With an Indonesian brief arguing that the concession itself was unconstitutional and without many precedents, arbitrators might well award no money at all. With the Indonesians having made it clear from the outset that they were willing to pay something in renegotiations, this seemed like a more certain route.

Third, and probably most important, ITT wanted to protect its other interests in Indonesia. The bitterness that would have accompanied arbitration might have so damaged the company's reputation that its other businesses would have suffered. We shall see that arbitration did destroy business prospects for later investors.

By the time of our next stories, arbitration had become a more sophisticated and powerful tool in a system for the protection of foreign investors' property rights. But, for many investors arbitration and other expanded protections would still prove less reassuring than they appeared.

Outcomes That Might (or Might Not) Have Been

With hindsight, ITT's management did not see the loss of its Indosat subsidiary as inevitable. Samuelson remarked to us,

> We would have been willing to soften the realities of the [1967] agreement if only we had someone with vision [in Indonesia] to interface with. I am sure we could have worked things out by addressing the question "how can we together make the situation smoother?" Unfortunately, there was a good deal of gamesmanship—on both sides. We [at ITT] would have liked in any case to retain [management] control to be able to run the company efficiently, which probably would not have been possible on the basis of equity participation by the Indonesian government. Imagine, voting scuffles and all!

Once high-level Indonesians had focused on the agreement, this outcome was probably not in the cards. Indonesia might have offered continued foreign ownership, under a strict regime of price regulation. But the country had no record with this kind of regulation. In an environment of corruption and favors, surely ITT would have hesitated to approve this alternative.

But could ITT have avoided all the government attention to its agreement if it had initiated some steps earlier?

The ITT/Indosat story raises a fundamental question that management is reluctant to face: What should a foreign firm do when it begins to reap a bonanza from its investment by virtue of what might in retrospect appear to be a rather generous contractual arrangement with a developing country, especially if it sees its bargaining power as weak? Should it quietly rejoice in its good fortune until the host country becomes aware of its success, or should it initiate change itself?

Gutsy managers might have proposed partnerships or revisions to the arrangements. The Medan–Penang cable could have been financed by selling part ownership of Indosat to the government, for example. ITT might have relaxed its strong preference for complete ownership and taken in an influential local partner whose interest would also be in continuing profits. We will report on later investors, with little bargaining power, who did exactly that. The step would come at a cost to investors, however: Local partners preferred not to put up money for their shares. More radically, ITT could have offered to surrender its monopoly when its bargaining power declined.

We doubt, however, that it is realistic to expect most managers to initiate changes that would sharply reduce a firm's profits, even if the reduction might ensure a future for the investment. Managers must explain to their boards, shareholders, and lenders the advantages of reducing profits. Doing so successfully to people who have little familiarity with politics in the country in question would take a very persuasive and brave proponent.

Maybe ITT could have quietly incurred the entire cost of building the strategic Medan–Penang cable and postponed the day when the whole arrangement would be challenged. Companies have often recognized the need for responding to government desires, even with unprofitable investments. In the early 1980s, Saudi Arabia managed to "persuade" a group of giant oil companies, including Exxon, to participate in developing petrochemical capacity, for example. The companies' mega-investments eventually flooded the world's polyolefins market and almost wiped out returns for the entire plastics industry for several years. But the oil companies recognized that a "no" would almost certainly have jeopardized the much more profitable oil supply and refining arrangements in Saudi Arabia. We will see similar decisions in later stories in this book, when some oil companies apparently undertook and renegotiated electric power investments in Indonesia for strategic purposes rather than out of great enthusiasm for the projects themselves.

Although proceeding with the cable might have delayed the inevitable, the Indosat deal was obsolete by 1980. The problems were fundamental. "It was only a matter of time," Jonathan Parapak said to one of us. This was a politically sensitive industry, one at the critical node of Indonesia's international communications. By 1980, foreign ownership seemed like a burden, not a necessity. Given the attitudes of the times, the foreigner had to be displaced.

In 1980, Indonesian decision makers were hardly at the forefront of the movement to take over the commanding heights of the economy. Other developing countries had long driven out almost all foreign investment from infrastructure. It was not news to ITT executives that Indosat was part of the very last chapter of a long story of takeovers of this kind of investment around the world. Only after a decade or more would foreign investment return, but it would again encounter problems.

After a brief follow-up on state-owned Indosat, we will explore more recent foreign investments, where the obsolescing bargain is very useful, but not sufficient, to explain what happened.

5

Indosat: A Successful State-Owned Firm

You can boo, but booing's got nothing to do with it.
—Bob Dylan, remarks at the Bill of Rights Dinner
    at the Americana Hotel, New York, December 13, 1963

Indosat did not collapse into the poorly run firm that is now the image of state-owned enterprises. To the contrary, it embarked on a bold new mission, invested in maintenance and new capacity, expanded rapidly, and kept up with new technologies. Moreover, it made money. But our story of Indosat ends with a twist of irony.

Indosat as a State-Owned Enterprise to 1985

Many Indonesians acknowledged openly and ungrudgingly that the organization and management systems ITT had left behind proved durable and successful. Foreign investment had worked; it had transferred skills and technology to Indonesians.

So encouraging were the early years of state ownership of Indosat that they challenge the idea that ownership per se—public or private—is the critical issue in the success or failure of infrastructure. Although the disputed Medan–Penang cable opened for service in March 1984, Indonesia refrained from imposing numerous unprofitable social goals on Indosat. Further, it resisted any temptation to provide subsidies. Nor did it insist on low regulated prices that would make it impossible to earn profits for reinvestment. Moreover, the enterprise retained the skills that the foreign investor had developed.

Critical Initial Decisions

Retaining ITT's Top Indonesian

With the Indonesian flag flying over Indosat on January 1, 1981, one of the first decisions was who would manage the state's newly acquired company. Jonathan Parapak, ITT's Indonesian manager, was the choice, and one likely made by the Indonesian president himself.

Parapak had technical skills, some government experience, and management training. Born in 1942 and educated in engineering in Australia, he had worked briefly in government before going to Indosat. Perhaps most importantly, he had been the beneficiary of ITT's in-company management training, working his way up from systems engineer, to manager of engineering, to director of operations and engineering, and eventually to the top post in Indosat. Now he was determined to demonstrate that public enterprises could be run professionally, productively, and ethically. In the process, he worked within the state system to get things done by dint of what he called "creative response to red-tape."

Dividing Up the Tasks

Another decision was the future relationship between Indosat and the old-line, government-owned Perumtel, which operated the domestic telephone system. The government decrees that converted Indosat into a state-owned commercial enterprise (*Persero*), the most business-like of the three forms of state enterprise in Indonesia,[1] seemed clear: Indosat retained responsibility for international telecommunications, while Perumtel was assigned domestic telecommunications.

The two companies, however, remained locked in negotiations throughout 1981 to define their relations with respect to services to be provided, use of equipment and facilities, maintenance, logistics, costs and compensation, and assignment and training of employees. Prior to nationalization, Indosat's arrangements with Perumtel had been rather simple: Indosat directly managed only the satellite ground station and the international technical maintenance center; it paid Perumtel a fee for domestic distribution and collection services; and it reimbursed the cost of Perumtel employees loaned to Indosat. Because the government mandated that Indosat would now assume full responsibility for all facilities and people connected with international telecommunications services, some of Perumtel's operations would have to be transferred to Indosat.

Perumtel management saw a separate state-owned Indosat as compromising its status as the sole national telecommunications agency. Moreover, like employees in many a state-owned firm, some Perumtel employees were not eager to move to a firm that was likely to be operated much like a private company, as Parapak explained, "because they would lose their traditional privileges, such as automatic promotions strictly on the basis of seniority." In the heat of negotiations, Perumtel even threatened to withdraw its trained employees from Indosat.

Perumtel and Indosat finally agreed at the end of 1981. Indosat would take on international telex and telegraph and coordination with overseas systems, which in the past had been under Perumtel's jurisdiction. The transfer required moving some 667 Perumtel employees to Indosat. A somewhat complex cost sharing and compensation formula was devised to replace the earlier percentage fee.[2]

Labor Policy

Parapak's new labor policies in Indosat were something of a reaction to his experience under the American-based multinational. He told us,

> Of a total workforce of 140 [for ITT's Indosat], only 40 were regular employees and the rest contract labor. You cannot build loyalty among your people if they are borrowed from others. Now the entire workforce consists of regular employees. We used to have a union in the old days, but no more. ITT was more interested in professional people. Start-up-top was the philosophy. As for others, it was "if-we-can-do-without-you-we-will" kind of attitude. We have changed that totally. . . . There is no more discrimination in our workplace.

While Perumtel offered a base wage with as many as 21 benefits, the system of Indosat was modeled on that of a private-sector firm, with few benefits but a higher base wage.

Parapak also turned his attention to building an appealing work environment:

> We visited the office premises regularly. We would come into a room and clean it up, tidy it up, change the lights, put aside worn out typewriters and dirty tables—we showed them a whole new way of life.

Aiming for a new work ethic, Parapak reported the results:

> Within the first year of our independent operations, absenteeism dropped from 18% to 2%. The waiting time on operator-aided calls was reduced from 10 to maximum of 3 minutes. . . . Settlement of international accounts used to take anywhere up to eight months; we brought it down to less than three months. Equipment reliability reached a near perfect level of 99.99%.

Beyond the Twenty-Year Horizon

ITT's investment plans for Indosat had always been constrained by the fact that the agreement would end in 1989. Parapak's vision began to soar when this barrier disappeared. Consequently, state-owned Indosat's actual capital outlays reached Rp84 billion, in contrast to ITT's planned investment of Rp4.3 billion of investment from 1981 to 1985.[3]

Revenues over the plan period turned out far better than the forecast as well—almost triple, in fact. In its first five years of state ownership,

Indosat's annual receipts rose 660%. Its profit performance between 1981 and 1985 was even more impressive, jumping 824% (see Table 5.1).

Even with new investments, over the first five years of state ownership Indosat paid the government dividends totaling Rp112 billion ($102 million, at the 1985 exchange rate) and corporate taxes of Rp125 billion ($114 million). The returns on the approximately $45 million the state had paid for Indosat were handsome. And so successful was Indosat in meeting international standards that it began to win tenders from international Intelsat.[4]

Unfortunately, these results were hardly typical for public-sector enterprises in Indonesia.

Corruption

Corruption was a debilitating disease in Indonesia, earning it the dubious ranking of the most corrupt country in the world in 1995.[5] ITT's bribes for the original Indosat contract hardly set it apart from other companies doing business in the country. Could Indosat, as a state-owned enterprise, escape the corruption that was so pervasive in Indonesia?

Parapak argued that keeping Indosat clean was not only possible, but that he had made it a personal mission "to prove that it can be done." Even during the ITT days, Parapak enjoyed the reputation, as one ITT manager diplomatically put it, of being "untainted by his environment." But the real test of his integrity came after he became the CEO of state-owned Indosat. He learned early on that he could not assume that Indosat would remain immune to unethical business practices, especially after the heavy influx of former Perumtel employees from a different culture. He said, "It is public knowledge that commissions, or 'gift envelopes,' are commonly exchanged" in the public sector. But he and other managers agreed to

Table 5.1 Indosat Revenues and Net Income (million rupiah)[a]

	1981	1982	1983	1984	1985	1981–85
Revenues forecast—1980 (under ITT ownership)	19,666	22,812	33,871	49,113	62,668	188,130
Revenues achieved (under state ownership)	26,679	66,902	111,060	140,732	176,056	521,429
Percentage improvement over forecast	36%	193%	228%	187%	181%	177%
Net income forecast—1980	4,469	5,518	8,794	13,675	17,325	49,781
Net income achieved	8,813	24,251	52,838	65,778	72,609	214,289
Percentage improvement over forecast	97%	339%	387%	381%	319%	330%

[a]U.S. dollar amounts given in the forecast converted into rupiah at the following exchange rates: 1983—US$1 = Rp800; 1984—US$1 = Rp1000; 1985—US$1 = Rp1100

Source: The 1981–85 business plan submitted to the ITT headquarters by Jonathan Parapak in the third quarter of 1980 and Indosat's annual reports for the same five-year period.

...tell our employees that none of us was prepared to accept any commissions, any gifts, any influence, or anything like that, either from people outside when they became suppliers, or people inside who wanted to be promoted or to be placed in certain positions [of authority]. And if anybody was interested in those sorts of things, [we must tell them] to please leave Indosat immediately.

True to his word, Parapak addressed a 1982 letter to everyone doing business with Indosat, circulating it within Indosat as well. The critical paragraph was this:

...the Board has made a policy decision that no officer or employee of Indosat is permitted to accept a commission, kickback, gift, favor, or anything else that would, or might be deemed to, influence and/or interfere with the execution of the functions related to purchasing, supply of goods, facility development, provision of services, collection of payments, etc. Giving or acceptance of the items in question will be firmly dealt with and the Board will immediately terminate all relations with the business associate, supplier, or contractor involved.[6]

To us, Parapak said, "One cannot, of course, count on the inherent goodness of people without at the same time ensuring that they earn decent wages: Pay your employees well and look after their general welfare—our salaries [in the mid-1980s] are some 30% higher than [those of] the public sector at large." Parapak also introduced a system of rotation whereby employees were not allowed to occupy sensitive positions for long periods. "You know the difference," he said, "between *tempat basah* [Indonesian for, literally, a wet place, a position where opportunities for collecting bribes are significant] and *tempat kering* [a dry place]. Why tempt people by prolonged exposure?"

But Parapak's system was not perfect. In subsequent conversations with Indosat's corporate clients during the summer of 1987, we had a distinct feeling that cracks had begun to appear in the solid ethical structure. One client, for example, gave us the following account of his experiences in dealing with Indosat representatives:

To gain access to the packet-switched network for data transmission, you have to register with Indosat and obtain a code. [When we applied] we were approached by an Indosat employee [who said], "it normally takes two months to get a code, but I can help [expedite it]...!" Similarly, when we sometimes experience carrier loss on the lease circuit, help doesn't come from Indosat [without consideration].

Still, we believe that instances of this type constituted aberrations. Other clients confirmed the organization's generally respectable image.

An Important Caveat

Good management and the lack of harmful government intervention played a major role in Indosat's performance, but there was another important

Table 5.2 Direction of Telephone Traffic (April 1987)

	Indosat (Traffic to the United States)	ATT (Traffic to Indonesia)
Total calls	47,427	112,771
Total minutes	299,771 (20%)	1,162,357 (80%)
Average length per call	6.32 minutes	10.30 minutes
Average charge (collection rate)	$2.35 per minute	$1.35 per minute[a]

[a]Various types of rates—economy, discount, and standard, for the initial minute as well as rates for each additional minute—have been averaged out over a 10.30-minute call.

factor, and one that casts something of a shadow over the enterprise. An inherited tradition that Indosat chose not to modify in the post-ITT era was the use of monopoly power to charge its customers high prices.

Around the world, international telecommunications services had long been priced well above their cost, with the resulting contribution used to support domestic and especially consumer services.[7] But, Indosat's rates were especially high. One indicator is the fact that foreign firms in Indonesia, and their expatriate personnel, showed a preference for international phone calls to be into, rather than out of, Indonesia (see Table 5.2).

Indosat's high rates probably harmed the larger cause of national development. In the corporate world, efficient telecommunications enables decision makers to minimize uncertainty and improve coordination of activities in offices, factories, and the marketplace. Indeed, at the time the *Economist* said, "the telephone and the information network that it represents have become . . . one of the world's most effective productivity raisers."[8] But telecommunications costs can also be a company's biggest single non-labor cost item after real estate,[9] and profits can easily erode if these costs are not kept in check. Lower rates might even have increased Indosat's profits from international traffic. With communications satellites, in particular, costs flatten out fast. But Parapak argued that high charges could discourage too many calls and thus save foreign exchange for the country, a standard that still carried weight in Indonesia. Even if one agrees with the goal, the conclusion is still hard to accept. Enhancing the ability of businesses to compete in the global marketplace was especially vital for a country trying to reduce its reliance on oil as the predominant source of export revenues. In fact, that Indosat had maintained the monopoly mentality had inherited from ITT was probably the most serious charge laid against the company by its critics.

One might wonder how Indosat could maintain high tariffs while many other state-owned enterprises have been unable to charge customers prices that would enable them to pay for investment needs. In the case of electricity, as we shall see, prices in Indonesia were kept so low that the state-owned power company could not cover its costs and expand capacity as needed. Politics provides the answer, we suspect. Increases in electricity and fuel prices affected many Indonesians; so price increases were met with strong reactions, even riots. In contrast, Indosat's customers did not include a wide swath of the population. There would be no popular uprising against high charges for international phone calls because they fell mostly on business people, and especially on foreign business people.

Nevertheless, Indosat proved that state ownership could work in spite of what was to become the conventional wisdom. The company was managed well, but its profits were also attributable to its ability to exploit a monopoly position. Many other state-owned enterprises have been less fortunate.

Indosat from 1985

Spreading Its Reach

Parapak continued as president and CEO of Indosat until 1991, when he moved on to broader assignments. He remained on Indosat's supervisory board, however.

In 1985, Indosat opened its second gateway, in Medan; in 1992, its third, in Batam; and in 1995, its fourth, in Surabaya. Through these ports, Indonesia used satellite, submarine cable, and microwave to communicate with the rest of the world. By 1989, all its switching and transmission equipment had been converted to digital. International direct dialing service, first introduced in 1981 for Jakarta-based customers on a limited scale, was by 1995 available throughout Indonesia and covered 80% of all outgoing international calls.

Unlike many state-owned telecommunications companies elsewhere, Indosat jumped into cellular operations when they were taking off. It held controlling shares in Telkomsel, the country's largest operator, and Satelindo, with Deutsche Telkom. By 2002, it had become the country's largest internet service provider, and had begun to offer World Wide Web consulting services to businesses.

An Odd Twist

By the late 1980s, fashions had come full circle, as we will see in Part II of this book. The new so-called Washington Consensus on how development should be encouraged lauded private ownership. Like other developing countries, Indonesia was being pushed by the World Bank and aid organizations to privatize its infrastructure. Private ownership, however, took on some odd meanings.

All along, Indonesia had lagged a bit in following new trends. The nationalization of Indosat had been one of the last of the widespread nationalization of utilities. Similarly, the re-privatization of Indosat took place rather late in the return to private ownership. Most of the telecommunications systems of Latin America, for example, had already been privatized by the time the Indonesian government got around to selling its controlling interest in Indosat.

There may be some advantages in moving slowly. Government and its advisors had the opportunity to learn from bitter public disputes elsewhere. The 1980 nationalization of ITT's subsidiary had gone quite smoothly and had not been accompanied by a domestic outcry against foreigners and their "lackeys," as happened in many other countries. This not only avoided a bad investment climate, but it also made it politically palatable for Indonesians to retain ITT's former manager and many of its management practices in the newly state-owned enterprise.

Even though Indonesia's reluctance to re-privatize Indosat and other state-owned firms had frustrated multilateral institutions, caution seemed especially appropriate with respect to Indosat, which had performed quite well. By the mid-1990s, however, it did seem time for a change. The company needed a large injection of funds to keep up with new technologies. Further, the country's increased dependence on multilateral institutions meant that the government had to respond to demands for serious privatizations.

In October 1994, the Indonesian government took the first steps to privatize what it had so carefully nationalized almost 15 years earlier, offering 35% of its hard-won shares in Indosat—but not control—to private investors. Partial privatization of Telkom came next, after Indosat.[10] Soon Indosat and Telkom shares were trading on the Jakarta and Surabaya stock exchanges, and, through American Depository Receipts, in New York. In 1999, a new telecommunications law would phase out Indosat's and Telkom's "exclusivities" and open the sector for competition, while providing some compensation to investors. As a result, Indosat and Telkom began to encroach on each others' territories.

In 2002, the Indonesian government sold off an additional 42% ownership in Indosat, making it the first major Indonesian state-owned firm transferred to majority private ownership. As a result, Singapore Technologies Telemedia acquired controlling interest in the company.[11] The new owner of "privatized" Indosat was, ironically, itself controlled by the Singapore government.

A Reverse Twist

But, in a July 2005 reversal, the Indonesian government announced its goal of buying back control of Indosat. It was constrained by the cost and by its eagerness to encourage Temasek, the owner of Singapore Telemedia, to invest in other activities in Indonesia. At the same time, Telkom was also proposing to buy back some of its shares. The stated purpose was to increase government control. Cynics, noting the government's 51% ownership of Telkom, feared that management wanted to escape public disclosure rules, especially on the New York Stock Exchange.

Twists similar to those that characterized the Indosat story occurred elsewhere, as infrastructure also moved from private to public and eventually back to private ownership. In the 1990s, privatization of several telephone companies in Latin America had placed them in the hands of Compañía Telefónica de España, the Spanish company that ITT had acquired in 1924 and lost to nationalization in 1945. When privatization became fashionable, in 1987 the Spanish government sold part of its interest in the company, but it retained management control. Thus, over the decades, the telephone companies of Argentina, Chile, and Peru went from ITT control, to state ownership, to control by a former ITT subsidiary that itself was controlled by a foreign state. Even after full privatization of the Spanish company in 1997, the government retained a "golden share" that gave it influence over some strategic decisions. Privatization and state-ownership had become somewhat confusing terms by the time the twenty-first century arrived.

ITT's Fate

If Indosat's story has a happy conclusion, the same can hardly be said for ITT. This *bête noire* of the 1970s Left turned into a pussycat as it went the way of many other conglomerates. Proving unwieldy to manage and yielding to the new antipathy toward diversified firms, ITT was broken up into more focused pieces. At the end of 1985, ITT and the French Compagnie Générale d'Electricité formed a joint venture, Alcatel Alsthom, which combined their telecommunications and electronics businesses. Within four years, ITT's entire remaining worldwide telecommunications products business went to Alcatel. In turn, in 1992 Alcatel sold what had formerly been ITT's "customer premises equipment" business in the United States to a group of private investors, who formed Cortelco Kellogg, later Cortelco. For a while, it licensed the ITT trademark from ITT, but it appears no longer to use the name.

In 1995, the remaining ITT Corporation was divided into three companies: ITT Corporation (with hospitality and gambling properties), ITT Hartford (insurance), and ITT Industries. Only ITT Industries, with miscellaneous industrial and defense products, would retain the ITT name.[12] Nothing like the old and powerful ITT would survive to participate in the new wave of private investment in infrastructure of the 1990s.

Part II

Return of Private Ownership of Infrastructure: Electric Power, 1990–1997

6

Back to Private Power

Government ownership of utilities has always been the first goal of the socialists and communists.
—President J. E. Corette of Montana Power Company, 1959[1]

Long before Indosat was reprivatized, a new ideology had begun to take hold in development institutions. From the mid-1980s, private ownership and foreign investment began to be touted as solutions to many problems of the Third World. Starved of capital for projects they wanted, many officials in developing countries were sold; they turned from efforts to evaluate potential foreign investments to marketing programs designed to attract ever more foreigners. The new attitudes encouraged enthusiastic home countries and multilateral institutions to turn attention to providing guarantees of property rights so that they could increase the flow of investment into the developing world.

In no sector was the enthusiasm of development institutions for private foreign investment greater than for infrastructure, particularly electricity. The consequences were in some cases disastrous. Experiences in Indonesia echo those in many other countries and raise serious questions about when privatization is appropriate, how it should be implemented, whether there are better ways to finance and develop infrastructure, and even whether the new guarantees to foreign investors could survive.

The End of Private Ownership of Infrastructure

With the nationalization of Indosat in 1980, Indonesia had joined most of the rest of the developing world by placing infrastructure into state hands.

From the early 1970s into the mid-1980s, state ownership dominated infrastructure in Asia, Latin America, and Africa, as it had long done in Europe. While in the United States much infrastructure remained privately owned,[2] it was very heavily regulated by the state.

Even countries with unwavering trust in a capitalist market system insisted on either state ownership or state regulation of infrastructure. The intellectual arguments for government involvement derive primarily from perceived "market failures." It is extremely important to note that most infrastructure is characterized by at least some degree of natural monopoly. Because it makes no economic sense to duplicate electric power lines, city gas distribution systems, and highways, competition—the essential guardian of consumer interest—is impractical. Absent state regulation or state ownership, monopolies would exploit their position. Most countries chose state ownership.

Many economists have been less enamored of the additional grounds for government intervention, but there are other reasons for state ownership or regulation. Both demand for and supply of much infrastructure respond slowly to price changes. Customers will light their evenings, shower their bodies, or call their business associates regardless of price hikes for electricity, water, or telephone service; similarly, customers are unlikely to shower more often or turn on more lights if prices decline. Sure, demand may change, but only over a long time period. On the supply side, obtaining all the necessary permits and rights and constructing new facilities—more roads or power plants, for example—is time consuming. Consequently, supply does not expand quickly in response to shortages reflected in price increases. Moreover, investment is "lumpy"—that is, small amounts of capacity cannot be efficiently added. In many infrastructure sectors, both demand and supply are very inelastic, at least in the short run. As a result, price serves as a poor regulator when demand and supply become imbalanced.

Inelasticities, along with high fixed costs, low marginal costs, and the fact that electricity cannot be easily stored, provide a recipe for price instability. Shortages drive prices way up before capacity can expand to meet demand, and surpluses drive prices way down because demand increases little. Moreover, price instability and capacity shortages for something as basic as electricity have troublesome spillover effects on the rest of an economy. The heavy hand of government, in one form or another, has provided a possible remedy for this serious problem.

On top of that, infrastructure is expected to serve social or political goals beyond those that market-driven investors might accept on their own. The demand that Indosat lay the Medan–Penang cable was not an isolated case. Governments insist that affordably priced electric power be available to remote communities, regardless of whether it is profitable to install lines that reach them. A government-owned enterprise can undertake the task, or regulatory agencies can demand it of private actors, as they have in the United States.

Developing countries, in particular, saw additional reasons to turn to state enterprises. Private ownership with government regulation, as in the United States, seemed ill-adapted to the scarce administrative skills and the corruption so pervasive in many poor countries. Private investors would hesitate to turn their futures over to regulatory bodies that might prove untrustworthy. Further, weak domestic capital markets were unlikely to provide the huge sums of money required for private ownership. Consequently, private development would mean foreign ownership, but foreign ownership of sectors critical to the economy was widely viewed, in the 1960s and 1970s, as dangerous to independence, especially in newly constituted countries.

Prior to the mid-1980s, developing countries had alternative sources of funds: The World Bank, other multilaterals, and even private banks were willing to lend to governments so that they could build and own infrastructure, and loans came without the foreign control associated with direct investment.[3] No wonder this was, for a period, a favored choice of the developing world.

The New Ideology: Private Ownership Again

The 1980s brought new views of the proper role of governments in economic affairs. The Reagan and Thatcher revolutions called for market solutions to almost everything, including infrastructure. Their free-market theorists argued that market failures were exaggerated, but in any event the old policies of government intervention caused still more "failures" and pressures for even more intervention. The results were worse than the original problem. If government would step back, it was believed, markets would take care of most issues. Thus, privatization and deregulation became magic bullets for some very difficult problems.

Although the growing "Washington Consensus" covered a wide range of policies, the preference for private ownership was prominent among them.[4] The new ideology quickly dominated the policies of U.S. foreign assistance; multilateral agencies—in particular, the World Bank and the International Monetary Fund (IMF)—were quick converts as well. Yet the new enthusiasm for privatization seemed like testing new medicines on the poor. Developing countries were pushed to privatize their infrastructure in ways that had hardly been attempted in many industrialized countries.

The new policies garnered at least some support in developing countries, and a few countries embraced them with open arms. Although Indosat may have been working fine, many other state-owned enterprises were not. Some had turned into employment machines, with high wages and excess labor. Political control over prices led many to lose money and left them unable to expand services. A government might even find temporary relief for its budget problems by selling off some state-owned companies.

The environment had also changed. Fear of domination by foreign firms had declined, especially in Asia and Latin America where officials had gained skills and self-confidence. In a very few countries, growing domestic capital markets even raised the possibility of domestic private ownership of large projects.

With the new consensus, the World Bank ordered a review of the inefficiencies of electric power in the developing world.[5] The findings justified what was already becoming the new policy of the World Bank Group: It would, whenever possible, support private generating companies, rather than providing funds to governments or state-owned entities. According to former executives of the Indonesian state-owned electricity company (PLN), from 1990 the World Bank made it clear that it would make no more loans to Indonesia for state-owned generation. The debt crises of the early 1980s had reduced governments' access to private banks. Now they were losing the principal alternative source of money for state development of infrastructure.

However, observers realized that private investors might hesitate to undertake large commitments when, unlike ITT, they had no technological edge that could secure their property. Although host countries might make promises, governments could change their laws and commitments, and they had done so with abandon in recent decades. International institutions and home governments began to construct new rules for the market.

Securing Property Rights for the New Investors

The results emerged rather haphazardly, but the new system of property rights appeared to offer credible assurances to investors.

First, international arbitration grew in importance as new arrangements provided governing rules and many countries signed commitments to honor awards made by arbitrators. Further, the spread of bilateral investment treaties (BITs) and regional economic agreements assured a growing number of foreign investors that they would have access to international arbitration. No longer would each investor have to seek individual assurances of access to arbitration, as had petroleum and mining companies, and even ITT.

Second, governments and multilaterals found ways to expand their political risk insurance to cover "creeping expropriation." Changes in investors' contracts could end up triggering claims. In addition, multilaterals and export agencies of home countries increased their lending to private investors for infrastructure projects. Such credit from home countries or multilateral financial institutions and official insurance looked rather like guarantees. No host country, many investors reasoned, would squeeze a project that involved money or insurance from the World Bank and aid donors.

Finally, and apparent only in the 1990s, the United States in particular began to offer much more support to its investors than it had at any time since before World War II.

Still, enthusiasm and new assurances did not solve all problems in sectors as complicated as infrastructure. A 1990 World Bank conference report[6] expressed puzzlement that negotiations had become so tedious, saying the fears that governments would not follow "the rules of the game" were "grossly exaggerated." They added, "Few governments have signed contracts and then clearly repudiated them." The authors ended with "Nevertheless, it is exciting to contemplate shifting to the private sector the provision of certain services which have traditionally been delivered by the public sector." Repudiation was, of course, soon to come; and the process of shifting to the private sector was to prove much more "exciting" than this first brush with reality dared suggest.

Indonesia's Power Sector

Indonesia's renewed interest in private infrastructure emerged first in toll roads. As a preview of what was to come, in 1987 the initial road project went to a firm controlled by President Suharto's eldest daughter Siti Hardiyanti Rukmana, known as Tutut.[7] Funds reportedly came from two government-owned banks, a state-owned cement company, and a Suharto foundation. When one of the banks turned down Tutut's first request for an interest-free loan, the bank's president was dismissed.

Similarly, the personal interests of the president's family in privatization would plague all infrastructure. In earlier days, a large portion of income from corruption had been used to buy political stability by supporting the official political party and buying off potential dissidents. As Suharto's children grew up, however, they introduced a new type and probably a new level of corruption: They took equity positions in any potentially profitable large enterprise, and eventually even in smaller ones. Their business empires were supplemented by real estate, jewelry, racing cars, and other assets that reflected a level of conspicuous consumption largely absent in the past. Infrastructure offered a new opportunity for expanding the children's portfolios.

It was the colorful minister for research and technology, B. J. Habibie (see Box 6.1), who pushed hardest for private sector participation in electric power.[8] After unsuccessfully promoting a private nuclear power plant, in 1987 Habibie was appointed to chair the so-called Team 35 to deal with the problems of slow implementation of electric power projects. Membership excluded the powerful minister of finance[9] and all other technocrat economic ministers. This no doubt intentional omission of the technocrats reduced oversight of hanky-panky and also marked the start of the intra-government tensions that would underlie all power negotiations.

Box 6.1 B. J. Habibie

B. J. Habibie was one of the more colorful characters of Suharto's Indonesia. Born on the island of Sulawesi in 1936, he was spotted early when Suharto was serving in the military. He was sent to Germany, where he received a doctorate in engineering in 1965.[a] Habibie stayed on to become a vice president director at the German aircraft manufacturer Messerschmitt. After he became convinced that Indonesia's development required "jump-starting" the country with high-tech industries, he was invited in 1974 by Suharto to return as an advisor to the president and Ibnu Sutowo, head of Pertamina. In 1978, Habibie became minister of state for research and technology, pushing state development of an aircraft industry as well as other high-tech businesses. His emphasis on high tech in a very poor country made him controversial, and his off-budget financing of favored ventures did not endear him to the economic technocrats.

An adoring biography of Habibie inadvertently says a good deal about the person. For example, it quoted his wife:

> [T]here can't be two captains on one ship...I am aware that I should not be in his way....He always was a person who is enthusiastic about building up his country and nation....I must prepare his clothes for wearing, his shoes have to be ready there also. His meals must be served by me he loves such small gestures [sic]. Therefore, I who know him well, must adjust myself. Shouldn't married people stick to the motto of *"the big you and the small I?"*[b]

One advisor described Habibie in arguments as "jumping up and down," and summed up his many contacts with Habibie in one statement: "He was a lunatic." The technocratic ministers would surely have agreed with the advisor, but some others considered Habibie to be a brilliant visionary. And some, especially foreign businesspeople, saw great money-making opportunities in his visions, whether he was a lunatic or not.

German firms worked hard to cultivate him, and they were willing to pay. *Der Spiegel* got hold of documents confirming a remittance to Habibie of 200,000 marks from Ferrostall in 1991.[c] A former chairman of Siemens is quoted as saying, "We brought him along, we built him up, then he turned and put the bite on us. Now he's got a castle in Germany that makes mine look like a garage."[d]

---

[a]A. Makmur Makka, *Habibie: From Pare-Pare via Aachen* ([Jakarta]: C. V. Swakarya, 1989), English edition.

[b]Makka, *Habibie.*

[c]Theodore Friend, *Indonesian Destinies* (Cambridge, Mass.: Belknap Press for Harvard University Press, 2003), p. 395.

[d]Quoted in Friend, *Indonesian Destinies,* p. 395.

PLN's Limits

In 1964, Indonesia had assigned electric power to the separate state-owned company Perusahaan Listrik Negara (PLN). In subsequent years, PLN was turned into an increasingly independent entity,[10] taking on the label of a full limited liability corporation in August 1994, but with all its shares in government hands. It had long been managed from the former head-quarters of the old Dutch electricity company, an attractive gingerbread Victorian building in downtown Jakarta. With time, PLN had become a company of 55,000 workers,[11] and its management had spread into several buildings. In the mid-1990s, its headquarters was consolidated and moved to a rather nondescript modern building south of the city. Ever conscious of its origins, however, PLN retained the original Victorian building and made sure that it was brightly and colorfully lit for holiday occasions.

In spite of its official status, PLN was never really the only supplier of electricity. Many industrial firms had set up their own generators, some-times as their principal supply and sometimes as back-up to unreli-able public power.[12] In fact, estimates claimed that 40% to 50% or even more of industrial needs originated from captive or related private sources.[13] In addition, PLN bought in a very small amount of power for its own distribution.

By some measures, PLN had not done so badly. An "index of elec-trification" climbed from 10 in 1981–1982 to 30 in 1990–1991.[14] Generating capacity had grown from 3,934 megawatts in 1983–1984 to 9,117 in 1990–1991.[15] In earlier days, the dry season had led to long brownouts on Java, the most populous island, as hydro reservoirs were drawn down and residual water was used for priority irrigation. Additional oil-fired ca-pacity greatly alleviated seasonal problems.[16] Those with firsthand ex-perience of Indonesia in the bad times of the 1960s and early 1970s noted a marked improvement in the reliability of electric power in later years. Still, backup generators in industrial plants testified to managers' shaky confidence in public power.

From 1989 to 1991 serious problems began again. Brownouts and long waiting lists for new connections for industry appeared as demand outgrew capacity.[17]

PLN's finances were in shambles. One of PLN's problems was euphe-mistically labeled as "leakages." Some leakages were technical, re-sulting from poor maintenance and lack of investment. Some, however, resulted from poor people tapping into PLN's lines with abandon, paying nothing for stolen power. Moreover, rates for the poor were set at very low levels; they paid little even if they did not steal.[18] But for many who paid, power was not cheap. Retail consumers were charged both for the installed capacity of their homes and for power used, and fixed charges increased sharply with capacity. Bills of $500 or more per month were not at all unusual in the early 1990s for an air-conditioned house that met expatriate standards. But many rich and powerful Indonesians ignored

---

Box 6.2 Delhi Leaks

A study of Delhi's electric power system concluded that about half of total power was not paid for. The study identified four sources of leakage. First, some people simply connected directly into the power lines. Second, small firms used very simple technology to tamper with meters, leaving only about a third of actual consumption recorded. Third, larger firms bought more sophisticated technology that slowed electric meters; the devices could be turned off remotely in the event inspectors arrived at the factory gate. Fourth, better-off consumers collaborated with employees of the electricity company, who would record incorrect meter readings to create "provisional bills." In turn, the employees reportedly collected a monthly fee from customers for their "services."

If poor people who hooked into the lines were caught, there was little penalty, and they would simply hook in again. Cheaters in small industries were difficult to catch for they would pull out the special wire in the meter when inspectors visited the neighborhood. With 30% of customers in Delhi having provisional bills, offenders could be chased down, but strong labor unions made it next to impossible to dismiss employees who were involved in the corruption.

Although the study was done in Delhi, an article in the *Jakarta Post* suggested that the problems in Indonesia were quite similar.[a]

Source: Shana Sadiq, "Hidden Firm-Specific Variables and Non-Technical Power Loss as Residual Risks Affecting the Efficiency and Financial Structure of Utilities in South Asia: Case Study Delhi, India," Department of Resource Economics, Tokyo University, April 2003.
[a]A'an Suryana, "PLN-Police Sign Deal to Curb Power Theft," *Jakarta Post,* February 8, 2003.

---

their high electricity bills, adding significantly to those so-called leakages.[19] (For the results of a study of similar leakages from the power system in Delhi, see Box 6.2.)

PLN's prices for electricity were, of course, controlled by the state. Politically sensitive, they were kept low. Publicly available data were not very revealing, but it was said that PLN made an 8% rate of return on its Java/Bali grid[20] and broke even, more or less, on its off-Java facilities, where tariffs were the same as on Java, while costs were higher.[21] Even this performance was possible only with the help of large state subsidies. As a result, PLN was chronically short of money for investment and found borrowing difficult. Unlike Indosat, PLN was not far from the stereotype of state-owned enterprise in developing countries.

Table 6.1 Annual Growth Rate in Real Gross Domestic Product (%)

	Year			
	70–75	75–80	80–85	85–90
Real GDP growth	8.05	7.92	4.74	6.25
Real GDP growth/capita	5.34	6.13	2.46	4.39

Source: Theodore Friend, *Indonesian Destinies* (Cambridge, Mass.: Belknap Press for Harvard University Press, 2003), p. 510.

The shortage of investment funds portended serious problems. Some projections predicted annual growth of 10% to 12% in demand for electricity; by 1993, actual growth exceeded expectations, reaching an astounding 17%.[22] With the economy expanding at up to 6% annually in the 1980s (see Table 6.1), it was abundantly clear that Indonesia was going to need new sources of power.

For Suharto, electricity became an issue of state when forecasts reported that PLN could not meet the demand in the rapidly expanding industrial estates and labor-intensive export processing zones. The president was extremely worried about jobs, especially on Java with its huge numbers of young entering the workforce. Private investment offered a possible solution to what looked otherwise like an intractable power problem with implications for political stability.

Luckily, fuel for private power would not be scarce. Although old coal sources the Dutch had exploited had been almost forgotten, recent exploration was uncovering significant supplies in parts of Kalimantan, and Indonesia had already developed production in Sumatra. Gas was available in the archipelago, in some cases near enough to population centers for power generation. Finally, Indonesians were eager to tap the underground heat sources that were associated with the "Ring of Fire," as the volcanic chain of the Pacific is called. To the government, coal, gas, and geothermal sources were particularly attractive because they could free more of Indonesia's oil to earn foreign exchange on the export market.

The 1994–1999 FiveYear Plan claimed that PLN had doubled its installed capacity from the 1987 level of 6–7,000 megawatts.[23] It called for increasing this capacity by 11,700 megawatts by 1999, with new investment projected at more than $13 billion. PLN would have found it difficult to raise this level of funds anyway, but now the World Bank's hesitancy to lend for state-owned development made the problem more severe. Although international banks were scrambling to lend money to rapidly growing Indonesia, they preferred the private sector or insisted on government guarantees for loans to state-owned enterprises. Anyway, borrowings of state-owned firms were formally limited as a result of past unpleasant experiences.

With few alternatives, Indonesia would turn to privately owned facilities for a substantial part of new capacity.[24] The public learned of the interest in March 1989 when PLN announced its projections. A year later, in April 1990, the president himself formally issued the welcome to foreign investors.

Organizing for Private Power

To deal with the new investors, the government created two teams. The first was Tim Persiapan Usaha Ketenagalistrikan Swasta, soon known by an acronym jarring to English speakers, PUKS; this team was headed by Artono Arismunandar, the Director General for Electricity and New Energy in the Ministry of Mines and Energy.[25] With a brother as a general, a wife related to Suharto's wife, and even rumored status as a successor for Suharto, Arismunandar was in a position to push projects in the right direction. He avoided doing soand eventually told a critical advisor that he did not want to get his fingers burned by crossing important people. He was not alone; no Indonesian seemed willing to cross those "important people." This reluctance would place a heavy future burden on Indonesians.

The Indonesian team picked up a foreign advisor, Peter Jezek, at the end of September 1990, drawing on funding from USAID and the U.S. Office of Energy.[26] Jezek was eventually to become a real mystery figure to Indonesians and to other advisors (see Box 6.3).

Jezek quickly argued that limiting the PUKS team to members of the Ministry of Mines and Energy and PLN was a serious mistake. Concerns about power would inevitably attract the interest of other ministries: in particular, the economic technocrats. Jezek reports that he tried to reach the technocrats himself through Hollinger, who was still an advisor to Sumarlin, by this time the minister of finance, but his efforts were rebuffed.

In May 1991 the Ministry of Mines and Energy issued formal invitations for private companies to submit proposals to build new generating facilities. The new opening would lead to a scramble for contracts, with the almost inevitable accompanying corruption. Scrambling, however, did not mean competitive bidding for most of the projects.

Privatization would indeed bring money that PLN was unable to borrow. But PLN would have to pay even larger sums for private power than it would have had to pay to service debt from borrowing. How it could do so was a question left unanswered. The problems of low tariffs, poor bill collection, and leakage from distribution were very real and were not considered at all in the rush to private power. Unfortunately, Indonesia was not alone in undertaking privatization without a serious analysis of what problems privatization was supposed to cure and what new problems it might impose.

Warnings

Far from all Indonesians were converted to the new Washington Consensus. Indonesians turned to private power mainly because they needed

Box 6.3 Peter Jezek

Like Vladimir Gold, Peter Jezek was born in Czechoslovakia. He came to the United States in 1968, leaving Prague just before the Soviet invasion. He reports that he was sentenced to prison in absentia for his participation in the uprising. In the United States, he earned a Ph.D. in geology. He first went to Indonesia in 1971 for, as he put it, "all kinds of activities," one of which was "geophysical exploration." At some point, he had worked for Stone & Webster and had been designated as project manager for a geothermal project, but it did not go forward. In 1975, he traveled in the islands of eastern Indonesia, finding himself in Timor at the time of the Indonesian takeover. He had started working on private power in Indonesia in 1985, evaluating proposals for a facility on Batam Island and for the potential nuclear plant that had attracted Habibie's interest. He also worked on private power in Pakistan for five years; as he put it, he eventually began shuttling back and forth between the two countries. Unlike Czech-born Gold, Jezek was in no way a shadowy middleman acting on behalf of foreign investors, but he did become a puzzle for many. He was willing to challenge officials for whom he worked and occasionally went public with troublesome issues. According to some people we interviewed, by the end of negotiations for Paiton I, Jezek feared for his own safety, because he had learned too much about the unattractive details of power projects. Another source claimed that Jezek had told him that the U.S. ambassador was trying to get him thrown out of the country. When Jezek returned to Indonesia as an advisor after the Asian Currency Crisis had struck, his struggles with other advisors and his eventual sudden departure would turn him into something of a mystery figure.

capital and because of the personal interests of some influential and well-placed individuals. One clear sign of the lack of deep commitment was the fact that the private sector was invited to participate only in new projects. Enthusiasts would find Indonesia torturously slow in privatizing existing government-owned infrastructure.[27]

Alarms sounded quickly. Jezek, the advisor to the Ministry of Mines and Energy, thought Indonesia should start with small and medium projects to learn. He argued that limited experience in Latin America and Pakistan[28] showed the dangers of jumping in without clear policies. But his desire for careful planning was met with disdain by his minister, Ginandjar Kartasasmita: "If we listened to people advocating planning, we would still be living under [the] Dutch colonial yoke."[29]

Hollinger prepared a report for the minister of finance that supported private infrastructure but also warned of the possible pitfalls.[30] It emphasized that Indonesia was entering territory that had been barely explored by other developing countries.

Inside PLN there was also resistance to private power. Nengah Sudja, the director of research at PLN, told us that he presented a paper at ITB (Indonesia's leading technical university) that asked, What kind of animal is an independent power producer? What is the difference from current arrangements? The answer, he concluded, was simply higher costs.

Hollinger's report may have reached other technocrats, but it is unlikely that it made it to the "engineers," in particular Habibie or the mines and energy minister Ginandjar. It is even less likely that objections from PLN skeptics were read by political figures. The technocrats may have argued their points in debates with the "engineers" before Suharto, but the economy was booming, so the influence of the technocrats was waning (see Box 6.4). Habibie's preference for large projects carried the day, and private investment seemed the only source of the needed funds.

Contracting Generation

The basic structure for privately owned electric power generation in Indonesia was decided rather quickly. Indonesia could choose to invite the private sector to generate, transmit, and distribute electricity; or it could limit private participation to one stage. One argument favoring only generation was that it was less politically sensitive, for consumers would not have to face bill collectors from foreign companies. Also, competition among generators was theoretically possible. Indonesians chose generation, however, for no other reason than that was where they needed money.

Still more choices had to be made.[31]

The Power Purchase Agreement

In the early 1980s, reforms in the United States had led to long-term contracts for private firms to build generating capacity and supply electricity to distribution companies. The contracts were "take or pay," prices were indexed to critical cost variables, and they typically ran for 10 years or more.[32] They ensured that generators had more predictable prices than what regulators might offer because even U.S. regulators might respond to political whims. Still, regulation practically guaranteed that distributors would have adequate cash flows to meet their commitments under the purchase agreements. And even if a distribution company ran into trouble, generators' claims ranked higher than the claims of lenders.[33] With this kind of security, private investors in generation could easily raise low-cost capital. Out of these experiments emerged some American firms—such as Enron, Entergy, and AES—that were ready to take on markets abroad when they opened to independent power producers.

Box 6.4 Decision Making under Suharto

Under Suharto, the decision process on important economic issues differed from what Americans know. Ministers tended to fall into two groups. The economic technocrats tended toward a common position. Another group, sometimes called the "engineers" (Adam Schwarz named a similar grouping the "nationalists"),[a] would often coalesce around a different policy. Representatives of the two groups would argue their cases to the president.

The technocrats preferred competition, free markets, open borders, and little licensing, whereas the engineers pushed for high-tech industries, direct government support, and protection through import licenses, tariffs, and capacity licensing.

President Suharto allocated victories between the groups, carefully keeping the contending powers in balance. The edge tended to go to the technocrats when economic times were bad and to the engineers when times were good. The technocrats became adept at using crises to get their way, pushing for whatever reforms they thought they could get through when times were bad.

Most importantly, when Suharto had listened to his ministers' opinions, he made a decision rather quickly, then he turned the task over to a particular minister to carry out. Everyone quickly fell in line.

When the power agreements were being negotiated, times were good. Thus, the 1993 cabinet was eventually described by one of the technocrats (Emil Salim) as a "cabinet of engineers," led by Habibie and Ginandjar.[b]

[a]The engineers could be subdivided into those who supported "megaprojects," almost regardless of the industry, and those who pushed for high-tech projects. The two subgroups, however, were generally allied. See Adam Schwarz, *A Nation in Waiting: Indonesia in the 1990s* (St. Leonards, Australia: Allen & Unwin, 1994).
[b]Theodore Friend, *Indonesian Destinies* (Cambridge, Mass.: Belknap Press for Harvard University Press, 2003), p. 139.

Market Systems

In the 1980s, the United Kingdom took a different, and more complicated, approach, seeking to build competitive markets for electricity. Private generators sold to distributors through a central pool, with prices determined by demand and supply. Further, large users of electricity could buy directly from the pool or directly from generators, bypassing the heretofore monopoly distributors.

Eventually, some U.S. states began to adopt parts of the U.K. model. The best-known effort was, of course, that of California. Unlike the British, however, California did not allow long-term contracts between suppliers and distributors, and the state capped the retail price of electricity, fearing the political and economic consequences of the kinds of swings that might otherwise result from an inelastic market.

Regulation

There was a sharply different model: A country could skip both competition and contracts by creating an independent regulatory body to set tariffs for privately owned power, usually with guidelines such as return on investment: in other words, the model widely followed in the United States before reform began.

Reaching a Decision

Indonesians chose something close to the first stage of U.S. reforms. The state-owned power company would contract with independent power producers to pay for a given amount of power, whether it needed the electricity or not. The "take-or-pay" arrangements, opposed by some within PLN, would specify minimum payments that would ensure that the investor could meet his fixed costs, including debt service and a target return on investment, no matter how much electricity PLN needed.

Although Indonesians gave no serious consideration to alternatives, the arguments for long-term contracts seem overwhelming. It is hard to imagine that foreign investors would have had any more trust in an Indonesian regulatory system than would ITT. An effort to create real competition by having suppliers bid to sell electricity seemed far too complicated for Indonesia at the time. Economist Paul Krugman concisely laid out the conditions necessary to build a competitive market for electricity: a robust transmission system and a watchdog agency with adequate powers to prevent and punish price manipulation, free of ties to the companies it is supposed to police.[34] In Indonesia, collusion and corruption would surely have proved deadly. Moreover, the problems of operating a market system had not been shaken out even in the industrialized countries; California's later experiment was to collapse in 2000.

Potential investors liked the choice of "power purchase agreements," or PPAs, as they are called in the industry.[35] Their formulas would determine the price PLN would pay for electricity for 30 years. The details of those formulas would, of course, be of great importance because they would determine which party took on various risks: Indonesians through their government enterprise, the government itself, Indonesian consumers, or the investor.

Moreover, this time around investors were convinced by the new international guarantees that contracts would be honored, whether they had bargaining power or not.

Indonesia's advisors were right that the government was entering largely uncharted waters. The power sector was much more complex than toll roads, where Indonesia had some experience. Only scattered information was available about the terms negotiated for the few private power projects in other developing countries. Indonesians did not know the histories of investments in the 1920s and earlier nor would they have viewed them as relevant. In spite of the lack of information, by 1997 Indonesians had signed contracts for 27 power plants, representing close to 11,000 megawatts and an investment of $13 to $18 billion.[36] Still more were under negotiation when things began to unravel.

7

Paiton's Power: The Cost
of Poor Preparation

*The first principle of contract negotiation is don't remind them of what
you did in the past; tell them what you're going to do in the future.*
—Stan Musial

With slow growth in home electricity markets, cheap money, and a go-go atmosphere, foreign investors responded eagerly to the new call of emerging markets. Assurances of property rights added to investors' eagerness to undertake projects in risky places. On the other side, Indonesian officials were unprepared for the complexities of power negotiations and encountered pressure from the U.S. government to sign deals that benefited U.S. companies. And, most importantly, the personal interests of some Indonesians overrode the good of the nation. All this was to become clear in the very first negotiations.

With technology minister B. J. Habibie's enthusiasm and in spite of the principal advisor's recommendations, in April 1990 President Suharto approved moving ahead on a huge generating complex known as Paiton I, to be located in East Java.[1] This project would comprise two generating units of around 600 megawatts each. According to plan, the site would eventually have eight units, with a total capacity of 4,000 megawatts, about 60% to be privately owned.[2]

Indonesian's state power company, PLN, would build and run the site's first four 400-megawatt units, which were to cost around $1.1 billion and be in operation before foreign investors started.[3] The Asian Development Bank and the World Bank had signed loan agreements for these state developments the previous year, and they proceeded apace. At least for a while, this would end multilateral loans for such projects in Indonesia.

Getting the first private deal right would be critical because it would be seen as a model for subsequent power plants.

Preparation

The Tasks

Enthusiastic letters from interested companies began to arrive almost immediately after the president had announced the new policy. Inquiries and visitors were directed to an array of offices. Jezek frantically argued for "a single point of contact for potential sponsors of private power projects,"[4] but for a while to no avail. The eagerness of foreign firms encouraged some Indonesian officials to believe that a few invitations to desirable investors would quickly and painlessly cause power plants to spring up all over Java. The country's growing electricity shortage would be eliminated, with little effort from the government.

This sunny outlook did not last long. Jezek had been right in his earlier warnings that the size of commitments would attract the interest of other ministries. The Ministry of Finance worried about the financial implications of any government guarantees and special tax provisions; the Environmental Protection Agency was concerned about the risks to the environment; and the state investment agency was anxious about yielding its authority to approve or reject any foreign investment.

Consequently, the preparation team grew. In November 1990, representatives from the technology and finance ministries joined.[5] In 1993, membership had expanded to 15 people; eventually it reached 25.[6] As the team grew, secrecy disappeared, repeating the Indosat experience. However, unlike with Indosat, the electricity team had no unambiguous boss. Although the team was now chaired by the head of PLN (Jamin, at the time), it soon became obvious that the government itself, not PLN, would really decide things.[7] But exactly who in government would make decisions was less clear, as the ministers struggled for influence.

If bids from investors were to be compared, the country would need terms of reference to tell companies exactly what they were bidding on. Soon after his arrival, Jezek had begun meeting with the preparation team to ready those terms. After drafting a version for discussion, he grew worried as officials within the Ministry of Mines and Energy kept responding that the proposed terms were "good." He replied that they were not "good," rather simply a starting point.[8] Eventually, he became so frustrated that he refused to release his most recent draft. He was ordered to produce it from his laptop.

As draft terms were circulated more broadly within government, the lack of consensus grew ever clearer. An illustration: The draft indicated that the government would guarantee PLN's performance in power purchase agreements. When the draft reached the Ministry of Finance, the minister replied with a clear and unambiguous "no" to the idea.

Worried about what they saw in the proposals, the technocrats asked their own advisors for comments. The Harvard Group's response added to the alarm, and even raised questions about the whole idea of private power.[9] But the Group was to have no influence in the matter. The resident team lacked specialized skills,[10] and, more importantly, the team worked for the economic technocrats who were in the end largely shut out of events. According to one account, Ginandjar Kartasasmita, then minister of mines and energy, said, "Either I decide or they [the technocrats] decide."[11] The rival technocrats and engineers had not settled their differences, and tensions between the two camps would continue to be a formidable barrier to agreements that would protect Indonesia's interests.

In the end, Indonesians failed to offer bidders standard formats for financial and technical proposals. Another of Jezek's recommendations was ignored: There was to be no prequalification process. Jezek believed that Indonesians "knew little about the individual [prospective] developers"[12] and thus needed a basis to determine which of the aggressive firms were actually capable of undertaking such a huge project. These omissions proved costly.

Adding Advisors

Tensions between groups of ministers interfered with what might have been a rational selection process for additional advisors. Presumably to allay the concerns of the Ministry of Finance, consultants for contract documents and on pricing issues were to be managed by Jusuf Anwar, the general secretary of that ministry (who later became the minister). Jezek requested short-term technical assistance through USAID or the U.S. "Office of Energy";[13] USAID made a commitment for a $7.75 million grant. The minister of finance submitted the official government request required by USAID, but the head of the national planning agency, another technocrat, responded, "Take it out immediately. If Ginandjar needs money, he should go through me. I can get World Bank money."[14] The tension led to the rejection of grant money in favor of loan money.

In November 1991, PLN added a Frankfurt-based engineering firm, Lahmeyer International, to its advisors. As an illustration of the hiring process, the following story was told to us: When the firm's people were passing through Jakarta to show their finance model, they made a presentation to the Directorate General of Electricity and Energy Development in the Ministry of Mines and Energy and to PLN. After an hour's presentation, the firm was hired.[15] In the end Lahmeyer gave a great deal of advice on conducting negotiations and on strategy, often working with Jezek.[16] Before its contract ended in November 1993, it produced a valuable report with lessons from the experience.[17] Yet the firm's bills— covered under a World Bank loan—remained unpaid for two years. When pressed to pay up, Arismunandar, representing the Ministry of Mines and Energy, responded that such pressure was not properly Javanese.

Meanwhile, the Ministry of Finance added the law firm White & Case, but not without a dispute over who would pay its bills. White & Case had developed a close relationship with Pertamina, the national oil company, in the 1970s, and had then worked with the central bank and the Ministry of Finance. The ministry had long trusted the firm, and, it seems, so had the Suharto family. Nevertheless, the firm, we have been told by an advisor, was reluctant to take on this new assignment. Presumably, the issue was potential conflict of interest.[18]

Possible conflicts of interest in this case would seem small in light of later events. Almost any law firm with expertise in electric power had worked for potential investors and would do so in the future. The worry on the government side was always that private companies were more important clients and would thus call the shots. At least White & Case's long history of representing the government provided some offset. Whatever the reason, the White & Case lawyer we interviewed for this research (who was involved only in subsequent events) was enthusiastically pro-Indonesia. We will return later to the perplexing issue of lawyers' conflicts of interest.

One of White & Case's early assignments was to prepare drafts of the power purchase and implementation agreements. This work was supposed to be coordinated with Jezek and short-term consultants in his office as well as consultants in the Ministry of Finance. This was not an easy assignment, given the tensions between the consultants' two employers.

The Ministry of Finance brought in yet another group on its tab, which the Indonesians had long called the "three houses," the "Advisory Group," or the "Troika," comprising investment bankers Lazard Fréres & Co., SG Warburg & Dillon, and Lehman Brothers.[19] Interestingly, Indonesians claimed that the Troika was reluctant due to their preference for macro issues and financial reform over involvement in individual negotiations. Given their expertise, which lay much more in micro issues and in negotiating, this explanation is puzzling. We suspect that concern over potential conflict of interest might have been behind their hesitancy. After all, investment bankers constantly deal with large firms such as those that might become involved in the power projects.

For sure, the sum of Indonesia's advisors represented a great deal of skill. But hired separately, having never worked together, and having no clear hierarchy, advisors formed cliques, with different policy orientations and different loyalties. The negotiating team itself had recognized problems with the advisors by late 1992 and proposed that Jezek assume responsibility for coordinating all the advisors. Jezek, however, noted that this would not work, because the advisors were funded from different sources and "therefore seem to have different 'allegiances'."[20] He was right. They were never to work effectively together as had the advisors on the Indosat nationalization.

Policy issues had still not been sorted out[21] when, on September 23, 1991, two proposals appeared for Paiton I. Events were outrunning preparation.

Negotiating with BNIE

One proposal for Paiton I came from a consortium known as BNIE (PT Baya Nusa Intercontinental Electric), with a projected cost of $2 billion to $2.5 billion, twice the original PLN estimate. The leader was Intercontinental Electric, Inc., a U.S. company controlled by the Roy family, movers in a Boston-area entrepreneurial group.[22] President Suharto's second son, Bambang,[23] was to be the local partner through his own business group, Bimantara.[24] Big Indonesian bears were circling around the potential honey pot.

Intercontinental

Intercontinental had never built a power plant outside the United States,[25] nor had the company shown interest in international expansion for electric power, in spite of its name. Then Stephen Roy met Gordon Wu, a Hong Kong developer of Asian power plants.[26] Wu, on a visit to Boston, convinced Roy that Asia was the place to put cash from lucrative U.S. deals. Wu himself was not interested in joining with Intercontinental; he did his projects without rich-country partners, as we will see. So the Roys would have to conduct their own search. They sought assistance from the consulting group Hagler, Bailly & Company.[27] There, Roy was to meet an employee who would be of some help later.

Intercontinental was one of many entrepreneurial firms that were ready to try their hand in newly popular infrastructure investment in developing countries. In fact, some of the firms were created for no other purpose and had no experience in building infrastructure, but rather planned to draw on their contacts to assemble deals. Several were a product of the "Washington tradition of revolving doors"[28] (see Box 7.1). Utility firms joined the fray because the U.S. power market was growing only slowly and money was cheap. For a number of the firms, the herd instinct prevailed over analysis, as it was to do so frequently in the go-go 1990s.

Intercontinental differed from some other firms in that it had actually invested in generating facilities in the United States. Moreover, Intercontinental's owners had at least some overseas experience: Stephen Roy had directed family interests in the Middle East, partnering with the Korean firm Daewoo.[29]

One key to the Paiton I contract seemed to lie with Minister of Technology Habibie. There are differing accounts of how Stephen Roy met him. The most likely in our view is that the two men met in mid-April 1990 at a White House–sponsored environmental conference.[30] A letter from Roy to Habibie refers to the Washington meeting, and adds a bold claim: "International Power Corporation is the leading power project development company in the United States...." It went on, "[W]e sipply [sic] over 1300 megawatts of power to major electric utilities in the Northeast...."[31]

Indonesian law required that a foreign investment such as this include a minority of Indonesian equity.[32] Although the original purpose of the

Box 7.1 New Infrastructure Investors

One example of the new breed of firm created to exploit the new opportunities for private infrastructure was the Emerging Markets Corporation, or Emerging Markets Partnership, an investment group organized around Moeen Qureshi, former official of the World Bank, and Lloyd Bentsen, former U.S. secretary of the treasury and governor of the Inter-American Development Bank. Other participants, in one way or another, included Donald C. Roth, former treasurer of the World Bank, and Maurice R. Greenberg, chairman and CEO of American International Group (AIG). The following individuals, preeminent leaders in their fields, have served as chairmen of the company's advisory boards:

- Asia I and Asia II: Dr. Henry Kissinger
- Latin American Fund: The Honorable Lloyd Bentsen
- Emerging Europe Fund: M. le Gouverneur Jacques de Larosière
- African Fund: His Excellency Nelson Mandela

Although short of technical expertise in building infrastructure, the big names recognized the need for money and brought in General Electric Capital Corporation and the huge insurer AIG.[a]

In addition to large utilities, small entities emerged to take on the new markets, as illustrated by the Tennessee Valley Infrastructure Group. These groups usually started with expertise in electric power and sought out contacts abroad for sales of members' services and equipment.

[a]Jeff Gerth, "In Post–Cold-War Washington, Development Is a Hot Business," *New York Times*, May 25, 1996, p. 1.

requirement had been the development of local business, a foreign investor might turn the requirement to its advantage. In particular, the president's interest could be piqued if his family would benefit from a profitable deal. The enthusiasm for power on the part of influential Indonesians was so strong that, according to one lawyer involved, electricity projects were soon to be offered to potential investors with the name of the suggested Indonesian partner already attached. The president's son Bambang was an obvious choice for this one (see Box 7.2). He had tried earlier to work with Gordon Wu's Hopewell Holdings to obtain Paiton I, but the effort had come to naught. He would be a largely silent partner in the new consortium. "Silent" seems to have meant quite silent—it is not clear that the Roys even met Bambang until considerably later.

Box 7.2 "The Family"

Suharto had six children. Their assets in 1999[a] were estimated as follows:

Bambang	$3,000 million
Sigit	$800 million
Tommy	$800 million
Tutut	$700 million
Titiek	$75 million
Mamiek	$30 million

One book on Indonesia attributes the start of the children's business ventures to opportunities at Pertamina, the state-owned oil company. After its head, Ibnu Sutowo, was fired in 1976, Pertamina was forced to export through two separate companies. By the 1980s, Bambang and Tommy held substantial shares of these companies. Allegedly, the Suharto family had 170 contracts from Pertamina, covering insurance, security, and other "services." They were said to yield $50–99 million per year. Through Bimantara Citra, Bambang had accumulated major interests in oil shipping and marketing, entertainment, telecommunications, infrastructure, finance, automobiles, and electronics.[b]

Bambang, born in 1953, never attended university. He has been described as "shy" and "insecure," yet he seems to have inspired fear. When an *Asia Week* reporter asked one of Bambang's business partners about him, the response was, "You're kidding, I've got my kids to think about." In response to the same question, a Western businessman answered, "Pick another topic."[c]

By the mid-1990s, Suharto's grandchildren were also beginning to seek their fortunes. One scheme was a tax on alcohol to be collected by a private firm owned by a grandchild. The proposed "liquor sticker," as expatriates dubbed the tax stamp, finally fell victim to conflicts with others in the Suharto clan who held interests in Bali tourism, which might have been injured by the tax.

---

[a]John Colmey and David Liebhold, "Suharto Inc.: Special Report," *Time Asia,* May 24, 1999, available at http://www.time.com/time/asia/asia/magazine/1999/990524/cover1.html (accessed April 2006).
[b]Theodore Friend, *Indonesian Destinies* (Cambridge, Mass.: Belknap Press for Harvard University Press, 2003), p. 251.
[c]The account of Bambang comes from Keith Loveard, "Suharto's Son Rises," *Asia-Week.com,* April 12, 1996, available at http://www.asiaweek.com/asiaweek/96/0412/feat1.html (accessed December 2004).

An investor might view these partnerships as one method of ensuring property rights, a more sophisticated one than the bribes that ITT paid at the outset of its venture. Partners with ownership have an interest in future profits, not just in the original deal. If they are sufficiently influential, they could intervene with the government to ensure that the project remains profitable.

Discussions Begin

Minister of Technology Habibie invited Roy to Jakarta on May 6, 1990. According to an advisor for Indonesia, the next day, Roy and a Hagler Bailly employee met with the head of the preparation team,[33] and Roy followed up with a request for exclusive negotiating rights for 150 days, adding that preparing the proposal and negotiating would cost him over a million dollars.

Things began to move very fast. According to one report, mines minister Ginandjar summoned Stephen Roy to meet him in Washington (see Box 7.3). As the story was told to us, when Roy arrived (on June 21, 1990) at the hotel in the Watergate complex, he asked reception for the minister's room number. The response was "the seventh floor." He repeated the question with an emphasis on *number*, and was told he did not need it: "Ginandjar has the whole floor."[34] The meeting reportedly went well, and Ginandjar suggested that Roy visit with the team in Jakarta again, leading to a meeting with the head of the negotiating team on August 7.

A consultant to the Roy family, Henry Lee, helped cement relations. A lecturer at Harvard's Kennedy School, Lee had been director of the energy office and special assistant to the governor for environmental policy in Massachusetts. He came with impeccable credentials, but no experience in Indonesia. Through the Roys, Habibie asked Lee to conduct a study of a controversial petrochemical project,[35] in order to help out Bambang, one of the project's sponsors. Peter Gontha, the CEO of the petrochemical project and a partner in the Bimantara Group, eventually became the principal go-between for Roy and the elusive Bambang, according to an advisor in Indonesia.

U.S. Support

Intercontinental turned to the U.S. government for support. On Intercontinental's behalf, a Washington lobbying firm contacted U.S. Vice President Quayle and convinced him to "put in a word" for the company's proposal in his upcoming visit to Jakarta.[36] He did so in May 1991. In addition, Intercontinental crossed to the other side of the political aisle for help from U.S. Senator Brock Adams (D-Washington State), who directed a letter to the Indonesian ambassador to the United States saying that U.S.–Indonesian trade relations would improve if the Intercontinental group were awarded the project.[37]

Box 7.3 Ginandjar Kartasasmita and Team 10

Ginandjar Kartasasmita, an air force officer educated in Japan as an engineer, had become an increasingly powerful figure, especially after 1983 when he became vice chairman of the newly created and infamous "Team 10," named after the presidential decree that created it. To counter widespread concern that ethnic Chinese were the principal beneficiaries of economic growth, the team was to encourage the accumulation of wealth in the hands of *pribumi* (non-Chinese) Indonesians. To do so, it established a procurement system for all government contracts worth more than 500 million rupiah. For small projects, only the "weak group" (non-Chinese Indonesians) would be allowed to bid. For medium-size projects, *pribumi* Indonesians would receive a 5% preference on bids. For major projects, the new team was to decide on project allocation but favor *pribumi* Indonesians if purchases were from domestic sources.[a]

Run by State Secretary Sudharmono (head of the official Golkar party from 1983 to late 1988, and later vice president), the team was soon to control aid contracts as well. It turned into a system of patronage hardly matched elsewhere in a country that was already remarkable for its corruption. It served as a principal device for Sudharmono and his allies among the "engineers" to build political and economic empires and to provide Suharto with another source of support.[b]

From 1983 to 1988, Ginandjar held the position of junior minister for promotion of domestic production, a job the technocrats loved to call "junior minister for protection." He added the chairmanship of the investment agency (BKPM) to his titles in 1985. He was well liked by foreign business people: He spoke English well, he was personable, and he allegedly accepted a known fixed payment for appointments, which removed the guesswork of determining an appropriate "gift" for visits. In 1988, Ginandjar gave up these positions to become minister of mines and energy.

---

[a]For more information about Team 10, see Jeffrey Winters, *Power in Motion: Capital Mobility and the Indonesian State* (Ithaca, N.Y.: Cornell University, 1996).

[b]For corruption allegations against Ginandjar, see Suwarjono, "Freeport Inquiry: 'How Much Did You Get Pak Ginandjar?'" *Detikworld.com*, July 13, 2000, available at http://www.angelfire.com/journal/issues/irian071600.html (accessed April 2006).

This much help for a U.S. investor was rather standard. However, U.S. government support for its investors would eventually go much further, and at a cost to U.S. and Indonesian interests.

Seeking Power

Intercontinental had made a presentation to the negotiating team on December 18, 1990. Nine months later, the consortium submitted a formal proposal. The price proposed by Intercontinental ranged between 6 and 9 cents per kilowatt hour (cents/kwh), depending on the scenario. A commonly cited figure is 8.2 cents.

President Suharto favored Intercontinental, so much so that he met personally with Roy on October 10, 1991. According to one account, Roy informed the president that he had $2 billion ready. Roy exited the meeting in high spirits, even going so far as to tell an advisor to the Indonesians not to continue to investigate the proposal because the project was his,[38] adding that he would not stand for World Bank evaluation.

Roy's confidence did not seem misplaced. The president ordered the team to go for the deal, and, on October 18, the consortium was given exclusive rights to negotiate.[39] Late in the month, the power teams terminated all efforts to evaluate the proposal, "by GOI [government of Indonesia] instruction,"[40] and the company was invited to begin negotiations on November 16, 1991. Suharto's enthusiasm was probably not kindled by the price offered. U.S. government support may have helped gain his endorsement, but, probably more importantly, the president liked the company's alliance with his son. The president's preference carried weight, to say the least, because the president himself had to sign off personally on every large foreign investment project in the country.[41]

The consortium followed up with more presentations to the negotiating team, but they were also described as vague and as not answering questions raised by the team.

Collapse

In spite of support from Indonesia's first family, the U.S. vice president, and a U.S. senator, the potential deal with Intercontinental suffered a slow death. From late October 1991 the proposal seemed to be moving ahead; then for a while it appeared to be off.[42] On the last day of 1991, a second group was invited into negotiations, to begin discussions in early January. By mid May 1992, the negotiating team had announced that the second consortium was the preferred bidder,[43] but the Intercontinental group was not formally dropped as a contender until August 11, 1992.[44]

Although the new consortium began discussions with Bambang's company,[45] they came to naught; instead, another child of the president would join this second consortium. This was neither the first nor the last time that the president's children competed for a project. Losing out on this one, Bambang would get his own power plant later.[46] Indeed, there would be enough deals for each member of the president's family to have one or more power projects, if he or she wanted it.

In the end, doubts about the capacity of Intercontinental, a small family firm, to handle the huge project had won out, even over Suharto's support. One interviewee reported that Sumarlin, the minister of finance, doubted the company's capacity and had called for more bidders. Another report was that the director general for electricity in the Ministry of Mines and Energy had turned against Intercontinental's group, also suspecting that it could not raise the money.[47] Belief that Intercontinental had submitted unprofessional and incomplete proposals also subtracted from its credibility.[48] Doubts counted for more in the face of a proposal from a rival group with very large financial resources and "real corporate fire power," in the words of an advisor.

If Indonesians had had a prequalification process and had thus recognized the potential problem earlier, they would have saved time. Still, political influence and the enthusiasm of U.S. officials might have won out for a while. As one advisor put it, "The Roy proposal created a snowball. You couldn't stop Roy plus the U.S. government once it started rolling." But snowballs do not hold up in the tropics—this one eventually melted.

The aborted negotiations with Intercontinental were costly to the Indonesians. They not only absorbed critical time of the preparation and negotiation teams, where skills were very scarce and when preparation of policies and regulations should have been of the highest priority, but they also meant there would be pressure for the next negotiations to proceed very quickly lest the feared power shortage materialize.

The failed negotiations had also drawn attention away from mounting difficulties at PLN, where the greatest problems actually lay. Finally, the Intercontinental negotiations brought the U.S. government firmly into the picture for power investments. It did not withdraw with Intercontinental— far from it. Not only would U.S. involvement continue, but it would be quite different from that of the ITT days. A new attitude was emerging.

8

Paiton's Power: A New Contender

Please allow me to introduce myself
I'm a man of wealth and taste
—Rolling Stones, "Sympathy for the Devil," 1968

With U.S. government help, the second contender for Paiton I would strike a deal that promised huge profits and few risks. Lacking the kind of technological edge that protected ITT, investors would include influential domestic parties in the equity and add a set of defenses based on the new international property rights. They would ensure themselves access to international arbitration and encourage future backing from the U.S. and Japanese governments should trouble arise.

The BMMG Consortium

The new consortium would be called BMMG, to reflect its partners' names: BHP, Edison Mission Energy, Mitsui, and General Electric Capital Corporation.

Edison Mission Energy

The lead foreign sponsor, Edison Mission Energy (Mission), was part of the Edison Companies. Its size suggested that it could raise the needed funds.[1] Mission had been founded only in 1987, but one of its subsidiaries, Southern California Edison, had operated under that name since 1909 and claimed to be California's second largest investor-owned utility company.

Unlike ITT, Mission was neither a widely diversified company[2] nor one with extensive international experience. Later, it would enter Thailand,

Turkey, the Philippines, several European countries, and New Zealand, but thus far it had only purchased a power project in Australia

Mitsui

The large Japanese company Mitsui knew of Mission's interest in Asia[3] and had learned of the Paiton opportunity through contacts with Graeme Robertson at Batu Hitam Perkasa, the eventual coal supplier (see Box 8.1). Unlike Mission, Mitsui had wide-ranging interests in developing countries, especially in Southeast Asia. One advisor reports that the company brought to the consortium a very special asset: an established intelligence network in Indonesia. Mitsui's own interest in the project probably lay largely in construction and equipment contracts.[4]

General Electric

General Electric also brought to the consortium experience in developing countries. It had operated in Indonesia since the late 1960s,[5] but around 1991, CEO Jack Welch had selected Indonesia as a "must" market.[6] As a result, GE was to seek deep and diversified involvement in the country, starting with ties to the state-owned aircraft producer, headed by B. J. Habibie, and spreading to a range of manufacturing, from lighting to medical equipment. It would eventually enter a joint venture with Habibie's Indonesian Agency for Strategic Industries to produce gas turbines[7] and another joint venture with the state-owned railway company to manufacture locomotives.[8] GE had a wing, General Electric Capital,[9] that could provide money for power projects, making it a sure bet that GE would become the principal supplier of major equipment. Moreover, GE Capital thought of itself as having considerable expertise in evaluating big projects, wherever they were located.

GE had even had extensive experience in infrastructure projects in the developing countries. By the end of 1929, the company had controlled at least half of U.S. investment in overseas electricity facilities through its subsidiaries Electric Bond & Share and American & Foreign Power Company.[10] Of course, GE's earlier investments in Latin America, Asia, and elsewhere had been sold off or expropriated as private ownership of infrastructure had fallen out of favor. Like many corporate executives in other firms, GE top managers knew little of their company's much earlier overseas experience and showed equally little interest in learning about it. If there were lessons from the past, as we believe there were, GE would have to relearn them.

At GE Power Funding, interests in Paiton I were handled by Frank Blake,[11] described by one of his long-time associates as "intellectually honest, but fairly unsentimental and tough. Just the type that Jack Welsh liked." Although Mission's representative was the principal spokesperson in negotiations, GE's was always present as well. According to one consultant, tension between GE's representative and Mission's was glaringly obvious on several occasions. One important task of the GE negotiator

Box 8.1 Graeme Robertson

Graeme Robertson, another colorful character, told us that he had come to Indonesia from Australia in 1972 to teach. Needing more income, he soon picked up jobs evaluating projects for potential foreign investors. One task was to examine whether Indonesian coal posed a threat to New Hope, the Australian coal company in which his father was involved. Along the way, he seems to have taken up with an older well-to-do Indonesian "girlfriend." Upon meeting another Indonesian, Fena, we were told, Graeme dropped the old girlfriend while she was attending a course abroad. Robertson said to us that Fena was the daughter of a Javanese princess; others added that her father was a wealthy Dutch expatriate. The jilted girlfriend seems to have taken badly to Graeme's new interest and went after him on immigration, tax, and other charges, forcing him to leave the country. With the help of Fena's friends (one interviewee called them "shady"), Graeme returned and married Fena in 1979.

According to Robertson, his scholarship and entrepreneurship combined when he sent someone to search for the mine site mentioned in Joseph Conrad's *Victory*, suspecting that strip mining could now extract what had been left behind. But Conrad provided few clues for locating the mine:

> On the nights of full moon the silence around Samburan—the "Round Island" of the charts...the most conspicuous object was a gigantic blackboard raised on two posts and presenting to Heyst, when the moon got over that side, the white letters "T. B. C. Co." in a row at least two feet high.... There was a coal-mine there, with an outcrop in the hillside less than five hundred yards from the rickety wharf and the imposing blackboard.[a]

Robertson told us the site was found on the Malaysian island of Labuan, but Malaysians feared the environmental impact of strip mining, nixing any further development. Nevertheless, Robertson went on to obtain coal interests from Spanish concession holders of the site in Kalimantan that was eventually to supply Paiton I. He brought New Hope into the deal, but, needing influential Indonesian partners, he also invited Liem and other important Chinese businessmen to join. As we shall see, he eventually provided another asset of value to Mission's chief negotiator, namely, Fena.

By 2002, Robertson had purchased expensive properties in Bali and Jakarta and was supporting art and social projects, in particular The John Fawcett Foundation for Humanitarian Projects in Indonesia. Other interviewees alleged to us that his success was tied up with some shadowy Indonesian characters and that he had left a string of angered business associates. Whatever the truth, he had moved up far from a teacher's salary.

[a]From Chapter 1 of Joseph Conrad, *Victory*, first published in 1915. Robertson detractors challenge the claim that this was the mine in *Victory*, adding that the Labuan mine had been closed by 1912.

seems to have been to protect the company against charges of corruption. This could surely cause tensions.

The Local Partner

Indeed, as ITT showed, one way to obtain a deal in Indonesia was to pay a bribe. Investors were discovering a better route, however: Make income of influential local partners contingent on future profitability of the investment. BMMG took on an influential company, Batu Hitam Perkasa (BHP),[12] as an equity partner. It would profit if the project itself remained profitable.

BHP had been contacted through the American Chamber of Commerce.[13] One asset it brought was an Indonesian named Hashim Djojohadikusumo. According to a Mission letter to OPIC, Hashim came recommended by the U.S. embassy.[14]

Hashim was not just any Indonesian. His father was one of Indonesia's most famed economists, Professor Sumitro. When Suharto brought him back from exile to make him minister of trade, he was restored as a respected and vocal figure.[15] More importantly, Hashim was the brother-in-law of President Suharto's second daughter, Titiek.[16] Titiek had married Hashim's older brother Probowo, a military officer, in 1983. According to Indonesian reports, Hashim's businesses served as a source of funds for *Kopassus*, the army's special forces unit[17] (see Box 8.2).

As we have said, most Indonesians who were able to obtain important business licenses and access to funds were ethnic Chinese, non-Chinese (*pribumi*) cronies of the president, or military officers. Hashim belonged to the second group. He had been a beneficiary of the new opportunities created for *pribumi* business people in the 1980s. Through his family ties, he had access to and the trust of the president, assets that would turn out to be important in the upcoming negotiations.

Hashim's sister-in-law, Suharto's daughter Titiek, was the subject of many stories. Movie stars and art seem to have been two of her passions. *Time Asia* quotes a companion as saying, "She loves big chunks of jewelry."[18] Another popular story was that she hated dogs, and therefore slept in a separate room from husband Probowo and his Alsatians.[19] Whatever was true about her personal life, she held equity in BHP and the coal company. Government requirements[20] would make sure that BHP's affiliate would fuel Paiton I.[21] As a shareholder, Titiek could be counted on for help obtaining the project and for more assistance if the investment ran into trouble.[22]

Agus Kartasasmita, the brother of the minister of mines and energy Ginandjar, also held an interest in BHP. We do not know when Agus obtained his holdings or whether he was important in clinching the Paiton deal. Influential or not, his presence became fodder for later critics of the arrangements.

A closely linked company, P.T. Adaro Indonesia, would actually supply the coal from the once-Spanish concession.[23] Adaro was a joint venture

---

Box 8.2 Hashim Djojohadikusumo

Hashim Djojohadikusumo was only 36 years old in 1991. With a bachelor's degree from Pomona College in California, he had served a two-year stint as trainee with Lazard Frères and returned to Indonesia in 1978 for his first step in business, variously described as comic book publishing and working for his father's consulting firm. He moved up some notches by venturing into sugar and palm oil projects and a trading company with Malaysian businessman Robert Kuok. Hashim's first big-time project was Semen Cibinong, a large cement producer, which he bought (41.46%) in 1988. He was soon to have substantial interests in petrochemicals and several banks,[a] and his trading companies would become deeply involved with former Soviet republics.[b] Hashim worked with his sister-in-law, when it was useful; thus, Titiek, a daughter of President Suharto, eventually joined with him to develop Jakarta's modern Senayan shopping mall.[c]

An American, Gordon Bishop, who had partnered with Hashim for a batik fashion business, described Hashim's methods: When Hashim ran into some financial trouble in other businesses, he started to milk the joint venture. Reportedly, Bishop was told to go along with the scheme or leave the country within 72 hours. Another time, while Bishop was in a coma from severe injuries suffered in a car accident, Hashim canceled his medical insurance. Bishop's description: "I knew Hashim when he was a nice guy, but he got bigger and bigger and bigger.... [Earlier] others had taken advantage of him.... There's nothing worse than a nice guy who decides to never be nice again, who decides to be a tough guy."[d]

Robertson had invited Hashim to join his group, because he needed some "protection," as he put it to us, if the project grew large. In 1989 or 1990, Hashim acquired part or all the 20% interest that the Spanish investors had retained.

[a]Bank Papan Sejahtera, Bank Industri, Bank Pelita, and Bank Universal.
[b]For his business ties, see "Hashim's Business Empire Is Collapsing," *Gatra*, March 29, 1999.
[c]For a report on Hashim, see "Triumph of a Native Son: A Young Suharto Intimate Builds a Conglomerate," Asiaweek.com, available at http://www.asiaweek.com/asiaweek/95/1020/biz3.html (accessed August 2004).
[d]Story and quote from Theodore Friend, *Indonesian Destinies* (Cambridge, Mass.: Belknap Press for Harvard University Press, 2003), p. 217.

---

with New Hope Corporation, Ltd., of Australia, operator of three coal mines in Queensland.[24] Unsurprisingly, Titiek and Hashim held interests in this company as well (see Figures 8.1 and 8.2).

Hashim and associates assumed little risk with Paiton. The financial arrangements that brought them into the project, soon to be echoed in a wide

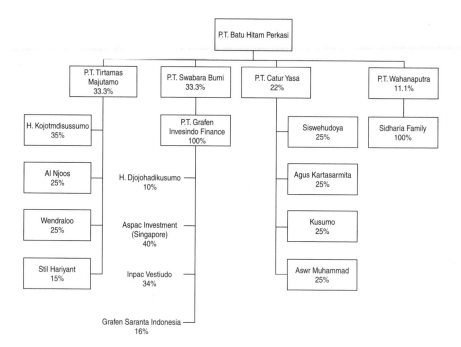

Figure 8.1 Ownership of BHP Source: http://www.softwar.net/paiton2.html. (viewed 8/04) and *Confidential Offering Circular* (1996) of Paiton I.

range of later deals, went as follows: The foreign equity investors extended a loan to the Indonesian partner, who could then put up these funds for shares. In the Paiton case, Mission, GE, and Mitsui loaned $49.6 million to the local partner. The partner agreed to a "market rate of interest" (although some reports say that the rate was 1.5% per year) and to give up 65% of dividends as interest and loan repayment until the "debt" was repaid.[25] The approach became known as "carried-interest arrangements."

Of course, the arrangements were in reality no more than gifts to influential partners. The partner had to put up no money. Whenever the investment prospered enough to pay dividends, some of them would go to the partner. No dividends meant no money for the partner; but there would also be no obligation to repay the loan, except out of a portion of future dividends. Because the full benefit of the shares came only after a portion of dividends had been withheld to service the nominal debt, perhaps one might describe the arrangements as a delayed gift, but a gift nonetheless.[26]

Some investors were offered an alternative. Two investors told us that a foreign company could simply give a designated local partner[27] something on the order of 5% interest[28] as an alternative to 15% under a loan arrangement. An investor in one power project explained his choice: Having 15% of the equity locally owned looked better politically than having only

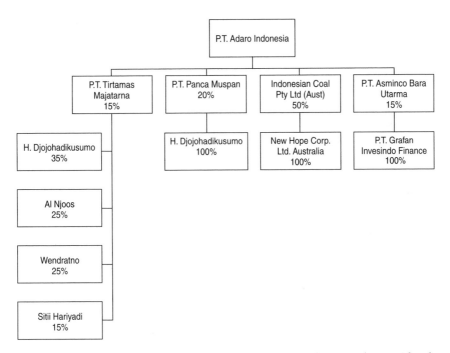

Figure 8.2 Ownership of Adaro Source: http://www.softwar.net/paiton2.html. (viewed 8/04) and *Confidential Offering Circular* (1996) of Paiton I.

5% local ownership, even though narrow financial calculations might support the 5% choice.[29] He failed to add that the 15% ownership would also increase the partners' interest in maintaining future profitability.[30]

A reader might well ask how U.S. investors could get by with these gifts. After all, the U.S. Foreign Corrupt Practices Act (FCPA) of 1977 was supposed to put an end to corrupt payments that undermine capitalism abroad. Although managers could actually go to jail under the Act, U.S. investors in Indonesian power did not even try to hide these arrangements. Some reported them to the U.S. Securities and Exchange Commission, and they were known to OPIC before it committed to a project. We asked the U.S. justice department why they were not illegal. The reply ran as follows:

> Whether a gift, loan, or payment to a relative or crony would be a violation of the FCPA would depend on whether it occurred at the direction of the official or whether some form of benefit inured to the official.[31]

The president surely never issued a directive ordering shares for his daughter; that was not the way things worked in Indonesia. Suharto was even unlikely to have benefited directly from equity given to his daughter. But, like most fathers, he surely took pleasure in seeing assets going to his children. Regardless of who benefited, the justice department's special logic presumably made investors passably comfortable with the arrangements.

In some other power projects, local partners would be cronies rather than members of the First Family. In these cases, it would be even more difficult to prove a direct benefit to the president from gifts of shares. But a richer Chinese businessman would have more funds from which the president could request assistance, as he was wont to do when he needed money for some particular purpose. Because any such quid pro quo is only implied by the mutual obligations that are so strong in many Asian cultures, and particularly when the Chinese profit at the discretion of the president, any benefit to the head of state would be devilishly hard to prove in a U.S. court. Presumably, lawyers for U.S. investors figured the same way. We have even been told that American trade officials met in the embassy with American managers to guide them on avoiding problems with the Foreign Corrupt Practices Act by using partnerships.[32]

Nevertheless, GE seemed worried about terms of the loan and pressed Hashim to sign anticorruption declarations. Hashim apparently refused to do so, pointing out that Mission had not asked for anything similar. In spite of GE's caution, investors moved right ahead with similar arrangements for virtually all the power deals.

We asked American managers in Paiton for their thoughts on the arrangements. The response was a version of "everyone else is doing it, even in the Philippines." Few readers would take the Philippines of the time as a model of propriety. On the other hand, refusal to participate in the arrangements would have meant no project for most investors. No matter how managers justify their actions, these arrangements point out a gaping hole in the U.S. Foreign Corrupt Practices Act.

Counsel

Mission sought assistance from an outside law firm, Skadden, Arps, Slate, Meagher & Flom. Its assignment of Raymond Vickers to the case was troubling. Vickers had previously worked for the Indonesian government before moving to Skadden (and he eventually became house-counsel at Mission). Working on the company side in a negotiation with a previous client could raise questions, at least within the United States. It is not clear how Vickers could build a divider in his head to separate his intimate knowledge of the Ministry of Finance from the Paiton negotiations. This and other seeming conflicts of interest in these power cases raise uncomfortable questions about whether American lawyers apply ethics rules less rigorously abroad than in the United States. We approached Vickers for an explanation, but he did not respond.[33]

The Government Side

Advisors

Even though the government-owned electricity company, PLN, would be the sole purchaser and the distributor of electric power, and thus had to sign the power purchase agreement, PLN would not control the negotiations. PLN's, director[34] and others we interviewed said that the government, mainly the director general in charge from the Ministry of Mines and Energy, really negotiated the agreements. The shortage of skills in both PLN and government agencies meant that success could depend on effective use of advisors. As we have seen, however, these were a skilled but disorganized crew.

Advisors increasingly tangled with each other, especially with those who reported to different bosses. Advisors to the Ministry of Mines and Energy reported especially strained relations with Hollinger, whom the minister of finance had asked to sit in on negotiating sessions. Reflecting the tensions, more than one advisor claimed that Hollinger used them to collect information and build contacts but offered no information or contacts in return. One advisor reminded us several times that Hollinger had worked alongside Mission's counsel, Vickers, earlier, and that they were friends, both with houses in the same town in the south of France.

To some extent, the tensions reflected slightly different stances. Hollinger looked at the Paiton project more favorably than did Jezek, but they also reflected different loyalties, the lack of a hierarchy among the advisors, and even quite different views of the proper role for advisors. Jezek and some other advisors did not hesitate to speak to the press, for example; others strongly believed that advisors should stay in the background and avoid any kind of publicity.[35] And there was no single boss to clarify expectations.

Jezek's role appeared to change as new negotiations started. His skepticism about huge power plants[36] was at odds with Ginandjar, for whom he worked. He recalled that Ginandjar had told him "Indonesia had nothing to learn from the private-power experiences of Pakistan, the Philippines, and Latin America, because Indonesia wasn't a banana republic."[37] In fact, one advisor reported to us that Jezek was so uncomfortable with the way things were going that he chose not to participate in the negotiations. But the USAID mission director had passed on a message, on September 13, 1991, from U.S. Ambassador John Monjo:[38] Jezek was not to assist in the Paiton negotiations.[39] He was facing a problem we have frequently seen. As soon as U.S. commercial interests are involved, the embassy or USAID makes sure an advisor on its payroll follows the U.S. line or withdraws, regardless of the interest of the country supposedly being helped. Still, at the invitation of the Indonesian government, Jezek attended a number of negotiating meetings "as an observer."[40] His role may, in fact, have changed less than it appeared.

Of course, advisors working for the same boss could cooperate. The investment banking Troika and White & Case (both employed by the Ministry of Finance) produced a joint report on nascent Paiton negotiations[41] questioning the ability of PLN to distribute all the power from the large projects being considered, warning of high prices for domestic coal, proposing linking the price to international price standards, and arguing, as had Jezek, for better policy guidance from the government and for a clear framework for decision making.

This report for the minister of finance did reach the minister of mines and energy. Ginandjar's response was that the issues had been taken care of, or were to be covered in a presidential decree that was already in draft form. In this atmosphere of competition and tension, advisors in the Ministry of Finance and probably the minister himself had not been given this draft decree.[42] Unsurprisingly, Ginandjar rejected linking the coal price to an international standard. There were too many influential people tied up in the Adaro mine and related facilities for this kind of constraint. The tone of Ginandjar's response was that of someone who resented the intervention of outsiders in a family matter. It was indeed something of a family matter, of course, with the participation of Ginandjar's brother, the president's daughter, and another indirect relative in the deal. But, perhaps equally or more importantly, Ginandjar had little tolerance for the intervention of other ministers into what he considered to be his territory: He belonged to one camp of ministers, the finance minister to a different camp.

Although technocrat ministers also asked the Harvard Group to comment on both the report and Ginandjar's response,[43] Jezek told us that he never saw the Harvard comments, which probably did not reach the Ministry of Mines and Energy at all. Jezek did, however, have access to the draft decree (he may, in fact, have even prepared the first draft), and he prepared memos of his own in response. Of course, the finance minister's advisors, in turn, never received those papers. Advisors would remain trapped in the local power struggle.

The World Bank

Although not technically an advisor in the negotiations, the resident representative of the World Bank also had concerns about what was happening. After Jezek raised issues with a World Bank official visiting from Washington, on December 13, 1991, the official met with Habibie and others to discuss Paiton. By 1993, the local World Bank office was taking a stronger stance, saying that the Indonesian government should "urgently reject the time schedule and the tariffs of all private projects," or else "they would run the risk of inevitable and major increases in the cost of electricity."[44] This was in spite of the World Bank having pushed for private investment in the developing countries. The Ministry of Mines and Energy showed little interest in the World Bank's concerns.

World Bank opposition was expressed more strongly in November 1994, when an official said that the deals being considered would cost $800 million per year more than world standards suggested they should, and again in February 1995.[45] Although there is no evidence that World Bank headquarters in Washington took up opposition in any serious way, with two exceptions the World Bank Group would, in the end, express its displeasure by refusing to provide support to any of the private power investors.

An Abortive Effort at Policy Formulation

Although this event was not mentioned by others, Paiton managers told us that electricity became a very serious concern of state on Heroes' Day (*Hari Pahlawan*), November 10, 1991. As President Suharto was giving his celebratory speech at one of the national monuments, the lights suddenly blacked out. The irate president dismissed Djiteng, the head of PLN. But the blackout may not have been the only reason: The president had been annoyed by the head's aggressiveness with respect to another power project that involved a crony.[46] The president appointed Zuhal, who had been attached to the Ministry of Mines and Energy and had been doing research at the University of Indonesia on electric power. Zuhal had run some of the early meetings of the negotiating team for Paiton I. PLN employees, who had demonstrated against Djiteng's departure, viewed Zuhal as an outsider, adding to complications in a rushed and unprepared environment.

Indicating the lack of preparation, draft agreements reached investors only five days before their proposals were due.[47] The accompanying terms of reference assured them that the government would guarantee PLN's commitments, although this was still vigorously opposed by the Ministry of Finance. Moreover, companies were being asked to bid in the absence of a clear legal framework.[48]

The president issued a decree on July 9, 1992,[49] that was supposed to settle policy matters and create a solid legal basis. Vague and offending few, the decree failed to provide guidance on allocation of risk, terms for *force majeure*, foreign exchange adjustments, or environmental standards.[50] In other words, it was silent on major unresolved issues. But it was quite clear on two points: In contradiction to what investors had just been told, the government would not guarantee PLN commitments under power purchase agreements, and the price to PLN had to be denominated in rupiah.

By the time meetings with the Mission-led consortium began, the government team and its advisors had prepared a few technical and strategy papers and had a financial model to evaluate offers. One advisor had recommended that the negotiating team be limited to five members plus supporting advisors, and that discussions be split into parallel sessions on technical and financial issues. Limiting participation was to prove difficult because it would mean excluding officials whose interests were affected.

Further, the Indonesian team was facing another problem that had appeared in the ITT/Indosat negotiations: Every document they produced seemed to be in the hands of company managers within hours.[51]

Negotiations

Negotiations for Paiton I began with the Mission-led consortium. The serious bidding process that had been contemplated fell by the wayside. Even then, negotiations took one and a half years and became quite adversarial at times.[52]

Costs of Being Unprepared

Mission was to find the negotiating environment in Indonesia very different from anything it had ever encountered. Robert M. Edgell,[53] an executive vice president, led the consortium's side. Of the Indonesian negotiations, he was to say, "There were times when I got frustrated, because it takes a long time to get decisions made in this government...."[54] Citing the number of "points" he had accumulated at Jakarta's Grand Hyatt Hotel (see Box 8.3), Edgell was later to report that he spent 500 days in Jakarta over the three-year period of preliminary discussions and the negotiations.

Advisors to the Indonesians had sympathy with managers. In one report, Jezek said, "In general the parties submitting... proposals are left 'in the dark' for long periods of time without knowing what the fate of their proposal is."[55] Things would only get worse once Suharto was gone.

Especially frustrating for investors, Indonesians made commitments and then withdrew them. At one point during the negotiations, for example, Arismunundar, the head of the Indonesian team, reached out his hand and said, "We have a deal." Mission's Edgell sent out an announcement from his hotel room after the meeting. The next day, the head of the Indonesian team failed to show up at the scheduled meeting. He had insisted that a foreign advisor tell Edgell that there was no deal yet. No Indonesian was willing to present the facts or apologize.

Indonesians also grew irritated. According to one advisor, Edgell was "emotional, but almost certainly well intentioned at the outset," but when Habibie, Ginandjar, and the government team leader continued to act in unbusinesslike ways, Edgell finally began to respond in kind. According to an Indonesian, Edgell was, on occasion, very "rough" (*kasar*) in his style.

Because the negotiations pitted aggressive American business people against Indonesians, many of whom are quiet, reticent, and super polite, some degree of conflict was probably inevitable. Still, the tone got worse, not better, as the negotiations proceeded.

Offers as Moving Targets

Tensions also reflected the wide distance between the parties' goals. Mission had entered the negotiations with an offer of 7.3 cents per kilowatt hour (cents/kwh), but the offer eventually rose to as high as 10.32 cents. Some observers have criticized Mission for increasing its price when it became the only contender for Paiton I. To be fair, however, the requirements for the project itself provided a moving target. For example, it was not so clear

Box 8.3 A Changed Jakarta

By the 1990s, development had turned Jakarta into a very different city from what ITT's managers had encountered over two decades earlier. The old, depressing Jakarta airport had been replaced with a lovely French-designed facility on the outskirts of the city. Customs and immigration had been cleaned up, at least for arriving Westerners. Clearly marked and metered taxis lined up for airport arrivals. Pedicabs had been banned from the city streets. Mostly modern Japanese cars and locally produced Kijang (sport-utility vehicles using Japanese technology) regularly backed up for an hour or two during rush-hour jams.

For business people, Hotel Indonesia was now "out." The government had put money into building the more stylish Hotel Borobudur, located next to the influential Ministry of Finance. The Borobudur was soon followed by a number of more upmarket hotels, offering different styles for the visitor. As the options grew, the Borobodur remained the hotel of choice mainly for foreigners on a budget, like those constrained by U.S. state department per diems.

Opened in 1991, the Grand Hyatt became one of the principal business visitors' hotels, and it reflected the new Jakarta. A genuine high-rise on Jakarta's busiest traffic circle, it stood as a gateway to a row of tall new office buildings that now lined the divided, multilane Jalan Jenderal Sudirman, which stretched to the leafy 1950s suburb of Kebayoran and provided access to new "McMansions" and gated communities further south.

No longer a hardship post for Westerners, Jakarta and particularly the shopping mall[a] attached to the Grand Hyatt offered it all—including a Japanese department store and supermarket with Asian and Western food, and Alfred Dunhill, Cartier, and Bulgari shops. To put it bluntly, the Grand Hyatt was gaudy, like much of the new Jakarta that rapid growth had produced. But the amount of electricity required to light the Hyatt's giant chandeliers must have been a great stimulant to businessmen who would arrive to negotiate power plants.

[a]The reader may not be surprised to learn that Bimantara, led by the president's son Bambang, held a substantial stake in the mall and, perhaps, the hotel, with funding priced at far below market rates.

at the outset that whoever built Paiton I would also have to build a great deal of surrounding infrastructure for the whole complex.[56] At an early point, the capital costs had been estimated at $1,405 million, but they grew with discussions. For example, the consortium added $72 million for delays in reaching agreement, $62 million for scrubbers, $64 million for shared facilities, and $88.2 million for scope changes. The government specified sources for some equipment, telling the consortium to buy boilers from Combustion Engineering/ABB rather than from the its preferred supplier, Foster and Wheeler. The local affiliate of Combustion Engineering/ABB that would build some of the components had ties to Habibie.[57] This change in suppliers reportedly added another $25 million to costs.[58]

The demand that Paiton I reduce the average pollution for the entire complex to an acceptable level, offsetting the allegedly high level of pollution from PLN's part, meant that Paiton I would have to use low sulfur coal. Because the fuel already had to be sourced in Indonesia, the requirement sealed Adaro's position as the coal supplier. Costs of coal to the project would reflect the interests of influential owners of this company and be passed on to Indonesians by the consortium.

Managers also claimed to us that they had been assured that the Mission-led group would get four of the Paiton units if it submitted attractive offers for the first two. Managers hinted that their original offer had been lower, based on assumptions of joint economies and fewer coordination problems, if they could also build the second two units. Finally, Paiton's management contended that the charge for electricity had to go up when the government made it clear in 1992, with the presidential decree, that it would provide no guarantees for PLN's commitment.

It might seem that a gap of the magnitude that divided the parties—5.2 cents on the government side and a target price of perhaps 6 cents, against a 10.3 cent offer from the company—might have been so discouraging that discussions would end. Not so. By the end of the third round of negotiations, the president had issued his approval for the project, and the investment authority, BKPM, had granted a license. These were signals that agreement had been largely reached, even though there was still no accord on price.[59]

But negotiations suffered a setback when the president named a new cabinet in March 1993. Sudjana, a military officer, took over from Ginandjar as minister of mines and energy. One advisor reported Sudjana as "pretty straight, though he tended to rely more on reading books to learn about the issues faced in electric power." Some others were much less sanguine. In any event, Sudjana seemed suspicious of, or uncomfortable with, foreign consultants. He brought along an Indonesian advisor of his own, Adnan Ganto, who had been with a British investment firm. New personnel meant that relations had to be worked out anew, among the advisors and within the negotiating team, and with the managers.

A Busy Recess: Using Power

A recess was called after the fourth round of negotiations. At this point, the consortium's offer stood at 9.98 cents/kwh for the first six years, 8.73 cents for years 8 to 13, and 5.7 for the remaining 15 years. Dissatisfied, the government team requested the consortium to reconsider its offer and submit a new proposal by August 7.

Even during the recess, the parties continued to communicate. By mid-1993, Indonesia's chief negotiator said that Indonesia would accept a price of 8 cents per kilowatt hour, clearly abandoning its old target price. Mission said "no," and was ready to cash in on the influence that local partner Hashim was supposed to bring to the deal. To activate Hashim, Mission executives criticized him for not going over the head of the negotiating team and taking the consortium's offer directly to Indonesia's president.

But nothing was simple. The president's son Bambang reentered the picture. He still wanted a power project. The government appeared ready to award two additional units at Paiton to a consortium that included Siemens and Bambang's Bimantara. This would mean that the offer of four units for Mission's group, if it was ever truly made,[60] would disappear. The anticipated economies would not materialize, and there would be more parties to coordinate at the site. Further, Bimantara was trying to gain the rights to construct shared coal receiving, storage, and handling facilities. Suspecting that Bambang would extract a few pounds of flesh from this deal, the Mission-led group viewed the proposal skeptically.[61]

Until now, President Suharto had limited his involvement to frequent questions about why the negotiations were progressing so slowly.[62] In July 1993, however, Hashim took up Mission's challenge and sent a letter to the president, arguing that the government should agree to a higher price than its negotiators were proposing. He claimed that a 25% rate of return to investors was appropriate, given the risks involved. He failed to say whether the return was on investors' equity or on all assets, or what price would yield that return.[63] Nevertheless, he followed up by personally meeting with the president.

Exactly what was said in that meeting is not public, but Hashim emerged to say that the president had set the absolute cap on price at 9 cents. In this kind of bargaining, one might have expected a proposal to meet halfway. Instead, this was largely a capitulation to the company.

On August 6, the consortium responded with the proposal in Table 8.1.[64]

Four days later, Hashim again wrote to the president, translating the offer into a "levelized" price of 8.5855 cents, including "PPN" (value added) tax. This was soon followed by another letter on August 19 asking for a response. Zuhal, director of PLN, told us that he then received a letter from the minister of mines and energy telling him the price and to sign. He was sure

Table 8.1 Paiton I Price Proposal (August 6, 1993)

	Years 1–7	Years 8–13	Years 14–30
New price (including PPN tax)	8.7900 cents	8.6200 cents	5.6900 cents
New price (excluding PPN tax)	8.5600 cents	8.4100 cents	5.6900 cents
Old price (excluding PPN tax)	9.9642 cents	8.7085 cents	5.6900 cents

*Value added tax (Pajak Pertambahan Nilai).

Source: Letter from Hashim S. Djojohadikusumo to President Suharto, August 10, 1993.

that the letter had been instigated by Hashim and perhaps Titiek.[65] Once the president's position was clear, discussions of price were concluded within a month, settling at 8.56 cents for six years; 8.41 cents for the next six-year period, and 5.54 cents for the remaining 18 years.[66] The power of the local partner had paid off handsomely for the investors.

Round 5: Pressure for Progress

Even with the price agreed, a few issues still remained unsettled: The most important issue was the handling of currency risk. Thus, the fifth round of negotiations began on September 16, 1993. International relations and rumors of new policies provided reasons to hurry matters along.

It had long been recognized that some components of the electricity price would be indexed to foreign exchange, whatever the authorizing decree had to say about the matter.[67] Investors wanted to allocate currency risks to the Indonesian side, arguing that the financing commitments would be denominated in foreign currency. Mitsui was interested in yen, and the project would likely have some yen-denominated loans. So the consortium raised the issue of indexing not only to the dollar but also to the yen.[68] On top of this, investors also sought government assurances that foreign exchange would be made available and again requested government guarantees for PLN's obligations. These were not new issues, but the negotiating team had no authority to yield on them. Recognizing this, members of the consortium had begun to meet with officials of the Ministry of Finance, circumventing the negotiating team.[69]

The company was growing eager for a completed and signed power purchase agreement. First, it was reportedly worried that the government might "change course" in its power plans[70] and opt for a competitive system rather than power purchase agreements. Business people love the idea of competition but prefer not to face it. Power purchase contracts sounded like a better deal to investors. Second, tensions between Indonesia and the U.S. government were mounting over labor policies. The United States was threatening to cancel the country's privileges under the Generalized System of Preferences (GSP), which allowed duty-free import of many Indonesian products to the United States. Cancellation or suspension would put a number of Indonesian exports at a serious disadvantage vis-à-vis those of competitors, and just possibly would turn Indonesians against a U.S. company such as Mission. So there were two reasons to hurry.

Calling on the U.S. Government

Like the first consortium led by Intercontinental, Mission's group had sought U.S. assistance in getting the Paiton deal. Arguing that Intercontinental offered more U.S. content in its proposal, the Department of State had turned down Mission's request for trade development funds in 1991. But Mission really wanted political help. Following Intercontinental's successful overture to the U.S. vice president, Mission contacted Quayle's deputy chief of staff on October 23, 1991, to suggest that Quayle send a letter to Suharto "to correct the misperception that the Administration is favoring one U.S. company over another." The move worked. In less than a week, the U.S. embassy told Ginandjar, Habibie, and the finance minister that the U.S. supported both companies equally. Soon the Indonesian ambassador to the United States received a letter supporting the Mission-led consortium from Senator Harry Reid (Democrat, Nevada). Mission could play the same game as Intercontinental, and probably with more influence.

Mission had plenty of access to the U.S. government and was showing no reluctance in using it. Warren Christopher, who had been a director at Edison International, a Mission company,[71] was now the U.S. secretary of state; this former director could be useful. Exactly how helpful Christopher was in the negotiations we will probably never know, but he would reappear later.

As if one secretary of state was not enough, the consortium sought help from Kissinger & Associates. Henry Kissinger had contacts in Indonesia and had advised Freeport McMoRan, the mining company that had entered Indonesia as Freeport Sulphur about the same time as ITT and had developed a huge and controversial copper and gold project in Indonesian New Guinea.[72] Mission also turned to at least two lobbyists from the Bush I administration to improve access to U.S. officials.[73] Both were present when Mission executives met with officials in the U.S. Department of Commerce. The efforts produced results. In January 1994, three U.S. official government delegations pressed the deal with Indonesians.[74]

It is difficult to measure the importance of U.S. intervention in this particular negotiation. Jezek said it was "very important," and we tend to believe him, given his close involvement in the events. But this was only the beginning of U.S. government help.

Concluding a Deal

The negotiating teams continued to work out the details of the agreement. Two items, usually "boilerplate," covered dispute settlement and *force majeure*. Although the first of these turned out to be rather standard, the second was not.

The dispute settlement provision was, to say the least, long. It took more than four pages to spell out three steps to be followed "should a dispute or difference of any kind whatsoever" arise out of the agreement,[75] including any dispute over the validity of the agreement. If the first two failed, the matter was to go to arbitration under the United Nations Commission on International Trade Law (UNCITRAL) rules. Each party would nominate an arbitrator, and those two would choose a third; failing to choose, they would turn to the International Centre for Settlement of Investment Disputes (ICSID) for a name. As was common practice, arbitration would be in a third country, in this case, Sweden. Because the use of arbitration was growing, the clauses would seem to provide a more realistic approach to settling any future dispute than did the reference to arbitration in the ITT/Indosat case.

Hardly standard was the *force majeure* clause.[76] A lawyer commenting on the Paiton I agreement told us, "I have never seen [a *force majeure* clause] that is so one-sided. Someone would have to prove God exists before he could invoke this clause." White & Case, as counsel for the Ministry of Finance, was, we are told, instrumental in drafting the provision, which also took up more than four pages. One important imbalance: It did not allow PLN to claim *force majeure* as a reason for failing to fulfill its obligations if the cause was any Indonesian government action; Paiton I, on the other hand, could claim *force majeure* as an excuse for failing to fulfill its side of the bargain if acts of government, including any new environmental regulations, affected it.

The agreement and its related documents had grown to more than 300 pages,[77] in contrast to the 11 pages of the ITT/Indosat agreement. Like ITT's agreement, this one was also in English, reflecting the fact that many of the clauses had come from the company side or Western advisors to the Indonesians, as well as the fact that the foreign lawyers and managers were not fluent in Indonesian. No local language version would carry equal weight, as might have been demanded in Latin America. Given the complexity, one must wonder how many Indonesians fully understood the implications of the lengthy contract in a foreign language.

Understood or not, the power purchase agreement was signed on February 12, 1994.[78] Ironically, the United States formally challenged Indonesia's GSP standing three days later.[79] A conspiracy theorist would suppose that Mission had been able to delay the U.S. action until its deal was done, but we have no evidence on either side of such a theory.

Overall, the negotiating process sounds much like the bargaining process in a traditional Indonesian food market, except for the fact that the outcome—particularly on the all-important issue of price—was determined by the president with his family and cronies, not by the parties in the face-to-face negotiations.

9

Paiton's Power: More Home Government Support

...my colleagues at State know there is no higher priority than sitting behind what I call the "America Desk"—which is my shorthand for the job of not just promoting American business but also ensuring that our business people can compete and win on a level, fair, and open playing field.
—Warren Christopher, former U.S. secretary of state and
   director at Edison International, a Mission company[1]

In September 1994, a ceremony marked the official start of construction of Paiton I. Attending were the U.S. ambassador and representatives of some institutions that might put up money, along with the secretary general of the Ministry of Finance.[2] One might have expected higher level Indonesian officials for such a large project, but this was really only a ceremony. No contract for construction had been executed[3] and the all-important financing was still missing. The U.S. government would become much more deeply involved before the project could proceed. In fact, this chapter will show that the involvement was so deep that one must question the meaning of "turning to the private sector" for infrastructure.

Deliverables for Official Visitors

Before putting up around $2 billion, lenders wanted assurances beyond a contract with a financially shaky buyer, PLN. They had probably already exercised strong influence to ensure that electricity payments were indexed to inflation and the foreign exchange rate. But an additional kind of security would be some complementary financing and insurance from multilateral and bilateral organizations. This would provide a seal of legitimacy and some protection of property rights, as a wise sovereign would hesitate to squeeze a project if that would mean squeezing major lenders to the country. Or at least so investors could assume.

But the multilaterals themselves were balking. In September1994, U.S. Ambassador Barry stated that the project faced two problems: the "skittishness" of the Asian Development Bank (ADB) because of the involvement of the Suharto family, and a delay in obtaining financing from the U.S. Export-Import Bank (Exim).[4] The country office of the World Bank had, of course, already stated its objections to the venture, and the Bank was unlikely to provide money through its International Finance Corporation.

The U.S. Export-Import Bank, happy to participate in the project led by an American investor, countered that the ADB's concern was with a very "minimal" involvement of Indonesia's first family. With indirect equity holdings of Suharto's daughter Titiek reported as 0.75% of the total equity, this "minimal" holding represented a little more than $15 million dollars.[5] The report failed to mention Hashim's relationship to the president's family, Agus's relationship to the minister of mines and energy, or the involvement of powerful people in the coal terminal and shipping. Because a little hint of questionable participation did not dampen the enthusiasm of U.S. officials, they pressed the ADB to go ahead with loans for the project. Ambassador Barry reported "working with" Linda Yang, the U.S. executive director at the ADB, who was "doing all she can."[6] Whatever she did, she failed to convince the multilateral bank to lend.

In the September meeting at the U.S. Department of Commerce, officials and company managers agreed that they needed a deal with money behind it before the upcoming November Asia Pacific Economic Cooperation (APEC) summit in Jakarta.[7] U.S. President Clinton would attend. The commerce department and no doubt the embassy wanted to add this project to their list of "deliverables" for the president's visit. Deliverables had become a measure of officials' diligence, and few important visitors inquired seriously whether they were good for development or even real.

The commerce department, under Ron Brown, supported the deal. Mission Energy appeared on a list of donors to the Democratic National Committee, which Brown had chaired. Mission's CEO, John Bryson, had contributed to both Clinton's campaigns and to his legal defense fund.[8] Perhaps related to these contributions, or perhaps not, inside the Department of Commerce, the Advocacy Center was asked "to keep tabs on the project until the mission"[9]—that is, until Clinton's upcoming visit to Indonesia.

The Department of Commerce had created the Advocacy Center in 1993. Its Web site announced "assistance can include a visit to a key foreign official by a high-ranking U.S. government official; direct support by U.S. officials (including commerce and state department officers) stationed at U.S. embassies; and coordinated action by U.S. government agencies to provide maximum assistance."[10] An American company seeking assistance was asked questions to determine whether the transaction was in the U.S. national interest, an interest measured largely by U.S. content in the transaction. Little attention was paid, it seems, to whether the transaction was in the interest of the foreign country. An applicant was told only to "highlight the competitiveness of your bid in terms of technology and price." However, an applicant did have to certify that officials had not and would not be bribed.

The Advocacy Center and other strong U.S. support for American investors abroad reflected new U.S. policies. To some extent, those policies were playing catch-up with those of other governments who had long provided support to their firms abroad. In a visit to Jakarta as U.S. secretary of state, Warren Christopher summed them up:

> Every day, in one way or another, Embassy Jakarta goes to bat for American businesses and helps you try to score orders and secure investments—from the Paiton power plant in East Java, to the communications networks in West Java, to the forestry communications in Eastern Indonesia.[11]

The chief political counselor in the American embassy was quoted as saying that "protecting the interests of major investors and creditors was at the center of the table in everything we did. Concerns about stability made it to the margins. Concerns about human rights, democracy, corruption never made it onto the table at all."[12]

Comfort and Guarantees

The lack of Indonesian government guarantees had now become a major holdup for finance. Potential private lenders—the Japanese, in particular—were insisting on them, even though the governing decree for electric power had prohibited guarantees. When investors had raised the matter again about six months before the power purchase agreement had been signed, the minister of finance had still balked.

Nevertheless, the Japanese Exim Bank and the Japanese Ministry of International Trade and Industry (MITI) continued to push for guarantees. In March 1995, a high-level GE manager wrote the chairman of the U.S. Exim Bank about the issue,[13] mentioning recent meetings in the Ministry of Finance and with Habibie to seek an extension of the deadline for financial closing from February 12 to March 31 and to explore compromise language for a guarantee.[14] In seeking U.S. Exim Bank support, the manager said,

> Ken, your and US Exim's leadership is critical to get this deal done. Frankly, JEXIM's current controversial political position in Japan, combined with their less innovative thinking on project financing in general, means they need (and may actually want) you to step forward. A successful Paiton close will probably help them politically no matter who takes the lead.

He added,

> Ken, I'm very worried, based on input I've received in Indonesia and around Asia, that this deal will go to the Europeans (Seimens [sic]/Bimantara) if we don't close by March 31st.

Experienced in this area, GE understood U.S. politics: Support your appeal with a warning that business might go to Europeans.

Less than two weeks later, Mission's CEO[15] sent a letter to Ronald Brown thanking him for his help and suggesting "substantive talking points for your telephone call to Mar'ie Muhammad, the Indonesian Minister of Finance." Among the points mentioned in the letter was the following:

> The U.S. Government, from the President on down, has put a high priority on the Paiton Project—the U.S. Export-Import Bank (Exim) and the U.S. Overseas Private Investment Corporation (OPIC) have given the Project more support than any in their history—and we would be very grateful if you could approve the revised form of Consent so that this project can close on March 21.[16]

In sum, the U.S. government was pushing the Indonesian government for guarantees that were contrary to the authorizing decree and national policy.[17] This reflected an interesting view of privatization.

Notes of a Paiton manager from a meeting with Ambassador Barry in the U.S. embassy soon thereafter suggest the extent to which the U.S. government was monitoring the Indonesian government on behalf of Paiton's investors.[18] The notes report that Jusuf Anwar, the secretary general in the Ministry of Finance, had not yet discussed the issue with the minister but that he had authorized White & Case lawyers to talk with Paiton lawyers about assurances. They also relate conversations with Widjojo (incorrectly reported as a past minister of finance) on the subject.

In fact, with the counsel of White & Case,[19] a compromise had been hammered out within the ministry. The commitment, called a "letter of comfort," would state rather vaguely that the "government would cause PLN to honor its obligations."[20]

Not satisfied, the Japanese continued to seek more concrete guarantees. On March 8, 1995, three Japanese from MITI and the Japanese Exim Bank, one representative from OPIC, and four managers from the project sponsors met with the secretary general of the finance ministry and an advisor from the Troika (from Lehman Brothers). The Japanese wanted "assurance that GOI performs in full PLN's obligations," guarantees that foreign exchange would be made available, guarantees against expropriation, waiver of sovereign immunity, and coverage for war, rebellion, and similar. With respect to nonpayment, the secretary general responded to the lenders that they were considering a very hypothetical situation, remote from reality. Even if PLN were to go bankrupt someday, he said, the country would possibly also be facing the same problem. He added that "This is beyond the imagination of the government." Even though the Asian Currency Crisis was only two years away, the events were indeed probably beyond the imagination of anyone involved at that time.

The secretary general pointed out that Indonesia had no exchange controls, that laws covered expropriation, that Indonesia belonged to

ICSID and dispute settlement was covered in the power purchase agreement, and that the company could buy insurance against war risk. He reiterated a deep concern: "If MoF [the Ministry of Finance] issues some sort of assurance, there shall be 5,000 requests queuing...." And, he pointed out that guarantees might violate pledge covenants in existing government borrowing. In short, he said "no."

The Japanese did not grasp this "no," it seems. The deputy governor of the Japanese Exim Bank met with the secretary general the next week. We have no record of that meeting, but it seems that the ministry official held the line. On March 20, 1995, Jack Welch, GE's CEO, wrote Habibie on the matter, saying that another manager had mentioned that "GE and Mission were trying to broker a compromise 'side-letter' which would provide some broadened language for the lenders without significantly changing the [government of Indonesia's] obligations under the PPA [power purchase agreement] and other agreements."[21]

The minister of finance ended up signing letters of comfort, with no additional side letter. What exactly is a letter of comfort like that which emerged out of these negotiations? In considering the meaning, it is important to realize that the minister of finance knew what guarantees were, the governing decree had not authorized them, and he declined to sign them. Jack Welch's letter provided an answer for the time being:

> It is my view that the [Government of Indonesia], despite the compromise 'consents' language being currently proposed [that is, the letter of comfort the minister was willing to sign] has not meaningfully enlarged its responsibility to support the project from the series of agreements hammered out with the sponsors last year.[22]

In its 10-K filings with the U.S. Securities and Exchange Commission, Edison International reported: "The state-owned electricity company's obligations are *supported* [italics added] by GOI [Government of Indonesia]." The statement would surely have read "guaranteed" had the company believed that it really held guarantees. Further, Edison's 1995 annual report speaks of the company's success in "achieving debt security [for Paiton] in the absence of sovereign guarantees." And its confidential offering circular, dated March 21, 1996, clearly indicates that the comfort letter was not a guarantee. Mission would later waffle on its interpretation, and the meaning of the comfort letters would become a subject of intense debate in another case.

U.S. Government Finance

The U.S. government continued to be involved in completing the financing. A March 30, 1995, memo from the U.S embassy in Jakarta to "Sarah Kemp, US & FCS" said, "Advocacy is ongoing and still may need further Washington assistance." US & FCS was the Foreign and U.S. Commercial

Services in the U.S. Department of Commerce, a unit charged with promoting U.S. exports and protecting U.S. business interests abroad, with a focus on small and medium-sized U.S. companies. Whatever the explanation for this unit's involvement—Paiton would generate U.S. exports, particularly turbines—it seems that private development of infrastructure would not be left to private investors.

Ron Brown himself continued to help. When it became clear that the Asian Development Bank would not provide funds, Brown pressed for $1.8 billion in limited recourse project financing from U.S. Exim Bank, OPIC, and the Japanese Exim Bank. The U.S. government organizations responded: US Exim offered a construction loan and $540 million of political-risk guarantee. OPIC also joined in with money and guarantees (certificates of participation), even though it also knew of ADB's concerns.[23]

Officials of US Exim discovered that the American government enthusiasm for the project was not shared by all Indonesians. One report said, "When the representative of the U.S. Exim Bank visited Indonesia, several experts of the government and PLN pointed out to her that the country did not need Paiton I."[24] Yet some $500 million in "U.S. content" (that is, U.S. business) was purportedly involved,[25] and perhaps campaign finance money as well. With the commerce department pressing hard for the project, Exim could overlook any doubts that Indonesians might express.

With its own money committed, the United States increased pressure on the Japanese to join in. The American ambassador to Indonesia, Barry, asked his counterpart in Japan, Walter Mondale, to urge the Japanese Exim Bank to put up money.[26] The result as of April 21, 1995: $990 million. With this signal, eight Japanese commercial banks signed on for an additional $360 million. The Japanese Ministry of International Trade and Industry kicked in insurance for the loans.

President Clinton's visit to Indonesia on November 16, 1994, was cheered up by an impressive assembly of deliverables: Reports count $40 billion of business arrangements signed on a single day. Clinton himself signed the arrangements for loans to Paiton from the Export-Import Bank, initially $425 according to a White House press release. Also present to see the results of his department's support was Ron Brown, and perhaps Warren Christopher.[27] As is so often the case, the deliverables were not quite what they appeared to be: OPIC and Exim Bank commitments were no more than "letters of advice." It was not really a done deal, but it looked good nonetheless, and the event provided good press.

Christopher's speech in Indonesia reflected the new U.S. policy that had so helped this investor:

> In the not-too-distant past, the promotion of U.S. business interests abroad was rarely at the top of the diplomatic agenda. I believe that the Clinton Administration has changed that for good.[28]

Regardless of intent, that change may not have been "for good."

The New Company

Mission and the other members of the consortium had formed the PT Paiton Energy Company (PEC),[29] an Indonesian entity, to undertake the project. The shares in the new company were initially held as follows:

Edison Mission Energy	32.5%[30]
Mitsui	32.5%[31]
GE	20.0%[32]
Batu Hitam Perkasa (BHP)	15.0%

As is usual in such a project, each owner would have opportunities to make money beyond its dividends. Mission would hold the contract to manage and operate the plant; for this service, it would receive an annual fee of $3,250,000.[33] Mitsui would take the lead role in the construction contract and could capture profits associated with this work. GE could earn margins on turbines and other equipment. BHP's affiliate, Adaro, would supply coal, at a price that would reflect its influence. In theory, lenders could act as a brake on cash drawn off by equity partners. In practice, they were likely to monitor these flows only if the project were to falter on servicing its debt.

Wrapping Up the Package

Presumably private lenders decided that U.S. and Japanese government participation in loans and insurance, a powerful local partner, a comfort letter, and provision for international arbitration provided sufficient protection of their property rights. Although ITT's arbitration clause had looked experimental in the late 1960s, times had changed and arbitration was being used more frequently to settle disputes between investors and host governments. Because the United States and Japan provided large amounts of assistance to Indonesia, presumably their involvement would also underwrite the terms of Paiton's contract. And the consortium's local partners were well connected in the political system. The comfort letter might, however, have given some pause. We have been told that Japanese lenders and guarantors increased their fees because of the lack of guarantees,[34] so they must have believed that the letter meant little.

In any event, lenders were sufficiently comforted to go ahead, even eagerly. According to one source, 48 international banks wanted a piece of the deal.[35] The announcement of Paiton I's financing, in July 1995, listed two coordinating banks (Chase and the Industrial Bank of Japan), eight "lead arrangers," 28 "arrangers," nine "lead managers," and four entities as "agency lenders/guarantor/insurer." These latter were the two Exim banks, Japan's MITI, and OPIC, the U.S. government agency that guaranteed banks' senior debt and provided $200 million insurance (convertibility and political violence only) to Mission and GE.[36] The banks' enthusiasm may have been the result of the go-go mood of the time and perhaps the tendency of bankers in a consortium to make the often faulty assumption that another bank has done serious analysis of risk. Of course, the funds were project finance, without guarantees from the equity investors. But why worry, with Japanese and U.S. loan guarantees?

In spite of its opposition, the World Bank even became involved in the end. The Multilateral Investment Guarantee Agency (MIGA), the World Bank's insurance wing, offered a $50 million policy to an affiliate of General Electric Capital Corporation, for a portion of its $61.2 million equity investment in Paiton. In justifying its guarantee, MIGA argued that the project "will further develop the coal industry and allow the country to maintain its oil export levels."[37] No mention was made of whether the prices for coal and electricity were reasonable or whether PLN could even pay for the electricity at those prices. MIGA had, according to one of its managers, been too eager to increase its business to engage in questions about the project itself. Of course, MIGA's involvement added another piece to the investors' set of defenses, should Indonesia ever decide to renege on its deal.

With everything lined up, financial closure took place in April 1995, but not without a hitch. Three days after the closing, the Ministry of Mines and Energy ordered PLN to inform the project sponsors that the power purchase agreement was canceled, because the closing had supposedly taken place some four hours after the deadline. We were told that Adnan Ganto, the advisor brought in by Sudjana, the new minister of mines and energy, had urged the minister to cancel the project so that it could be given to Gordon Wu, the Hong Kong investor who had originally inspired Intercontinental to go to Asia.[38] Jezek and others fought the cancellation, and the government eventually reversed itself. Later, Adnan found another project for Wu, and established an unenviable reputation among foreign advisors.[39] The event also rattled investors' confidence in the government's ability to manage the power sector.

In the end, "private investment" in power depended heavily on government. Of the total projected project cost of about $2.5 billion, private principals offered $680 million in equity and subordinated debt,[40] and private banks put up an additional $180 million in the form of Rule 144A bonds.[41] Thus, the total private contribution was $860 million, or only about one third of the total funding. Of the $1.82 billion external debt financing,[42] the Japanese Exim Bank, MITI, U.S. Exim, and OPIC provided or guaranteed the balance (for details, see the appendix to this chapter), even though they knew of possible corruption. In sum, like the privatization of Indosat to a company owned by a foreign government, private power seems to have taken on an odd meaning, this time with two thirds of the money coming from or guaranteed by foreign governments.

Showing good manners, Mission's CEO expressed his gratitude to the U.S. government in a letter to Ron Brown: "The US Government, from the

---

Box 9.1 Robert M. Edgell

A very special bonus went to Edgell, Mission's chief negotiator: He gained a new wife. The story is one that several interviewees eagerly told us. On arrival in Indonesia, Edgell was reportedly not enamored of Southeast Asia. Soon, according to one advisor, Edgell commented that he could not understand why so many foreign men had Indonesian girlfriends. It seems, however, that he began to understand.

Graeme Robertson, the Australian coal entrepreneur, had married an Indonesian, Fena (see Box 8.1). She was described to us as a "foxy lady," and the couple were known for their dress and style, winning the "loveliest couple" award at AmCham's Christmas Ball. But Robertson told us that her ambition was to leave Indonesia, while he was eager to become an Indonesian citizen and remain there. Sometime during the power negotiations, Robertson's wife and the married Edgell took to each other. The result was two divorces, one for Edgell and one for Fena. Fena then married Edgell, soon produced a baby, and brought with her the children from her marriage to Robertson.[a] Fena accomplished her goal of leaving Indonesia, and Robertson became an Indonesian citizen in 1995. Edgell settled in what was described to us as a posh office in Singapore. His newfound enthusiasm for Southeast Asia would probably matter when the Paiton deal began to fall apart. People who knew him said that he was so satisfied that he was determined to keep the project going. Edgell himself told us that Fena helped to increase his understanding of Indonesians.

[a]Robertson's version was that he had promised Fena to find her a good husband, when it became clear that they had different goals—and that he had done so.

President on down, has put a high priority on the Paiton Project—the U.S. Export-Import Bank (Exim) and the U.S. Overseas Private Investment Corporation (OPIC) have given the Project more support than any in their history. . . ."[43]

Help in the negotiations and in assembling the finance was only the beginning of the involvement of the U.S. government in Indonesian power, as we shall see.

Personal Celebration and Caution

There were other, more personal reasons for satisfaction. Mission's managers received bonuses. Their bonuses, managers told us, were based on financial performance and goals for new business, among other criteria.

They were not so deal-driven as those given at Enron for its power projects. Enron's executives, it seems, received a straight percentage of the projected net present value of projects they negotiated. Mitsui's executives were rewarded with special commendations from their superiors.[44] We assume that GE's managers were also adequately compensated, but we have little information as to how.[45] Edgell also received a bonus of a more personal nature (see Box 9.1).

Almost as a footnote, there was to be another, last-minute shift in partnerships. In January 1996, in a lucky or prescient move GE reduced its share of Paiton I from 20% to 12.5% by selling some of its interest to Mission. In the same year, it sold most of its remaining 12.5% interest to TransCanada PipeLines, a company that was adding electricity generation to its gas transport business and venturing abroad. GE, left with only 2.5% of the equity,[46] had probably already accomplished its main goal: ensuring sales of its equipment to the facility.

The optimism that accompanied the financing announcement was a bit spoiled by a foreign advisor, who said that signing the power purchase agreements without an adequate set of power-sector regulations was "like building a skyscraper without driving piles."[47] Dejected, Jezek wrote in his final report,

> it was not productive to continue with the advisory activities under the prevailing conditions of politicisation and unwillingness or inability of the [government of Indonesia] to take corrective measures. It was once stated that insanity is defined as "doing the same thing over and over again but expecting different results" ... Efficiency and skills, and not political connections should guarantee success of private sector companies. . . .[48]

When Jezek was asked to extend his assignment, he declined and headed for Thailand. His advice had crossed officials' interests so often that he reported to us that he had been warned by a well-connected American, "You had better watch your behind. Ginandjar is upset and will have you killed."[49] But Jezek would eventually return.

Appendix 9.1 Paiton I Project Costs

Project Cost Breakdown	US$ Million	Percentage of Total Base Cost
EPC construction contract	1,772.30	70.9
Value added taxes	53.70	2.1
Interest during construction	308.20	12.3
Up-front financing fees	144.30	5.8
MITI fee	12.30	0.5
Commitment fee	29.30	1.2
Agency fees	3.70	0.1
Development expense	43.20	1.7
Development fee	11.80	0.5
Owner's engineer	15.00	0.6
Operation and maintenance staffing	15.00	0.6
Working capital	25.30	1.0
Insurance	30.00	1.2
Administration cost	26.00	1.0
Pre-completion labor	6.60	0.3
Contingency	3.30	0.1
Total base project cost	2,500.00	100.0
Contingencies and cost overruns	300.00	

EPC: engineer, procure, construct; MITI: Japanese Ministry of International Trade.

Source: Diana Yuliyanti, "Project Finance for Independent Power Producers in Developing Countries: The Paiton I Power Generation Project in Indonesia," dissertation submitted for Masters of Science in Civil and Environmental Engineering, Massachusetts Institute of Technology, February 1, 2001, p. 73. The data came originally from the *Confidential Offering Circular*, March 21, 1996. Reprinted with permission.

Appendix 9.2 Project Financing Plan II for Paiton I

Financing Source	US$ Million	Percentage of Total Base Cost
Senior debt		
JExim facility		
Tranche A	540.00	21.6
Tranche B	360.00	14.4
USExim construction facility	540.00	21.6
OPIC facility	200.00	8.0
Bonds	180.00	7.2
Total senior debt	1,820.00	72.8
Subordinated debt		
Mission	176.00	7.0
Mitsui	143.00	5.7
GECC	55.00	2.2
BHP	—	0.0
Total subordinated debt	374.00	15.0
Equity		
Mission	122.40	4.9
Mitsui	99.45	4.0
GECC	38.25	1.5
BHP	45.90	1.8
Total Equity	306.00	12.2
Total base project equity	680.00	27.2
Total base project cost	2,500.00	100.0

BHP: Batu Hitam Perkasa; GECC: General Electric Capital Corporation; JExim: Japanese Export-Import Bank; USExim: U.S. Export-Import Bank.

Source: Diana Yuliyanti, "Project Finance for Independent Power Producers in Developing Countries: The Paiton I Power Generation Project in Indonesia," dissertation submitted for Masters of Science in Civil and Environmental Engineering, Massachusetts Institute of Technology, February 1, 2001, p. 74. The data came originally from the *Confidential Offering Circular*, March 21, 1996. Reprinted with permission.

Appendix 9.3 Debt-Financing Breakdown for Paiton I

Debt Source	Principal Amount (US$ million)	Percentage of Total Debt
JExim facility		
Tranche A	540.00	29.7
Tranche B	360.00	19.8
USExim facility	540.00	29.7
OPIC facility	200.00	11.0
Bonds	180.00	9.9
Total debt financing	1,820.00	100.0

JExim: Japanese Export-Import Bank; OPIC: Overseas Private Investment Corporation; USExim: U.S. Export-Import Bank.

Source: Diana Yuliyanti, "Project Finance for Independent Power Producers in Developing Countries: The Paiton I Power Generation Project in Indonesia," dissertation submitted for Masters of Science in Civil and Environmental Engineering, Massachusetts Institute of Technology, February 1, 2001, p. 75. The data came originally from the *Confidential Offering Circular*, March 21, 1996. Reprinted with permission.

Appendix 9.4 Interest Rates and Terms for Paiton I Debt

	Interest Rates (%)				Repayment Years
Debt Source	Precompletion	Years 1–4	Years 5–8	Years 9–12	
JExim					
TrancheA	9.44	9.44	9.44	9.44	1999–2011
TrancheB	4.88	11.13	11.25	11.38	1999–2011
USExim	9.38	11.50	11.50	11.50	1999–2011
OPIC	6.18	12.29	12.29	12.29	1999–2011
Bonds[a]	10.46	10.46	10.46	10.46	2008–2014

[a]The bonds were initially purchased by CS First Boston Corporation, Chase Securities, Inc., BA Securities, Inc., Barclays de Zoete Wedd Securities, Inc., Credit Lyonnais Securities (USA) Inc., and UBX Securities LLC.

JExim: Japanese Export-Import Bank; OPIC: Overseas Private Investment Corporation; USExim: U.S. Export-Import Bank.

Source: Diana Yuliyanti, "Project Finance for Independent Power Producers in Developing Countries: The Paiton I Power Generation Project in Indonesia," dissertation submitted for Masters of Science in Civil and Environmental Engineering, Massachusetts Institute of Technology, February 1, 2001, p. 75. The data came originally from the *Confidential Offering Circular*, March 21, 1996. Reprinted with permission.

Appendix 9.5 Financing from Equity Holders for Paiton I

Project Sponsor	Subordinated Debt		Equity		Ownership Interest (%)
	US$ million	%	US$ million	%	
Mission	176.00	47.1	122.40	40.0	40.0
Mitsui	143.00	38.2	99.45	32.5	32.5
GECC	55.00	14.7	38.25	12.5	12.5
BHP	0	0	45.90	15.0	15.0
Total	374.00	100.0	306.00	100.0	100.0

BHP: Batu Hitam Perkasa; GECC: General Electric Capital Corporation.

Source: Confidential Offering Circular (1996) for Paiton I.

10

Evaluating Paiton I

Gilded tombs do worms enfold.
—William Shakespeare, "Merchant of Venice,"
 Act II, Scene vii

In almost no time, Indonesians and others began to criticize the terms of Paiton I. Although one can quibble with critics' calculations, almost any approach raised serious questions about whether the deal was good for Indonesia. The costs were high, even though major risks were assigned to the host country. The way risks were allocated for this and the other 26 Indonesian power agreements ensured that the Asian Currency Crisis would bring them all down. Collapse would come even before projects had been finished.

Price and Politics

To be effective, critics of foreign investment need simple numbers, even if they are less than perfect. (For some details of the agreement, see the appendix to this chapter.) Two approaches fit the bill: (1) Compare the price of Paiton's electricity with prices of electricity delivered by other generators, and (2) argue that Indonesia could have built the project itself with only a few years of the sums Paiton would remit to foreigners over the next 30 years.

Determining a single price for Paiton is not as easy as it might seem because nominal prices were to decline over time.[1] Not surprisingly, the company offered the lowest figure: an unexplained 6.3 cents per kilowatt hour (cents/kwh) over the 30-year period of the agreement. An arithmetic average of the prices for each of the 30 years turns out to be 6.72 cents. PLN

145

reported a "levelized" price of 7.37 cents, also without explanation.[2] A sophisticated analyst might apply a discount rate to weight the earlier prices more heavily than later ones. Not surprisingly, however, many critics focused on the highest figure available: the starting rate of 8.56 cents/kwh.

Critics made various comparisons. A World Bank publication reported that "Wholesale IPP [independent power producer] tariffs in Malaysia and Thailand range from 3 c to 4 c per kilowatt-hour...."[3] An Indonesian article claimed 1994 prices in Thailand of 4.2 cents; in Pakistan of 6.5; and the Philippines of 5.7.[4] Another document, by a foreign nongovernmental organization, said that Paiton's price was 60% higher than those in the Philippines.[5] In any of these comparisons, Paiton I was vulnerable.[6]

Another standard was prices for other electricity projects in Indonesia. One study reported that Paiton's charges were 32% higher than those of comparable projects.[7] In another domestic comparison, Paiton I's price was matched against the offer at Paiton II of 6.60 cents/kwh.[8]

A sophisticated analyst might start with the quoted prices but adjust them to reflect different investments for surrounding infrastructure, for payments to other Indonesians that are not net costs to the economy, and so on. But sophisticated comparisons are not the stuff of politics, nor were the necessary data readily available to critics.

Avoided Costs

Early on, advisors had urged Indonesians to compare prices of private power with "avoided costs"—that is, with costs that PLN would incur if it were to generate the power itself. Right after the final signing, the *Jakarta Post* had carried an article telling of criticism in the House of Representatives (DPR): Paiton's price of 8.56 cents/kwh was cited as "far higher" than the average cost of Rp 107.31 (4.9 cents) for power PLN generated on Java.[9]

The rub: Almost everyone agreed that PLN's reported costs did not accurately measure actual costs. Bookkeeping was terrible, and government subsidies could not easily be disentangled. Cost estimates varied so widely that they could not inspire confidence. At the low end, a study determined that PLN could generate power for 4.11 cents/kwh.[10] Another study, at the opposite end, calculated necessary tariffs based on a "competitive return to equity," adjusted for all subsidies to PLN and assigned costs of exchange rate risks to a state-owned project. It arrived at a price 45.5% higher than PLN's revenue.[11] This implied a cost at retail of about 10 cents/kwh, or a wholesale cost of about 6.7 cents.

Both of these extreme estimates of avoided costs yielded a figure lower than most calculations of Paiton I's levelized tariff. Attacks of this kind were complicated, but they carried at least some credibility.

Payback

Payback provided another simple calculation for critics. A PLN professional reported that the principal fixed payments included in the Paiton tariffs amounted to around $600 million per year.[12] He then claimed costs of building a similar facility at Tanjung Jati B at $1.2 billion. Therefore, about two years of fixed payments for Paiton I would be enough to build the entire Paiton I. This was also a calculation that could be easily grasped, in spite of its several problems.

Cost of Capital

Because money was the principal contribution of the investors, an evaluation could also compare the cost to Indonesia of Paiton's capital with the costs of capital for other projects and with costs of alternative sources of funds.

Rate of Return

Dividends and debt service paid abroad represent net costs of foreign investment to a host country. With a few assumptions, one can estimate these payments for Paiton I. Assume, first and reasonably, that the fixed capacity payments in the four-part Paiton tariff represent payments of interest, principal, and dividends. If one accepts the perhaps exaggerated claim that capital invested was actually $2.5 billion, we estimate that the stream of fixed capacity payments adds up to an internal rate of return on total assets of about 20% per year.[13] One can then estimate an expected pretax (cash flow) return on equity[14] of about 38%. If the return is reduced by 15% to account crudely for free shares to local partners, the rate is still a healthy 32%.[15] Taking a different approach, a graduate student at MIT estimated a 24.76% return on equity.[16] These estimates do not include any profits captured in construction, equipment sales, and various fees.

Our rough estimates are consistent with reports from managers involved in Tanjung Jati A and C, who told us that they expected an internal rate of return of 28%, at an electricity price of 5.7 cents/kwh. They added that "Paiton I must have been hugely profitable at its [much higher] price."[17] Regardless of how crude our estimates have to be, the expected return on equity must have exceeded 30% by some significant margin, even though equity holders faced no liability for Paiton's nonrecourse project finance. The return on total assets was surely at least 20%.

Comparisons

Projects Elsewhere

These expected returns were at the high end of returns projected elsewhere. A Philippine coal-fired project appears to have expected earnings of around 23% on equity.[18] Two authors reported that infrastructure investors (in developing countries) seek an internal rate of return of 15% to 18% on all assets, and 25–35% on equity.[19]

Borrowing Cost

From the point of view of the Indonesian economy, the returns to investors ought to be compared with costs of alternative sources of capital. In this case, we will argue that a relevant comparison is with the costs Indonesians would have incurred if they had actually borrowed to build the project. Indonesia could surely have borrowed dollars at a much lower cost than 20%. If the government were to guarantee the borrowing, a standard is the sovereign borrowing rate of, say, 9% in 1996.[20] Based on these comparisons, one must conclude that private money for Paiton I carried a very high cost.

To be sure, a country could reasonably decide to pay more than the sovereign borrowing rate for foreign direct investment, particularly if (1) the foreign investor brings assets—such as technology or market access—that do not accompany borrowing; (2) the foreign investor assumes more risks than does a foreign lender; or (3) the foreigner adds to efficiency. Investors in Indonesian power projects did not bring scarce technology; PLN had built and operated power plants in the past, and could do so again.

The allocation of risks in the Paiton agreement were more like those of debt than the usual foreign direct investment. A country might pay more for direct foreign investment than for debt if the investor assumes risks of demand shortfalls, price fluctuations, and foreign exchange movements. However, the power purchase agreements allocated these risks to Indonesians, not the investors.[21]

To be fair, investors in Paiton I did face some risks. In particular, they had to construct a plant that met certain standards, and they had to meet a particular schedule. They had to make sure that systems were in place for coal to be available as needed. But risks associated with construction and systems were largely under investors' control, and they had built similar facilities before. Beyond that, the investors faced primarily risks associated with PLN's ability and willingness to pay, but any lender to PLN would have faced these same risks.

Company managers did claim efficiency. They told us that they would run Paiton I with a third the number of people that similar state-owned generating facilities employed. But in the scheme of things this mattered little. The original plans for Paiton I called for four expatriate and two Indonesian managers, and four expatriate and 17 Indonesian operators.[22] Thus, foreign ownership might save the salaries of 42 Indonesian operators and 12 Indonesian managers. These savings would have to be balanced against the additional costs of expatriate managers and operators. Under any reasonable assumption, the cost of expatriate employees far offsets the low wages of additional Indonesian employees in each category. Thus, there would likely be no financial gain from the decreased employment.[23] Moreover, because labor costs of power plants are, according to a rough calculation, only perhaps two tenths of a percent of total costs,[24] if there were any gains they would be overwhelmed by the cost of capital.

Foreign owners might have brought additional operating efficiencies, but efficiencies matter from a national point of view only if some share of the resulting gains is passed on to Indonesia. In this project, the high price of electricity means that the investors capture any gains from efficiency. Although the conclusion proves upsetting to private managers and especially to engineers, when all gains from efficiency are captured by the foreign investor, there is little reason for a host country to prefer an efficient operation over a less efficient one. In the end, it is the costs to the country that matter, not savings in labor or other technical measures of efficiency. Without regulation or tougher negotiation on prices, private monopoly simply captures the rents from efficiency gains.

Foreign investors in electricity might overcome other problems in the sector; they could, for example, be more diligent in collecting bills from customers than was the state-owned company. But the investors in Paiton were not in the distribution business, so they were in no position to solve one of the sector's major problems.

Finally, one has to consider the issue of guarantees. If one considers the comfort letter to have been something short of a sovereign guarantee, which was clearly the intent of the minister of finance, then one ought to add some margin to the cost of sovereign debt to reflect risks to Paiton's owners that PLN might be unwilling or unable to honor its contracts. It is difficult, however, to justify a figure double the cost of sovereign debt, especially in light of the protections seemingly offered by arbitration and the involvement of U.S. and Japanese government credit and insurance agencies. On the other hand, if one considers the comfort letter as a guarantee, as investors would later claim them to be, then the returns to investors ought not to have been much, if any, higher than that of sovereign debt.

Regardless of the comparison chosen, the deal struck for Paiton I seems an expensive way to obtain money to expand Indonesian power.

Where Did All the Money Go?

Not only was the expected rate of return high, but everything was pricey.

Project Costs

Referring to the amount of investment, a "part-time project partner" at Lehman Brothers said: "All things considered, the project seems to be very costly."[25] Later, we will see that an outside engineering consulting firm (hired by Indonesians) came to a similar conclusion, after a detailed investigation. At $2.5 billion, Paiton I cost much more than Indonesia's Tanjung Jati B, which critics of Paiton I reported as costing between $1.2

and $1.5 billion for similar capacity.[26] Critics also cited the lower costs for Paiton II, reported at $1.67 billion.

Paiton I managers countered by saying that the additional infrastructure required of them added about 0.72 cents/kwh to the tariff.[27] This implies a cost for extra infrastructure of about $300 million.[28] There are various explanations for other costs, and because they come from different sources, we cannot tell whether they are duplicative. Charges for delays in reaching agreement, scrubbers, shared facilities, and scope changes were mentioned in Chapter 8.[29] In a letter to the president, Hashim attributes 0.57 cents of the tariff in the first years to new environmental demands and 0.62 to higher interest rates.[30] Paiton managers also reminded us about $25 million attributable to having to buy more expensive boilers. Although this was a substantial bonanza to individuals who might have shared in the premium, in the overall costs of the power project this figure is small.

Because foreign shareholders provided equipment, construction, and services, some of these charges may have been inflated. Mitsui and General Electric surely had incentives to bill higher than normal prices for construction and equipment; similarly, Mission could take out profits through management fees. Such transfer prices could reduce taxes as well as political risks from high reported returns. Of course, profits transferred in this way did not accrue to the local partner.

Although we can identify some likely sources for high project costs, a detailed and fully credible explanation has never been provided. We can only speculate. Whatever their origins, the costs were reflected in the price PLN, and eventually the Indonesian customer or taxpayer, would pay for electricity.

Coal Price

Charges for electricity from Paiton I also reflected the coal prices from the affiliated supplier.[31] Paiton managers emphasized to us the quality of the coal, the ability of the supplier to set aside reserves, and requirements of lenders for stockpiling and delivering coal. But one advisor to the Indonesians is quoted as saying that, when advisors questioned the coal price during negotiations, "We were slapped back so fast our heads were spinning."[32] Given that the coal would come from a mine partly owned by Hashim and the president's daughter, that it would have to pass through a coal terminal affiliated with the same owners and would be shipped on transport owned by cronies, there were powerful interests supporting high prices for delivered coal. And there was no competitive bidding for the supply contract. One source estimated that coal was priced at 30% to 40% above the going international rate. More specifically, a PLN official said that Paiton was paying $34.90/ton for coal that could be bought elsewhere at $21 to $24/ton, figures largely confirmed by management later.[33]

If one starts with the estimate of 1.637 cents/kwh for coal, and assumes that it was overpriced by 30%, then 0.49 cents/kwh of the electricity tariff is due to excess charges for coal. Half a cent may sound small, but it represents considerably more than $100,000 per day.

Conclusion on Economics

There can be little doubt that the terms of the agreement offered handsome returns to the investors. Although the project was treated like a foreign direct investment, it carried few of the risks normally associated with this kind of investment. The usual foreign private investor bears risks of demand, price, and exchange rate. Faltering demand, unexpectedly low prices, or a falling exchange rate would mean smaller dividends to owners. The investor expects a high return in exchange for bearing these risks. In contrast, a lender shifts these risks to the borrower. Dollar debt has to be serviced no matter what happens to demand, prices, or exchange rates. The lender, of course, receives a lower expected return in exchange for not bearing these risks. The Indonesians got the worst of both sources of capital: They took on the major risks that they would have incurred if they had borrowed to build the project; at the same time, they agreed to pay returns on capital that were those of foreign direct investment.

The cost of the project and returns to capital are, in the end, reflected in the price for electricity, where pennies per kilowatt matter. At a price of 5.5 cents/kwh instead of 8.56, PLN would have saved the tidy sum of almost three-quarter million dollars *per day* in the early years of production.[34] And, remember, this was only one of more than two dozen similar commitments by PLN. Indonesians would pay dearly. However, managers and lenders appeared to care little and to understand even less about the impact of the arrangement on the Indonesian economy.

Government: Competence and Corruption

Why did Indonesians sign an agreement that seems so one-sided? It must have been obvious that PLN would find it difficult to pay more for electricity than it was collecting from its customers. And the allocation to Indonesians of what might normally be commercial risks assumed by direct investors should have raised red flags.

Tender

Some advisors blame Indonesia for not putting the projects up for tender, as they said they would. But a real bidding process seems never to have been in the cards. Preparation is essential if comparable tenders are to be sought; Indonesians fell short as they began to seek investors. Probably more importantly, there were too many outstretched hands. The president's family and other influential Indonesians were as eager to share in the pot of gold as were foreign investors. Not only might negotiations create a larger pot than tenders, but they would make it easier for powerful Indonesians to lay claims on part of the contents.

Although a bidding process might have resulted in better deals for Indonesians, experience elsewhere shows tenders pose another set of risks for countries. Potential investors submit low bids and then initiate renegotiations after they have been awarded contracts.[35] Tendering is unlikely to have been problem free.

Organization

For effective negotiations, Indonesians needed a single body with authority, that allowed a voice for affected ministries and agencies and that had adequate funds to collect under one umbrella the technical and legal resources it needed.

In the renegotiations of ITT/Indosat, the government had created just such a structure. One minister was unambiguously in charge; other agencies had representation, but not decision-making power. Foreign advisors worked together well and reported to one boss. The negotiating team was very well prepared, and even had fairly extensive knowledge of the company with which they were negotiating. Moreover, the process appears to us not to have been undermined by corruption[36] and interference by other governments. This was very different from the power negotiations.

Information

Another problem for Indonesia, and for other host governments, was asymmetry of information. As we have said, Indonesians knew little about agreements negotiated elsewhere. In fact, those that existed had been concluded only recently, so even the advisors did not have access to them. Indonesia's information had to come primarily from press reports, with their barest of details. In contrast, company managers and their lawyers surely knew other contracts.

In the 1970s, the United Nations Centre on Transnational Corporations, recognizing a similar problem for mining negotiations, built a library of mining agreements for government negotiators. Although in the early 2000s the World Bank picked up the idea and started to build a similar facility for infrastructure agreements, its officials have been less successful. Although the organizer of the U.N. library was willing to make deals—trades with advisors and lawyers for confidential documents, for example—the World Bank has been much more proper in formally asking governments for copies and honoring nominal confidentiality. As a result, as of our writing, the World Bank's efforts have accomplished little.

Not Alone

As expected, the Paiton I agreement did serve as the model for some two dozen additional Indonesian power agreements, all concluded by 1997.

They brought additional investors from the United States and Japan, but also companies from Germany, the United Kingdom, and elsewhere. Prices and some other details differed by project, but risks were allocated along the lines of the Paiton agreement.

Indonesia was not alone in returning to private power. In the 1990s, 70 developing countries reached financial closure for a total of more than 600 private electricity projects, representing investment of some $160 billion.[37] This flurry of activity followed perhaps two decades with almost no private investment in power in the developing countries. Practically the only exception was Chile, which had created a private electricity market earlier, in the 1980s. Many of the new negotiations shared some or all the problems associated with Paiton I: personal interests of powerful officials, weak organizational structures, serious rivalries among ministries and agencies, lack of information about terms elsewhere, poor handling of consultants, and even home government pressure. In this environment, foreign investors were promised high returns even though they took on few of the commercial risks usually associated with direct investment. The result would be a shocking number of disputes as countries reconsidered what they had done. Bargains obsolesced quickly because investors brought no special technology that could protect them. But the structure of most agreements meant that financial crises would add a new kind of trigger for disputes.

Appendix: Tariff Structure for Paiton I

Makeup of Tariff

The tariff charged for electricity from the Paiton I project comprised four components:

Component A: capacity charge

Component B: fixed operations/maintenance charge

Component C: fuel charge

Component D: variable operations/maintenance charge

Each of these was expressed in lengthy formulas. The following simplification captures the essence of the pricing structure.

Component A

The capacity charge was by far the largest component and was supposed to cover the investments made in constructing the facility. Presumably, it was designed to be sufficient to cover debt service, taxes, and dividends to equity holders.

This component was the one that stepped down over time. Although Paiton claims that the government requested the step down, no doubt the structure reflected the project's debt service obligations and the eagerness of investors to get returns out early. The projections were that Component A would be:

Years 1–6	6.12 cents/kwh
Years 7–12	5.97 cents/kwh
Years 13–30	3.10 cents/kwh

Component A was an annual fixed amount. It would be reduced only if available plant capacity fell below the 83% specified in the power purchase agreement or increased only if the availability exceeded the specified amount. Although the figures were specified in rupiah, the component was indexed to the U.S. dollar.

Component B

The fixed operations/maintenance charge was also independent of deliveries of electricity. Half of Component B was dollar indexed, and each element was inflation indexed. It was subject to the same adjustments for capacity availability as Component A. This component was said to cover payments made under the operation and management contract held by Mission Operation and Maintenance Incorporated—in other words, a subsidiary of Mission. The management fee was not bid on, and it was not based on cost calculations or not easily checked, of course. This component of the tariff was expected to be 0.435 cents/kwh.[38]

Component C

The fuel charge varied with the amount of electricity delivered and covered the cost of coal. Sixty percent of the amount was dollar indexed, to be adjusted annually to the exchange rate. It was expected to be 1.637 cents/kwh.

Component D

The variable operations and management charge varied with the amount of electricity delivered. About 25% of this component was dollar indexed. Both the dollar and the rupiah amounts were inflation indexed. It was expected to be 0.285 cents/kwh.

Annual Fixed Cost

If no electricity is purchased, the charge is the sum of components A and B. The annual fixed costs (for the first years) would, according to the above figures, be

(Component A + Component B) × Hours in day
× Days in year × Capacity utilization
× Capacity in kilowatts
$= (0.0612 + 0.00435) \times 24 \times 365 \times 0.83 \times 1{,}200{,}000$
$= 581{,}453{,}000$

Part III

New International Property
Rights in Action, 1997–2005

11

Paiton I: Promises Fail

The contracts have to be honored.
—George Munoz, OPIC[1]

A fter several years of very strong economic growth, Southeast
Asia's long boom came to an abrupt end. The first alarm
sounded when Thailand's currency was devalued in July of 1997. As the
financial crisis spread through the region, Indonesia was hit hardest of all.
The collapse of the Indonesian rupiah brought down all 27 of the electric
power agreements that had so recently been concluded. Their debt-like
characteristics made absolutely sure of this.

Crisis

Before the crisis, the rupiah had undergone steady but slow depreciation,
more or less matching the rate of inflation. The central bank had announced
its expectations for the coming year and used its reserves to manage the
exchange rate. The predictability of rates enabled managers to calculate
whether it would be cheaper to borrow low-interest dollars or high-interest
rupiah. Many bankers and conglomerates happily borrowed in dollars
because the interest on dollar loans was low enough to offset the need for
more rupiah to service debt as the exchange rate slowly declined.

The Asian Currency Crisis brought an end to the central bank's ability
and commitment to manage the exchange rate. Henceforth, market forces,
including rumor and panic, would determine how many rupiah were required to buy a dollar. The rupiah sank from about Rp2,300 per U.S.
dollar in June 1997 to about 4,000 by September.

The collapse of the rupiah broke many Indonesian firms that had borrowed heavily in dollars.[2] Their rupiah earnings simply could not service their dollar debt at the new exchange rates. There was no exemption even for companies and banks tied to Suharto. As panic ensued, the economy itself turned sharply downward. Climbing unemployment led many low-skilled Indonesians to flee the cities to their villages for food. The unemployed who remained created a political time bomb for the regime as they struggled to support themselves.

On September 3, the government announced a package of economic reforms, but they failed to turn around the economy. By March 1998 the rupiah had fallen to 8,325; on July 12 it hit a low of around 15,200 per U.S. dollar. It eventually hovered between 7,000 and 9,000 per dollar for 1999 and 2000.[3] The impact was deeply felt as the gross domestic product fell almost 14% in the year after the crisis hit.

As economic activity declined, so did projected demand for electricity. While PLN's electricity sales had grown some 13% to 14% in 1996 and 1997, demand grew only 1.5% in 1998.[4] It seemed that Java and Bali would not need anything like the amount of power PLN would soon be obligated to buy.[5] With some 9,000 megawatts of private electricity capacity under construction or at an advanced stage of planning,[6] reports began to suggest that PLN had 50% more capacity overall than it needed for Java and Bali, even without the new producers.[7]

Still more important, because many of PLN's commitments were effectively linked to the dollar, in rupiah terms its obligations—for servicing its own huge debts,[8] for its fuel purchases, and for its private power purchase agreements—simply exploded. Indexing meant that the rupiah-cost to PLN of electricity from Paiton I rose almost proportionally with the fall of the national currency. But PLN billed its customers in rupiah. Right before the currency collapse, PLN's tariff converted to an average of around 7 cents per kilowatt hour (cents/kwh). According to one calculation, in early 1998 PLN's dollar-equivalent average selling price had fallen to about 1.7 cents/kwh,[9] but it had contracted to buy private power at 5.7 cents to 8.6 cents. PLN's obligations to the private power producers put the company in the same position as a firm that had borrowed dollars.

Although a huge price increase for electricity would alleviate PLN's problem, price increases required approval from the Ministry of Mines and Energy. An automatic tariff adjustment system, introduced in 1994, was supposed to adjust prices to changes in the rupiah/dollar exchange rate, inflation, and costs of private power for PLN; however, implementing regulations had never been issued, and rate adjustments remained at the discretion of the ministry.

PLN requested an increase, but the government faced conflicting pressures. On one side, PLN needed money. Moreover, the World Bank wanted prices up, if for no other reason than the fact that PLN owed multilaterals from past borrowing. Even before the devaluation, PLN was in violation of covenants in its World Bank and Asian Development Bank (ADB) loans. On the other side, not only could customers ill-afford electricity priced at three or four times (in rupiah) what they had been paying, but any government approval of significant tariff increases might be political suicide. Higher prices would affect millions of Indonesians at a time of economic disorder and growing challenge to Suharto. The beginning of 1998 was already seeing daily demonstrations across the country. Government officials were not suicidal, so they refused PLN's request.

For PLN, the consequences were disastrous. If it honored its contracts, it would have to pay 50% of its entire operating budget to the private power producers by 2000—this, for what already seemed to be largely unneeded power. Its own revenue was inadequate to meet its obligations.

Canceling or postponing power projects would alleviate some of the pressure. The failed reform package of early September had somewhat vaguely called for the suspension of some "mega-projects" as part of fiscal austerity. The International Monetary Fund (IMF) went further and pressed for specific cutbacks in large projects,[10] and it even appeared that cancellations of projects would be a condition of any IMF assistance.[11] Detailed decisions emerged later in the month, when a presidential decree[12] called for action on projects worth about $6 billion,[13] including postponements of 13 electricity generating projects and continuing review of six more. But another decree,[14] issued January 10, confirmed that Paiton I, already under construction, could continue.[15]

Any euphoria on the part of Paiton's owners would be short lived. In January 1998, a private geothermal power plant received notice from PLN that its payments would be calculated at 2,450 rupiah per dollar.[16] The message: Private power producers would receive more or less a quarter of the dollars they were expecting. Briefly—until March—the Ministry of Finance had topped up PLN's payments to make up the difference,[17] but the ministry's allocation of funds ran out. IMF pressure to hold down government expenditures precluded any substantial replenishment for this kind of outlay. PLN was on its own.

Paiton I was not yet producing, but its future income stream looked bleak. By the end of 1997, capital markets had already registered concern by downgrading Paiton's senior debt from "investment grade" to "speculative grade."[18] One purchaser of bonds on the secondary market told us that Paiton's bonds eventually traded as low as 16 cents on the dollar. The financial markets recognized that Paiton's only customer, PLN, was technically bankrupt.[19]

Officials were beginning to argue that Paiton's power purchase agreement could not survive as originally negotiated. PLN's CEO Adhi Satriya pointed out publicly what we said in the previous chapter with slightly different figures: The $995 million per year, which he claimed now represented the "fixed costs" for Paiton, was enough to develop a new power plant of 600 megawatts every year.[20] With attention focused on the agreement, the contracted price of electricity now looked exorbitant to

Indonesians. Moreover, a weakened Suharto could not keep the issue from the public as he had done earlier with the ITT/Indosat case.

Mission, Paiton I's lead investor, recognized the inevitability of change. In its March 1998 10-K filings with the SEC, the company announced its intentions to "revisit" its arrangements with PLN.

In some ways, Paiton was experiencing an echo of the obsolescing bargain that had hit the Indosat project 17 years earlier. But there were also important differences. Unlike ITT in 1967, Paiton's owners had no protection from any scarce technology or other assets that would have made their continued presence critical. This combined with high prices and high profits in a sensitive industry would probably have brought down the agreement in much less than the 13-year span of ITT's interest in Indosat. The onset of the Asian Currency Crisis meant that Paiton's owners came under attack before they had even finished building their plant.

The debt-like character of the power projects made the Asian Currency Crisis a particularly effective trigger for their collapse. The crash of the currency and the economy would lead most foreign direct investors to experience declining profits, dividends, and thus demand for dollars. Not so for the power projects, with their allocation of risk. If the agreements stood, foreign owners would receive the same flow of dollars regardless of the exchange rate and demand for electricity.

The international community had developed ways of dealing with at least some of a country's debt. If the Indonesian government had borrowed to build the power plants, it would have turned to the London Club or the Paris Club, which provide a set of conventions for rescheduling sovereign debt to bankers or official lenders. Or, if the obligations had been those of a purely private borrower, elsewhere bankruptcy could have resulted in discharge or restructuring of the debt.[21] But the Paiton project was labeled as direct investment and not subject to the usual vehicles for dealing with the fallout of economic crises.

It would take five years, three more presidents, and a great deal of management time before the problem could be resolved. Whether it was really resolved even then remains an open question. Moreover, the democratic Indonesia that emerged out of the turmoil from the crisis would be a much more complicated place for foreign businesses than was the autocratically run country of Suharto's New Order.

End of the Suharto Regime

Under political attack, in 1998 Suharto appointed a new cabinet that was "crony and family to a bizarre extreme," in the words of an Indonesia expert.[22] It included crony Chinese businessman Bob Hasan as minister of trade and industry and Suharto's daughter Tutut as minister for social welfare, for example.

A minister of a quite different ilk, Kuntoro Mangkusubroto, now headed mines and energy. He announced on May 20 that rupiah electricity prices would be raised an average of 20% in May, with further 20% increases in August and November. But after government forces had shot and killed four student demonstrators on May 12, demonstrations had grown to full-scale riots in various parts of the city. Flaming shopping malls trapped victims. In Glodok, the old Chinese quarter of Jakarta, looting and torching hit particularly hard. At least 174 died at the Yogya Plaza mall in East Jakarta.[23] In the suburbs, a few houses of wealthy Indonesians—especially Chinese Indonesians—burned. Stories of rapes and other attacks spread. For days, smoke and fear hung over this city of more than 12 million people. In all, more than a thousand Indonesians died as the military and police stood by and watched.

Some accused General Prabowo Subianto, the brother-in-law of Paiton's Hashim and son-in-law of Suharto, of instigating riots, although no charges stuck.[24] To be sure, military leaders—particularly Prabowo and General Wiranto—were locked in a power struggle. The winner could even take the presidency, should Suharto fall. In this climate, even a small price increase for electricity might make for more chaos; thus, the hikes were not implemented.

The government edged toward collapse. On May 20, former Minister of Mines and Energy Ginandjar drafted a letter, which was signed by 14 ministers, saying that they would not serve in a new cabinet.[25] Ginandjar was widely believed to want the presidency for himself.

As violence grew, Americans, other foreigners, and wealthier Chinese-Indonesians fled Jakarta, many for Singapore or Bangkok to wait out the unrest. Jakarta had become a rumor mill. One story had it that a U.S. embassy–sponsored evacuation flight was delayed in leaving Jakarta's airport until a bribe was turned over to airport authorities. Whatever the truth, the fact that the story was widely believed testifies to how pervasive and open corruption had become by this time.

Facing a monumental challenge to his own power, Suharto had little time for reviewing electricity agreements. Consequently, no progress was made in what seemed to be inevitable: arriving at some kind of new accommodation, or a complete break, with Paiton's foreign owners.

Habibie as President

The calls for Suharto's resignation could not be silenced without a bloody crackdown by his military. But the country was no longer shut off from world observation, as it had been in 1965 when Suharto's rule had begun with a massacre. Bowing to pressure, Suharto resigned on May 21, 1998, ending more than three decades in power. His successor was Vice President B. J. Habibie, the early proponent of private electricity and Paiton I.

Habibie, like Suharto, represented the ruling Golkar Party. The power base had hardly changed. Thus, unlike many a new government, this one could hardly denounce the old regime for negotiating bad deals. It was the economic crisis onto which the entire blame was shifted, not the ignorance, mismanagement, or corruption of members of the Suharto government.

Not all remained the same, however. The old decision-making mechanisms began to crumble. The new president would not have the almost absolute authority that Suharto had gained. His ministers struggled for control over the electricity renegotiations as they did over other economic decisions. Coordination across ministries grew ever more difficult, and reaching firm and lasting decisions on anything remained elusive.

Struggle for Control

One can only imagine the frustration that Paiton's managers felt as they confronted the confusion within the government. Officials offered no clear ideas of what they wanted in restructured agreements. Moreover, it became less and less obvious who was going to negotiate on behalf of the country. Some advisors were leading a move to turn negotiations over to PLN. Extricating the government from negotiations would make it clear that the government had no more liability as shareholder than would any other shareholder in a limited liability corporation. The minister of finance supported this approach.[26] Accordingly, ministers were urged to refuse to meet with visitors interested in the electricity problem, surely adding to Paiton's bewilderment.

But some ministers were reluctant to surrender influence over such large contracts. The minister of mines and energy, for example, pointed to PLN's lack of experience in running anything like these renegotiations and wanted his ministry to exercise control over the sector. To this end, Kuntoro had his own consultants produce a paper, "Power Sector Restructuring Policy."[27] It proposed that the ministry restructure the sector along the lines of the California system, with bidding by private generators to supply the distribution system.[28] His Directorate General for Electricity and Energy Development would, unsurprisingly, be the initial industry regulator; eventually, a supposedly independent agency would report to the ministry.

In theory, Paiton's management could have offered its own proposals to move things along. As we pointed out in the Indosat story, however, corporate management generally finds it very difficult to take the initiative in proposing something that would reduce investor returns. Explaining such a move to lenders and board members is a formidable challenge that most managers try to avoid. At any rate, a company proposal would have been met only with disorganization and, likely, silence on the other side. The Indonesians were just not ready.

Under the autocratic Suharto, struggles like this had usually been settled quickly.[29] The president himself would decide who was to conduct negotiations as he had done in the Indosat case—end of dispute. Yes, Suharto had failed to put a single minister in charge of the original Paiton negotiations, but disagreements on major issues—the price of power, in particular—had gone to the president for the final decision. In contrast, the new president did not have the weight required to make and enforce such decisions. As a long-time Indonesia observer put it, "As Suharto's vice president, [Habibie] had no initial legitimacy and was unable to develop any...."[30] The authoritarian legacy of Suharto's New Order government was much weaker than many had supposed.

In the Habibie government, a new player emerged and joined the rivalry: the State Ministry for State-Owned Enterprises. Because this ministry took over from the Ministry of Finance the job of representing the government as shareholder in state-owned enterprises, not surprisingly its minister claimed a large role in the discussions involving state-owned PLN.[31] He suggested that the president establish a more formal set of structures that would involve most interested parties.[32]

The result was a three-tiered approach, which seemed to complicate things even further. A decree in late 1998[33] created a ministerial committee, to be chaired by Hartarto, the coordinating minister for development supervision and state administrative reform. This was a man firmly in the camp of the engineers, as opposed to the Berkeley Mafia technocrats.[34] Moreover, his son-in-law was a partner in another power company, to be discussed later. Kuntoro Mangkuksubroto, the minister for mines and energy, and the minister in charge of state-owned enterprises would be vice chairmen. Other members would include Bambang Subianto, the minister of finance; Zuhal, the minister for research and technology; Rihardi Ramelan, the minister for trade and industry; and Budiono, the minister for planning and national development.[35] The team was publicly announced in January 1999.

A steering committee, headed by the minister of mines and energy, would report to this ministerial committee.[36] Its members would include the minister for state-owned enterprises, the president-director of PLN, and staff people from the ministries represented on the ministerial committee.

The third tier was the negotiating team, centered in PLN. It would be led by Hardiv Situmeang, PLN's director of operations, from the Batak ethnic group of North Sumatra, a group with a reputation of being much more direct and aggressive than the retiring Javanese. Hardiv was very widely respected for his intelligence and technical knowledge.

But creating a structure did not guarantee that all would run smoothly. For example, the then minister of mines and energy told us that when he learned early on that the son-in-law of the head of the ministerial committee was involved in one of the generating projects, he asked the head to resign. When the dispute reached the president, however, he backed the committee head. After losing a second dispute, the mines minister said he agreed to remain on the committee in name only to save the president the embarrassment of his resignation.

To make matters worse, the negotiating team itself had little authority. It had to seek approval for any commitment from the steering committee; the steering committee was in turn to ask approval from the ministerial committee. It was not at all like the short lines to real authority that had moved the ITT renegotiations along so quickly.

Assembling Advisors

Nevertheless, the head of the negotiating team, Hardiv, began to move. First, he assembled a group of advisors to help him.[37] But advisors would change as the governments changed. Sometimes, the result was a volatile mix, as incumbents survived while new advisors with different approaches and different allegiances signed on.

Hardiv located Faramarz Yazdani, who had advised the California Public Utilities Commission. Some advisors believed that Yazdani's Iranian origins gave him special credibility in Indonesia, which is also predominantly Muslim and oil producing. Yazdani would be the longest lasting and one of the most influential of the advisors. Even so, his influence waxed, waned, and waxed again as regimes and PLN bosses changed.

Hardiv also had picked up an advisor with a legal background, William Bradley, who was on assignment in the Ministry of Mines and Energy under a contract paid for by USAID.[38] Hardiv reports that Bradley proved very helpful in working out a plan for dealing with the problems.[39] Maybe he was too good: At one point, USAID told him that the agency could not have U.S. taxpayer money supporting a lawyer helping the Indonesians against U.S. companies. At USAID, commercial concerns again won over development goals; the agency was behaving like it had earlier with Jezek. In response, Hardiv simply hired Bradley directly.[40]

Yazdani suggested a law firm with which he had earlier worked, and McKenna and Cuneo was hired late in 1998. Its advice would eventually prove controversial, and other law firms would later appear on the scene.

John Sroka, an Australian, was added to the advisory group as "corporate advisor." He had already been brought to PLN under a World Bank contract to help restructure the company. Sroka was criticized by some advisors for not having expertise in privatization, but he quickly gained a reputation for being tough on investors and remained on the job until 2000.

The most experienced advisor, Peter Jezek, was to return. In September 1999, Kuntoro brought him back to the Ministry of Mines and Energy. As previously mentioned, in 1995 Jezek had departed for Thailand and Vietnam, discouraged by what he considered to be his lack of influence and perhaps fearing bodily harm. Upon his return, he was again to play a significant role, but also leave a trail of mystery.[41]

Recognizing that the Indonesian government lacked negotiating skills, Kuntoro arranged for the World Bank to sponsor an initial visit from a Cambridge (Massachusetts) consulting group that specialized in negotiation, Lax Sebenius LLC. They seemed a good choice. Lax, Sebenius, and

Kuntoro had all studied under Howard Raiffa, a noted mathematician and negotiations expert. A team visited the principal Indonesian parties in July 1998 and made a return trip in October. It is not clear who paid for the second trip, but it was possibly USAID, where Kuntoro had good relations. At the time, Stapleton Roy, a man popular with Indonesians, was the U.S. ambassador; in fact, a number of officials in the U.S. embassy had considerable sympathy with the Indonesian side,[42] although that sympathy was to be largely silenced later.

On this second trip, Lax submitted proposals for a nonlegalistic strategy. Some investors would receive compensation in the form of bonds indexed to the Indonesian gross domestic product (GDP). According to Kuntoro, the proposals were too complicated to sell to other ministers or to the investors and their bankers. Moreover, some Indonesians found the consulting fee proposed by the consultants extremely confusing to determine, and they believed it could add up to staggering sums.[43] The firm was not hired, and the Indonesians never retained advisors specialized in negotiations.

But Lax's visits reminded all of a problem that continued to plague negotiations in Indonesia: leakage of government documents and discussions. Lax told us that his memo to the country's president was in the hands of one company by the same evening. Similarly, the *Jakarta Post* quickly published reports of the proposed engagement, including the consultants' suggested compensation. Leaks would continue, as one of the authors of this book discovered: A memo that he wrote in August 1998 was leaked to the *Wall Street Journal* and to Mission's management. In both cases, the leaked document was a copy sent to Ginandjar's office.[44] During the earlier ITT negotiations, contents of government discussions had been leaked to the company, but if anything had leaked to the press in those days, they surely would not have had the courage to publish it. This was another sign that times were changing.

Building a Strategy

Indonesia had negotiated 27 similar power agreements, and all of them were now under attack. Dealing with some two-dozen different contracts and an even larger number of investors was a formidable task. Major issues arose immediately: whether investors should be dealt with as a group or separately; whether the route to new agreements ought to be litigation or negotiation; and, if negotiation was the goal, how to force companies to the table.

Seeing major financial implications in renegotiations, the technocrat ministers asked the Harvard Group (in August 1998) for a position paper on general strategy. After they reviewed the resulting memo,[45] they arranged a meeting between a Harvard advisor and the head of the PLN negotiating team. As a result, one of the authors of this book met with Hardiv one evening in early September at the Borobudur Hotel for a discussion, which continued late into the night.

The Harvard Group's paper made the following recommendations to the Indonesians:

1. Renegotiate the terms of the power purchase agreements to reflect terms elsewhere that emerged under competitive bidding.
2. Think of the capacity payment element of the contracts as debt, subject to the same kind of rescheduling that would apply to Indonesia's other debt obligations.
3. Avoid fights over the legality of the agreements, if possible.
4. Build a team headed by a strong official with authority and compatible strategy, technical, and legal consultants.
5. Gently remind investors reluctant to renegotiate that bankruptcy is a messy but possible option and that public exposure of corruption underlying the agreements would not be in their interests, should a legal battle develop.
6. Look to the experience from Indosat/ITT to draw lessons on conducting renegotiations.

The memo also warned that a U.S. senator, Trent Lott (Republican, Mississippi), and a congressman, Newt Gingrich (Republican, Georgia), had already spoken in support of U.S. power investors. It also raised the possibility that firms with political risk insurance might behave differently from others. But the Harvard Group played almost no additional role in renegotiations.[46]

With his advisors, Hardiv and his team drew up a set of proposals for a new power purchase agreement and submitted them to President Habibie for approval. It is not clear whether the president ever responded. The president seemed unable to make such a momentous decision on his own. Moreover, it was still not at all clear where authority resided in a government that was in disarray.

Meanwhile, with its facility soon to come on stream, sometime in 1998 Paiton's owners did decide to make a proposal of their own, offering to lower the price of electricity to 3.3 cents, adding that this would allow the company to cover only its operating costs and interest payments. This dramatic cut would still require PLN to come up with substantially more rupiah than it would have needed at the pre-crisis exchange rate. Moreover, this generous-sounding offer was not what it seemed: Paiton insisted on its right to recoup the foregone payments at a later date.

Indonesians had decided for complete restructuring of all electricity contracts, not a temporary price reduction, but they feared that the companies would unite against them. Determined to deal with each company individually, they sought a way to isolate them.[47] A controversial confidentiality agreement was to be the mechanism. Under it, the companies would agree not to reveal to anyone, including other investors and the U.S. embassy, anything about their discussions with the Indonesians, and not to turn to arbitration. Debates over the proposed confidentiality agreement probably sidetracked discussions, as investors resisted. In the end, the worry about united companies was misplaced. The companies were not united at all; their own strategies differed considerably, for reasons we will eventually explore.

Home Government Help

Meanwhile, Mission was reinforcing its defenses. Even before real renegotiations had begun, managers tried to seize an opportunity to capture a little help from the U.S. government. As deputy secretary of the U.S. Department of the Treasury, Lawrence Summers visited Jakarta on January 13, 1998, and met with Suharto. American investors tried to convince him to raise the issue of the electric power contracts with the president. Summers is said to have responded, "We have bigger fish to fry. The IPPs [independent power producers] are not on our radar screen."[48] In other words, the Department of the Treasury was not going to let intervention on behalf of individual U.S. investors compromise the overwhelming U.S. interest in avoiding regional instability. For a brief period, and at least for this deputy secretary (and later secretary) of the treasury, broader foreign policy interests overruled commercial interests.

Mission nevertheless gave the appearance that U.S. help would be forthcoming. In June 1998, Ronald Landry, CEO of the operating company, warned: "If the government reneges on this contract, they will get absolute turmoil," threatening intervention by the U.S. and the Japanese governments.[49] The company was moving away from the accommodating attitude that it had shown in its 10-K. In fact, after the first meeting with Paiton's management, one of PLN's American lawyers was to say that that he had never seen such aggressive behavior.

Mission managers began to organize the threatened U.S. intervention. On August 6, 1998, Edward Muller, CEO of Mission's parent company, met with U.S. Secretary of Commerce William Daley. Warren Christopher, who had returned from the Department of State to Mission as a member of one of the group's boards, may also have attended the meeting; the available documents are not clear on this.[50] In any event, Daley, who had taken over Ron Brown's job after Brown died in an airplane crash in Bosnia, seemed cautious, responding that he could not commit to advocacy on behalf of Mission alone because other independent power producers' contracts might be affected when Paiton's plant came on line (scheduled for May 1999). Thus, he would commit the U.S. government only to generic calls for the Indonesians to honor their contracts.

Mission soon sent Christopher to Jakarta, in September 1998.[51] Before his arrival, the commerce department circulated a memo, with the same date as the Daley-Muller meeting,[52] to remind U.S. officials that Christopher was now (again) on Mission's board of directors. Given the ambiguous relations in Indonesia between business and government, however, the Indonesians could be forgiven for confusion over whether

Christopher's visit to Jakarta was supposed to be a visit from the U.S. government. In fact, a few Indonesians apparently failed to grasp the fact that Christopher was no longer secretary of state.

After the visit, investors in other power agreements wanted to know what had transpired. Landry, Paiton's CEO, told the other companies that Christopher spoke "on behalf of the IPP's when he said that any solution reached with Indonesia must: be a 'win-win' solution and not embarrass Indonesia; protect the USG, other government agencies and the financial community; maintain debt coverage and the sanctity of the contract; focus on financial rather than legal issues."[53] He did not explain how sanctity of contract and the clear inability of PLN to meet contractual obligations could be reconciled. The only serious possibility would be that the government was seen as a guarantor, even though Mission had indicated earlier that support letters were not guarantees. Managers may have hoped that the government would voluntarily take on the obligations of PLN, as it had done in the case of Pertamina's debt crisis in the 1970s. But with the government itself short of funds and operating under IMF-imposed fiscal constraints, a voluntary bailout of PLN seemed unlikely.

In any event, Christopher's visit had little direct impact. Nevertheless, the gift he brought along—a scale model of the power plant—was a big hit. And, according to our interviews, a number of Indonesians read the visit as a signal that the power problem would not be limited to Indonesia and the private companies. Rather, this was a matter of interest to the U.S. government, which would likely make its overwhelming power felt.

Although the embassy did not view Christopher's visit as U.S. pressure, Washington soon began to exert pressure of its own. The Exim Bank, which had committed $540 million to the construction of Paiton I, had a new head, James Harmon,[54] who showed little hesitancy to squeeze reticent borrowers. The restraints on U.S. policy that were reflected in Summers's rebuff of the investors' call for help had, in fact, mostly disappeared. Gone was the old fear that support for investors would help the Indonesian Left, threatening a friend and oil producer. By this time, commercial interests had become dominant in U.S. policy.

The new attitudes were reflected in Harmon's dealings with the Indonesians. The *Asian Wall Street Journal* was soon to say that Harmon "has played the hero in Asia's economic crisis and he has played the bully."[55] Indonesians we interviewed would say he earned the "bully" appellation in their country. He was determined to build a coalition of the usually competing official creditors to enforce their claims. Following a meeting of creditors in Tokyo, he reported that "the U.S. Exim Bank and 18 other credit agencies committed themselves in Tokyo to 'greater cooperation on maintaining and increasing trade finance, resolving workouts, and other issues.' "[56] Indonesians thought the message was clear enough.[57]

The U.S. insurance agency and lender the Overseas Private Investment Corporation (OPIC) also became involved. It had $200 million at risk in Paiton I and had, as we will see, issued insurance for other power projects in Indonesia. In mid-July 1998, it sent an "Advocacy Mission" to Indonesia; missions returned in September and again in November.[58] By December, OPIC officials' public pronouncements turned to an ironclad principle: "The contracts have to be honored," said George Munoz, OPIC's president.[59] Munoz's approach and, many would say, ill-mannered behavior would leave a particularly nasty taste in Indonesia. One rather mild foreign advisor to the Indonesians later described him to us as quite simply "a bastard." Another advisor termed him "arrogant," and added a description unsuitable for print. Munoz would throw diplomatic behavior to the winds, in a country noted for the gentleness and politeness of its people.[60]

Growing U.S. official support for the Mission-led group reflected the new U.S. policy toward its investors abroad. The Department of Commerce had helped Paiton's investors in the original negotiations; but by the time the renegotiation of Paiton I began, U.S. government agencies and the embassy were even more willing to push the Indonesian government. The Department of State mounted no resistance, as it would have in the Cold War days; instead, the embassy joined the shoving.

Negotiate or Litigate: Flop-Flopping

Paiton's owners had included in their contract a provision entitling them to proceed to international arbitration should a dispute arise. Unlike in ITT's time, arbitration now had teeth, or so it seemed. The Indonesian government also had the right to initiate arbitration under the terms of the contract; however, if the approach were to be legalistic, Indonesians preferred to turn to local courts because they promised more understanding for the fix in which PLN and the government found themselves. By February 1999, foreign legal advisors were urging the minister of mines and energy, Kuntoro, to go to court. If Indonesians waited until Paiton could claim nonpayment of an invoice, the argument went, the foreign company would have a more plausible claim in arbitration. But, Kuntoro and many other Indonesians viewed litigation as a last resort, favoring negotiation.

Negotiating

Regardless of rights, both sides started discussions, appearing to share the hope that legal action of either kind could be avoided. The Indonesian negotiating team had issued a press release on December 22, 1998, saying that it would soon invite the producers to discuss possible resolution of the contractual issues.[61] Their hopes got a big boost a few days later when the *Asian Wall Street Journal* published an article that accused the investors of corruption and the U.S. government of interference.[62] Given the slow pace with which things were moving, external support was especially important. It would be 12 months before the Indonesians could claim another success; and the resulting elation would be quickly shattered by a surprising decision of the next president.

Meanwhile, the insolvent PLN asked for an 18% increase in power prices, another request that was rejected by the minister of mines and energy.[63] By mid-1999, the local tariff still translated only to somewhat over 2 cents/kwh;[64] PLN's financial problems and the need for resolution continued unabated.

Paiton was formally invited to renegotiate in March 1999,[65] but early meetings did not go smoothly. One can speculate that renegotiation was especially difficult because some of the managers and officials now involved had also negotiated the original agreement. For Mission and General Electric (GE) managers, it must have been difficult to accept the fact that a deal they had negotiated and sold to top management, shareholders, and lenders (and for which they had presumably received bonuses) only four years earlier had to be scrapped. On the Indonesian side, the ministers of mines and energy and finance and the head of PLN were new, but a few officials and their advisors in the new meetings had also been involved in the original negotiations. This was unlike the ITT renegotiation, where 13 years had passed and the negotiators on both sides had little personal reputation or pride at stake. In the ITT situation, even Hunter, who might have had the most commitment to the old deal, was removed by the company from its negotiating team to smooth the process.[66]

The first agenda item, as far as some Indonesians were concerned, was the proposed agreement on confidentiality and a commitment not to go to arbitration. An investor in another power project (Tanjung Jati B) rather quickly signed the commitments, and Paiton also tentatively agreed, in a letter dated April 22, 1999. But its managers soon changed their minds.[67] The drive for a confidentiality agreement continued to sidetrack later discussions as well.

The next month, Paiton's need for some kind of payments arrangement, even if temporary, grew urgent. When the first 615-megawatt unit was ready for commercial operation in May, Paiton duly notified PLN that it was ready to deliver electricity.[68] The second 615-megawatt unit would come on stream in just two months.[69] Once it was in operation, Paiton needed cash to service its debts.

Litigating?

Discussions between Paiton and Indonesian negotiators broke down in early May. The company's line was toughening again, possibly as a result of events connected with the simultaneous dispute over CalEnergy's two power projects. CalEnergy had very quickly turned to arbitration rather than trying to renegotiate. On May 4, an arbitration panel had issued its first ruling, awarding CalEnergy more than $500 million for the investment it claimed to have made plus a part of its projected future profits. (See Chapter 14 for the full story.) This award must have influenced what the owners of Paiton viewed as their best alternative to no agreement

("BATNA," in the jargon of negotiation specialists). Perhaps seeing new possibilities, Mission announced that it would seek $4 billion in damages from PLN. Edward R. Muller, president of Mission, reinforced the fears that this meant arbitration: "[Mission] cannot allow PLN and the Indonesian government to just career along without making a serious attempt to fulfill the contract. . . . It is way too convenient for PLN to say the power contracts have become too difficult to stick to, let's do away with them. Until both parties agree to alter the contract, it has to be honored." He added that the IMF could provide money to the Indonesians to pay what was owed under the contracts.[70] Muller's statement was not popular with the Indonesian side; if the IMF ever heard about the proposal, its enthusiasm would have surely been rather muted.

Whether the company was playing "good cop, bad cop" or whether owners simply took different positions is not clear, but the Indonesian partners followed a conflicting line. Suharto's daughter Titiek was now gone from the deal,[71] but Hashim remained and explicitly differentiated Paiton I from other investors such as CalEnergy, saying that "We don't have any plans [to go to arbitration]. They [other power producers] are confrontationists. . . . Our partners are not that type. We can make compromises. We realize the current difficulties are beyond PLN's control. That's why we are negotiating."[72]

Suffice it to say that the Indonesian negotiators were already puzzled and confused by the different behavior of investors in various electric power projects. Instead of a united front across the 27 projects, they now they faced a mix of responses. Some investors that had invested little simply walked away from their projects; some seemed willing to renegotiate; and some turned to confrontation, exercising their rights to go to arbitration. In Paiton I, the owners did not appear completely united even within the single consortium.

Negotiating Again

For whatever reasons, Paiton's owners soon backed off from their belligerent stance and from the principle of "sanctity of contract." They again appeared ready to revisit the arrangement.

We can only speculate that Mission had decided that it wanted to continue in the electric power business in Indonesia, and it recognized that bitter legal battles, such as CalEnergy had initiated, would end its prospects. In contrast to CalEnergy, Mission's continuing expansion overseas might also have influenced its decision. In 1997, Mission had purchased the remaining shares of an Australian power venture and added an investment in a transmission system in the same country. It was building a gasification project in Sicily, a co-generation plant in Turkey, and continuing the development of a co-generation plant in the Philippines and a generating project in Thailand. Its affiliate Edison Capital was investing in the Netherlands, South Australia, and Latin America. In fact, overseas commitments accounted for a large part of the company's earnings growth.[73] Although Mission's conceding to reconsider the Paiton agreement could tempt other countries to renegotiate deals, managers may have worried more about earning a reputation for pugnacity.

Edgell, Mission's original negotiator, could also have had a personal reason to try to keep the project and thus the renegotiations going. He seemed happily settled in Singapore with his Indonesian wife and new family. With Paiton I as one of his babies and the company's largest investment in the region, Edgell's position would remain secure if a revised deal could be concluded.

Unfortunately for peace, however, the Indonesian team backed away from one of its commitments: that it would not accuse investors of being involved in "KKN" (corruption, collusion, and nepotism). PLN began to argue that the free equity (based on loans) to well-connected Indonesians had enabled power prices in various projects to be marked up. An advisor to PLN was quoted by the *Financial Times* as saying, "They got away with murder. The penny will eventually drop that we are now talking of a new environment. There is no sense in saying 'We signed these contracts in good faith.'"[74]

U.S. and Japanese Backing

Although Mission appeared ready to compromise, investors' and lenders' governments had yet to move beyond the idea of sanctity of contract. By July 1999, diplomatic pressure on the Indonesians was growing stronger, especially from officials of the government credit and insurance organizations of five rich countries. They had banded together to form what they called the Joint Export Credit Agencies Mission. Japan, Indonesia's most important overall creditor, played a lead role within the consortium. From July 11 to 15, representatives of four countries (United States, Germany, Switzerland, and Japan) visited the finance minister, the CEO of PLN, and others to warn them that failure to honor contracts with power suppliers would discourage new foreign investment and would lead to a halt in government-to-government loans to Indonesia.[75] An aggressive, rather un-Japanese letter, called "Proposed Measures for Immediate Issues of Paiton I Project" arrived from Japan's Exim Bank. Although it recognized the need for rescheduling payments under the power purchase agreements and, less clearly, the need for a review of tariffs, it also asked for government guarantees on rescheduled payments and implied that Japan's support for Indonesia at the CGI (Consultative Group on Indonesia) meetings—where development assistance was allocated—was at risk if it failed to accept the proposals.[76] In the period of 1996 to 1997, commitments at CGI had amounted to close to $8 billion, almost $2 billion of which was from Japan. This or another letter to the minister of finance added that a refusal to pay would "impair Indonesia and our ability to work with you in the future."[77] To their surprise, Indonesians found the government credit and insurance agencies to be taking a harder line and to be more unified than were the companies.

The visit and letter came two weeks before Indonesia's annual negotiations with donor governments at the CGI meetings. International pressure continued in the Paris Club discussions, where attempts were under way to restructure Indonesian government debt.[78] Of course, the Paris Club was supposed to be a forum for dealing with a borrowing country's sovereign debts to official institutions, not private foreign direct investment. This did not stop the U.S. delegation from bringing up the controversy over the power purchasing agreements.

Moving to Litigation

In spite of foreign governments, Paiton managers and the Indonesians again moved closer together. By the end of July, they seemed to have reached a firmer understanding that they would continue to negotiate rather than move to arbitration. In a meeting on July 26, Paiton committed to not issuing a dispute notice, the first step toward arbitration, as long as PLN met certain conditions. And PLN backed off the corruption issue.

However, the truce broke down and the debate turned ugly again the next month. PLN CEO Adhi Satriya accused the power producers of "world class mark-ups" and threatened cancellation of contracts if corruption was uncovered. He was now using the term "mark-ups" to mean that the companies had recorded their investments at inappropriately high values on their books.

Adding a complication, he said that take-or-pay agreements would have to end anyway because new plans for the sector called for a shift to competitive bidding to supply electricity to PLN. Indeed, the idea of a market system for power was gaining ground. At least by August 1997, the ADB was pushing Indonesia toward a merchant system modeled on that of Victoria in Australia.[79] The ADB (with the support of the Japan Bank for International Cooperation) wanted Indonesians to have the system in place by 2003, a speed that the World Bank field office found "ridiculous."[80]

In spite of the posturing, public statements, and new complications, PLN and Paiton managers were still talking. Not surprisingly, Paiton did not want to give up the guaranteed market, but it offered to accept a merchant system, under the condition that the transition period would be at least 10 years. And it expressed a willingness to agree to a price reduction for the intervening period. In exchange, it asked that the investors be offered some additional investment opportunities in Indonesia, a proposal PLN rejected.[81] Deadlock returned.

In response to the new standstill, Paiton managers ratcheted up the tensions a substantial notch. On August 18, 1999, they took the first step toward arbitration by sending a notice of dispute to PLN. PLN viewed this as a breach of the July 26 truce agreement.

Largely on the sidelines, but growing increasingly concerned, the technocrat ministers again asked the Harvard Group for comments. The resulting memo, from advisors far from the front line of negotiations, recommended that the government hold off on initiating legal action itself, predicting that Paiton's owner could be convinced to back off from arbitration with a reminder that any corruption would become public if arbitration went ahead and that a company victory in arbitration (which the advisors thought likely) would only mean that PLN would declare bankruptcy, something the foreign investors might fear.[82] Whatever the merits of the Harvard memo, it had little impact because it had been requested by the technocrats, not by the ministers who were making decisions in the power cases. Probably it never reached them.

The U.S. government also turned up its pressure on Indonesia. It attempted (but failed) to block a $400 million loan from the ADB to Indonesia.[83] The arrival of a new U.S. ambassador in the fall of 1999 changed attitudes. Robert S. Gelbard, a career foreign service officer, came to the post from being the president's special representative on Kosovo and having been assistant secretary of state for international narcotics and law enforcement affairs. He brought a style appropriate to the Kosovo problems and his prior enforcement job, and not that of the Peace Corps position he had once held. His brashness and aggressiveness were in sharp contrast to the style of his immediate predecessors. One prominent Indonesian deeply involved in the renegotiations described the new style: "Before, Ambassador Barry was a friend of Indonesia, and Ambassador Stapleton could distinguish the United States from U.S. companies; Gelbard is not and cannot."[84] Kuntoro, who was by his own statement friendly with the embassy, said that Gelbard was "very American," adding "you have to yell back at him and he will listen." He was, Kuntoro added, not very good with most Javanese. This can hardly be viewed as great praise for an ambassador to a government run largely by Javanese.[85]

The U.S. government escalated its threats during a Singapore meeting held in November 1999 and attended by a group from OPIC and the Indonesian "Minister of Economic Affairs," presumably Ginandjar.[86] It warned that it would formally invoke the Helms-Gonzalez Amendment to the 1994 Foreign Assistance Act.[87] This would require that U.S. directors vote against loans from international financial institutions to Indonesia. The only out would be an explicit waiver from the U.S. president.[88] What had transpired extralegally in the ADB would become official policy. Other steps would likely follow: The United States could cut off all aid and withdraw from Indonesia privileges under the Generalized System of Preferences, causing Indonesia to lose its duty-free access to the U.S. market for a significant volume of exports. It could also tighten Indonesia's textile quotas, which would threaten jobs for the poor.

Lest Indonesians fail to get the point, the next month officials from export credit agencies again visited Jakarta, from December 8 to 11,[89] meeting officials and company managers, and visiting the geothermal project of an American-controlled oil and gas group.[90] The agencies soon wrote the coordinating minister for the economy, the finance minister, the new minister for state-owned enterprises, the head of BAPPENAS, and the minister of energy and mines saying that "the private power problem . . . should be settled as among first priority and as soon as possible."[91]

On the negotiating front, bitter arguments had become common between Paiton managers and Indonesians. Reflecting the tone, one advisor was quoted as saying, "The reality is that they are trying to screw money out of a poor country for electricity which is unwanted, overpriced and agreed under 'unclear' circumstances. The government has not given any guarantee to PLN or the IPPs."[92] Nevertheless, Paiton managers again tried for peace, backing off the dispute notice and proposing a standstill agreement under which both parties would commit themselves to negotiation.

The company's conditions for a standstill agreement, however, were too much for PLN's team. When PLN refused, Mission's negotiators again ran out of patience and threatened to sue for $4 billion if PLN failed either to pay an invoice that had become due on August 15 or to begin negotiations by September 20.[93] The threat led to what both parties seemed to want to avoid, another move toward the legal process. Not having received payment at the current exchange rate, on September 27, 1999, Paiton issued a second notice of dispute.[94]

Meanwhile, renegotiations with at least one other power company were moving along. On September 29, 1999, PLN and El Paso's Sengkang reached an interim agreement, the first case to show real progress in negotiation. A temporary tariff would allow the producer to pay for gas (the fuel at Sengkang) and operating costs, and to make interest payments on its debt.[95] This presented a possible model for a temporary solution with Paiton.

In the first days of October, Paiton appeared to agree to hold off arbitration a little longer. But, alas, things fell apart again on October 6, when Paiton continued to refuse the confidentiality and no-arbitration agreement PLN was still pushing.[96] Indonesians claim that Paiton was playing them along, asking for small changes in the agreement and when they were granted, asking for still more, with no intention at all of signing.

With talks seemingly dying, PLN decided to file a suit first. PLN negotiators took this step very reluctantly, strongly preferring renegotiation. In fact, litigation was still a contentious issue among Indonesia's advisors. Although the Indonesians' main foreign law firm had advocated the court approach, some others still preferred arbitration or renewed efforts to renegotiation. But Indonesian resistance to litigating faded as officials concluded that Paiton's owners were not negotiating in good faith and that they had been holding off arbitration only until their case would be stronger. Now, Indonesians concluded, they would have to rush to court before the company initiated arbitration.

In the Central Jakarta District court on October 7, Indonesians claimed that the power purchase agreement had "violated law No. 15/1985 on power and is in contravention of morality and public interest."[97] They alleged that the agreement was one-sided and the result of corruption, collusion, and nepotism and asked the court to declare the contract "unlawful, unfair, and not transparent" and "void and not enforceable."[98] PLN argued that arbitration was an inappropriate way to resolve the dispute because the agreement itself was unlawful. If the agreement was void in the first place, its dispute settlement clause was also invalid and irrelevant.[99]

With legal action under way, the United States momentarily backed off. Knowing what was about to happen, the coordinating minister for development supervision, Hartarto, called the U.S. ambassador the day before PLN filed its case to say, "PLN has informed me that PLN is taking Paiton I to court, I am sorry to say." The U.S. ambassador seemed disappointed and responded, "O.K., please decouple us [the United States] from the company."[100] This new hands-off attitude in the U.S. embassy was to be only temporary.

PLN sought to bolster its legal case by submitting to the court a report from the SNC-Lavalin Group, a Canadian engineering and construction company. It provided what the now-free Indonesian press interpreted as shocking data,[101] estimating that the appropriate cost of Paiton I was $1.033 billion, plus or minus 20%, far from Paiton's claimed cost of $1.772 billion (excluding the financing costs and other charges that brought the cost up to the reported $2.5 billion). One item in the company's accounts labeled "project development cost" amounted to $22.2 million, and was not further documented. Many Indonesians assumed this was for bribes, whatever the truth.[102] Based on the report, the government argued that "engineering, procurement, and construction costs of Paiton were inflated some 72 percent."[103] The international press coverage generated by the Canadian report added to Indonesian's confidence.

Paiton managers immediately attacked the study, saying it relied "solely on the cursory descriptions" of the plant in the power purchase agreement.[104] The Canadian company responded that it had visited the plant and used its extensive databases from other projects.[105] In our interviews, Paiton managers derided the report, claiming that PLN's units 1 and 2 had cost just as much as Paiton I, if the costs of the PLN facilities were scaled up to the equivalent capacity and adjusted for a 7% annual inflation rate.[106] Further, managers said that, because they could not pass through in price increases any cost overruns, they had no reason to overstate them. Of course, a passable MBA student could come up with the reasons we mentioned in the previous chapter to overstate costs.

PLN was much less prepared to present its second legal argument, corruption. The State Supervisory Board on Finance and Development[107] was assembling a report that would name 14 officials allegedly involved in corruption in Paiton I. The list supposedly included Ginandjar and Sudjana, the two ministers of mines and energy,[108] but PLN did not have strong evidence in hand to support charges.

In spite of the mounting legal battle, some discussions continued between the disputants. Paiton soon made another offer: to accept $154.5 million as capacity payment for the next 13 months and to reduce fuel charges from 1.63 to 1.10 cents/kwh.[109] The formal letter containing the offer included a proposal for a long-term settlement as well, supposedly at 3.3 cents/kwh.[110] But, we were told, the offer was accompanied by an increase in the take-or-pay portion, meaning more electricity that PLN did not need. We do not know the details of this offer, but whether it was good or bad, PLN was not yet ready for a deal. And, in any case, a big change was about to take place.

12

Paiton I: Backing Away from the New Property Rights

The thing about democracy, beloveds, is that it is not neat, orderly, or quiet. It requires a certain relish for confusion.
—Molly Ivins, book author and columnist[1]

O ctober 1999 marked the end of one-party rule in Indonesia. The country's transition to democracy brought additional problems for business managers, as it opened the way for new interest groups—the press, nongovernmental organizations (NGOs), labor unions—to challenge the Paiton I accord. Indeed, as authoritarian governments elsewhere have yielded to more open regimes, and as governments have divested authority to regional entities, managers of multinationals have faced similar problems. In this changing environment, the Paiton dispute took new turns.

Although Paiton's investors had built defenses using the new international system of property rights, in the end the new assurances such as arbitration and insurance provided only limited protection for the company. In contrast, other electricity investors that we will examine later did rely heavily on the new assurances. Government officials, private managers, and those who would improve the system need to understand why the new property rights played different roles for different investors.

The Paiton dispute raises important questions about why foreign firms undertook such risky projects in the first place. One factor in the decision must have been their trust that the new assurances would be effective.

Blind Leadership

In the hotly contested 1999 national election, the most votes were gathered by the Indonesian Democratic Party (PDI) led by Megawati Sukarnoputri, first daughter of Indonesia's first president.[2] But the new president was to be elected by parliament, not by popular vote. In the showdown, parliament chose Abdurrahman Wahid, popularly known as Gus Dur, of the National Awakening Party (PKB). To calm the restless country, he named Megawati Sukarnoputri as his vice president, but the relationship between the two rivals was never to be very good.

Gus Dur, a Muslim cleric, led the nation's largest Muslim organization, Nahdlatul Ulama (NU). Educated in Indonesia, Egypt, and Iraq, he spoke for moderate Islam, and in this he represented the majority in overwhelmingly Muslim Indonesia. But Gus Dur had suffered two strokes and was, for all practical purposes, blind (said to be the result of diabetes).

The new president was not very interested in economic matters, and understood even less about them.[3] He was as likely to seek mystical help as solid economic advice. Theodore Friend says one confidant was an American promoter of hospices, and he described her as a New Age philosopher "repelled by materialism and bureaucracy of American medicine."[4] This was not an auspicious start for a presidency faced with a full-blown macroeconomic crisis, but perhaps no worse than Suharto's early-1998 flirtation with a dollar-based currency board that would magically solve the country's payments problems.[5]

Gus Dur's cabinet choices reflected the chaotic political situation.[6] As one well-known economist cleverly put it, the cabinet was "the maximal result of the compromise." Gus Dur himself said it was "the best of the compromise."[7] In practice, if not in name, this was a reconciliation and coalition government, one that had to accept Megawati proxies and representatives of the formerly governing Golkar party, as well as officials from heretofore underrepresented provinces. As a result, politics dramatically constrained the president's choices.

To foreigners, a surprising appointment was Kwik Kian Gie as the coordinating minister for the economy. A Chinese-Indonesian who had been a vocal critic of Suharto's economic policies, Kwik had survived by not pushing his opposition too far. With the exception of crony businessman Bob Hasan, appointed to Suharto's very last, "bizarre" cabinet, ethnic Chinese had been systematically excluded from influential positions in recent governments. On top of that, Kwik's strong support of Megawati meant that he would be viewed as a partisan in the rivalry between the president and vice president and thus an ineffective coordinator, regardless of his title.

The political coalition and weak president strained Indonesia's government apparatus, which contained no mechanisms to settle the disputes that arise within such an arrangement. European countries with coalition governments, for example, include nonpolitical and powerful permanent secretaries to resolve differences across ministries. Indonesia lacked these or any other devices for building consensus and cooperation.

No surprise, the compromise cabinet was unable to work together on economic issues. Past economic coordinating ministers had hardly coordinated based on authority, but they had usually come from a group of like-minded technocrats, the Berkeley Mafia and its hangers-on. The separate faction of "engineer" ministers at times had their own coordinating minister, who served a similar role. Now, with more diverse ministers holding economics portfolios, the so-called economic coordinating minister began to build his own in-house staff. Instead of coordinating, his was becoming a separate ministry.

To solve the coordination problem, the president created a new body, the National Economic Council (Dewan Ekonomi Nasional). This new layer of government only made matters worse. Because it was not a council of insiders, tension arose quickly between it and those officially in the cabinet. On top of that, the president created still another council, this one of business people. Many inside government viewed the new unit as the voice of the Chinese-Indonesian conglomerates. Widely despised, they appeared to be granted actual representation in the new regime.

Perhaps in reaction to the failure of coordinating efforts, perhaps out of a desperate desire for credibility, the president also turned to high-profile foreigners for counsel, among them Singapore's Lee Kuan Yew, former Federal Reserve chairman Paul Volcker, former U.S. Secretary of State Henry Kissinger (although he was already advising Freeport McMoRan, one of Indonesia's very large foreign investors, and had worked for Mission), and financier George Soros.[8] Because none of the prominent advisors could spend the time needed to develop a deep knowledge of Indonesia, their advice would have to be very general. There is no evidence that they ever added anything constructive. In fact, Volcker seemed to have grasped the basics quickly and told the president that he could not give advice as the president had no structure under him to carry it out.[9] Even if the outsiders had tried to play a major role, cabinet officials would surely have undermined them, just as they had the two Indonesian councils.

At the same time, parliament and a free press were asserting themselves much more than in the past. As a result, Paiton would be negotiating not only with a disorganized government, but also with media and a parliament (and eventually NGOs) that were no longer subject to the will of a strong president.

Indonesia was evolving into a different kind of emerging market, paralleling changes in a number of other developing countries. Managers have not always been quick to recognize the deep effects that emerging democracy has on them, and they often have been hesitant to embrace the changes.

Retreat from Arbitration and the Courts

Gus Dur would change things at PLN. It seems that, in early December 1999, Laksamana Sukardi, the minister for state-owned Enterprises, Kwik, and Lt. Gen. Susilo Bambang Yudhoyono, the minister of mines and energy,[10] called

PLN director Adhi Satriya to a meeting in the national planning building. Following the president's instructions, Kwik told Satriya that litigation in the Paiton case was not to continue. Satriya responded that the ministerial committee and then-President Habibie had approved the legal approach. When Kwik continued to press, according to one advisor, Satriya stood up, said "then I have to resign," and walked out.

PLN was doing well enough in the Jakarta court. In early December, a provisional ruling had ordered Paiton to refrain from arbitration. To back its ruling, the court threatened to impose a $600 million fine on Paiton if the company attempted action against PLN. One U.S. legal advisor says the lawyers were hugged as heroes by PLN employees in the elevators of headquarters when they arrived for work the next day. Some believed that this was a significant victory, sending a wake-up call to Paiton and other companies that they had to negotiate "in good faith and on commercially reasonable terms."[11]

Nevertheless, Gus Dur followed up the Kwik meeting with a direct order to PLN to stop the court case and all other legal processes involving electric power agreements.[12] The president then insisted on removing Satriya from PLN. One advisor would say that Satriya's statements to the press had "set the country on fire." Satriya unambiguously resigned on December 20.[13] After he learned of Satriya's resignation, the head of the negotiating team, Hardiv Situmeang, also resigned, against the urging of some of his advisors. In his letter of resignation to the minister for state-owned enterprises, Hardiv mentioned his professional ethics, his public accountability as a director of PLN, and his moral responsibility. Rather less quietly, Satriya issued a public statement that the president's decision to withdraw the court case worked against PLN's interest.

Gus Dur appointed former Minister of Mines and Energy Kuntoro as the new head of PLN. With the legal case still in court in January, U.S. Ambassador Gelbard called Kuntoro to argue that it should be stopped immediately. Kuntoro told us that he registered his agreement with the ambassador, but responded that he had received no confirmation from Paiton's management that they would drop their arbitration demand if PLN withdrew the court case. Gelbard gave his word that the day after the court case was stopped Paiton would terminate arbitration.[14] Kuntoro responded that he would "be finished" if this did not happen. Gelbard answered that he represented the word of the U.S. government. Kuntoro told us that he could trust "Gelbard to deliver on his promise." Although the U.S. government had no authority to assure that a U.S. company would drop an arbitration case, Paiton managers told us that they had always kept Gelbard informed of the status of negotiations, presumably enough to give Gelbard confidence in his promise.

Ending the legal process was a rather dramatic about-face for Indonesia. Understanding why Gus Dur halted the case, even though it was going well, could provide clues about the workings of the new regime, yet the full story remains elusive. Most Indonesians we spoke with believed that their new president had succumbed to tremendous pressure from the U. S. government, especially when he had visited the United States in November 1999 for eye treatment.[15] Certainly, Gus Dur spoke with President Clinton on that trip, but what Clinton said to him is not in the public record. We asked Gus Dur himself in June 2003 why he dropped the case, and his response, that the legal route would have taken too long, sounded so much like an American answer (in that the Jakarta court was, in fact, soon to issue its final decision) that we followed up by saying that many in Indonesia thought his order was the result of U.S. pressure. Known for his humor, he said that he and Clinton had seen "eye-to-eye on everything, with the exception of Monica Lewinsky." We leave to the reader the interpretation of this blind Javanese politician's evasive answer.

Although U.S. pressure likely played a role, Gus Dur probably had a strong preference for negotiation over confrontation.[16] His Javanese and clerical background may have convinced him that discussion could solve all. We were also told that Kuntoro, who had turned down counsel's advice to initiate legal action in early 1999, had assured him that the problem could be resolved without a legalistic approach. But the president might also have feared that a court case could expose corruption on the part of government officials on whom he still depended. Although it is impossible to assign weights to these various influences, all probably affected the decision.

PLN formally withdrew its legal case on January 20, 2000. As the U.S. ambassador had promised, Paiton, in turn, dropped its demand for arbitration. And the parties agreed to continue to try to settle their differences through negotiation. A number of people on both sides must have felt a great deal of relief. The future looked much more promising.

Not everyone was happy, however. Eager to allay concerns that he was doing nothing about pursuing corrupt officials and unhappy with the withdrawal of the PLN case, Indonesia's attorney general, Marzuki Darusman, was soon (May 2000) to complain: "We are in possession of unambiguous evidence for corruption. So far, however, we have been forced by political pressure to suspend our investigations until an interim agreement has been concluded. Once we are able to proceed with the investigations, it will become clear which companies have been paying bribes."[17]

The Indonesian parliament also spoke up, expressing its "regret" over the decision to drop the legal case; the house speaker Akbar Tandjung said parliament would summon officials to explain the decision and to investigate the "resignations."[18] Amien Rais, the speaker of the People's Consultative Assembly, stated that "he suspected 'foreign powers' were behind the resignations."[19] But the investigations supported by the attorney general did not proceed, and any evidence of corruption was never made public. Ironically, the house speaker was himself convicted of corruption in 2002, a conviction that was eventually itself overturned. (For more on corruption and Indonesian regimes, see Box 12.1.)

Box 12.1 Justice, Corruption, and Property Rights

Development economists often assume that the only way to ensure property rights and development is to have "rule of law" under something like a Western-style legal system.[a] They have even debated which kind of Western system is better.[b] Suharto's Indonesia proved that corruption and the absence of a Western-style legal system were no overwhelming obstacles to business. After all, with the economy growing by some 7% per year for 25 years, many investors must have felt reasonably secure in their property rights.

An informal system operated, as it does in a number of countries. Under Suharto, business was considered to be a serious matter. Anything that squeezed business to the point that it could not survive was viewed as a threat to the country's and Suharto's well-being. On serious matters, Suharto himself served as a court of appeal. When major business conflicts arose, crony and family partners provided access to the president, who would settle them, whether the disputes involved Indonesians or foreigners. As a part of this informal system, much of the corruption was organized from the top and distributed downward. A business would have to pay, but for firms with connections the informal system ensured that the sums were limited to a level that a firm could bear.[c] Affordable amounts could be quite high, especially because the country had low effective taxes. Oil revenues helped finance visible expenditures, and corruption the invisible ones.

Of course, this informal justice system failed to protect the ordinary citizen, whose house might be broken into or whose stock for small-scale trading could be stolen. In parts of the country, *adat* (customary law and procedures) handled "petty" cases effectively. In urban environments, vigilante groups—perhaps with police support—arose from time to time to render justice when matters got out of hand. The result was very safe streets and neighborhoods in Indonesia's huge, sprawling, poor cities in spite of the corrupt police and legal system.

This informal and centralized system collapsed with the fall of Suharto. There was no longer a figure with the authority to administer justice and to coordinate and cap corruption. With business at the mercy of corrupt courts, disputes could fester interminably.[d] In fact, corruption probably increased with the end of authoritarian government. Formal decentralization of government made matters still worse. Bureaucrats at local levels had new authority and no brakes. Like their compatriots in Jakarta, they also wanted a share of the riches.

With no authority figure to ensure property rights for investors, the new democracy now desperately needed a formal legal system and enforcement of laws on corruption.

(continued)

> **Box 12.1** (continued)
>
> [a]For a number of examples, see *Finance & Development*, June 2003, particularly the interview with Allan Meltzer and articles by Arvind Subramanian and Hali Edison. On the other hand, Rodrik explicitly recognizes that property rights may be sufficiently secure for investors under different systems, pointing to China. See Dani Rodrik, Arving Subramanian, and Francesco Trebbi, "Institutions Rule: The Primacy of Institutions over Geography and Integration in Economic Development," mimeo, October 2002. Available at http://ksghome.harvard.edu/~drodrik/institutionsrule,%205.0.pdf.
> [b]Much of the best work has been done by Rafael La Porta, Florencio Lopez-de-Silanes, and Robert Vishny.
> [c]Similar caps seem to have been absent in some other countries such as Nigeria.
> [d]Like that of Manulife. For this and some other notorious cases, see Hans Vriens, "Megawati Breaks a Business Impasse," *The Wall Street Journal*, October 7, 2002.

New Advisor Turmoil

A new head of PLN and a new attitude toward renegotiations brought new advisors and new roles for old ones. Tensions only grew.

To start with, Kuntoro had to appoint a chair for the negotiating team. He chose Syamsuddin Warsa, a member of the team all along and once the construction manager for the PLN portion of the Paiton project. Kuntoro and Syamsuddin inherited Hardiv's old advisor Yazdani as well as Sroka and the team's legal advisors. But the law firm fell into the "tough" camp, too much so for the new government and PLN management. With another two months on its contract, it was dismissed and Cleary, Gottlieb, Steen & Hamilton was hired. In spite of allegations of conflict of interest, Kuntoro decided to go ahead with this firm.[20] Kuntoro also added two firms to help with financial analysis, but other advisors reported to us that they had little impact on important decisions.[21]

Peter Jezek mysteriously disappeared in July 2000. He had been deeply involved in the original negotiations, probably threatened with bodily harm, left for Thailand, and returned in 1999 to work with PLN. This time he left no note of explanation, provided no forwarding address, and failed even to collect his last paycheck. One advisor told us that Jezek had had a stroke; another, that he had had a massive heart attack; a third, that he had been threatened a second time and feared for his life. Kuntoro and Hardiv tried without success to contact him. All who knew Jezek thought that he was in the United States, but they said that he seemed to want to keep his location secret. He was, and he did.

Kuntoro brought in Bill Hollinger, the same person who had served as advisor in the Indosat case, during the early planning for private investment in electricity, and again for the original Paiton negotiations. Kuntoro hoped that Hollinger would fill the serious gap left by Jezek's disappearance. There is no question about which side Hollinger was on, but he had more trust in business and business managers, and more friends among them, than did other advisors. Because he had been a consultant in the original negotiations, he might also hesitate to take a position that the outcome had been all wrong. Whatever other reasons could have influenced views of him, his milder attitude toward investors and his style were enough to make him suspect among other advisors.

Kuntoro, himself technically trained, knew the importance of technical skills. He soon discovered that Hollinger could not supply them. Henceforth, Hollinger's role would be to draw on his international contacts and his relations with company people. Because much of the specialized knowledge and power experience resided in what we have called the "tough" camp, Kuntoro discovered that he could not dispense with them. Although Yazdani, Sroka, and Hardiv were now in the out-of-favor group for their positions, Kuntoro continued to draw on them for technical matters.

Reflecting their different substantive views, their different loyalties, and their different ideas of the proper role for consultants, the advisors often made critical comments to us about each other. Two advisors, we were told, formed an "anti-investor cabal." One advisor expressed doubts about the loyalties of another advisor, and repeated a charge that he only collected information from others but gave out no information in exchange. After Jezek disappeared, one advisor tried to trace the previous employers on his resume, eventually concluding that the number of dead ends indicated that he was a CIA agent. This contention only added more mystery to Jezek's disappearance.[22]

To be sure, working conditions heightened tensions among the advisors. Jakarta's new hotels were world class (see Box 12.2), but facilities in PLN's headquarters were primitive. Lawyers said PLN had no computers for them, and not even paper—they had to bring their own. But working conditions had certainly been no better for advisors during the ITT/Indosat renegotiations, and disputes had hardly been noticeable. First, during ITT/Indosat, the advisors' long association with their principal Indonesian clients was reflected in a shared basic attitude toward problems. Second, one person had been in charge of assembling the specialist advisors, choosing people whom he knew, with whom he had worked earlier, and whom he trusted. Any differences in views could be managed. In the power case, however, even Kuntoro's careful management could not eliminate tensions and improve the effectiveness of the group.

Other Tensions

Among Indonesians, old battles continued, but with some new characters. The economic coordinating minister, Kwik, wanted the negotiating team to report directly to him, while the head of PLN sought to control it. Kwik's response, that PLN was not an "operational entity," contradicted one of the possible lines of defense for the government should the case return to litigation: that PLN was a separate, limited liability corporation and its shareholder, the government, was therefore not responsible for

---

Box 12.2 Jakarta Revisited

As executives returned to Jakarta to salvage what they could from their investments, they found a city that had continued to change. The booming 1990s had provided business visitors with a wide choice of luxury hotels and restaurants with almost any kind of food. Some hotels, like the Regent, were isolated from outside shops and poor Indonesians. A business manager staying in them needed a car and driver or a willingness to take the "executive" Silver Bird cabs to reach meetings or noncaptive restaurants.

Jakarta's transportation had also evolved. Pedicabs were long gone from the city's streets, and the two classes of taxis were all metered. Old three-wheel, two-cycle Bajaj—similar to motorized pedicabs—still added to noise and air pollution off the main streets, and the narrower ways in poor neighborhoods could be negotiated on the back of motorcycles, which stood at corners ready to take on passengers. The poor overloaded the buses and vans that crawled through the now jammed streets. While middle-class Indonesians often drove Kijangs, the rich, of course busy on their cell phones, were chauffeured around in the usual Third World assortment of Mercedes, BMWs, and similar autos. No subway or elevated "Skytrain"—as in Singapore or Bangkok—would provide an alternative to the nightmare traffic. Jams meant over one-hour commutes for many expatriates, and the traffic largely drove managers' hotel choices. Development had its costs, and the economic crisis alleviated traffic and pollution only slightly.

---

its obligations. The conflict over control was severe enough to prompt Ambassador Gelbard to visit Kwik, not once but twice, to argue that the team should report to Kuntoro. For sure, this added to the ambassador's reputation with Indonesians for meddling in internal matters, although this time he probably had the right idea, for both Indonesia and the investor.

The disputing government parties eventually resigned themselves to a modified and clumsy arrangement. The negotiating team would report to PLN's board of commissioners,[23] which in turn would report to the ministerial team. The negotiating team would have a staff and a "daily technical team" that would report to Syamsuddin and to the directors of PLN. In practice, however, the negotiating team short-circuited this compromise: Kuntoro oversaw day-to-day negotiations, while the negotiating team informally reported directly to both the steering committee and the ministerial team. As a result, negotiators were able to create a somewhat sensible approach out of a rather Byzantine compromise.

The new cabinet took a much more active role in the renegotiations than had the previous one, but new problems also emerged. As anticipated, Kwik, a Megawati loyalist, did not always work well with the president. Moreover, Kwik seemed indecisive to many.[24] Just as things began to settle down, another general overhaul of the cabinet, in August 2000, led to Kwik's departure and the appointment of Rizal Ramli in his place. Everyone had to adjust again to new leaders.

On the other side, Paiton's management was facing its own internal complications. Government negotiators often forget that private parties can be as divided as their own ministries. In this case, lenders were a problem. With little cash coming to Paiton, project managers were unable to meet debt service obligations in full and the equity owners, of course, had no commitment to step in with funds. That is the point of project finance.[25] Moreover, adding to the difficulties, some of the senior debt in this and other power projects had been sold by the original lenders. A thin private secondary market had developed as investment groups bought downgraded obligations. As a result, even more parties gained an interest in the outcome of negotiations.

One possible threat to Paiton came from the complex default provisions that such debt usually carries. If one lender to a project declares its loans to be in default, typically most or all other obligations are automatically considered in default and can be declared immediately payable. Up to this point, Paiton's management had been able to hold off its creditors, who probably saw an earning project as likely to return more to lenders than one in liquidation. U.S. Exim Bank had extended its deadline to refinance its original construction loan, relieving some pressure. Two more extensions carried the company to December 2001.[26] Apparently other lenders reached temporary agreements about the same time, accepting interest payments only.

Resumption of Negotiations

With the court case dropped, negotiations had gotten off to a fresh start in a kick-off meeting with the foreign investors.[27] Kuntoro personally addressed the assembled group, saying that he "means business." He added that he did not want discussions "polluted" by the investors' local partners, who had not even been invited to the meeting.

By this time, local partners had largely disappeared from the scene anyway. Paiton's Indonesian partner had been notably absent from renegotiations all along. Hashim was even "out of the deal."[28] In the new democracy, relatives of Suharto or his officials would not only have little influence, but their presence could be an embarrassing reminder of allegations of corruption and cronyism.

Settlement was looking more likely. On February 21, 2000, Paiton and PLN signed an interim arrangement to cover the rest of the calendar year, calling for a total fixed payment of $115 million[29] plus 2.6 cents per kilowatt hour (cents/kwh) for any power actually accepted by PLN.[30] The idea was that payments would cover the actual production cost of electricity (fuel and variable operating and maintenance costs) and a small portion of capacity payments, which would go toward interest obligations. The parties agreed that a subsequent temporary tariff would have to enable Paiton to make principal payments as well. With this agreement and with some recovery of demand, PLN began to accept electric power from the facility.[31]

Gus Dur was said to have been "so happy" when he was told of the interim agreement, seeing his approach vindicated. Unfortunately, he had been told only of the variable price and not the $115 million fixed payment. In June, someone finally informed him of the additional payment. This surprise news apparently contributed to his faltering confidence in PLN's CEO Kuntoro.

The temporary agreement, however, led the parties to reaffirm their commitment to try for a long-term settlement and avoid legal processes. New negotiations, they decided, would commence soon, in April 2000.

There had indeed been substantial progress. Most importantly, the debate was now over what a new contract might look like. The rigid view of sanctity of contract had melted. Both sides recognized that the arrangement had to be adjusted to reflect new realities. Paiton's owners had even offered the outline of a new long-term deal: lower the tariff for its power in exchange for an extension of its contract from 30 years to 60 years.[32]

Home Governments Again

Although negotiations were progressing, the U.S. government grew more strident than ever. In January 2000, OPIC had again sent representatives to various ministers to press for settlements. It added a threat of seizing Indonesian assets abroad if the government did not meet its payment obligations to the power companies.[33] On March 8, 2000, the German, Japanese, and Swiss export credit agencies also arrived to defend their interests in various projects.[34]

At about this time, U.S. Ambassador Gelbard voiced his defense of U.S. companies in such strong terms that he lost a good deal of credibility. An Indonesian newspaper[35] quoted Ambassador Gelbard as being "dismayed" by "unsubstantiated" allegations that American companies had engaged in corrupt practices. The ambassador, according to the article, "denied allegations of corruption leveled against U.S. companies operating in Indonesia.... I don't believe there is *any* [emphasis added] corruption."[36] Americans were amused. Indonesians, less so. Rather, many were very angry at the contention of American innocence during the Suharto years, and especially from the ambassador of a country that had chastised Indonesia in the past for corruption.

Eventually Mission brought back a former U.S. official to lobby for them—Henry Kissinger. Although Paiton managers mentioned the relationship to us, neither the company nor Kissinger & Associates would provide further details. One might puzzle over possible conflicts of interest. Kissinger's firm would have been advising the company side in the Paiton renegotiations, even though Kissinger had recently—and may have still—served as advisor to Gus Dur.[37]

Meanwhile, in January 2001, Paiton and the Indonesians struck another interim agreement, calling for fixed monthly payments of $108 million for the next six months as well as payment for any power delivered. Differences between what had been contracted and what was actually paid would accumulate as "overdue."[38] The document included the goal of reaching a final agreement by June. The deadline was not to be met, as Gus Dur changed personnel again.

More Turnover of People

On March 2, 2001, the president removed Kuntoro as head of PLN, replacing him with the company's marketing and distribution director, Eddie Widiono. Kuntoro later blamed his dismissal on his refusal the previous June to give the Klaten-Tasikmalaya transmission-line contract to the highest of three bidders, as he claimed Kwik had written to him to demand.

The story behind the transmission line illustrates some of the issues with Indonesian governance. In Jakarta, Gus Dur had met an American businessman, Harold Jensen, from Salt Lake City.[39] They had built a relationship based on their common interest in how the state deals with minority religions.[40] Jensen, a Mormon, had invited Gus Dur to Salt Lake City for treatment at an eye clinic there. The president went in 1998 and again in 1999, when he stayed at Jensen's home. Jensen organized surgeons, paid for treatments, and covered other expenses. Jensen just happened to represent the Swedish-Swiss company Asea Brown Boveri (ABB), which wanted the contract for the transmission line.[41] As Kuntoro told us the story, after Gus Dur had returned to Jakarta, he had Alwi Shihab, the minister of foreign affairs, arrange a dinner for Jensen to meet with Kuntoro. Kuntoro recounted to us that the American "acted as if he was [the country's] president."[42] The result: Kuntoro says he walked out, without touching even the appetizers.[43]

Kuntoro said his fate was sealed the next month when he challenged the president's insistence that he use Austrian export credit funds for another Sumatran project, the Musi River hydro project in Bengkulu. The president responded that this was the second time he had refused his instructions. After Kuntoro stood firm on the issue, he remained in PLN only until the president could line up a replacement.

A new head of PLN meant still another shift in advisors. Hardiv was appointed as director for planning at PLN and continued to be active in the renegotiations. The temporarily out of favor advisor Yazdani saw his influence return, and Hollinger was not retained. Although the new head of PLN was viewed by some interviewees as more "compliant" than Kuntoro, the "tougher" advisors were in the ascendancy.

Roles for New Actors

Press

Indosat's owners had never faced a free press, but Paiton's would, and one that was clearly on the side of tough negotiations and opposed to U.S. intervention, and on the offensive against corruption.

The Indonesian press had already reported parliament's complaints of U.S. interference, claiming that six U.S. senators had written a letter to President Habibie warning him to take care of the power sector problems, in particular Paiton I.[44] The press had also reminded the public of the original support for the project given by former U.S. Vice President Quayle, by former U.S. Secretary of State Warren Christopher, and allegedly by former U.S. Secretary of the Treasury Robert Rubin.[45]

The court case had attracted press attention. Somewhat confusingly, the *Jakarta Post* seemed to favor its withdrawal, even though Paiton was "considered not only the most blatant case of KKN, but also the most uncooperative...."[46] The newspaper then reported the president as saying, "The power tariff scheme [in Paiton's contract] is entirely *gombal* [rubbish] and was produced by the corrupt old regime. But, like or dislike it, we have to honor it."[47] Exactly what "honoring" meant was less than clear, as the president went on to say that the contracts had to be renegotiated. The newspaper concurred, saying the contracts "would bleed the state company and the nation for decades as the power rates they charged were prohibitively high."[48]

The press also picked up corruption as a favored topic, with respect to the power projects and otherwise. One of the major Indonesian-language papers, for example, cited the claim of a parliament member that between $15 million and $50 million in bribes were involved in the power projects, surely a dramatic understatement if one adds the value of the equity shares provided cronies and members of Suharto's family.[49]

The press added greatly to the pressure on Gus Dur to bring some of the corrupt figures of Suharto's regime to trial. Paiton's partner Hashim had crossed Gus Dur earlier (in late 1998) by thwarting an attempt by a company controlled by Gus Dur, his brother, and other NU party leaders to take over a company controlled by Hashim and Suharto's daughter Titiek. Hashim was arrested in March 2001 for violations of banking rules in Bank Industri.

Also in for arrest on April 6 was another figure involved in the Paiton story: Ginandjar Kartasasmita, the minister of mines and energy when the Paiton negotiations began and brother of an equity holder in Paiton's coal supplier.[50] Accusations against Ginandjar were nothing new.[51] As we have pointed out, he was said to have made his start with Team 10, the notorious group reputed to take a percentage of all significant government contracts. Other accusations arise from his days at BKPM, the investment coordinating board. Whatever the truth of the accusations, Ginandjar was arrested but never tried. Holding a military commission,

---

Box 12.3 Ginandjar Kartasaasmita at Harvard

At the time of his arrest, Ginandjar was a fellow at Harvard's Weatherhead Center for International Affairs, but he had gone to Indonesia for a visit. He had been invited to Harvard by economist Jeffrey Sachs during Sachs' visit to Jakarta as head of the Harvard Institute for International Development (HIID), much to the chagrin of many of the institute's professionals who were well aware of corruption allegations.[a] By the time Ginandjar arrived at Harvard, HIID had been closed; thus, he ended up at the Weatherhead Center with a commitment to write a book. In mid-2006, the book was still "in process." Ginandjar was eventually elected as a Golkar representative in the newly created upper legislative house, the DPD.

[a]See "Development Troubles," *Harvard Magazine*, September/October 2002, 105(1), pp. 61–62, for a house publication's sanitized version of Sachs's troubled management.

---

he could be arrested only with permission of the armed forces; however, he had been taken in three days before the permission was issued, so he was therefore released (see Box 12.3).

Democracy was a new world for the Indonesian press, but it never succeeded in its efforts to bring many Suharto era figures to trial.

Labor

New freedoms of expression extended to labor as well. Under Suharto, labor unions had been subject to the government's iron hand. Strikes were generally forbidden, and on the rare occasions when unions violated government wishes, the military reacted harshly. Now, with the military weakened and a new government, unions assumed a larger role. In April 2001, the union that represented PLN workers, filed a civil lawsuit against the minister of mines and energy and Paiton,[52] charging that the original arrangement violated the 1945 Constitution as well as a law on electricity that included a statement saying "a contract should not financially burden the public."[53] Although the Central Jakarta District Court ruled that the union had no standing to bring the action, the case served as a further reminder that democracy was bringing new players to the table.

Nongovernmental Organizations

The NGOs would have to be added to the list of parties managers must consider. Some international NGOs had already criticized the power contracts from a safe distance, but now they and domestic NGOs could do business inside the country. One domestic NGO, the Working Group on Power Sector Restructuring (WGPSR), was turning its attention to the power agreements, targeting the efforts of the Asian Development Bank to push Indonesians to liberalize the electricity market.[54] Although NGOs would not have a large voice in the renegotiation of Paiton, their influence would continue to grow in the new Indonesia and in other developing countries that were becoming more democratic.[55] By 2004, long after Paiton had been settled, they had established panels in Indonesia that were supposed to be consulted with regard to any new power plant.[56]

Moving Ahead

Although Indonesia was still negotiating with 17 other power projects, Paiton I and two other projects headed the agenda.

In late June 2001, Paiton reportedly offered a long-term tariff of just above 5 cents/kwh, while PLN offered a little lower figure. Paiton even proposed delaying the implementation of the long-term rate until January 2002 and providing power in the meantime at 4.12 cents for six months. The parties were now close.

It may be that Gus Dur's decision to withdraw from legal battles was beginning to pay off, but in July 2001 parliament voted to oust the president. Two corruption charges against the administration, although never proved, had started the ball rolling. Perhaps more important in the end, the economy had not recovered and the president's "imperious" style was resented by the newly self-confident parliament.[57]

Megawati Takes Power

Paiton managers now faced their fourth president in a little more than three years: former vice president Megawati Sukarnoputri. In spite of her name, she came with no special knowledge of electric power,[58] and like Gus Dur she understood little of economics or finance. Her business experience comprised a flower shop that she had opened in 1979 to supply Jakarta hotels.[59]

A new president meant still more turnover within government. Megawati made two especially strong appointments, to the positions of coordinating minister for economic affairs and minister of finance.[60] With the coordinating position came chairmanship of the ministerial team to oversee the electric power negotiations. But what the power companies saw was again a revolving door. This was the third head of the team within a rather short period.

Much as she might have wished otherwise, Megawati's honeymoon as president did not include any rest from electric power. Almost immediately the *Wall Street Journal* produced an article that called for the United States to help her by brokering revisions of the contracts negotiated by U.S. investors during the corrupt Suharto days. The article partly blamed the United States for problems arising from the 1997 crisis, and said it had a "moral obligation to do what it can to help the new president straighten them out."[61] But the newspaper's views were not shared by U.S. officialdom. OPIC and Exim Bank were not about to let up their pressure; nor did it seem that Ambassador Gelbard was inclined to help the Indonesians.[62]

Megawati seemed curiously detached from the running of government. In his book on Indonesia, Friend reports one story that, true or not, reflects a common view of her presidency. The story goes that when she made her first visit to New York, she was asked to a meeting with American businesspeople to reassure them about their operations in Indonesia. She declined, spending the time shopping at Bloomingdale's. On that trip, she reportedly arranged to have (and presumably paid for) a special showing of *The Phantom of the Opera* for her entourage.[63] Moreover, her regime was also not entirely free of Javanese mysticism. Friend also reports a story that the minister of religious affairs was convinced that a certain inscribed rock in Bogor was hiding enough money to pay the country's total indebtedness (over $150 billion).[64] Exploring the rock might be an easier solution to the country's economic problems than trying to deal with the complexity of foreign investment contracts. It seems that the treasure was not found.

For a while, the new government faced virtual paralysis. With time, however, Megawati's confidence in the new coordinating and finance ministers seems to have grown, and more and more decisions were delegated to them.[65] This was helpful in the renegotiations.

But having just dumped a president, parliament was even more conscious of its power and introduced a little more confusion. In November 2001, the press reported that a parliamentary committee was debating a draft law that might shove the Paiton negotiations back to their starting point. It would fully liberalize power generation, converting to a merchant system, which was something that had been threatened before, of course.[66] If the proposed system were to come into being, formula prices and take-or-pay would be dead. A very few Indonesians and certainly multilateral finance institutions had retained their fascination with a market-oriented system, in spite of the overwhelming barriers in Indonesia to any near-term success.[67]

Winding Up Negotiations

In spite of the new confusion, negotiations with Paiton proceeded under the assumptions that Paiton would continue to operate under a power purchase agreement. With the distance between the two sides narrowing, PLN and Paiton entered a series of interim agreements, in January, July, and September 2001.

By September the positions seem to have stood as follows: PLN was offering to buy electricity at 4.65 cents/kwh and to make payments of $3.3

million monthly for arrears and restructuring costs. Paiton's offer stood at 4.93 cents/kwh, with monthly payments of $4 million. The monthly payments over the next 20 years were, according to Mission, the difference between the amounts received during the renegotiation period and what would have been due under the new agreement, plus interest on those payments.[68] In addition, Paiton was asking for a 10-year extension of the project and for a capacity factor of 85% rather than the original 83%.[69] The economic coordinating minister responded in October that the Paiton offer was acceptable.[70]

The end was clearly in sight on December 14, 2001, when PLN and Paiton signed a "Binding Term Sheet" setting out the main provisions of an amendment to the power purchase agreement with Paiton's most recent offer.[71] The revised agreement would expire in 2039, 10 years later than the original date. The sheet also included a "standstill" agreement on legal proceedings, a version of the long-sought confidentiality agreement, and implementation provisions and conditions that had to be met before the final agreement could materialize.[72]

Negotiators did not quite meet their self-imposed deadline of March 31, but a new power purchase agreement, reflecting the terms of the Binding Term Sheet, was signed before the end of June 2002, to take effect on December 23.

Cleaning Up

Paiton managers still had much to do. One need was to revise company debt. The U.S. Exim Bank provided an additional loan of $381 million, and the owners negotiated a new amortization schedule with lenders. A large part of the tradable bonds had been acquired by a hedge fund, Farallon Capital Management, which appears to have cooperated in the restructuring.[73] The task was completed on February 14, 2003.[74] In the end, the U.S. Exim Bank, the Japanese Bank for International Cooperation (JBIC), Nippon Export and Investment Insurance (NEXI), and OPIC were the four largest lenders. All, obviously, were government organizations. With the changes in financial structure, this "private" investment remained dominated by government funds.

Another matter to clean up was the arrangement for coal. The original deal had required that Adaro's coal[75] be shipped through Indonesia Bulk Terminal and be carried on specific ships to the plant. Both the terminal and the ships were owned by affiliated (and previously influential) parties.[76] Paiton management was now saying that the old arrangements were resulting in coal that was $10 to $12 above market prices—just as critics had earlier alleged.[77] The once-powerful parties had little remaining influence. Moreover, one of the old arguments for an exclusive deal with Adaro and affiliates was collapsing: that dedicated reserves and stockpiles, dedicated barges and other vessels, the intermediate terminal, and a single supplier were needed as safeguards for regular supplies.[78]

Paiton could now seek alternative suppliers, changing relative bargaining powers and enabling a new deal with the old supplier. The result: The price of coal would be determined at Paiton's jetty, at market prices.

To be sure, Paiton would have to pay a settlement to end the old coal contracts. Adaro's owner, Batu Hitam Perkasa, had already threatened commercial arbitration against Paiton for breaking the deal, seeking $250 million. But by mid-December 2002, Paiton and BHP had agreed on a settlement.[79] The anticipated settlement costs may have been added into the restructuring charges and thus into the monthly payments due from the Indonesians.[80]

Company Victories

At the completion of renegotiations, both the Indonesians and Paiton's owners could—and did—claim that they came out well. Edison Mission would hold onto its position as a leading producer of electricity for the Indonesian market, and for 10 years longer than originally contemplated. Landry, Paiton's president-director, thanked the coordinating minister (Dorodjatun), the minister of mines and energy (Purnomo), and PLN's president (Eddie Widiono) for their support. Edgell, the original negotiator who had, according to one advisor, championed continuing with the project, said, "The investors in Paiton Energy are extremely pleased with the successful restructuring of Paiton Energy. This achievement should send positive signals to the investment community that Indonesia is an important destination for long term equity investment."[81] This has to be interpreted as saying that Paiton's investors would still make enough money, even after cutting the price of electricity. Edgell seemed personally delighted, an advisor said, because he could remain comfortably in Singapore with his Indonesian wife and family. His new love for Indonesia and Southeast Asia surely contributed to his willingness, even as an original negotiator, to back away from a rigid view of contract and encourage progress in renegotiations.

In the end, Paiton's managers could claim another victory, one they never spoke with us about. In spite of all the tension and accusations during the renegotiations, this company's managers had earned the respect of most Indonesians with whom we spoke. After the new arrangements were concluded, we heard no claims that Paiton's managers were culturally insensitive, arrogant, or deceptive. As a result, these managers did not end up spoiling the future of Mission, General Electric, or Mitsui in Indonesia.

Indonesian Victory

On the other side, the new price for electricity appeared to be a significant victory for the Indonesians. Indeed, it was considerably lower than the original price. Under the previous agreement, the "levelized" price was between 6.3 cents/kwh and 7.37 cents/kwh, depending on how one averaged. Under the new agreement, PLN would pay a price of 4.93 cents/kwh each year over the new 40-year period. PLN calculated the savings at a little more than 30%.[82]

Elusive Stability

Avoiding the Problem?

In the best of worlds, the parties ought to have negotiated a deal at the outset that would have lasted. Academics advocate contracts that cover all contingencies; in contrast, real negotiators find it very difficult to come to terms with remote but potentially catastrophic events. Often, one or the other party rejects even the possibility that such events could materialize. In this case, collapse of the rupiah remained an unmentionable in the original negotiations and thus could not be realistically handled by contingency clauses. To be sure, some minor changes might have reduced political sensitivities. For example, Paiton's owners could have insisted that the cost of additional infrastructure not be incorporated into the electricity price but rather that it be shown separately, as a monthly loan repayment, for example. By lowering the price of electricity by around 0.75/kwh, the adjustment would have made the price of Paiton electricity seem somewhat more competitive with other sources. One can think of additional options.

But it was not the best of worlds. Writing all contingencies into the contract was never in the cards, and a little window dressing would probably have done little to save the agreement. Once the Asian Currency Crisis struck, debt agreements fell. Although the large projected rate of return was a matter of negotiation, allocating risk like debt may have been an inevitable result of high leverage and project finance. The structure, however, meant that the agreement was bound to fail with a serious currency crisis.

One might wonder what would have happened if the crisis had not occurred. Our bet is that the agreement would have been renegotiated in a few years, for it would have obsolesced rather quickly, given that foreign investors brought little more than money to Indonesia.

The renegotiated arrangement for Paiton I may have been no more stable than the old one. Almost as soon as the thick revised agreement for Paiton was stapled together, Indonesian critics emerged to challenge its terms.

One popular charge involved the monthly payments. Critics insisted that they should be allocated to the cost of contemporaneous power deliveries, making the electricity price not the 4.93 cents reported by management but 5.45 cents.[83] Further, critics pointed out, in the new agreement PLN committed to make capacity payments for 85% of the capacity of the facility, up from the original 83%. Critics adjusted the price figure to 6.03 cents/kwh to account for what they claimed to be a realistic maximum capacity factor of 75%.[84] Careful statements of these charges were far too complicated for politically motivated public statements, but they were fodder for sound bites that were difficult for managers to refute.

Comparisons with other countries also returned quickly. In the summer of 2002, a parliamentary commission's expert reported that even the 4.93 cent figure from management compared unfavorably with Malaysian tariffs of only 3.2 cents. An attack on the new agreement also appeared in a small book that reported total costs of other projects as shown in Table 12.1.

Prices for electricity from the original power projects would also be compared with proposals from new investors. First among them were investors from China, who were offering to produce power with much smaller investments and considerably lower tariffs. Whether they could deliver remained to be seen, but the tentative offers were there for anyone who wanted to attack Paiton I.

The nominal prices of a contract like Paiton's were, of course, not those actually paid. Some components were indexed; some were fixed regardless of the amount of electricity PLN took. According to one report, the actual price in 2000 for Paiton I electricity was 12.22 cents/kwh, as fixed costs had to be allocated over a smaller amount of power than anticipated.[85] Publicity for the real prices will almost certainly provide another basis for attacking the revised agreement, as it did in India's Dabhol contract with Enron.

Moreover, PLN's financial problems were not over; in fact, little had really changed. A cash crisis at PLN could easily turn attention again to Paiton. The idea of creating a merchant market for electricity had also not died. Conversion, if it ever happened, would also make the power purchase agreements obsolete.

In the new Indonesia, public scrutiny would turn to any agreement that is very visible and that involves large sums of money. Payments of millions of dollars per day were at stake in this plant alone. Whether the various comparisons of rates and costs and the calculations of returns are fair or not matter little when the issue is political, as it had inevitably become.

Table 12.1 Comparison of Power Costs

Project	Capacity (megawatts)	Total Cost (US$ billion)	Cost per Kilowatt (US$)
Paiton I (as reported)	2 × 615	2.5	2,032
Paiton I (SNC-Lavalin estimate)	2 × 615	1.6	1,310
Guang Zou (China)	3 × 660	1.9	969
Pangasinan (Philippines)	2 × 609	1.4	1,149
Pulau Lekir (Malaysia)	2100	1.8	876
Suralaya (West Java)	3 × 600	1.6	891

Source: Dr. Ing. Nengah Sudja, *Menggugat Harga Jual Listrik Paiton I* (Jakarta: INFID, 2002), Table 6, p. 30.

Kuntoro, an astute commentator on Indonesia, summed it all up in our interview: "Since the fall of Suharto, Indonesia has found it difficult to have one policy on anything." Indeed, any investor in a large, politically sensitive project in the new Indonesian democracy could be confident that his arrangements would be revisited, revisited, and revisited.

Why Did Investors Take on Such a Politically Risky Project?

With hindsight, one wonders why foreign investors went ahead with Paiton I in the first place. Unlike ITT in 1967, in the 1990s Mission and similar investors were entering infrastructure sectors where they held no unique technologies that might protect them. And, as PLN advisor Sroka was later to put it, "The first rule of commerce is that if you are selling a commodity, you cannot afford to sell it to a buyer that cannot afford to pay."[86] It should have been clear at the outset that electricity prices would not provide PLN the funds to service all its power contracts. If pressed, managers might have said that the government would soon approve rate increases, but the record could hardly support such optimism.

It is possible that investors really did not understand the risks they were facing. Mission had no experience in the developing world, and, as we have said, managers in GE showed little interest in learning from their "ancient" history of investments in Third World infrastructure.[87] Still, managers did not have to look back far. Paiton I was not the first of the new wave of private infrastructure investments to end up in a dispute. That honor may belong to the 1993 dispute, mentioned earlier, over the deal that Japanese Kumagai Gumi had struck to build and operate the Bangkok second-stage expressway. Widely publicized, that conflict could have provided some warning.

Portfolio Explanation

Of course, managers may have known perfectly well that Paiton was risky, but viewed the project as part of a portfolio made up of many investments with large, uncorrelated risks but also high expected returns. Possibly. Mission's (Edison International) 1997 balance sheet showed common shareholders' equity of about $9 billion. Mission's investment in Paiton was reported as $490 million. Thus, it represented more than 5% of the consolidated company's equity.[88] This was a significant bet on its own for Mission. After negotiating Paiton I, however, Mission proceeded to develop projects in at least nine countries outside the United States by 2004. Paiton I did eventually belong to something of an international portfolio.

Incentives and Risk

Corporate incentive systems can play a role in how managers investigate or weigh risk. We have been told that Enron paid managers 10% of the net present value of the Dabhol (India) power renegotiations: half to the managers directly responsible and half to top managers. Even if the agreement collapsed in the future, a manager such as Rebecca Mark would keep her bonus. With this type of incentive, there is little reason for a manager to pay serious attention to risk. The likely result would be managers negotiating the best-looking deal possible, ignoring the risk, and collecting the bonus—and hoping they were in a different position by the time the deal collapsed.[89] As we said earlier, we do not know exactly how bonuses were calculated for managers who negotiated the original Paiton agreement. We were only assured by one Mission manager that they were "considerably smaller than what Enron paid." Another manager said that they were not deal based, like Enron's. Still, it is difficult to imagine that bonuses did not affect the negotiators' view of risk.

Moral Hazard

The new assurances encourage something for which economists have a rather odd name: moral hazard. This phenomenon accompanies almost any kind of insurance. If managers really believe that the new international property rights will secure their investments, they have little reason to worry much about risks. If unfortunate events occur, the "insured" investors will be compensated anyway. It is much like someone who decides to build in a flood zone under the assumption that government flood insurance will compensate him if his property is damaged. The risk of flood plays a much more minor role in his decision than it would without the insurance. We will soon see that new assurances for investors are fraught with this and other kinds of moral hazard that likely lead to perverse decisions.

The Times

Finally, one must remember the times. The returns expected of power plants in the Third World must have seemed quite extraordinary to American utilities in the 1990s. Yields on electric utility investments in the United States ran around 2% on assets and 10% on equity.[90] Investment money was cheap and plentiful, and managers were desperate for growth. Word of golden opportunities in the developing countries surely tempted otherwise cautious managers. Returns of 35% or so might reasonably lead even conservative managers to bet 5% of their equity.

Moreover, as competitors rushed in to grab the riches, any managers who hesitated faced another kind of risk: to their careers. If the newly popular investments turned out to be the bonanzas that they were made out to be and a manager had failed to join competitors, the hesitant manager might in the end look very bad indeed. On the other hand, if the projects failed after a manager had invested in them, he or she could always point out that no one could have known better because all the smart competitors had done the same thing. Thus, the bigger career danger was not investing in something that might turn out well. There is no doubt that this kind of bandwagon effect caused banks and investment funds to take on huge risks abroad. Almost certainly a similar phenomenon drove foreign investors in infrastructure.

The New International Property Rights

The decisions of infrastructure investors cannot be chalked up only to inexperience or ignorance, faulty incentives, the bandwagon effect, and portfolio management. Investors in Paiton and other infrastructure projects built walls of protections that appeared to ensure their property rights: that is, the security of their contracts. Paiton's owners had influential local partners with an interest in future profits. On top of that, they had guaranteed access to international arbitration, some political risk insurance, and a great deal of money from official institutions that would, most investors believed, ensure foreign government support in the event of trouble. Encouraging this kind of investment was exactly what the new international system of property rights was supposed to do.

Lulled by such guarantees, investors may have taken much too narrow a view of risk. In other words, there was indeed a moral hazard problem. As the CEO of a power project in Pakistan (HUBCO) explained, he felt there was no need for HUBCO investors to look at economic or political risk because "the project is guaranteed by a sovereign government; that government had never defaulted on an obligation; the World Bank was involved in designing, financing and guaranteeing the project; and there was demand from Wapda [the Pakistani power authority]."[91] But in the end the various "guarantees" guaranteed much less than some investors had supposed. For all, U.S. government support was helpful. Yet, in the end, Paiton's owners did not turn to arbitration when their contract was challenged. At the time, they wanted to remain in the international power business and in Indonesia. It is likely that they understood that U.S. government support was general and could be blamed on all investors. A bitter arbitration, however, would damage the owners' future business interests. In the next chapters, we will look at investors who decided differently, and turned to arbitration and insurance.

Coda

Maybe Edison Mission grasped the continuing vulnerability of their overseas projects. For whatever reason, at the end of 2004 the company sold its non-U.S. power investments to a partnership of Britain's International Power PLC (70%) and Japan's Mitsui (30%). The sale would include 13 power plants in nine countries, including Paiton I. Although Mission temporarily held onto investments in the Philippines, Thailand, and Turkey, the expectation was that they would also soon be transferred to this or another buyer.[92] The California-based Mission was retreating to its original market in the United States. In 2005, TransCanada, which had acquired GE shares in Paiton I in 1996, also drew back from its international plunge, selling its interest in Paiton I to subsidiaries of the Tokyo Electric Power Company.

Edgell, chief negotiator for Paiton, decided to stay with his new life in Singapore. With Mission no longer active in the region, he retired from the company in March 2005 to form a company of his own. His firm was engaged by the new owners of Paiton I to help move along the proposed Paiton III. In 2006, however, Edgell did move, to Atlanta, Georgia, to become Mirant's executive vice president and U.S. regional head. His new location was far from his Bali and Australian properties. Accordingly, his and Fena's 2850 m^2 Australian mansion went on the market for almost A\$ 20 million (about US\$ 15 million).

13

Karaha Bodas Company: Turning to Arbitration

One doesn't live a marriage by running to the divorce court to settle disputes.
—Stewart Macaulay[1]

Paiton I was only one of 27 Indonesian power agreements struck down by the Asian Currency Crisis. Unlike Paiton I, the owners of the Karaha Bodas geothermal power project decided to go to arbitration. The decision suggests a link between corporate strategy and how companies use the new international property rights. In the end, Mission did not draw on the new property rights as much as it could have, probably because using them might have terminated its business in Indonesia and perhaps even damaged its opportunities in other developing countries. Reputation seems to have mattered much less to at least two of Karaha Bodas's owners.

The cases in this and the next chapter illustrate serious problems associated with the new property rights. In particular, they reflect a very rigid view of contract, they can result in inappropriately large awards, and they are fraught with moral hazard. The story of this project also points out the frustrations investors encounter when host governments believe that the application of the new property rights is not fair to them.[2] As of summer 2006, eight years after the Asian Currency Crisis struck Indonesia, the struggle over this project was ongoing. Having failed thus far to collect the arbitration award, investors must have also wondered whether the new rights would serve their interests as they had anticipated.

The Partners

One of the two principal foreign investors in the Karaha Bodas Company (KBC) was New York City–based, privately held Caithness Energy. The company provides little information about itself. It had begun in mining and then turned to generating electricity from renewable energy sources, primarily in California and Nevada. The only public indication of its size we have discovered is the amount of power it controls: As of 2001, Caithness claimed more than 465 megawatts from geothermal projects, 160 megawatts from solar projects, 210 megawatts from wind projects, and 315 megawatts from gas-turbine projects. It reported an additional thousand megawatts of generation under development.[3] In other words, it was not a major player.[4] The Internet tells us that its CEO, James D. Bishop, was an avid sailor, and a graduate of Yale (class of 1956) and Harvard Business School's MBA program.[5] The insulting and eventually threatening reaction of one of the company's lawyers to our request for information discouraged us from directly approaching management.[6] We interviewed only a public relations firm hired by the company's lawyers, and it claimed to know little about the secretive Caithness.

In 1996, Florida Power & Light (FP&L) joined Caithness in the venture. FP&L was a public utility founded in 1925 out of the consolidation of properties once owned by American Power & Light, a former General Electric subsidiary. American Power had been active across Latin America in the early part of the twentieth century, but those ventures were long gone. FP&L had grown rapidly with the expansion of Florida's population; it was eventually to supply electricity to roughly half of Florida's customers and to expand within the United States. As far as we can determine, it had remained a U.S. producer until it decided to enter Asia with Caithness. FP&L politely declined our request for interviews.[7]

Karaha Bodas was not to be the only joint venture of Caithness and FP&L. They were partners in a generating facility in California, had committed to develop jointly geothermal projects in the Philippines,[8] had both been generous contributors to the campaign of California Governor Davis,[9] and held substantial management ties.[10]

For the Indonesian venture, the partners created a Cayman Islands company, called Karaha Bodas Company L.L.C. (KBC), in which FP&L and Caithness would each own 40.5%.[11] Presumably the location offered confidentiality and tax benefits.

KBC would include one more foreign partner: Tomen Corporation,[12] a Japanese company with diversified interests in Indonesia and elsewhere, would hold 9%. At about the same time as the KBC project was being negotiated, Tomen was negotiating a power project in the Philippines.

The balance of the power project was to be held by an Indonesian partner, PT Sumarah Daya Sakti, a rather mysterious firm. One Indonesian involved in the power negotiations described this partner to us as a "company of ladies and dentists" from Solo.[13] In fact, the dentists were the ladies—"dragon ladies," as an advisor called them. In a colorful article, the leading Indonesian news magazine described the predecessor company, PT Indo Marinda Abadi, as having been established by a group of wealthy doctors and career women in Solo, in 1988.[14] The same

Indonesian interviewee told us that several, if not all, members of the group had close ties to President Suharto's wife, who was also from Solo.

According to some sources, by 1990 Tantyo Sudharmono held the license for the Karaha Bodas site and had acquired control of what had become Sumarah.[15] Tantyo was the son of Sudharmono, Indonesian vice-president at the time. Sudharmono was not just any vice president.[16] He had earlier been state secretary, the longest serving ever. As such, he had administered "Team 10," which controlled all government procurement over a certain value[17] (see Box 7.4).

Further, Tantyo's brother-in-law, Loedito Setyawan Poerbowasi, was also an owner, according to some sources.[18] He was appointed as a director, signed the KBC contract, and received some $2.5 million in fees for "services," based on a percentage of the cost of the project.[19]

American managers' scant knowledge of the partner and the deal that had been struck add credibility to the belief that Karaha Bodas managers had not sought out the partner for its skills in geothermal power.[20] The Indonesian news magazine report on the deal may have had it right,[21] that the company was "simply named as partner upon arrival of foreign contractors." Of course, the fact that Tantyo held the site license provided a rather compelling reason to include this partner. Much like partners of other projects we have discussed, this one received a loan from other equity holders so that it could buy shares, incurring an obligation to repay only out of future dividends.[22]

The Agreements

Because Pertamina, Indonesia's national oil company, held rights to geothermal energy sources, producers had to operate as "contractors" to Pertamina. This was arranged under a Joint Operation Contract between Pertamina and Karaha Bodas. Another agreement, called an Energy Sales Contract, gave KBC the right to build, own, and operate power plants and transfer power to Pertamina, which then sold it to the state-owned power company, PLN. In the process, Pertamina captured 3% or 4% on sales plus rent for the land; moreover, the projects would revert to Pertamina at the end of the contracts. Pertamina seems also to have retained the right to acquire a 10% interest in the venture for 10% of geothermal expenditures above $12 million.

Otherwise, the financial terms of geothermal contracts were very similar to those that governed Paiton I: Tariffs for KBC's electricity were effectively in U.S. dollars, and they were "take or pay."[23] But investors did bear an additional risk: that the underexplored geothermal sources might not be adequate for the proposed plants.

Pertamina, sometimes called "a state within a state," was powerful, similar to state-owned firms elsewhere that had large positive cash flows. As a result, it had led negotiations of geothermal contracts. According to

a former head of PLN and several other commentators, Pertamina contracts involved more corruption than did other deals. One lawyer for the
Indonesians estimated that for each 100 megawatts of capacity about $1
million was demanded in "unofficial" payments; this, beyond free or loan
shares, was provided to local partners.[24]

The contracts for the development of this geothermal project in West
Java were signed December 2, 1994,[25] and called for payments from PLN
at 8.46 cents per kilowatt hour (cents/kwh) for the first 14 years, 6.58 cents
from years 15 to 22, and 5.64 cents from years 23 to 30. Debt financing was
expected from Credit Suisse First Boston (CSFB). Some owners were
covered under a $75 million private political risk insurance contract, a fact
that was to come out only quite late in the subsequent battle.

The agreements included a rather odd provision: "Within 3 months of
the effective date, COMPANY shall provide PLN a schedule reflecting
COMPANY's estimate of the times and amount of delivery of electricity to
PLN."[26] In other words, PLN committed to a price without a production
schedule. PLN had anticipated the first electricity by December 1996. But,
by August 1997, the plan was as follows: units 1 and 2, 110 megawatts, to
be ready in August 1998; units 3 and 4, 110 megawatts, in April 1999; units
5 and 6, 110 megawatts, mid-2000; and unit 7, 70 megawatts, mid-2001.

Crisis

With the Asian Currency Crisis, Karaha Bodas appeared in the first round
of postponed projects.[27] The company and Pertamina lobbied for reinstatement of the project. Efforts included a visit by at least one of the
American managers to President Suharto himself. In November, a new
decree seemed to reinstate the project,[28] but a list of suspensions issued in
January[29] again included the project. Lobbying efforts were renewed in
Indonesia and also in the United States. A Washington lobbying firm took
up the case, and letters were sent to Vice President Al Gore and various
senators requesting their intervention with the International Monetary
Fund (IMF) or the U.S. government.[30] Managers defended their investment by pointing out that no relatives of the Indonesian president were
involved; however, they failed to mention that the interests of relatives of a
former Indonesian *vice* president were.[31] After a Caithness manager was
later asked whether this was being "transparent," he answered a follow-up
question on the meaning of transparency: "What [transparency] means to
me is that business deals are negotiated by both parties for both parties'
best interest."[32]

Senator John Kerry dealt with the matter by writing the IMF on behalf
of the company.[33] Lobbying, however, did not reverse the government
decision. PLN confirmed the postponement on March 6, 1998, warning
the company that if it proceeded with construction it would be doing so at
its own risk.

When the project was put on hold, KBC was not close to completion.[34] It had, however, begun drilling to determine whether the geothermal resources were adequate. As a result of this work, on September 18, 1997, it had submitted a "Notice of Resource Confirmation" for 55 megawatts. On December 16, it issued a new notice for "probable estimated reserve" for 240 megawatts and stated its intent to develop 210 megawatts. In March or April 1998, the company submitted a revised program and budget.[35]

Deciding against Renegotiation

With no change in the official status of its project, on April 30, 1998, the company notified Pertamina and PLN that it was filing for arbitration in Geneva, the location specified in its agreements.

Why did KBC decide so quickly—within a month of the final list of postponements—to go to arbitration? Company managers did not provide explanations to us, so we can only speculate. Their lobbying efforts to restore the project suggest that, in the early stage of the crisis, FP&L and Caithness were still willing to go ahead with the investment under its original terms. Like our next case, however, managers seem to have decided against continuing once serious problems arose. As far as we can tell, they made no effort to explore what new terms might eventually be offered in a renegotiation. They must also have been discouraged by the fact that capital markets were not eager to supply funds for crisis-stricken Indonesia. Moreover, both major owners were, it seems, ready to retreat from the developing world. FP&L had had a power plant in Colombia, which eventually disappeared from the company's SEC filings. It had established a number of other affiliates in the Cayman Islands with names of Latin American countries. All, however, were listed as inactive. By 2002, neither company had any power plants at all outside the United States, according to their annual reports and Web sites.[36] In fact, FP&L was making public statements that could be read as suggesting that it had never made the mistake of venturing abroad.[37]

To be sure, in its public relations statements, KBC offers a somewhat different explanation as to why the company would not negotiate its differences with Pertamina: The company no longer trusted Pertamina because it had avoided its legal obligations.[38] The statement concludes: "Simply put, there is nothing to renegotiate." Nevertheless, the haste and the statements of Karaha Bodas's management at least suggest that owners might have had objectives that were different from the investors who chose to renegotiate and remain in Indonesia. For KBC's owners, collecting insurance or an arbitration award, we suspect, provided a decent alternative to a negotiated settlement at a time when their enthusiasm for developing country markets was probably already waning.

One must wonder whether the Japanese partner supported the legalistic approach that the majority partners were initiating. Although Tomen was having financial problems,[39] it was not withdrawing from the Third World. Its public statements in 2002 reported conventional power plants in the Philippines (opened, as planned, in 1997), Pakistan (also 1997), and Thailand (under construction). The aggressive behavior of Karaha Bodas seemed very un-Japanese. We will note later that it is exceedingly rare for Japanese investors to proceed to arbitration in disputes with host governments. Likely, Tomen's small minority position and its other problems meant it had little voice in the decisions.

Whatever tensions might have existed among the partners, the combative attitude of FP&L and Caithness did not endear them to foreign investors in other Indonesian power projects. In our interviews, one manager with another American-owned power company in Indonesia described Caithness as "nasty people." This manager was concerned that KBC was creating tensions that would hurt relations of his company with Indonesia.

Arbitration

Once KBC had decided against renegotiation, arbitration may have been an inevitable step for collecting political risk insurance. Because the coverage came from purely private insurers, Lloyd's, Indonesians were unaware of its existence and saw only a company that was insisting on arbitration.[40]

The basic idea of investor–state arbitration is simple: Each side chooses an arbitrator, and the two arbitrators or a neutral body then picks a third. The three listen to arguments and make a decision, which the conflicting parties have agreed in advance to accept, subject only to some very restrictive rules about review.

At the outset, the choice of arbitrators posed a problem in this case. The KBC side named Professor Piero Bernardini.[41] Believing that the cases against three different parties (the government, Pertamina, and PLN) should not be consolidated and unsure which of the three should designate an arbitrator, Indonesians failed to meet the rather short deadline imposed on them. As the terms of the contract allowed, the claimant asked the International Centre for the Settlement of Investment Disputes (ICSID) to appoint an arbitrator on behalf of the Indonesians. The ICSID named Professor Ahmed S. El Kosheri.[42] The two arbitrators then selected the third, Yves Derains[43] (France), as chair.

The government added to its stable of lawyers an arbitration specialist with Essex Court Chambers in London.[44] The eponymous Jakarta firm of Adnan Buyung Nasution ("Buyung"), a human rights activist once exiled for resisting Suharto's abuses, counseled PLN; and both this Indonesian firm and Cleary, Gottlieb, Steen & Hamilton worked for Pertamina.[45] KBC, or its owners, turned to Schiller & Flexner; Jones, Day, Reavis & Pogue; and Reed Smith LLP for counsel.[46]

In its revised claim, KBC asked for an award of its investment (claimed to be $96 million) and for future profits (projected at $512.5 million).

Because the owners could not produce a signed original "letter of comfort," in the first round of the arbitration the tribunal ruled that it had no jurisdiction over the government. The tribunal proceeded to dismiss several procedural objections entered by PLN and Pertamina, including that of improper consolidation of cases against PLN and Pertamina.

Indonesians argued that the KBC contract violated Indonesian law and was thus invalid; however, testimony by Robert Hornick, an American lawyer who had practiced in Indonesia some 20 years earlier, carried the day, convincing the arbitrators otherwise. They also claimed that KBC could not have raised the funds to go ahead with the project once the currency crisis had struck, and therefore they should not be awarded profits from a project that they could not have finished. KBC countered that FP&L would have supplied the funds itself; the arbitrators accepted this contention of a FP&L executive at face value, in the absence of requested documentation. A skeptic might wonder whether FP&L would, in the end, have put up large sums of money at a time when it appeared to be losing its enthusiasm for developing-country markets.

Indonesians also charged that the exploration wells should have cost about $32 million, but the company's books showed outlays of close to $100 million.[47] They argued that some of the expenditures were "wasteful" and that payments made to the Indonesian partner were "undocumented and unwarranted" and thus questionable. The tribunal concluded that even if some expenditures were wasteful, they were spent by the firm to accomplish its task and that payments to the local partner were not "questionable" because they were "openly declared." In short, payments that are public cannot be corrupt. We leave it to the reader to evaluate this argument.

For the June 2000 hearings in Paris, the company presented present value calculations from Richard Ruback, a Harvard Business School professor. In December, the panel issued a final ruling awarding the company $261 million.[48] Of the firm's claimed $94.6 million expenditures,[49] $1.6 was struck by the arbitrators. The sum of $150 million was for lost future profits, having been sharply reduced from the original claim by some poorly explained calculations.[50] Finally, the tribunal added interest and arbitration costs.

Even if we accept the conclusion that the events were tantamount to expropriation, we believe that basing the award on the sum of investment and some function of hypothetical future profits is simply wrong from an economic point of view. We find little excuse for the size or the underlying logic of this award (see Box 13.1).

Appeals

Indonesians fought back. Carolyn Lamm with the firm White & Case, a lawyer who later joined the Indonesian side, summed up the Indonesian claim: "An investor who doesn't actually build a power project, nor has

Box 13.1 Calculating Damage Awards

Lawyers disagree on how to calculate awards to an investor when a contract is breached or a project is expropriated.

In both the KBC and CalEnergy cases arbitral panels drew on a principle of Roman law and modern civil codes, *damnum emergens* and *lucrum cessans,* investment and profits. This may be appropriate for some trade cases, as it was originally applied, but its use for investment cases is debatable. If Indonesia entered a contract to buy a customized airplane from Boeing, for example, and then suddenly cancelled it, Boeing might be granted the "investment" made thus far to build the plane (more accurately, costs incurred) and anticipated profits. The profits would have been earned over a short period, could be forecast with some degree of confidence, and might have been genuinely foregone.[a] But even in this case, Boeing would be expected to mitigate damages by seeking another customer for the airplane; its award would be reduced by its likely recovery.

To understand why the same principle should not be applied to long-term investments such as the power arrangements, consider a parallel example: an individual saver whose bank account is covered by deposit insurance. Say the saver's bank fails, and deposit insurance pays both the amount of the deposit and foregone interest for 30 years into the future. The award leaves the saver better off if the bank fails than if it does not, because the saver can now "invest" the principal and the compensation for foregone interest in another bank and earn interest again. Of course, for good reason the U.S. Federal Depository Insurance Corporation does not pay future interest when a bank fails.[b]

In describing the KBC award, an angry Indonesian provided a more colorful analogy:

> Driving down a very bumpy road you unexpectedly hit a chicken and it is killed. The farmer comes out and you apologize and offer to pay him for the chicken. But he says the chicken might have lived for 5 or 6 years, could have laid an egg every day, half of which could have become other chickens which could have laid more eggs and so on. So he wants a million dollars compensation.[c]

Presumably such an award would encourage a wise farmer to spread feed corn across a nearby highway.

Excess awards in investment disputes can have similarly serious implications. First, the host country has to pay more than it should. Moreover, the expectation of such awards would create incentives for inappropriate corporate behavior. Large awards are likely to lead firms to resist renegotiation and mediation.[d] Indeed, why should investors agree to a new deal, if they

(continued)

Box 13.1 (continued)

could recapture their investment plus future profit without risk and work? A clever investor would even seek projects with the greatest political risk, and perhaps behave in ways that increase the likelihood of government takeover. Finally and perhaps most importantly, excessive awards discourage governments from ending contracts when such action is economically efficient or from introducing desirable regulations.[e]

[a]In the CalEnergy cases described in the next chapter, the arbitrators modified the handling of future profits by drawing on the concept of "abuse of rights," reasonably arguing that it "would be intolerable in the present case to uphold claims for lost profits from investment not yet incurred . . . as though the claimant had an unfettered right to create ever-increasing losses for the State of Indonesia (and its people) by generating energy without any regard to whether or not PLN had any use for it. . . ." The abuse of rights doctrine was not applied in the KBC case, as far as we can tell.

[b]For arguments that the investor is obligated to put the returned investment back to use, see Derek Bowett, "Claims between States and Private Entities: The Twilight Zone of International Law," *Catholic University Law Review,* 1986, 35, pp. 929, 931–932. The argument is picked up in Thomas R. Stauffer, "Valuation of Assets in International Takings," *Energy Law Journal,* 1996, 17, pp. 459–488, as follows: "Why, therefore, should the private claimant expect the tribunal to award him loss of profits under the terminated contract for the same period during which the same capital is earning a second set of profits? On the assumption that he has put his returned capital to good use, the claimant, in effect, is claiming a double recovery for loss of profits. Such a claim seems both illogical and unethical."

[c]The chicken story appeared in an unpublished May 13, 2003, version of "Questioning the Electricity Price of Paiton I," given to us by Nengah Sudja.

[d]The issues of principles and calculation (for example the discount rate) are complex. For more on the subject, see Louis T. Wells, "Double Dipping in Arbitration Awards? An Economist Questions Damages Awarded Karaha Bodas Company in Indonesia," *Arbitration International,* 2003, 19, pp. 471–481. We have yet to discover a really thorough, detailed treatment of these issues in a law journal.

[e]"Notice how careful the law must be not to exceed compensatory damages if it doesn't want to deter efficient breaches." Richard A. Posner, *Economic Analysis of Law,* 3rd ed. (Boston: Little, Brown, 1986), p. 108.

lost significant amounts of money on the project shouldn't win an award for 30 years of damage rendered by an improperly constituted tribunal, in an improperly consolidated proceeding, without regard to Indonesian law (the applicable law specified in the contract) and following a denial of due process."[51]

Under the governing 1958 New York Convention, it seems that a party to arbitration can seek annulment of an award in the country where the arbitration was held, or under the laws of which the arbitration was held.[52] Facing a tight schedule and believing that it lacked resources to undertake multiple routes simultaneously, Pertamina's lawyers sought redress in Swiss courts.[53]

The Swiss refused to hear the case, on a technical glitch. Indonesia had to transfer 100,000 Swiss francs to the court by a certain date. Cleary Gottlieb was to transfer funds out of amounts it was holding, but inexplicably the funds were not credited to the court's account until after the deadline. Thus, the court would not hear Pertamina's application.[54]

Enter Private Insurance

From here, the story of Karaha Bodas takes a different path from our next case. The existence of $75 million of political risk coverage with Lloyd's did not come out in the arbitration.[55] At some point, Karaha Bodas's owners had collected on the insurance, but found it attractive to continue to chase the much larger award.

As KBC's owners have not granted interviews, we can only speculate on the reasons for and even some of the details of the subsequent events. Because the private insurance group had no clout to force the Indonesian government to reimburse them, one can imagine that they saw little point in taking over the project and its claims under rights they likely had under the policy. The best bet for the insurance group must have been to let KBC pursue the entire arbitration award in exchange for a commitment that KBC's owners would repay the $75 million to the insurance company if they collected. As long as the investors thought the odds of collecting more than $75 million were sufficiently high to justify their legal expenses, and as long as they were not interested in future business with Indonesia, they must have found it reasonable to proceed down the collection route, especially as the award was against Pertamina as well as PLN. Pertamina had valuable assets abroad.

Karaha Bodas turned to the collection task, pursuing Pertamina's overseas assets. It filed to seize Pertamina assets in Hong Kong, Singapore, Canada, and the United States. The United States looked especially promising because Pertamina received payments from U.S. oil companies through its New York office. With government funds in Pertamina's bank accounts at risk, the Ministry of Finance again called on White & Case, its favorite foreign law firm. Any conflicts of interest probably mattered little; the ministry wanted its long-trusted lawyers on the case.

The collection story is a long and tedious one, most of which is available in court documents. We will provide only a brief summary, but first we describe some efforts to settle out of court.

Negotiation of the Unwilling?

As the legal web grew more complex, some Indonesians did not give up hope that the matter could be settled through negotiation. However, Indonesians and at least some of their advisors showed little understanding of the project's owners.

In an effort to settle, PLN engaged a consulting firm in Jakarta, PT Harvest International Indonesia, belonging to Harvey Goldstein. Goldstein was another colorful character, who had settled in Indonesia some 30 years earlier. An American with a strong Bronx accent, he was the subject of many stories about his history, some of them likely to be urban myths. He was said to have dealt in military weapons in the 1970s; others said that he had come to Indonesia as a Mossad agent for Israel; still another said that he had convinced some ministers that he was a CIA agent. Whatever the truth, he had settled in Jakarta to build a consulting firm that had worked successfully with a number of American investors;[56] some others viewed him with great skepticism.[57]

A PLN official told us that Goldstein collected 1 billion rupiah from PLN for the mediation task and sent an emissary to Florida to meet with FP&L to discuss possibilities, including asking for more fees for himself.[58] Not surprisingly, FP&L flatly rejected any dealings with him. Interestingly, Caithness's lawyer denies that this mediation effort even took place.[59] If the effort is not fiction, Goldstein may have been a poor choice for the task, but it is unlikely that the KBC owners would have dealt more kindly with another mediator.

Trying to revive the project, in March 2002, the Indonesian president issued decrees that would allow the project to proceed, anticipating new negotiations with the project's original owners. In the summer of 2002, the government offered the company an option to continue with the project or hand it over to another investor, who would then settle with Karaha Bodas.[60] In January 2003, Dorodjatun Kuntjoro-Jakti, the economic coordinating minister, wrote U.S. Secretary of State Powell to express an interest in having him facilitate a settlement. In June 2003, Ainun Na'im, the senior vice president and chief financial officer for Pertamina, still had hopes: "KBC has the opportunity to settle the case by actually completing the project and making true on its commitment to producing electricity for the country."[61] As far as we can determine, neither of the principal investors expressed any interest at all in continuing with the power plant. Why should they, when they could collect the investment made thus far and a substantial part of future profits without having to build and operate the facility?

The U.S. embassy acted as if it was equally naïve with respect to prospects for negotiation. Several times it tried to get the disputing parties together. As late as August 2002 embassy officials asked the Indonesians to put a proposal on paper for settlement. KBC, they added, had hesitated to put anything in writing.[62] After rejecting an Indonesian request that the government intervene in U.S. court hearings (see later), the U.S. government again offered to help facilitate a settlement.[63] Indonesia accepted. But none of these efforts could go anywhere without the participation of both sides, and the investors still showed no interest.

Where the Indonesian partner stood in all this is confusing. In some of the projects, such as Paiton I, local partners more or less disappeared from the action after Suharto fell. Not quite so with KBC's partner, Sumarah. Loedito, the son-in-law of the former vice president, is reported as eventually writing the minister of mines and energy that the company will "reject all business affiliations that would cause losses to the government of Indonesia."[64] One might interpret this as saying he would even turn down any share from the arbitration award. But soon Mariati Murman Heliarto, one of the dentist founders, filed a complaint. She would not talk with reporters from *Tempo* magazine, but it seemed she was not so willing to give up her share of, potentially, tens of millions of dollars. Unlike the very wealthy children of the president, the dentists and some other participants in Sumarah probably saw the possible compensation as significant.

Collection Efforts

Karaha Bodas filed in a federal court in Texas to seize Pertamina assets, but Indonesians fought back. International rules do allow enforcement of an arbitration to be contested in a national court where collection is being pursued, but the grounds for denying enforcement are very narrow: One is that the award is contrary to public policy.[65] Pertamina argued that making a poor country pay such an award, especially when it was ordered to change the contract by its government and ultimately by the IMF, was contrary to U.S. public policy. Nevertheless, on November 30, 2001, the U.S. District Court of Houston ordered enforcement of the award.

Pertamina turned to the Indonesian courts, filing suit on March 14, 2002, in the Jakarta Central District Court asking that the arbitration award be annulled and requesting that the company be prevented from enforcement efforts anywhere. Filing this case was controversial. First among the opponents, we have been told, was the ministerial team overseeing the renegotiations of the power agreements. But the team's influence over rich and powerful Pertamina did not match its control over PLN. The second opponent was the Texas court, which ordered Pertamina to withdraw its Jakarta case. When Pertamina failed to do so, the Texas court found Pertamina in contempt. On Pertamina's appeal, the U.S. Court of Appeals for the Fifth Circuit overruled the Texas court and on June 19, 2003, lifted the injunction against Pertamina's Jakarta case.[66] The appeals court had turned to the New York Convention that governed international arbitration and affirmed the right of a party to arbitration to use the courts to defend itself against flawed arbitration decisions. Further, it rejected the right of one country's courts to prohibit action in another country's courts.

The Jakarta court affirmed its jurisdiction, and on August 27, 2002, vacated the decision of the arbitration panel.[67] The court ordered KBC not to take action to enforce the judgment and imposed a fine of $500,000 per day for any violation. Pertamina had stood in contempt of the U.S. court by fighting the case; now KBC's owners would be in contempt of the Jakarta court if they tried to collect. The injunction, however, had little bite; KBC's foreign owners presumably had no intention of setting foot ever again on Indonesian soil.

In December 2003, the Fifth Circuit U.S. Court of Appeals said that Indonesia "did not have primary jurisdiction" to set aside the award, upholding the Texas federal court's decision to enforce the arbitration decision.[68] In rejecting the view of several experts that the Convention granted Indonesia primary jurisdiction because its law governed the arbitration, the court explained: "Under the New York Convention, the parties' arbitration agreement, and this record, Switzerland had primary jurisdiction over the Award."[69] In other words, U.S. courts could not prohibit Pertamina from pursuing a foreign case, but they would not honor the foreign court's decision.

KBC had already (in February 2002) served restraining orders on New York bank accounts of Pertamina. The Indonesian government responded that the funds belonged to the government, not Pertamina. In its own defense, Pertamina turned to its argument that the contracts were canceled at the insistence of the IMF, saying that Pertamina had been unable to perform under the contract because of *force majeure* from outside the country. This position found some support even in KBC's own statement: "As part of an IMF recommendation for the stabilization of the Indonesian economy, former President Suharto issued three Presidential Decrees that ended with the suspension of this project."[70] Pertamina's lawyers called on the IMF to testify on its role in the postponement, or at least to prepare an *amicus* brief. To convince the IMF to support them, Indonesians approached Dono Iskandar Djojosubroto, their IMF representative, for assistance, but he declined to intervene, and the IMF refused to appear, claiming that the suspensions were the government's decision. This is no doubt technically true; the country could have decided against the IMF demand, but that decision might have been very, very costly.[71]

Accusing the IMF of "washing its hands of the problem," Pertamina's angry president sought authorization from the Indonesian parliament for the government to sue the IMF for "not having the goodwill to help the country recover from the crisis."[72] This turned out to be a dead end.

The U.S. District Court in New York allowed the claimants to attach no more than 5% of Pertamina's accounts, agreeing that the government had a property interest in the remainder.[73] But even 5% would, over a short time, add up to the amount of the claim, given the large oil proceeds that passed through Pertamina's bank accounts. Less successfully, KBC sought to seize payments owed Pertamina by its oil-producing partners, subsidiaries of Chevron Texaco, BP, and Exxon Mobil.[74]

The Indonesians tried another defense. In December 2002, their embassy in Washington asked the U.S. government to intervene on Indonesia's behalf, seeking a statement of national interest like the one that had been prepared by the U.S. government in a case brought in U.S. court by Aceh villagers against Exxon Mobil. The KBC dispute, a part of the argument would go, is negatively affecting bilateral relations between the

United States and Indonesia. Apparently, the U.S. government showed moderate interest in another part of the argument: that as a result of the process the U.S. courts were ordering money held that belonged to the Indonesian government. The United States government reportedly feared a precedent that might allow other countries to seize its funds abroad. But in the end the effort came to naught. The request was not acted on, and the parties were urged to seek a settlement, a hopeless plea.

Pertamina tried to line up allies. By 2003, former ambassador Gelbard had gone to work for White & Case to help the Indonesian defense. This, the reader will remember, was the ambassador who was so vociferously supportive of U.S. companies while he served in his ambassadorial role.[75] Further, in 2003 Pertamina hired former senator Bob Dole,[76] widely known as a Republican presidential candidate and television promoter of Viagra, to lobby for its side. He was joined by Jonathan Winer, counsel to Senator Kerry, who, the reader will remember, had written the IMF in support of Karaha Bodas.[77] Dole's efforts in Washington emphasized the value of good relations with Indonesia in the war on terror. In other words, Pertamina and its advisors had now caught on to the possibility that U.S. foreign policy could be turned back from its promotion of narrow commercial interests since the fall of international communism to a new concern about new national interests, Islamic fundamentalist terror attacks.

While KBC was trying to seize Pertamina's accounts in the United States, its cases in Canada, Hong Kong, and Singapore aimed at seizing the oil company's ships and other assets.[78] KBC's efforts to collect the award elsewhere had brought to light the political risk insurance.[79] Upon this discovery, Pertamina complained to the New Orleans 5th Circuit Appeals Court that it had not been provided with this information at the beginning. Further, it reported that it had not been allowed to conduct discovery earlier to challenge the company claim that FP&L would have funded the rest of the project itself in the absence of outside finance. It added that the arbitral award was inconsistent with Indonesian law. But in March 2004, the court rejected Pertamina's arguments.[80]

False Conclusion

Early summer of 2004 appeared to mark the end of Pertamina's long battle. After a few victories and many defeats in various courts, significant Indonesian assets had been frozen in New York.[81] Indonesia's supreme court overturned the Jakarta court's annulment of the arbitration award.[82] Pertamina announced that it would pay the claim, and government officials seemed to confirm the decision. But in August Pertamina reversed itself and stated that it would not and could not pay.[83] A new police investigation in Jakarta was supposedly uncovering evidence that would show that KBC had bribed Pertamina officials to inflate values of investments recorded on its books.[84] Further, Indonesian tax authorities claimed taxes on any award actually paid.[85] The son-in-law of the former

Indonesian vice president was arrested (and soon released, after paying 1.2 billion rupiah).[86] Warrants were issued for the arrest of a Canadian and an American executive.

To add to complications, participants in the local Indonesian partner firm, Sumarah, were leveling charges and counter-charges at each other. The former director, Mariati Murman Heliarto, had earlier filed a criminal complaint against her successor, Loedito. Having received no response from the Indonesian police, she entered a complaint in the South Jakarta court in January 2004. In an understated report on the complaint, a newspaper article said that "the situation points out that the KBC matter is indeed laden with problems and intrigue."[87]

In early 2005, Pertamina's U.S. counsel, Cleary Gottlieb, withdrew from the case, claiming, to a U.S. court, that Pertamina had not paid them. Another lawyer on the Indonesian side, however, told us that Cleary Gottlieb had been paid about $8.2 million dollars, but another $3 million or so was indeed outstanding from still unverified bills. At this point, the Indonesian law firm Karim Syah took up coordination of the case and brought in Lovell's, a UK-based firm with New York offices to replace Cleary Gottlieb.

With optimism hardly warranted by experience, Indonesians again announced their intention to negotiate a settlement.[88] To an outsider, FP&L and Caithness Energy seemed to have made their position perfectly clear: They wanted all the award money, not a power project. Whether evidence of corruption could be produced and whether it would shake the owners' determination remained to be seen. As we completed this book, more than eight years after the Asian Currency Crisis had struck Indonesia, the battle over Karaha Bodas continued.

Conclusions

An Alternative Solution

A little speculation: If the Indonesians had known of the insurance at the outset, one can imagine that this case might have gone differently. The Indosat buyout suggests a possibility. Depending on the details of the insurance contract, if Indonesians had put before the insurers an offer for the amount of the claim that they would pay out—$75 million—the insurers might have been tempted to accept, take over the project, and not pursue more money. They would have certain and immediate reimbursement. Indonesians would have had to give up $75 million, but they could have avoided the eventual $261 million judgment. On the other hand, this course of action would have required a decision-making ability that Indonesians probably could not have mustered during that time of transition, even if they had known of the insurance.

It is important to remember that after the Suharto government collapsed no one had the authority to offer a settlement. Moreover, such a decision would also have run up against Indonesians' deep fear of precedent. If the government had made an offer to buy the company in this case, other independent power producers might have sought the same exit from their disputes, even if they had no insurance. This would have been budget breaking, at a time when the IMF was imposing tight constraints on spending. And it is doubtful that the World Bank or the IMF would have funded a broad program of buyouts. Buying up claims of private investors with state money is not what privatization was supposed to be about.

Inaction may also have resulted from common managerial behavior. Managers, whether public or private, often turn over a difficult issue to a court or other legal processes to avoid making a bold decision for which they might later be criticized. In the case of a government official, fear of parliament or the press may govern; for business managers, fear of stockholder, director, or lender reactions may dominate. Suharto, for all his faults, could have made such a decision; Habibie possibly might have done so; but Gus Dur, and later Megawati, were not secure enough to act boldly.

Finally, history offered little help to Indonesians. Officials involved in the power renegotiations knew nothing about the old ITT/Indosat experience. Lessons are not easily passed down within large organizations, government or business. But the pervasive secrecy in the Suharto regime made quite sure that younger officials inherited few lessons from past events.[89] Even in 2005 observers wondered whether Indonesians had really learned from their experiences with electric power; some astute commentators feared they were about to make mistakes similar to those of the mid-1990s.

Business Costs

The potential rewards to KBC investors have come with a cost. It is hard to imagine that either Caithness or FP&L has any future prospects for business in Indonesia. Reflecting the tensions over the case, a 2004 article in a leading Indonesian newspaper ended with "The nation and the people do not want to be lied to by a rotten company such as KBC."[90] But the investors appeared to have no interest in future business in Indonesia or the rest of the developing world, and presumably the managers can find alternatives to Bali's beaches for their recreation. Arbitration and insurance provided a potentially profitable exit. If the owners end up collecting the full arbitral award, they will surely view the returns as very satisfactory indeed.

Arbitration

Arbitration grew in importance as a tool for settling disputes within the United States for several reasons. It eliminates the need for disputants to wait in a queue behind many other claimants for a public court's time. Transcripts do not go on the public record. The process may be less expensive than alternatives. And, unlike judges and juries, arbitrators can be selected by the parties for their legal or technical expertise. Moreover, contractual arbitration provisions and national law combine to make decisions binding and enforceable.

On the international side, however, investor–state arbitration arose for somewhat different reasons. There was no mutually acceptable alternative that would relieve foreign investors of the fear that they would be treated unfairly in local courts; host governments were spared the ignominy of appearing in the investor's home courts.

Although arbitration is an ancient method of settling disputes, its use for problems between investors and host governments has a short history. In the early part of the twentieth century, home governments occasionally arbitrated on behalf of their investors, and there were a few private–state investment arbitrations in the interwar period. But arbitration would remain rare until an enforcement mechanism and rules were created. Entering in force in 1959, the New York Convention[91] eventually filled the gap on enforcement by committing members to honor arbitrators' awards. As mentioned in Chapter 4, in 1965 the World Bank had provided a set of rules, commitment to honoring decisions, and increased legitimacy for investor–state arbitration with the creation of the International Convention for the Settlement of Investment Disputes and then the International Centre for the Settlement of Investment Disputes (ICSID).[92] The basis of the modern system was completed when, in 1976, the United Nations Commission on International Trade Law (UNCITRAL) adopted its rules for the "settlement of dispute arising from international commercial relations" and, in 1985, its Model Law on International Commercial Arbitration.

Slow expansion of membership in the new conventions—the United States did not join the New York Convention until the 1970s—gradually led to a state-sanctioned private justice system, one that had become substantially developed by the time of the KBC and CalEnergy (see Chapter 14) cases.

Until the 1990s, virtually all state–host government arbitrations arose out of provisions in investment contracts themselves, like those in the Indonesian power agreements. Change came in 1990 when an arbitration was brought before the ICSID on the basis of a bilateral investment treaty (BIT). By 2005, most of the more than 2,000 BITs called for arbitration to settle disputes between investors and host governments. Regional economic agreements, such as the North American Free Trade Agreement (NAFTA) and the Energy Charter Treaty, have granted similar rights to investors.[93] By providing arbitration as an option to huge numbers of investors, treaties have greatly expanded access to the dispute settlement tool.[94]

Arbitrations of investment disputes multiplied rapidly in the 1990s. The ICSID received its first case in 1972; between 1972 and 1982, only 10 cases were registered. The next decade saw 18, still hardly a booming business. By the end of 1996, more or less when the Indonesian power plants were negotiated, the ICSID had seen only 36 cases in its entire history. However, by 2004, the ICSID had 71 cases pending, all registered in 1997 or later.[95] Of these, at least 35 involved infrastructure investments.[96] Although the ICSID figures illustrate the growth in investor–state arbitration, they do not come close to providing a full count of such arbitrations because many—like KBC's—were conducted outside the ICSID registry. Estimates of arbitrations based on BITs alone run around 160 as of 2004.[97]

On the other hand, investor–host government arbitration has not attained the goals of domestic arbitration. An Argentine award in 2005 reached some 140 pages of legal and financial argument, with 218 citations and references.[98] A seemingly simple process has become a highly legalistic, complex domain of a few specialist lawyers, and it is extremely expensive. Moreover, the rules are not crystal clear, as this case and the next story show.

In the end, the arbitration award in the KBC case, based on a rigid interpretation of contract, weakened Indonesian confidence in the new property rights system. For Indonesians, the first and most important issue was whether the contract should have been rigidly upheld, given the circumstances under which it was negotiated, its relation to authorizing decrees and laws, and the economic conditions by the time of dispute. Arbitration, as conceived today, does not readily address these kinds of fundamental questions. Second, the size of the award was unexpected and surely questionable. Third, Indonesians believed that the arbitration process was flawed in this case and in the next. Similar problems have begun to shake the confidence of other host countries in the system.

In a summary of the KBC story, an article in the *American Lawyer* says that investment lawyers agree that "in the long run, honoring contracts and treaties is the only way to bring lights to places like West Java."[99] George Munoz, president of OPIC, was quoted earlier as saying that "contracts must be honored." Nevertheless, we, along with many others, believe that there can be compelling reasons for not honoring certain contracts. When a contract is broken for good reason, there ought indeed to be fair and reasonable compensation to the aggrieved party. The remedies ordered by the KBC tribunal appear to us not to meet those criteria. Excessive awards not only impose direct costs on host countries, but they also can lead to perverse behavior by investors, discouraging renegotiations that might lead to assets being put to productive use. If such awards become common, they will encourage corporations to seek out risky investments and even to encourage governments to breach contracts. In sum, they pose moral hazards similar to those that often accompany other kinds of insurance coverage.

We will return in the final chapter to the implications of the current approach to "privatizing justice,"[100] arguing that investor–government arbitration often fails to settle disputes satisfactorily. Several host countries are rebelling against what seemed to be a promising tool, and arbitration's future is in question. It need not be so. We will suggest changes to alleviate some of the problems evident in this and the next story.

14

CalEnergy: Claiming Official Political Risk Insurance

[We] got a ruling against those bozos.
—Former in-house counsel for CalEnergy

This chapter examines another foreign investor that chose not to renegotiate. Although the investor proceeded to arbitration ahead of the Karaha Bodas Company (KBC), the driving force appears to have been its insurance from the U.S. government agency the Overseas Private Investment Corporation (OPIC). Like KBC's owners, this investor showed no interest in maintaining business prospects in Indonesia or elsewhere in the developing world.

U.S. intervention was particularly strong in this case and may have contributed to deteriorating relations with Indonesia at a time when cooperation between the two countries was of growing importance in the battle against radical Islamic terrorism.

The disputes in this and the previous chapter left parties bitter and angry. In this case, one result was elaborated stories of events; we were not always sure we (or the arbitrators) could sort truth from fiction.

CalEnergy

CalEnergy had been founded in 1971 as a consulting and service company for developers of geothermal power in North America. When, in the late 1970s, power deregulation opened opportunities in generation, the company acquired a U.S. geothermal project; but by 1990 the company's revenues had yet to reach the $100 million mark. Dramatic changes began in 1991 with the arrival of an aggressive chief executive, David Sokol. As a part of the new growth strategy, the company acquired Magma, another geothermal producer, and moved company headquarters from California to Nebraska. As expanding into Asia seemed to offer a golden opportunity for further growth, Indonesia and the Philippines attracted corporate interest.[1] With its moves into Southeast Asia, CalEnergy was jumping from its U.S. home into environments radically different from those where it had previous experience, and it brought along no cautious partner like General Electric.

We are not sure how CalEnergy made its initial contacts in Indonesia. One source vaguely states that "the introduction...was made through high level political lobbying."[2] An advisor to the Indonesians told us an independent promoter, based in California, sold CalEnergy on a project he had come up with.[3] It does appear that Donald M. O'Shei,[4] a retired brigadier general and West Point graduate, championed Indonesian and Philippine projects inside the company. Indonesian officials and their advisors described him to us as rude, loud spoken, prone to making disparaging comments about Indonesians, and eager to spend money in any way that might make things happen quickly. We never met him.[5]

The November 1994 visit of U.S. President Clinton to Indonesia saw the formal signing of arrangements committing CalEnergy's special-purpose Bermuda subsidiaries to develop geothermal steam fields and associated power plants at Dieng and Patuha, on Java, and at Bedugul on next-door Bali.[6] The final contracts were signed later, in December, marking the visit of U.S., Commerce Secretary Ron Brown.[7]

Two facts are essential in understanding CalEnergy's later decisions. First, the parent company eventually changed hands and revised its views about opportunities in emerging markets. When problems began to emerge, it followed the path of a number of other 1990s investors in infrastructure and retreated from Indonesia and other Third World projects. Second, the company carried substantial political risk insurance with the U.S. government's OPIC. This, it would turn out, covered some of the cost to the company of reversing its international strategy.

Dieng

The original plan was that the Dieng geothermal project would be owned by PLN and Pertamina. When the Asian Development Bank refused to provide financing, Indonesians turned to the private sector.[8]

Dieng would be built in stages. According to the Energy Sales Contract, the first unit would produce 20 megawatts and be ready 24 months after the effective date of the agreement; a second unit of 55 megawatts, at 36 months; 20 megawatts, at 54 months; 55 watts, at 66 months; 110 megawatts, at 84 months; and 140 megawatts, at 102 months.[9] Electricity was to be sold to PLN for 7.66 cents for the first 14 years; 5.97 cents from years 15 to 22; and 5.13 cents until the thirtieth year. The project would be financed

75% by borrowing, from Credit Suisse First Boston (CSFB), ABN, AMRD, BNS, Paribas, and Sakura Bank.

CalEnergy turned to, or was possibly assigned, influential partners.[10] PT Himpurna Enersindo Abado (PT HEA), a subsidiary of an association of retired Indonesian military officers, would hold 10% of the newly created Himpurna California Energy Ltd. (HCE). Ltd.[11] President Suharto was, of course, a general. Having been involved in a coup, he knew a great deal about them, and was careful to make sure that the retired officers remained happy—Himpurna was one of the vehicles for conveying happiness. In the words of an Indonesian business publication, "Old soldiers in Indonesia neither die nor fade away: they do business. Some do it as a matter of self-preservation, others for a little more."[12]

No one claimed to us that Himpurna had business skills that made it an attractive partner in the energy business. In fact, a former CalEnergy lawyer said that meeting with Himpurna was "like meeting with your grandfather." Among its several investments, near the Dieng site the partner had a small plant making bricks or fertilizer or processing mushrooms, depending on who told us.[13] Whatever the plant did, its skills were unlikely to be of use for tapping underground steam and generating electricity.

Himpurna's equity was "bought" with the proceeds of a loan provided by the foreign investor. In other words, it was similar to Paiton's arrangement with its local partner. Moreover, it seems that the company began paying the local partner $5,000 per month in dividends even before the project had been built.[14] That was, to say the least, a bit odd.

CalEnergy probably had little to fear from the U.S. Foreign Corrupt Practices Act. Although accommodating the government's desires, CalEnergy was not providing shares to an official or even to an official's relative. The U.S. Justice Department would not consider such a transaction to be a violation of the Act, even if the shares were in effect given away and there were no apparent business skills or physical assets acquired in return. This is what is; the reader can decide what "ought to be."

Patuha

CalEnergy's second geothermal project, Patuha, would produce a maximum of 400 megawatts and also cost about $1 billion.[15] It would also be staged, with capacity increasing in five steps over an 84 month period. Electricity would be sold for 7.26 cents per kilowatt hour (cents/kwh) for the first 15 years; 5.63 cents for years 15 to 22; and thereafter 4.82 cents. The first stage[16] was to cost $95 million, and subsequent stages $284 million. Loans, for 75% of the cost, would come from the same sources as Dieng's.

This project involved a different partner: at the outset, PT Enerindo Supra Abadi (PT ESA), an affiliate of an Indonesian engineering company.

The firm's president, Fadel Mohammad, was an executive of the ruling Golkar party.[17] PT ESA would receive 10% of the equity in Patuha Power Ltd. for "project development services" and an option to buy an additional 20% for cash. CalEnergy affiliates would hold the balance.

We were told[18] that Sudjana, upon becoming minister of mines and energy, insisted that the locally held shares be sold to Mahaka Energy, also an engineering company, rather than remain with the previous minister's choice. The books for the power project later showed an $8 million consulting fee, which Indonesia's lawyers and financial advisors thought was someone's bribe. A former CalEnergy lawyer, however, assured us that the sum was for a loan to Mahaka, something he viewed as quite different from a bribe. Mahaka's engineering skills may have been subordinate to the fact that the company was run by Muhamad Lutfi, the son-in-law of Hartarto, the powerful coordinating minister for development supervision and state administrative reform.

Lutfi turned out to be useful for both Patuha and Dieng. CSFB, the project's lead financier, said that a letter of comfort, similar to that covering Paiton I, would help in the financing. In April 1996, more than a year after the contracts had been signed, Lutfi went first to the minister of justice to seek letters for both Dieng and Patuha, and perhaps a third project, Bedugul. He was sent on to the minister of finance, then Mar'ie Muhamad, who strongly resisted. Lutfi finally summoned enough pressure to get what he wanted. Similar to Mission, CalEnergy reported the letter in its SEC 10-K as "a support letter from the Republic of Indonesia."[19] There was no mention of guarantee, but CalEnergy's description would undergo radical metamorphoses later. Obtaining the letter was only the beginning of the usefulness of the Hartarto tie.

Bedugul

CalEnergy's third project, Bedugul, plays no major role in our story.[20] But this geothermal facility also had an influential partner, PT Pandanwangi Sekartaji, a member of a business group owned by Suharto's eldest son, Sigit Hardjojudanto.

Crisis

On September 24, 1997, CalEnergy confidently announced that its investments should not be affected by the first presidential decree following the currency crisis.[21] Nevertheless, in the fourth quarter of 1997 the company took a one-time charge of $87 million, "[r]epresenting an asset valuation impairment relating to its assets in Indonesia."[22] In plain English, it was writing off investments, in spite of its outward confidence. In January, the final presidential decree confirmed that the first three units of the Dieng project were "continued," and the fourth was "suspended"; the first unit of

Patuha, where construction had not yet begun, was "under review," and subsequent ones were "postponed."

The write-off was not a signal that CalEnergy was surrendering. The company rapidly mobilized political support in the United States. In January, congressmen Jon Christensen and Doug Bereuter (both Republican, Nebraska, where the company was now headquartered) sent a letter to three ministers and the heads of the national planning agency, PLN, and Pertamina to "urge you in the strongest possible terms to remove CalEnergy's geothermal projects at Patuha and Dieng from the 'Review' and 'Postponed' lists established by Presidential Decree No. 39." The letter claimed that the projects had been "erroneously"[23] included in the delayed projects, they had been "negotiated at arms' length in a transparent process," CalEnergy claimed to have invested more than $300 million in the projects, and the company carried political risk insurance issued by the U.S. government's OPIC. Copies of the letter also went to the U.S. ambassador (Stapleton Roy) and the U.S. secretaries of state, commerce, energy, and treasury.[24]

As chairman of the House Subcommittee on Asia and the Pacific, Representative Bereuter's interest in Asian relations probably had more to do with access to markets for Nebraskan agricultural products than with building infrastructure. How he so quickly developed expertise on Java's Dieng Plateau and particularly on the "transparency" of Indonesian negotiations remains shrouded in the fog for which the Plateau is famous. Bereuter's letter did not lead to reinstatement of the projects.

On March 15, 1998, CalEnergy claimed that one 60-megawatt plant was completed at Dieng and that construction had begun for an additional 80 megawatts.[25] Further, the company reported starting to build the Patuha plant (although the Indonesians claim that nothing was built at Patuha).

No Renegotiation

Like KBC's owners, CalEnergy did not pursue renegotiations that might have rescheduled startups and perhaps lowered tariffs. In 1996 and 1997, the company had taken out political risk insurance from OPIC and associated private insurers for the two Java projects. A successful claim would provide an opportunity for reimbursement of its expenditures and an easy exit. There was a catch, however. To ensure it could collect, the owners needed a legal decision against the Indonesian government, not a state-owned enterprise. OPIC would pay up based on "denial of justice" if the government did not honor a legal award.[26] To justify a claim on the government, the company began to describe its comfort letters as "sovereign guarantees," a dramatic rephrasing of the "support letters" in its earlier description.

On August 14, 1998, after PLN failed to pay the first (disputed) invoice from Dieng,[27] the company initiated arbitration proceedings against PLN for both Dieng and Patuha.[28] CalEnergy's CEO explained: "The fundamental basis of the international power industry is the sanctity of contracts."[29]

Several Indonesians we spoke with viewed CalEnergy's defiant stance as a case of striking insensitivity to cultural norms and bureaucratic processes of its host country. Although cultural sensitivity does not seem to have been a strong point in the company's management, there is another possible explanation. The speed of the action hints that CalEnergy simply did not want a new deal.

The rush to external guarantees may have resulted from corporate changes during the year. In August 1998, the company announced that it would acquire the Iowa-based MidAmerican Holdings Group, whose subsidiary was the largest utility in the state. The merger, in which the parties assumed the MidAmerican name, was to be part of a new and quite different strategy, one that did not include expansion in developing countries. In fact, the company had already expressed an interest in "packaging" its overseas projects for sale.[30]

Indonesians had apparently not recognized the importance of changes at corporate headquarters,[31] and they were puzzled and angered by the quick move to arbitration. If they had understood the company's waning interest in the developing world, they might have been less puzzled, but perhaps equally angry.

CalEnergy may have been discouraged from renegotiating by the same kind of "moral hazard" that supported such risky investments in the first place (see Box 13.1). Insurers worry, for example, that homeowners with theft insurance will pay less attention to locking their doors or installing alarm systems than they would if they were fully responsible for losses. In the extreme case, an insured owner who discovers his art is fake might arrange for a fire in order to collect insurance. Although CalEnergy did not burn up its project or presumably do anything that was illegal, its insurance would surely reduce the incentive for the company to try to reach an accommodation with Indonesians.

Probably with little chance of success, Indonesians struggled to avoid arbitration. Ginandjar, then economic coordinating minister, called CalEnergy's Indonesian partner Lutfi: "tell your Americans to stop."[32] Remember, Lutfi was the son-in-law of Hartarto, member of the ministerial team overseeing renegotiations and coordinating minister during the arbitrations. Lutfi's response is not on record.[33] The U.S. embassy also opposed arbitration.[34] Stapleton Roy, an ambassador eager to maintain good relations with Indonesia, still ran the embassy. He clung to the increasingly old-fashioned concern that very strong official support for an American investor could come at a cost to more important foreign policy issues.

Because maintaining U.S.–Indonesia relations was not the company's problem, CalEnergy gave little heed to the embassy. Claiming insurance would be a rather sure sign that the parties were divorcing, but unlike Mission, CalEnergy seemed ready for divorce.

CalEnergy's arbitration would be eventful. Unlike on television, most legal procedures are exceedingly boring, but in this tension-laden case a dispute over location, conflicting claims about choice of arbitrators, charges of bugged rooms, and an allegation of kidnapping would add TV-like drama to the tedious legal issues.

First Arbitration

Arbitration clauses in the agreements called for procedures that followed the rules of the U.N. Commission on International Trade Law (UNCITRAL), for the governing law to be Indonesian (although disputes continued over which Indonesian laws should govern), and for the location to be Jakarta.

Lawyers

CalEnergy engaged the large international Latham & Watkins firm as principal counsel. Indonesians hired as their lead counsel Adnan Buyung Nasution's firm, and as assistant counsel, the local Karim Sani firm.[35] Lawyers from McKenna and Cuneo joined some of the Indonesian team meetings and seemed to have considerable access to Minister Hartarto during discussions.

Choosing a Panel

CalEnergy named to the arbitration panel an Australia-based engineer and professional arbitrator, Antonino Albert de Fina.[36] The government (the Ministry of Finance) ended up selecting an Indonesian, Professor Priyatna Abdurrasyid.[37] Jan Paulsson became the third arbitrator and chair, but the process of his selection and possible conflicts of interest involving his firm, Freshfields, Bruckhaus, Deringer, made his choice a subject of controversy.[38] Whatever truth there was in the allegations, the selection certainly did not raise any issue of competence.[39] Paulsson was experienced, extremely well regarded by the profession, and an editor of the prestigious journal *Arbitration International*.[40] In short, he was one of the big names in the field.

Procedural Issues

Procedural issues arose immediately. CalEnergy sought one arbitration for both Dieng and Patuha against both PLN and the Ministry of Finance (based on the comfort letters). Counsel for the government contested jurisdiction, objecting to a single tribunal for two projects governed by six documents and without Pertamina's participation. A procedural hearing produced an agreement that each CalEnergy subsidiary would go first against PLN and then only later and if necessary against the Ministry of Finance. In the end, however, arbitration for the two geothermal projects were, for all practical purposes, joined. And the arbitrators eventually made a puzzling declaration: that Pertamina's interests were not affected.

Rather than using the government-appointed Priyatna for the arbitration in which it was the defendant, PLN decided to name its own arbitrator: a former Indonesian supreme court justice, Setiawan, S.H.[41]

From the outset, Indonesians contended that the contracts were themselves invalid because they violated a decree[42] that required payment in rupiah and prohibited government guarantees, and another that required tendering. Although some Indonesians believed that this issue should be settled by Indonesian courts, they were also convinced that the arbitrators would decide that the contracts were invalid anyway.

Hearings

Enter Coudert

Before the Indonesian law firms had completed PLN's written defense, Indonesians agreed to add the U.S. law firm Coudert Brothers LLP, which had sought the job and claimed sympathy for the Indonesian side. PLN's hope was that this prestigious international firm would improve Indonesia's case. Upon joining, Coudert signed a letter of "no conflict" of interest.

Coudert's lawyers prepared a less rigorous defense, dropping contentions that the contracts were illegal, that Pertamina had to be joined, and that CalEnergy itself stood in breach of the contracts, for example. When their statement was submitted to the panel, Coudert had effectively taken over the case.

A shock hit the Indonesian side a week before the scheduled hearing. According to other counsel, Coudert suddenly resigned, reporting that CalEnergy had recognized its hand in the work, argued that the firm had a conflict of interest, insisted that Coudert step down, and threatened to take the matter to the California Bar Association.[43] The resignation left Indonesians without their principal counsel, at the last moment before the first hearing. It seems that one more U.S. law firm had viewed conflict of interest somewhat differently in an international setting than it would at home.

PLN and its advisors scrambled for more legal help, but most international law firms with knowledge in the field discovered conflicts of interest. Karim Sani finally identified Mason's, a "boutique" British firm.[44] John Bishop, a senior partner, hopped on a plane almost immediately for Jakarta, arriving the very next day; another partner arrived from Hong Kong later that same afternoon. According to a lawyer on the Indonesian side, Coudert lawyers were willing to give their replacements only a 20-minute briefing and offered no guidance to the documentation they left behind.

Bugging

The lawyers for both sides took rooms in the Regent Hotel for last-minute meetings and interviews with witnesses. Soon PLN's counsel came to believe that everything they said was immediately available to the other side. Convinced that the rooms were "bugged," they told us that they brought in investigators who identified electronic signals but were unable to locate the hardware itself.[45] The investigators were reportedly sure that extremely sophisticated equipment was in use, of a type "to which only the CIA had access." We cannot confirm bugging, but a manager with a different American-controlled power company told another researcher that bugging was common practice, and he named a large security firm to which his company would turn for the job.[46]

Costly Constraints

Indonesia's lawyers wanted to argue that the agreements were the product of corruption, but only the ministerial committee could authorize such a politically sensitive defense. Coordinating Minister Hartarto (father-in-law of a CalEnergy partner) had taken control of cases involving arbitration. Counsel urged Hartarto to have his son-in-law own up and tell the story of how the contracts came to be. We were told that Hartarto not only declined, but he refused to allow the corruption issue to be raised at all. In response, Buyung appealed to the president, who first agreed to raising the issue, but soon retracted after reporting he had talked with Hartarto.[47] The result was the death of potentially the most convincing argument for the Indonesian side. Although this decision saved the necks of some officials, their families, and their cronies, it may also have cost the Indonesian people hundreds of millions of dollars.

At roughly the same time, a decision was made not to allow counsel to argue that Indonesia was acting under orders from the International Monetary Fund (IMF) in suspending the projects, lest the IMF be annoyed.[48]

These decisions left CalEnergy's side with the task of countering claims that the agreement was in violation of the authorizing decree. Testimony by Robert Hornick, the same American lawyer who would testify in the KBC case, countered the Indonesian claim.[49]

Reaching a Decision

CalEnergy asked the tribunal for its investment thus far and the net present value of all projected profits, including planned capacity, for the remaining three decades of the contract, a total of about $3 billion for the two projects.[50] Indonesians responded by arguing that the only issue for the tribunal was whether PLN owed about $4 million for the company's first invoice. It is not clear that they carefully challenged the investor's request for the sum of investment plus future cash flow; they may not have taken it seriously, given their earlier conviction that the panel would rule the contract invalid.

After hearings and deliberations, the tribunal ruled that PLN had breached the agreements and owed $391,711,652 for Dieng and $180,570,322 for

Patuha.[51] The sums included investment plus a calculation of the net present value of future profits, supposedly adjusted to reflect the fact that not all the planned investment had been made and the fact that PLN might not have been able to use the planned output. The tribunal terminated the contracts and ordered the facilities already built to be turned over to PLN.

The CalEnergy-appointed arbitrator de Fina wrote an annex saying he favored a larger award, without naming a figure. One report was that he wanted to award the requested $3 billion. If this sum was intended to be punitive, it is not clear why he thought punishment was in order. Indonesian actions were clearly in response to an economic crisis and not an opportunistic step to enrich themselves. The rumored sum would amount to more than 1% of Indonesia's annual gross domestic product. This was a poor country, with large international debts and a deep recession, the target of a rescue plan by the IMF.

The majority award was itself large—more than the total U.S. official pledge for relief and reconstruction after the 2004 tsunami.[52] When we asked a former CalEnergy lawyer about the size of the award, the response did little more than vindicate observers who doubted the company's cultural sensitivity: "[We] got a ruling against those bozos."[53] In the end, however, the amount of the award turned out not to matter much—at least as long as it exceeded the value of the insurance the investor carried.

The Jakarta Court Acts

Despite the tribunal's statement at the outset, the award did affect Pertamina. Two of its contracts were terminated, its revenue from the projects stopped, and facilities contracted to revert to Pertamina were given to PLN. To protect its interests, on May 26, Pertamina filed suit in a Jakarta court asking for a provisional injunction against enforcement of the award through either the courts or a second arbitration against the government.

The Jakarta court responded that it would hear the concerns and issued an injunction against further action by any party pending its final ruling.[54]

Second Arbitration

In spite of the court's injunction, CalEnergy immediately proceeded to the second arbitration, against the government itself. A spokesman for CalEnergy claimed, "The government of Indonesia issued sovereign performance undertakings on behalf of our projects ... the government has over $18 billion in reserve, so it is clearly able to honor this obligation."[55] What the company had earlier called "support letters" had now morphed into "sovereign guarantees." The foreign exchange reserves were hardly impressive when one remembers that Indonesia's external debt stood at several times the reported number. The real message was that CalEnergy now needed a decision against the Ministry of Finance, which, if the government then failed to pay, would support its claim on OPIC insurance.

The panel for the more dramatic second stage of arbitration was already set: Priyatna, the government's designee, was simply substituted for PLN's arbitrator.

Undermining the Case

Minister Hartarto made another decision that would undermine the Indonesian case: No finance minister would be allowed to testify, neither Mar'ie Muhamad. the former finance minister who had signed the letters of comfort, nor Bambang Subianto, the current finance minister. The former minister would surely have said that he had been asked to sign sovereign guarantees, but Indonesian law prohibited him from doing so. Consequently, he had agreed to letters of comfort, which required only that the government act in its role as shareholder to instruct PLN to pay.

Moving from Jakarta

The new proceedings began in Jakarta, as specified in the contracts, but CalEnergy demanded a new venue, claiming that its managers were being harassed, a contention Indonesians deny. The company added that Jakarta was not an entirely safe place anyway. Indeed, demonstrations were common, but there were few threats to foreigners by this time.

Without Indonesian consent, the chair of the panel moved the main hearings to the Peace Palace in The Hague. Resembling a fairy-tale castle, the Palace houses the U.N. International Court of Justice and the Permanent Court of Arbitration.

The Indonesians were now caught in a dilemma. The Jakarta injunction prohibited further steps in the case. Any party who participated in the arbitration could be fined $1 million per day. The ruling arguably covered the CalEnergy companies, the Ministry of Finance, PLN, the three arbitrators, and counsel.[56] Having no intention of returning to Indonesia, CalEnergy's managers and lawyers could proceed to The Hague without worry.[57] For Indonesians—including the Indonesian arbitrator—and their counsel, the threat was more serious. If they failed to participate and the arbitration proceeded, Indonesians could not present their side of the story, and the most sympathetic arbitrator might be absent. On the other hand, if they participated, they would violate an injunction of their own court, and they might be subject to huge fines when they came home. Presumably, they could have asked the Indonesian court to lift the injunction, but the decision was made to honor it.

Kidnapping?

A bizarre series of events followed.

First, Indonesians engaged Dutch counsel to apply to Dutch courts to halt the proceedings. Petitions for court action with respect to arbitration must be entered in the courts of the country where the arbitration is held. Whether this was still Indonesia, or the Netherlands, or no nation was unclear. The Peace Palace was actually international territory. Although the Dutch court never explicitly ruled on its jurisdiction, it refused to halt the process.

When the Peace Palace hearings were about to begin, the arbitrator appointed by the Indonesian side, Priyatna, was visiting his son in the United States. By his own statement, he was "hiding out" to avoid "improper contacts."[58] He had planned to fly directly from Washington to Amsterdam to participate in the arbitration. Unable to contact him directly because his son in Washington and his wife in Jakarta had been instructed to say they did not know where he was, Indonesians (led by Hartarto, we were told) went against the advice of their local counsel and sent a courier to intercept Priyatna at the Washington airport and give him a reminder of the injunction.[59] The plane was held while the courier and Priyatna discussed the matter.

It appears that at least one issue for Priyatna was the money involved. He reports that he asked the Indonesian emissary, "OK, suppose that I do not attend, I will claim for lost income." He then mentioned an amount of money that he says "stunned" the courier, who said he would have to call Jakarta. Priyatna then reports that he bargained with the official on the phone about how much he would receive. Of course, an international arbitrator's fee may well have been a number that "stunned" an Indonesian bureaucrat, but Priyatna did not trust any commitment an official might make over the phone.[60]

During a telephone call to Jakarta, Priyatna says, "the person from the ministry of finance" insisted that he should not go to the arbitration. When Priyatna countered that he had to go, he reports that the official said, "Mr. Priyatna, you must go home to Jakarta where your family lives." The official added that Priyatna's son also had to go to the embassy from time to time.[61] It is not clear whether this was intended as a threat or a reminder that he would someday return home where he would be subject to the Jakarta court's penalties. Priyatna interpreted it as a threat; he explained to us that he took the implied threat very seriously because he once had had his house confiscated and been prohibited from leaving Indonesia when he defied Suharto's instructions in the late 1960s with respect to an investigation of corruption at Pertamina. But, of course, Suharto was no longer in power.

Priyatna flew on to Amsterdam. He says that he was met by an Indonesian embassy official on his arrival, and that they proceeded together to the Ibis Hotel near the airport. One account says Priyatna reported praying through the night flight and deciding to go home rather than to The Hague, and that he had told the Indonesian embassy in Amsterdam to cancel his hotel booking in The Hague. Priyatna's subsequent account says that two[62] "high officials from the Ministry of Finance/Jakarta" were waiting for him at the hotel and one said to him, "If Mr. Priyatna is not prepared to be absent voluntarily, we shall be forced to carry out a kidnap."[63] Whatever happened, after one night in the hotel, Priyatna left, with eight embassy people, for the airport. This seems not to be disputed.

Around flight time, one of the arbitrators, de Fina, went to the airport with Jan Albert van den Berg, a partner of Paulsson and the lawyer who had argued against Indonesia's attempt to block the arbitration in the Dutch court, and found Priyatna in the lounge. They talked for a while, and Priyatna then left for Jakarta.

The two remaining arbitrators convened and considered Priyatna's absence, reviewing reports submitted by van den Berg, a driver, and de Fina.[64] Testimony by an arbitrator seems a bit unusual, especially when the arbitrator was appointed by the party that might benefit from the statements. The accounts were consistent, but no one mentioned weapons or other signs of force. Be that as it may, the two arbitrators determined they could proceed without Priyatna (or any Indonesian representation), even though Indonesian counsel contends that this was counter to the governing Indonesian arbitration law.[65]

UNCITRAL rules seem to say that the proceedings should not continue until a new arbitrator has been appointed.[66] Practice sometimes differs: It seems that arbitrators will try to proceed in the absence of an arbitrator if they believe that the absence is due to extreme actions by one party.[67] Because Pertamina, not the government, had initiated the Jakarta court case, one might reasonably conclude that it was not an effort by the government to interfere in the arbitration. The two arbitrators dealt with this argument by saying that PLN and the Indonesian government did not appeal the Jakarta ruling or attempt to stay the injunction.

Regardless of who was responsible for the Jakarta court case, if Priyatna's absence was due to a government kidnapping, one might conclude that the action was an effort by one party to frustrate the proceedings. But whether Priyanta even had been kidnapped is debatable. "To kidnap" is "to seize and detain unlawfully and usually for ransom."[68] We found no evidence of any physical force or threat of such, nor is it clear that insisting he obey the order of a Jakarta court was unlawful. Priyatna was in public areas of the airport when he was leaving and thus had obvious opportunities to escape any alleged kidnappers. He was not physically detained and no one demanded ransom. To be sure, he was threatened with fines and one could possibly interpret comments he later reported as having been threats to his family. Kidnapping or not, the story has been elaborated on ever since, even to reports of weapons being seen in the Amsterdam airport lounge,[69] contemporary coverage in the Dutch press,[70] and the participation of Indonesian secret police.[71] We are not completely sure how these exaggerated versions originated or were spread.

The allegations of kidnapping were important not only for the arbitration in the Peace Palace; as we shall see, they probably influenced to some extent OPIC's decision to pay CalEnergy's insurance claim. The company certainly used them to create a great deal of bad publicity for Indonesia in the international press, especially as the story grew ever more sinister.

Ruling

The two remaining panelists issued a preliminary decision rather quickly, in September 1999.[72] It confirmed the panel's jurisdiction over the case "notwithstanding Indonesian court orders purporting to enjoin the arbitration...in violation of generally recognized principles of international law." The final ruling was issued on October 15, 1999, upholding the interim award of more than $500 million, and confirming that the Indonesian government was liable for the sum.

This was, of course, a default ruling; the Indonesian side had not been present to argue its case. As a result, the all-important issue of what a letter of comfort means was never resolved.

In his accounts after the events, Priyatna says that the most effective argument to the panel would have been that the contract was the product of corruption. He goes on to say,

> the existence of blank share certificates at Himpurna Cal Energy...the mode was payment of dividend in advance in the amount of US$5 thousand each month to the Himpurna shareholders. This can already be categorized as illegal practice, since payment of dividend is usually made after a company has gained profit. The power plant Dieng had not been realized, the foreign investor must already make payment to the local shareholders.[73]

Priyatna also reported in his memoirs an effort to convince Hartarto to allow the corruption issue to be raised in future cases and a subsequent conversation on the matter with the Indonesian lawyer Buyung. He relates Buyung's reply: "Impossible Pri, everyone is involved." Priyatna concludes, "in the end I knew that it was indeed made impossible."[74]

Of course, we cannot be sure that Indonesian counsel would have carried the day with the corruption argument, testimony from a minister of finance on the letters of comfort, and evidence of the role of the IMF. All, however, had been nixed before the tribunal ever met in The Hague. Keeping Priyatna from the arbitration was likely an unwise decision, but disallowing the strongest arguments had probably already ensured that the Indonesians would lose the case and pay heavily.

Follow-Up

Priyatna's own accounts do not stop with the arbitration. He goes on to tell about a phone call when he returned to Jakarta from someone with the World Bank saying that the U.S. government would give him protection. It is not clear why anyone from the World Bank would make this kind of offer on behalf of the U.S. government, nor even why Priyatna might need protection because he had done what he claims his government had asked of him.[75] Our inquiries at the World Bank field office produced flat denials of any such event, and claims that Priyatna's reports had many inconsistencies.

Priyatna also reports a call from "an emissary from the Secretary of State of the United States" with, it seems, a similar offer. Priyatna says he turned it down. In a third story, he says that the "Minister Councilor" from the Dutch embassy offered legal action against Indonesians in the Netherlands for the kidnapping on Dutch territory. Priyatna also says he rejected this offer "since the current administration was one that was expected to be clean, unlike the Suharto and the Habibie regimes when courts could be terrorized, coerced, pressured, I would not file any lawsuit at all."[76] The mysterious stories and some of his reports of events where he was not present[77] make one a bit skeptical of other details in his accounts.

Meanwhile, Indonesian counsel returned to the Jakarta court to seek an injunction against enforcement of the arbitration award. From a legal point of view, the arbitration's seat presumably remained in Jakarta, and the award was subject to review by Indonesian courts. But times were changing, in response to the new president's (Gus Dur) revised approach. The law firm Cleary Gottlieb had taken over as principal counsel on the case, and insisted that the objection to the panel's ruling be withdrawn from the Jakarta court, contending that a protest against the decision of an arbitral panel was an embarrassment to Indonesia. Against the strong advice of Karim Sani lawyers, the contest was dropped, ending legal challenges to the award.

Enter OPIC

CalEnergy had filed its insurance claims with OPIC even before the second arbitration had begun, saying that the Indonesian government had caused PLN to breach the contracts (among other charges).[78] OPIC officials were not taken by surprise; they had been keeping themselves informed, regularly visiting Jakarta to track the power issues.[79] They had their reasons, with exposure in four projects (Paiton I, Dieng, Patuha, and El Paso's Singkang).

CalEnergy began to organize political pressure on OPIC to pay. At least one meeting was held on Capitol Hill on the matter. But OPIC delayed, waiting for the completion of the legal process.

Once the second arbitration had been decided, CalEnergy filed a new claim, this time based on the failure of the government to honor the award.[80] OPIC did not take long in paying up.[81] On November 11, after little more than a month, the company issued a press release saying that it had received $290 million; OPIC paid $217.5 million and "private insurers" paid $72.5 million.[82]

In fact, OPIC had briefly hesitated, even to the point of preparing two draft documents, one supporting the award and one denying it. The arguments on the denial side included: The arbitral award was invalid because of the location where it was held; the "Paulsson risk," as it was labeled, meant that the decision to proceed without the third arbitrator might be in error; the government had appropriate defenses that had not been heard (in particular, the move from Jakarta and the injunction from the Jakarta court); and the corruption issue had not been addressed. Although OPIC refused to provide copies of these memos,[83] we have been told that the balance tipped toward paying because of annoyance over the alleged kidnapping of the Indonesian arbitrator and the lack of firm evidence on corruption. But in an endnote to its Memorandum of Determinations, OPIC said that "it is not necessary to determine whether the [government of Indonesia] acted in any way improperly in connection with the arbitrator's nonattendance at the hearings...."[84]

When we interviewed an OPIC official about the events, he said he remembered that one of the witnesses had reported seeing a pistol in the hands of one of the alleged kidnappers in the airport waiting lounge. Further, he believed that a police report had been filed in the Netherlands on the "kidnapping" and that there was an account in a Dutch newspaper of the events, including the sighting of a gun. We confirmed with Jan Albert van den Berg, one of the two witnesses at the airport, that no weapon was spotted; further, affidavits to the tribunal mention none. A witness denied the alleged police reports, saying that he had only been summoned earlier by the Haarlem district attorney for a statement about the legal effort to block the arbitration.[85] The only immediate news account, according to one of the arbitrators, was an editorial in the *Asian Wall Street Journal*. That story, stimulated by a CalEnergy press release, may have been the first public mention of a "kidnapping," and, probably incorrectly, it says that the Dutch police were notified.[86]

We doubt that the OPIC official's account of what he had been told of the events results from faulty memory; his recollections were otherwise virtually flawless. When asked the source of the stories, he responded that the information may have come to OPIC from CalEnergy managers or its lawyers. Whatever the source of the apparent fabrications, Indonesians had no opportunity to counter them. In fact, they had no voice at all in OPIC's decision to pay, even though they would soon be held liable for reimbursing any insurance payment made by OPIC.

With respect to corruption, OPIC's published defense of the award makes it clear that the issue had indeed been raised in its deliberations, pointing out that the contracts provide for nonpayment if "the preponderant cause [of the expropriation] is unreasonable actions attributable to the investor, including corrupt practices."[87] There were certainly reasons for suspicion, and OPIC was well aware of at least some of them even before it issued insurance.[88] When it considered the claim, OPIC knew of the nature of the joint venture parties, the "free" shares, and the dividend payments to the Indonesian partner before the project had any earnings. OPIC claims its request to Indonesians to provide evidence of corruption was met with silence. With Hartarto's position in the government, his family's involvement, and the general disorganization of the public sector, silence should have been no surprise.

Anyway, the OPIC official went on, corruption *caused* neither the presidential decree that affected the projects nor the Indonesian refusal to pay the arbitration award. He added the question: What would the Indonesians say if OPIC refused to pay because of underlying corruption, especially after they had decided not to use corruption as a part of their defense in the arbitration? We respectfully disagree with the first response: If corruption was present, it presumably influenced the terms of the agreement, and those terms were very relevant both to the decree and any award. As to the second response: Surely U.S. decisions with respect to corruption and insurance should not be based on conjectures about sensitivities of foreign officials. Under the U.S. Foreign Corrupt Practices Act, the U.S. Justice Department can bring its own charges and conduct its own investigation without having to rely on the support of corrupt foreign officials. It is not clear why OPIC should act differently when there are substantial hints that corruption is present.

In publicly explaining its award, OPIC pointed out that charges of corruption had been levied against almost all the power producers, but none had been proved. OPIC's explanation adds, "Not only is it not illegal to have local partners, it is in many situations intelligent and indeed commendable business practice. . . ."[89] An OPIC official argued to us that free shares are not all that unusual, even in Texas oil fields. The explanation failed to mention the relationship of the partner to a high-ranking government official. We are unconvinced by any version of the argument that the possibility that everyone else is doing it excuses a company's actions.

Of course, we cannot know what the outcome of a thorough investigation would have been. Any corrupt payments uncovered may well not have violated the Foreign Corrupt Practices Act—we have seen one of its gaping holes.

The decision on paying must have posed some difficulty for OPIC. Refusing the claim, based on corruption or flaws in the arbitration, might discourage similar future claims. A refusal, however, would likely have initiated a protracted legal fight with the company, which OPIC might lose. Paying quickly would support OPIC's reputation among client investors and perhaps make some senators and representatives happy. And paying would most likely cost OPIC little beyond its administrative costs because OPIC could turn around and demand from the Indonesians whatever it gave the company. An OPIC official and a lawyer very familiar with OPIC both told us that the agency is not influenced by this kind of "moral hazard." But it is difficult for an outsider to believe that a decision would not take this into account, perhaps not explicitly or consciously.[90] Host governments ought to worry that "moral hazard" affects claims decisions when paying will cost the insurer little or nothing.

OPIC as Owner

When OPIC pays an expropriation claim, the insured's shareholdings and all claims associated with the expropriation pass to OPIC.[91] Thus, OPIC and the private insurers became the new owners of Dieng and Patuha.[92] The Asian Development Bank noted with some satisfaction that "It is now understood that OPIC will take over as the main sponsor in the project and may pave the way for a less confrontational approach to renegotiations on the PPA [power purchase agreement] with PLN."[93] It is hard to imagine that the tension could increase, but the change in ownership hardly shifted the dispute from war to peace.[94]

Claiming Payment

OPIC wanted its money from the Indonesians, but also it wanted an end to management problems because it was hardly equipped to run a power business. Expecting to take over, however, it had lined up advisors even before it acquired the shares. But it soon had its hands full with a business that had stopped paying its contractors some time ago. For example, DATI, a subsidiary of U.S.-based Parker Drilling, had successfully gone to arbitration in Singapore against CalEnergy.[95] At least 23 Indonesian contractors reported that they were owed a total of $40 million by the company.[96]

Indonesians told us that OPIC officials implied that the OPIC treaty between Indonesia and the United States[97] required Indonesia to reimburse OPIC. An OPIC official denied saying this, but admitted that he encountered difficulties in communication because it was unclear who was in charge in Indonesia. The treaty, in fact, said only that the U.S. government was entitled to take over CalEnergy's shares and claims if it paid on a political risk policy.[98] If CalEnergy had a legitimate claim, that claim passed to OPIC.

In theory, Indonesians could invoke a clause of the treaty to insist on arbitration or initiate a U.S. case to oppose any OPIC claim. If they exercised this right, they would have argued that CalEnergy had no legitimate claim against the government; therefore, OPIC had gained none by taking over the company's claims. A claim for expropriation could have arisen if PLN was considered the "alter ego" of the government or if the comfort letters were guarantees and legal under Indonesian law. The second arbitration, against the government, was, the Indonesians would have argued, seriously flawed.

Although some lawyers recommended resistance, it seems that Cleary Gottlieb, now the influential counsel, advised the Ministry of Finance against fighting. During the struggle, the U.S. embassy had vigorously supported OPIC, caring little about foreign relations. In fact, Kuntoro told us that when he faced pressure from the U.S. ambassador, it had always been about OPIC. Fearing retaliation by the U.S. government and probably having had enough of arbitration, Indonesians limited their reaction to a letter to OPIC setting out their arguments,[99] and backed away from legal action.

Meanwhile, OPIC officials were becoming long-distance commuters. They went to Indonesia for meetings on power in December 1999 and probably in January, February, and for certain in March 2000 to demand that they be made whole for their payments to CalEnergy. Moreover, OPIC wanted more than what it had paid out. Acting under a "claims cooperation agreement," the U.S. government agency saw itself as representing the private insurers' claims as well as its own claims.[100] They would share, pro rata, any reimbursement. Although an OPIC official denied that OPIC was committed to collect on behalf of the private insurers, the pro-rata arrangement is surely the equivalent of a commitment. If OPIC is to receive 100% reimbursement, it has to collect both what it paid out and what the private insurers paid. This was OPIC's first test of how such a compact would work.

Of course, Indonesia was not a party to the claims cooperation agreement. The original treaty called for consultations when a project was under consideration for insurance. An OPIC official reported that the agency had notified the Indonesian board of investments (BKPM) of its intent to insure the project, but it did not mention the private component.[101] BKPM was at best peripheral to the electric power agreements, and not involved at all in the geothermal agreements; in fact, it had gradually become peripheral to any important decision, as its approval for foreign investments had become largely a ritual. Because any notification to BKPM was surely lost in the bureaucracy, the lack of response should have been no surprise to OPIC. Sending the notification to BKPM was hardly a step designed to elicit careful consideration.

In light of the U.S. government's push for privatization and transparency in the Third World, it is not clear to us why OPIC and the U.S. government should use its power to collect on behalf of a private insurer. To be sure, its charter says OPIC is to encourage the development of private political risk insurance. A compact that ensures the use of U.S. government power to collect on behalf of private insurers might, however, be viewed as more than "encouraging" the private sector. And, in the name of transparency, one might expect OPIC at least to have informed Indonesians of this potential additional liability from the outset.

More Opaqueness

When OPIC came around to collect, Indonesian counsel asked for copies of the insurance contracts. Given the fact that hundreds of millions of dollars were at stake, it seemed reasonable to check that the company actually carried the insurance that it was said to have, that the events did generate a legitimate claim under the policy, and that the provisions of the insurance conformed to the terms of the letters that made up the treaty. But the counsel for OPIC refused to show the insurance documents. Instead, he produced only a model agreement, and gave no assurances that CalEnergy's policy matched the model.[102] His accompanying statement amounted to "if you sue us, you can have the contract." He told us, in hindsight, that he might have been "a bit harsh" on this issue. It seems that OPIC guidelines did allow him to show the contracts as a part of collection efforts, but he explained his refusal by saying that he did not want to get into a dispute with Indonesia's lawyers over "international law." Although his preference for avoiding dispute is commendable, the position seems to deny Indonesians the ability even to decide, without actually initiating a legal case, whether they had a case at all.

A former CalEnergy lawyer also argued to us that Indonesians should not be allowed to see the contract because release might cause a debate over whether an expropriation had actually occurred, as defined by the contract. That, in our view, is exactly the reason why Indonesians should have been allowed to see it.

To this day, OPIC considers its insurance contracts to be commercial secrets, even those on which it has paid.[103] But what is still secret and of potential value to competitors in this case is very difficult to fathom. CalEnergy no longer owns the projects and has even exited this kind of business. Again, U.S. calls for transparency seem to apply to others, but not to U.S. agencies.

Collecting from a Disorganized Government

OPIC officials' initial meetings with the Ministry of Finance went very badly. The agency offered Indonesia some time to pay, with no interest charged on the delay. The government, however, was in dire financial straits, with IMF pressure to hold down spending. OPIC wanted a commitment within a few days. The ministry's legal office (initially, under Agus Hariyanto), which was in charge of the discussions, did not have the authority to make such a decision; nor did the minister of finance, for that matter.[104] It was not even clear how a decision of this magnitude would be made. During that period, the country's decision-making mechanisms were in chaos.

The OPIC team reportedly grew frustrated with the lack of progress and the difficulties in getting appointments with important Indonesians. The economic coordinating minister, Kwik, for example, said he was too busy to meet with them. Eventually, Jezek, American advisor to the Indonesians, proposed that Laksamana Sukardi, the minister for state-owned enterprises, assemble OPIC and the credit agencies to tell them bluntly that it would take time to reach decisions, and that they must understand the government turmoil. The government would invite the agencies back to Jakarta within a specified time period, when it could have an agenda ready for discussion. The minister agreed to Jezek's "bullet points" for the presentation, but he did not show up for the meeting. A White & Case lawyer—that is, an American—had to read the statement on behalf of the Indonesians. The OPIC mission went home angered and, of course, without the commitment for reimbursement that it was seeking.

In May or June 2000, Indonesians sent a team, headed by Kuntoro and including at least two foreign advisors, to Washington to meet with OPIC's president, George Munoz, to try to settle the matter. When the group arrived at Munoz's office, he came out to meet them and told them that there was nothing to negotiate. He had made his offer; they could sit outside his office and discuss the matter among themselves as long as they wished. When they had decided to take his offer, they could "knock twice" on his door, and he would meet with them. With that, he went back into his office. Angered, the Indonesian mission walked out and returned to Jakarta.[105]

The U.S. embassy began to turn up the heat. U.S. Ambassador Gelbard stated in July 2000 that he was "running out of patience" with Indonesia's tardy payment to OPIC. He threatened them: "There is always the possibility of declaring expropriation. . . . If we were to do this, it would result in a dramatic deterioration of the rupiah and would hurt Indonesia very much."[106] In other words, Gelbard was threatening the application of the Hickenlooper-Helms Amendment, which authorized the cut-off of aid flow to a country that took U.S. property without prompt and adequate compensation.

The ambassador's comments generated a sharp response from Kwik, the economic coordinating minister, who reportedly "slammed" the ambassador for his threatening statements.[107] Bambang Sudibyo, the minister of finance, responded in anger as well, saying that the issue had become "political" as a result of the ambassador's statement, adding that parliament would have to approve any payment. (Ultimately, the decision would probably have had to come from the president.) He went on: "Go ahead and threaten us. You will not deal with me, but with the state."[108] Priyo Budi Santoso, a Golkar legislator, said that he would block government payment to OPIC and boasted, "If the U.S. government seizes our assets, then we will seize their assets here." These were not the kind of statements typical of reserved Indonesians; they provide a measure of their anger.

The only cool voice seems to have been that of Kuntoro, who said that negotiations were proceeding smoothly and that they were concentrating on reducing OPIC's claim.

Reaching a Deal

Negotiations were indeed proceeding, as Ambassador Gelbard must have known. Indonesians and OPIC ended up discussing several options. An OPIC official pointed out that elsewhere OPIC had promised a given sum of investment in the country—the project to be specified by the host government—in exchange for a reasonable settlement. Another suggestion was that OPIC and the government negotiate new contracts for the projects, with lower prices for the power, enabling OPIC to sell the facilities to a new private owner and recoup its money. Of course, OPIC was implicitly admitting that the original price for electricity was indeed too high. It was also admitting that it had options other than collecting from the Indonesian government. This OPIC official was at least attempting to defuse tensions.

With no progress on alternatives, Indonesians offered, in October 2000, to reimburse OPIC and the private insurance companies under terms typical of the Paris Club, which commonly govern the renegotiation of state-to-state debt. The terms were interpreted as payment over 20 years, with a grace period of four years and an interest rate 1% above that of the U.S. Federal Reserve Bank.[109] Because the take-or-pay, dollar-denominated contracts were much like debt, and the negotiations were now government-to-government, turning to the Paris Club for standards seemed a reasonable option, and one that is a common outcome for claims under German-sponsored political risk insurance.[110] Ministry of Finance officials met with OPIC in New York on election day, 2000. But OPIC rejected the proposal.

Negotiations continued for an additional nine months, with offers and counter-offers. After an agreed deadline had passed, Indonesians asked OPIC for a one-month extension, until July 31. During that period, OPIC gained a new president, Peter Watson. Still with no signature by July 31 and recognizing that political change was in the making—Megawati had taken over as president on July 23—Watson sent two OPIC officials to Jakarta with discretion to modify the terms of payment.[111] The change in OPIC leadership helped greatly. Less than a month earlier, Gus Dur had moved Rizal Ramli from coordinating minister for the economy to the Ministry of Finance. The new president, Megawati, had asked Rizal to stay on until she could form a new cabinet. Rizal signed the deal for the Indonesians on September 6. This was one of Rizal's last acts as minister of finance, and it took place without the knowledge of parliament. The central bank immediately responded that it would not pay until the new president and parliament approved. In spite of the bluster, to date Indonesia has regularly met the commitments agreed with OPIC.

The terms of the settlement remain confidential, something OPIC says the Indonesian side insisted on. The agreed payment has, however, been reported to be $260 million, with an interest rate of 6.21%, a three-year grace period, and 14 years of installment payments.[112]

Once Indonesia agreed to pay, OPIC reinstated eligibility for OPIC insurance. To what degree eligibility had actually been withheld during negotiations is not clear. OPIC had added more coverage for new investment in El Paso's Sengkang project in the meantime.

In any event, OPIC's new head, Watson, announced that this was the largest settlement in OPIC's history. He praised President Megawati for handling the matter promptly, and thanked Megawati's new coordinating minister for the economy, Dorojatun Kuntjoro-Jakti; her new minister of finance, Boediono; and her minister for state-owned enterprises, Laksamana Sukardi. Interestingly, he failed to thank the previous minister of finance, who may have risked his future to approve the settlement. In fact, Watson attributes the settlement to the change in government from Wahid to Megawati. We do not know whether Megawati had a role in the decision (although the new president did presumably approve the payment), but this is perhaps the kind of speedy shift in allocating gratitude that makes up "good diplomacy." After all, the agreement had indeed been signed under Megawati's watch, and it was the new government that now counted in U.S.–Indonesian relations.

Following Up

No one pursued the balance of the arbitration award. Remember, the award was for a total of over $570 million, but CalEnergy had received only $290 million from its insurers. One might argue that Indonesia still owed somebody $280 million.

Why, after so much legal struggle, was this money left on the table? CalEnergy's claims were transferred to OPIC after OPIC had paid up. But then OPIC could have tried to collect the balance of the award after it took over the projects and before the transfer to Indonesia. Either effort would have faced the contention that the arbitration was flawed and that it was subject to review in Jakarta, the arbitration's seat. More importantly, trying to collect more than it had paid out would probably have been too confrontational for OPIC, at least under its new head. The insurer was being reimbursed for what it had paid; any additional money might have to go to the insured anyway.

With the transfer of the project to the Indonesian government, the matter seemed to end, but at a high cost to Indonesian taxpayers. Indonesians brought Dieng back into production, but, they report, only after a great deal of difficulty with the secondhand Italian equipment CalEnergy had installed. As of 2005, Patuha remained unfinished. CalEnergy had never really moved on the third geothermal plant, Bedugul, on Bali. In fact, it had become the target of protests from Balinese who claimed that it violated religious beliefs associated with the mystically steamy site.[113] In 2004, rumors said that CalEnergy had sold the rights for this project to a group of Indonesians, including one Balinese, and perhaps the promoter who had brought CalEnergy to Indonesia's geothermal sites. Whether the plant could ever be constructed over the protests of Balinese remained unclear.[114]

Why Not a Deal Earlier?

With the advantage of hindsight, one must wonder whether Indonesians could have fared better if they had learned from the ITT experience in this case as well. Indonesians had hoped to negotiate new prices and a new schedule for these projects. Because CalEnergy was leaving Third World markets, however, Indonesians probably never had a chance with amicable negotiations. On the other hand, they might also have offered to buy out this project. The offer would have had to be for at least as much as CalEnergy hoped to collect on its insurance contracts—perhaps its BATNA (best alternative to a negotiated agreement). Indonesia would have saved legal fees, bad publicity from the alleged kidnapping, and the dispute with OPIC and the U.S. government. It might have had to pay immediately, rather than under the extended payout arrangement that was eventually agreed, but the savings might have justified giving up the extended payment terms.

One cannot know whether CalEnergy would have accepted the offer. It would have had some incentive to do so, as it could also have avoided the expensive legal process, eliminated the risk that the arbitration would have gone differently, or avoided the possibility that OPIC would deny the claim. It would have not faced the possibility of corruption charges, and it could have settled more quickly.

But the same reasons that held back a similar offer in the KBC case also apply here. Note that the minister of finance had not even been sure that he could settle with OPIC, although by that point the obligation was clearer and the threats against the country very real. Even if the president had been willing to make such a bold decision, it would have taken a great deal of nerve for an Indonesian official to say to the president, "We are likely to lose this case in arbitration, partly because we won't bring up the corruption issue and won't let the previous minister of finance testify. Thus, I recommend that we offer the company some quarter of a billion dollars."

Moreover, Indonesians we interviewed admitted that they understood little about the events going on inside CalEnergy. By the time they grasped the fact that negotiating a new contract was not likely to work, arbitration was well under way and the buyout option was probably moot. We have found that government negotiators rarely analyze corporate strategy and organization carefully, tending to view investors as all being similar and monolithic.

One more factor often leads managers—public or private—to the legal route. Although PLN preferred renegotiation, lawyers had led Indonesians to believe that they had a very strong case should it go to arbitration. They were convinced that the contract was not valid because it conflicted with authorizing legislation, and that it had, in any case, been breached by the company at Dieng.[115] Even if they had thought they might lose, Indonesians could hardly have predicted that the award would be as large as it turned out to be.

Official Political Risk Insurance

CalEnergy benefited from the new international property rights, drawing on expanded political risk insurance and home government support.

Official political risk insurance had evolved since the ITT story. In the case of the United States, OPIC was founded in 1971 as a government entity to take over an investment guarantee program previously run by USAID, whose program had, in turn, grown out of the Marshall Plan for Europe.[116]

Early political risk insurance from OPIC provided compensation to the insured for "expropriatory action" quite narrowly defined.[117] In fact, one arbitration between OPIC and an insured investor concluded that changes in contractual relationships as described in the "obsolescing bargain" literature did not amount to expropriation under OPIC's policy.[118] With time, however, OPIC began to use various mechanisms to cover "creeping expropriation."[119] In doing so, it insured against the kinds of contract changes that had been considered normal in the past. OPIC was taking an increasingly rigid view of contracts, much like that taken by the arbitrators in these cases.

The Indonesian experience with official political risk insurance has not been the only one that has made developing countries a bit wary. From the point of view of host countries, the new property rights system was not being very constructive. The moral hazard associated with the insurance surely had encouraged some investors to avoid renegotiation when economic crises hit Indonesia and other countries. And Indonesians saw themselves as having few rights when CalEnergy filed a claim with OPIC or when OPIC sought reimbursement from Indonesia.

Reform of official political risk insurance ought surely to begin with a review of how the policies are issued. An OPIC official admitted to us that they knew of possible corruption in the CalEnergy projects before the agency insured them. His justification for proceeding: Countries with U.S. foreign direct investment are better friends of the United States than those without. Whether the contention and implied causality is correct or not, we believe that it is a poor excuse for supporting corruption. Moreover, although the agency's application for coverage includes information that could be used to evaluate the economic impact of projects, it is not clear that acceptance is driven either by an evaluation of development effects or by the probability that the arrangement will be stable. It ought to be.

Further, and unlike many private insurers, public agencies appear to pay little attention to actual or potential moral hazards. If OPIC would insure only a smaller percentage of the equity, forcing more of the risk onto the investor, one aspect of moral hazard ought to decline. Second, allowing OPIC to seek something less than full reimbursement from host countries would reduce the perception that it faces no loss if it decides to pay claims.[120]

Moreover, OPIC could practice what the U.S. government preaches to developing countries: transparency. We see no good reason, for example, for OPIC's refusal to provide copies of insurance policies to host governments when an investor files a claim. If the policies ever contained any real business secrets, protecting them is surely irrelevant by this point in the life of the project.

In theory, host countries can appeal to arbitration themselves if they want to challenge the collection efforts of an official insurer. This is a clumsy method and one that host countries are wary of exercising, given possible retaliation by a home government.[121] Allowing the host government some degree of participation in the awards process would help alleviate the concerns. In the CalEnergy case, confidence would have improved if Indonesia had had the opportunity, before OPIC decided to make an award, to counter some of the stories that had reached OPIC about the alleged kidnapping.

Finally, collection compacts with private insurers seem to us to be carrying the government role in the private sector too far. Why, we ask, should the private sector be subsidized by the backing of home governments, at a cost in terms of foreign relations?

The next story will examine another case of official political risk insurance. Although the World Bank's Multilateral Investment Guarantee Agency behaved differently from OPIC, the outcome suggests some rather similar problems.

15

Enron: Another Kind
of Official Insurance

You don't want a silver kris *in your back.*
—MIGA official[1]

O ne more power project was the subject of an insurance claim. The story of Enron's attempt to build in East Java is mercifully brief compared with our other tales. The importance of the story lies primarily in why the Multilateral Investment Guarantee Agency (MIGA), the insurance agency of the World Bank Group, issued a policy for the project in the first place and in the cordial relation that MIGA retained with Indonesians when the conflict occurred.

The Enron Project

Originally, PLN, the state-owned electricity company, was to build and own a 500-megawatt gas-fired power plant in Pasuruan, East Java. But somehow a proposal from Enron Development Corporation was "brought to the attention of President Soeharto."[2] In 1994, Enron negotiated the basic terms for the plant, to cost some $520 million and sell electricity at 5.76 cents/kwh.[3] The contract would be for 20 years. The proposal was that $394 million in funds would come from Credit Suisse First Boston (CSFB) and Lehman Brothers' leadership. The final deal for East Java Power was not concluded and signed until November 18, 1996.

Enron sought (some interviewees told us "bought") powerful parties to back its investments. Enron would hold 50.1% of the equity (through Enron Java Power Corporation), with 25% held by the Indonesian Pasuruan

Power Company and the remaining 24.9% by Hong Kong–based Prince Holdings, Ltd.

Prince is a bit mysterious. According to the Indonesian business people we interviewed, the company was held either by Hutchinson Whampoa, Ltd., or directly by Hutchinson's chairman, Lee Kai Shing, along with the Salim Group, the company of powerful Suharto crony Liem Sioe Liong. A U.S. embassy report and PLN documents list the company as headed by Johannes Kotjo,[4] who was closely connected with Bambang Trihatmodjo, President Suharto's son. Whatever the exact ownership and control of Prince, it brought influence.

The participation of Pasuruan Power Company in the project further cemented Enron's political connections. This company's major shareholders were Anthony Salim, son of Liem Sioe Liong, the same Johannes Kotjo, and Bambang, son of President Suharto.

In the style for which Enron was to become known, it convinced the U.S. government to press for contracts in Indonesia. Secretary of Commerce Brown personally wrote the coordinating minister for trade and industry, Hartarto, to urge him to give "full consideration to the proposals." He explained, in one of his 1995 letters,

> Enron Power, a world renowned private power developer, is in the final stages of negotiating two combined cycle, gas turbine power projects. The first, a 500 MW plant in East Java, should begin commercial power generation by the end of 1997 if it can promptly negotiate a gas supply Memorandum of Understanding with Pertamina. The other project, a smaller plant in East Kalimantan [Indonesian Borneo], also awaits a gas supply agreement.[5]

In sum, *Power Play*, the title of a book on Enron's involvement in India, could apply equally to the company's approach to this proposed investment in Indonesia.[6]

Crisis and MIGA Insurance

Enron bought political risk insurance on the East Java project from the World Bank's MIGA. MIGA had been created in 1988, much later than the Overseas Private Investment Corporation (OPIC), and it reflected the enthusiasm for private foreign investment that gripped the World Bank during the period. By providing coverage against creeping expropriation, MIGA had added to the new international property rights. Enron was willing to pay for the protection.

Enron, like many other firms that venture abroad, must have considered MIGA's involvement as a guarantee, as much as insurance. In fact, so did MIGA, as captured in its name and the fashion in which it promoted itself.[7] It seemed unlikely that a host government that needed World Bank funds would cross MIGA by taking property that it insured.[8] The guarantee appeared to be very solid; MIGA had *never* had to pay a claim. But Enron's policy, which took effect in 1997, just in time for the currency crisis, would damage that record.[9]

When the crisis struck Indonesia, the unexpected happened: The Indonesians suspended the project, and, as far as MIGA was concerned, they breached Enron's contract. The company claimed that it had spent $25 million, even though *no* construction had begun. Critics said that the bulk of this money had gone to President Suharto's son to lay the "groundwork" for the project; we have seen no evidence, however, on either side of this contention. One might opine that some significant sum had been paid to Enron's negotiators, given the company's policy of paying bonuses to managers when a deal is concluded. In any event, Enron sought compensation from MIGA, asking for $15 million under its insurance contract.

Unlike OPIC, MIGA did not require a legal ruling to support a claim.[10] Bitter arbitration could be avoided, but the insurance contract did call for a short "cooling off" period. MIGA asked Enron to extend the period so that it could try to find an alternative solution, promising interest payments on any sum it eventually paid. The decision on a delay and a substitute project had to go to a very high level in Enron: to Rebecca Mark, according to a MIGA official. He made sure it was accompanied by a message that the company should carefully consider its position: "If you want to be able to have lunch again in this town, don't go for broke on a $15 million claim. Indonesia is a country with enormous resources. It needs Enron's skills."

MIGA clearly understood that an insurance award would likely end the company's business future in the host country. The official then implied that the Indonesians could fight: "They are used to carrying a *kris* in the belt. They could pull it out. You don't want a silver *kris* in your back."[11] Enron accepted the proposed delay, whether it was interested in the lunch option or feared the dagger.

MIGA used the time for an heroic effort to mediate a solution. A MIGA lawyer, Lauren ("Laddy") Weisenfeld, was dispatched to Indonesia to find a solution. His goal was to identify another project for Enron where it could recoup its losses. Peter Jezek and Weisenfeld came up with several alternatives. One was "marrying" Enron to a local firm that had a contract for a Sumatran pipeline,[12] but this would require some $100 million from Enron, more than they had in mind, especially for a deteriorating environment. Over the next nine months, projects were proposed (at least two by Enron, according to PLN) and eliminated, as MIGA and Enron extended the settlement period. One problem, according to a MIGA official, was that most likely projects would have to come from Pertamina, but it showed little interest. Even Kwik, the economic coordinating minister, could not induce the head of Pertamina to cooperate, we were told.

The struggle to come up with another project for Enron occurred at an inopportune time, for the company was undergoing change. Along with

CalEnergy, Florida Power & Light, and Caithness, Enron was evolving into a company with no long-term interest in continuing in Indonesian power, regardless of the opportunities it promised. One of its representatives reported that the company was leaving emerging markets because it could not earn the returns there that it could get elsewhere.[13] In fact, Enron's lack of interest in continuing had even deeper roots. The company was facing an intense internal struggle over its future: Would it focus on hard assets (such as power plants and pipelines) or on financial transactions (such as trading in energy futures)?

The traders would win the battle inside Enron over the future direction of the company. As a result, Enron would offer its overseas power plants for sale, considerably before its collapse into bankruptcy. We are not sure exactly when the victory for the traders was evident to Enron's managers, but the battles must have affected interest in alternative hard-asset projects in Indonesia.

When the last extension expired, MIGA had no choice but to pay, unless it were to claim that the policy was invalid. In fact, MIGA might well have done just that. Because MIGA policies carried clauses that paralleled OPIC's on bribes, it could have asserted that Enron's arrangements with its partners (the usual equity-for-loan deals) amounted to corruption and were thus contrary to Indonesian laws.[14] Then-president Gus Dur, however, had made it clear by this time that he did not want cases to be based on allegations of corruption. Thus, like OPIC, MIGA could not have relied on Indonesia to provide evidence. In the end, according to a World Bank official, as the amount of the claim was small, it was better simply to pay the agency's first claim and show the business world that MIGA insurance was good. He did not add that the payment would not cost MIGA anything anyway because MIGA would, like OPIC, turn around and demand that Indonesia reimburse the organization.

So, in June 2000, MIGA paid $15 million plus interest to Enron. It seems that all but $4 million of MIGA's obligation had been reinsured. Even in the short run, MIGA was out little.

Reimbursement to MIGA

MIGA soon sought reimbursement from the Indonesian government. Weisenfeldt took a draft agreement to the economic coordinating minister, Kwik, and the document sat for a few months. When Ramli replaced Kwik as economic coordinating minister, Weisenfeldt returned to Indonesia (in October 2000) to meet with the new minister as well as Purnomo Yusgiantoro, the minister of mines and energy, and Djunaedi Hadisumarto, the chairman of the National Planning Agency (BAPPENAS). Weisenfeldt reports pressing the coordinating minister to sign. A few months later, in January 2001, the minister of finance (by this time, Prijadi Praptosuhardjo, who held the position only briefly) finally did sign.

The Indonesian government agreed to reimburse MIGA over a three-year period for the $15 million (plus interest). In fact, Indonesia had little choice in the matter, given the pressure that the World Bank Group could muster if it chose to do so; but we have heard no claims that MIGA or the World Bank actually pronounced any threats. To be sure, Indonesia had been removed from the list of insurance-eligible countries. With the reimbursement agreement in hand, in February 2001 MIGA lifted its ban on insurance in Indonesia. Indonesia lived up to its commitment: MIGA reports having received the last installment on the payment in June 2003.[15]

On the surface, the events appear to reflect the same kind of "moral hazard" as governed OPIC insurance. With insurance to cover most of what it had invested and little interest in continuing with the project or a similar one, Enron had turned to its insurance coverage. Similarly, MIGA had little incentive to contest the claim. The fact that it could force Indonesia to reimburse it created another form of moral hazard. On the other hand, our interviews suggest that MIGA's decision to pay was driven largely by the relatively small size of the claim and its desire not to be seen as difficult by potential investor clients when it was faced with its first claim. Still, the decision to pay must be easier if the money, in the end, does not come from the insurer's pocketbook.

The styles of MIGA and OPIC in Indonesia were rather different. The drastic disparity in sizes of the sums involved may, of course, explain some of the differences. Whatever the reasons, the negotiations between MIGA and the Indonesian government remained cordial. One statement allegedly made by an Indonesian minister caught the flavor, as Indonesians saw the two events: "These guys from OPIC, five of them, all come in in dark suits, heavy attaché cases, drop them on the floor, we want to click our heels. You [MIGA] come in with jacket over your shoulder, alone, with a light folder for documents."[16]

At least from an international relations point of view, MIGA acquitted itself quite well. If it had made a serious mistake, it was in insuring the project in the first place.

Inside the World Bank

Indeed, we were puzzled as to why MIGA had issued the insurance. The World Bank's field office in Jakarta had questioned the power deals from the outset, as had visiting Bank missions from Washington. The local office's negative view of power terms seems to have convinced the International Finance Corporation not to provide money to Tanjung Jati B. The office's views, however, failed to keep MIGA from issuing insurance to both Enron and GE.

The World Bank was well aware of the poor financial condition of PLN, and it knew of the participation of the president's son and the shareholdings of crony businessmen in Pasuruan. With its stated goal of helping poor countries, it seemed like bad business and bad development policy for the World Bank's MIGA to insure a project where the customer was unlikely to be able to honor the contract, where the foreign investor brought little to the table other than money, and where the scent of corruption was so strong.

When we asked a MIGA official, in 2004, why the agency had issued a policy under these conditions, he told us that MIGA had been under great pressure to expand its business. He claims that the full information, with all its warts, went to the MIGA board for approval, and then to the World Bank's president himself. The official was unwilling to provide further explanation of the decision at the top, but it seems that the approvals came without further consultations with the Indonesia experts in the country office.

Until official insurance agencies, such as MIGA and OPIC, become tougher in making decisions about what investments to insure, claims like those of Enron and CalEnergy are likely to continue. We believe that it is easier to say no when an application for insurance coverage is being evaluated, even in the face of political pressure, than it is to deny the claims later. Events such as those involving Enron and CalEnergy are costly to poor countries and to international relations. Eventually, they will add to questions about the new property rights system.

16

Nationality, Corporate Strategy, and the New Property Rights

In the business world, the rearview mirror is always clearer than the windshield.
—Warren Buffett

By 2004, the restructuring of the 27 private power agreements was all but complete. Only the Karaha Bodas battle still raged. The overall outcomes support some important conclusions about corporate behavior and the new international property rights.

But first, brief summaries of two more stories will suggest that the nationality of an owner matters in a company's decisions with respect to the role of the new property rights and that it was possible for at least one investor to escape pressures to include questionable partners. Moreover, the notable absence of some major international power companies raises questions about why they chose not to join competitors in the world's fourth largest country.

Tanjung Jati B

No story of foreign investment in Asia would be complete without a Japanese project. Indeed, data for Indonesian investment approvals indicate that Japanese direct investment accounted for the largest amount of investment from any single country.[1] But this investment was primarily in manufacturing. In the power sector, Japanese money went to minority positions in a number of projects, such as Paiton I and Karaha Bodas. In only one case—Tanjung Jati B—did a Japanese firm assume the lead in a large project that had made significant progress by the time the currency crisis hit.[2] In this case, the Japanese government became active when a national investor was at risk, but both the Japanese investor and its government behaved rather differently from the Americans. The differences showed up in attitudes toward both contracts and dispute settlement.

Tanjung Jati B was coal fired and would have a capacity of 1,320 megawatts, similar to Paiton I. The agreement was signed on September 16, 1994,[3] and the project was to be completed in 1999. Moreover, it was also to be part of a complex of power plants, in this case to be located in Central Java. The project was originally planned to cost just under $1.8 billion. Although there is some disagreement in public reports, it seems that the price was to be 5.73 cents per kilowatt hour (cents/kwh), less than Paiton I's tariff.[4]

Wu and Southern

The original sponsor of Tanjung Jati B was Hong Kong's Gordon Wu, none other than the businessman who is said to have inspired Intercontinental to go to Asia and who had himself earlier sought Paiton I. Failing to obtain Paiton I when Ginandjar was minister of mines and energy, Wu returned when Ida Bagus Sudjana was appointed to replace Ginandjar, hooking up mainly with Adnan Ganto, Sudjana's advisor.

After an aborted second attempt to obtain Paiton I through Ganto, Wu did not give up on the site (see Chapter 9). At first, he sought permission to build another facility at the same location. Advisors to the Indonesians warned against this, arguing that the two private projects being negotiated already (Paiton I and Paiton II) and PLN's facilities were going to be difficult enough to coordinate without adding an additional private builder.

Wu identified Tanjung Jati B as an alternative. Rather than submit a formal proposal for the investment, he sent an offer in a letter of no more than six pages. Although the government was in lengthy negotiations with foreign companies for other power plants, Wu received an astonishingly prompt response that gave him preliminary approval to proceed. The speedy result, advisor Peter Jezek wryly noted, raises "serious questions about the transparency of the process."

Wu's ability to jump the queue caused some delays in other projects.[5] Whatever the cost, Wu's Hong Kong–based Hopewell Holdings Ltd. ended up with an 80% interest in Tanjung Jati B, which he would hold through his Consolidated Electric Power Asia (CEPA).

This project also included an influential local partner, Djan Farid, a close associate of Suharto's oldest daughter.[6] The daughter's exact interest is unclear, but others in the power business consider her to have been the actual partner. Farid's company and Wu incorporated PT Hopewell Impa Tubanan Power (PT HI Tubanan Power) to own the power plant.

Wu initiated discussions with the International Finance Corporation (IFC) for money. In the end, the coolness of the World Bank's country office led the IFC to decide not to finance any of the Indonesian power projects. The involvement of the First Family and cronies was too much.

Even without clear finance, some construction had begun by November 1996. But despite its early optimism about Asian power, or perhaps because of it, by the mid-1990s the Wu group was running into cash-flow problems. It had made many offers for power plants; more were accepted than it could handle. One advisor in Indonesia described Hopewell, Wu's main company, as "trying to become the McDonalds of electric power." Debt was climbing, while Wu gained a reputation of going ahead with projects against the advice of his technical experts.

Selling the CEPA holding company with all its projects would provide Wu an exit from his mounting problems. In 1996, a buyer appeared, in the form of Southern Company of Atlanta, which agreed to acquire 80% interest. CEPA served Southern's strategy of targeting emerging markets for power projects because CEPA specialized in exactly this kind of business. Its acquisition would catapult Southern into the top ranks of international power players. But Southern had serious misgivings about Tanjung Jati B.[7] The package of contracts and financing for the project had not been completed, and Southern executives feared that corruption was involved. Although Hong Kong investors did not face the constraints of the U.S. Foreign Corrupt Practices Act, Southern did.

Southern had specified that acquiring Tanjung Jati B with the deal would be contingent on all contracts and financing being in place by a certain date. Some $140 million was withheld from the purchase price for the contingency. Without a completed power purchase agreement by the specified date, Southern decided to delay a progress payment that was owed Wu. In the end, still pessimistic about this project, Southern bought full ownership in CEPA without Tanjung Jati B. Left with Tanjung Jati B, Wu transferred it from CEPA into Hopewell, another of his companies. A Southern manager told us that even after Southern was out of the project, it received a claim from someone for a $30 million "success fee." Southern responded that this was Wu's problem. Southern managers seemed pleased to be free of this troublesome project.

Southern held onto CEPA's projects in China, the Philippines, and Pakistan, through its subsidiary Southern Energy. But Southern's enthusiasm for the developing world was eventually to wear thin, like that of some other inexperienced international investors. It spun off Southern Energy, with its overseas projects, to become Mirant. Mirant retained interests in Asia, the Caribbean, and, for a while, Europe. By 2003, the company had dropped most of its European interests and was restructuring its debt in a struggle against bankruptcy. Southern itself was no longer a major player internationally; rather, it returned to its traditional U.S. roots.

Negotiating with the Japanese

Meanwhile, in April 1997, Sumitomo had begun serious construction work at Tanjung Jati B and had put up a $530 million syndicated loan and bridge funding. One report[8] says Sumitomo had completed 70% of the project when the Asian Currency Crisis hit Indonesia. In February 1998, negotiations began on the future of the facility. Those discussions, now with the Japanese, eventually took a turn that differentiated them from the others we have discussed.

Because Sumitomo had not been paid for its work, it stopped construction at least by May 1998.[9] Hopewell, the project's actual majority owner, declared *force majeure* in September of that year, when bankers would put up no more money and other contractors would also not proceed without being paid. Sumitomo appears to have assumed effective control in exchange for the construction costs it had incurred thus far. The Japanese company now had a reason to find a way to complete the project. It needed a business with income so that it could collect for its construction work.

Unlike other investors, Sumitomo itself initiated a proposal to the Indonesians. The company would seek low-interest loans from Japanese export credit agencies so that PLN could buy the project from Hopewell at a hefty discount and contract with Sumitomo to complete it. Reportedly, managers of Tanjung Jati B said that this buyout would allow the project to sell electricity for an unlikely low price of 2.3 cents/kwh.[10] Sumitomo proceeded to convince the Japanese government to offer a loan to PLN on concessionary terms.[11]

PLN showed some interest in Sumitomo's proposal, and discussions began about exactly what concessionary terms a Japanese government loan would entail. In September 1999, PLN announced a preliminary agreement to borrow something over $1.5 billion, at 1% interest, with a 10-year grace period, to be repaid over 40 years.[12] Of this, $1.15 million would be used to purchase the plant, which Sumitomo would complete for a total cost of $1.77 billion by 2003.[13] Given the importance of capital costs in a power plant, this concessionary loan could indeed enable Tanjung Jati B to sell power at a low tariff. The offer was tempting for Indonesians, but it came before the government had made overall policy decisions about the industry.

By sometime in 2001, the Indonesian government was no longer so tempted. The Japanese had made it clear that they were asking for government guarantees on the loan. Indonesians feared that yielding would set a bad precedent for other renegotiations; and, anyway, guarantees were counter to the original policy and decree on power. But if the liability for the loans was to be PLN's alone, it was the Japanese who would balk.

In September or October of 2001, a new proposal emerged. The Indonesian government announced that it would continue the Tanjung Jati B project under a 20-year "build, lease, and transfer" scheme. Although the lease fee was reported to be 2.26 to 3.25 cents/kwh of electricity delivered,[14] the exact meaning of this figure has not been made public. In any case, the low price reported certainly made the transaction easier to sell politically. As part of the deal, funding of $1.65 billion would be assembled by the Japan Bank for International Cooperation.[15] The arrangement appeared to be settled in November 2001, and the plant was rescheduled to go into operation in 2004[16] or 2005. Still, several details remained to be resolved: for example, the transfer of Hopewell's interest to Sumitomo had not been effected. More perplexing, Indonesian officials began an internal debate about whether a lease project like this would be subject to burdensome government procurement rules: in particular, to a 1982 regulation that required any foreign purchase amounting to more than $500 million to include a counter-trade element.[17] In that case, the Japanese would have to purchase some amount of Indonesian goods as part of the deal. This could bring down the tentative agreement.

Presumably a way was found to skirt the counter-trade requirement, but it took until May of 2003, when power shortages again loomed on Java, for the parties to clean up all the remaining issues and sign the lease agreement with PLN.[18] In the end, the price of electricity was capped at 5.6 cents/kwh; the fixed components amounted to 3.86 to 4.6 cents/kwh.[19] The date for commercial operation had now slipped to 2006. Other details have not been made public.

With a deal in hand, Sumitomo formally acquired Hopewell's 80% interest for $306.2 million. Of this, some $38 million would be paid to contractors and, vaguely, to "government authorities." Because Suharto's daughter, or her stand-in, had sold her interest in the project at some point,[20] Sumitomo ended up with 100% of the equity.

How should one interpret the deal? Rather than taking on a loan to buy back the project, PLN took on a lease commitment, which the government seems to have guaranteed. Sure, in substance the lease arrangement was no more than a loan. And the government guarantee of the lease was no less than the proposed and rejected loan guarantee. But Indonesians felt that they could call this a one-off deal, and that it would therefore not set a precedent for other settlements. The low-cost capital was attractive, and it had become clear that the power was needed. But the nongovernmental organization (NGO) that was alleged to comprise disgruntled PLN employees was quick to grasp the reality of the disguised guaranteed loan and soon began to criticize it.

Lessons

Negotiations with the Japanese were rather special. First, there was never any question about the willingness of the Japanese to renegotiate. They did not insist on "sanctity of contract," and, as far as we could determine, they never threatened to turn to arbitration. When it had become clear that changed circumstances meant that PLN could not honor the original deal, the Japanese recognized that something new had to be arranged. Settlement on a new deal might be difficult, and for sure the Japanese could be tough negotiators, but there was no grand legal principle involved.

One could argue that there was nothing especially Japanese or even Asian about the outcome. After all, Sumitomo was a company with extensive interests in Indonesia. Because conflict might have damaged its other projects, the company had a strong incentive not to be confrontational. Yet Mission, which also intended to stay in the country, had threatened arbitration and resisted proposed new terms to the point that the Indonesians went to court. We believe especially Japanese characteristics were evident: The Japanese have rather consistently tried to avoid confrontations over business matters.

The tendency of the Japanese to avoid arbitration is evident in the list of the companies that have taken disputes to the International Centre for the Settlement of Investment Disputes (ICSID). As far as we could discern as of June 2004, not one of the 159 settled or pending cases was led by a Japanese investor, nor was any arbitrator Japanese. When we asked a number of experts on arbitration of investment disputes for examples of Japanese companies that had turned to arbitration, they came up with only one: A Dutch subsidiary of Nomura, a Japanese company, had initiated arbitration against the Czech Republic.[21] Nomura, some say, is one of the most American of Japanese companies. Although arbitration seems to have arrived in Japan with British maritime transactions and Japan does have arbitration laws, we are told that arbitration has not become a common method of settling differences even within Japan. We can only conclude that the system of international arbitration that has emerged to ensure property rights to foreign investors has little appeal to Japanese companies. In fact, they seem to find American confrontational approaches rather repulsive.

Japanese dismay at the tactics of American firms is shown in rather charming language in a report with a Japanese author on power in Indonesia:

> While some Asian vendors appear to be interested in reaching compromise involving reduced tariffs, the American vendors were recalcitrant with support of US Commerce, State and Treasury departments. Their claims are rooted from the principle of sanctity of contracts, i.e. contracts are to be honored in good and bad times. The dispute between PLN and the American IPPs have forced both sides to seek settlement through arbitration agency as well as through the court.[22]

The Japanese consider their approach to be not only Japanese but also "Asian," as the excerpt suggests. Indonesians view themselves as being very different from the Japanese, and we have seen Indonesians take offense when Japanese say to them "we Asians"; however, in their tendency to avoid direct confrontation, the Japanese do share norms with Indonesians and many other Southeast and East Asians.

The differences between the roles of the Japanese government and the U.S. government in the power disputes are also striking. The Japanese export credit agencies joined with the American and European agencies when the projects involved were primarily U.S.-led (or European-led), and they were aggressive partners. In the case of the Japanese-led project, however, the Japanese government did not insist on sanctity of contract, but rather proposed alternative plans to solve the problem, and it did so long before a legal dispute would make accommodation difficult. By offering a low-cost loan to bail out the Japanese investor, the government made it possible for the Japanese company to save face and money, and concluded a deal that was probably good for Indonesia,[23] though at a cost to Japanese taxpayers.

To be sure, an Overseas Private Investment Corporation (OPIC) official reported that he had, at one point, also raised the possibility of its lending the Indonesian government money to buy the American CalEnergy projects. Indonesians did not respond positively and quickly, probably because (1) the proposal was clearly for a loan to the government, and policy prohibited such a commitment; and (2) the government had no effective decision process at the time. Counsel for the Indonesians believed that OPIC paid the company claim prematurely, ending the possibility of alternative solutions. Probably more important, Sumitomo wanted a settlement, but the American investor, as far as we can tell, showed little interest in any kind of negotiated settlement and thus did not push its home government proposal. In any event, the U.S. government soon abandoned its proposal and did not offer a clever alternative.

A Singular Investor: Amoseas

A quick look at the partners (Table 16.1) in the power projects supports the widespread belief of investors that incorporating powerful local partners was the only way to a deal. On the other hand, one foreign investor managed without taking in a partner closely tied into the Suharto clan: Amoseas, with its Darajat geothermal plant.

Amoseas was owned by Chevron and Texaco, major petroleum companies with years of experience in Indonesian oil production, including through another joint venture, Caltex.[24] The parent companies and their affiliates had long worked with Pertamina, the state-owned company that controlled both petroleum and geothermal resources. Amoseas itself had been created in 1970 for oil and gas exploration outside Sumatra, largely in the area from Irian Jaya to the Natuna Sea.

Amoseas also had a much longer history in Indonesian electric power than the other investors we have described. Its involvement in Darajat, a geothermal project near Bandung on Java had begun in 1984 when the company obtained contracts with Pertamina and PLN to build a 55-megawatt generating plant. Because this was before private generation had been authorized, the plant was owned and operated by PLN. Moreover, because the president's family and associates had not yet become captivated by the private benefits of power, none were involved in the deal. The plant had started generating in November 1994.

Table 16.1 Influential Indonesian Partners in Foreign-Owned Power Plants

Project	Principal Foreign Owner(s)	Influential Participant(s)
Paiton I[a]	Edison Mission Energy (US)	Hashim Djojohadikusumo (brother-in-law of Siti Hediati) Siti Hediati Haryadi (Titiek, second daughter of President Suharto) and Agus Kartasasmito (brother of Minister of Mines and Energy Ginandjar)
Tanjung Jati B[a]	CEPA (HK) ⇒Sumitomo (J)	Siti Hardiyanti Rukmana (Tutut, first daughter of Suharto)
Paiton II	Siemens (Germany)/ PowerGen (UK)	Bambang Trihatmodjo (second son of Suharto)
Pare-Pare	?[b]	—[c]
Sengkang[a]	El Paso (US)	Siti Hardiyanti Rukmana (Tutut, first daughter of Suharto)
Palembang Timur	Coastal (US)	Bob Hasan (crony Chinese businessman)
Salak	Unocal (US)	Bob Hasan (closest crony of Suharto)
Darajat[a]	Amoseas (US)	None
Sarulla	Unocal (US)	Tommy Suharto (third son of Suharto) and Bob Hasan (crony Chinese businessman)
Wayang Windu	Asia Power (NZ/ Singapore/ Malaysia) ⇒Unocal (US)	Bambang Trihatmodjo (second son of Suharto); another report says Tommy Suharto.
Sibayak	Enserch (US)	—[c]
Cilacap	Mitsubishi (J)/ Duke Power (US)	Bambang Trihatmodjo (second son of Suharto)
Tanjung Jati A	Tomen (J)/ National Power (UK)	Siti Hediati Haryadi (Titiek, second daughter of Suharto) and Bakrie (*pribumi* business group close to Suharto)
Tanjung Jati C	A Gordon Wu company (HK)	Siti Hardiyanti Rukmana (Tutut, first daughter of Suharto)
Dieng[a]	CalEnergy (US)	Himpurna (retired military officers)
Patuha[a]	CalEnergy (US)	Muhammad Lutfi (son-in-law of minister Hartarto)
Bedugul[a]	CalEnergy (US)	Sigit Hardjojudanto (first son of Suharto)
Karaha Bodas[a]	Florida Power & Light/Caithness (US)	Tantyo Sudharmono (son of the vice president) and possibly friends of Suharto's wife
Pasuruan[a]	Enron (US)	Bambang Trihatmodjo (second son of Suharto) and crony Chinese businessmen

[a]Described in text.

[b]We are not sure of the lead partner in the Pare-Pare project. Wärtsilä (Finland) had a contract to provide the power plant but reports that it was not the lead investor. Tomen (Japan) had an interest in the project.

[c]We could not identify local partners in Pare-Pare and Sibayak.

Source: Assembled primarily from information provided by one power investor.

Amoseas joined the new group of private power producers in 1995 when it negotiated an amended Energy Sales Contract for Darajat, which authorized expansion of steam capacity and a second power plant for an additional 70 megawatts, with an estimated potential output of 330 megawatts.[25] Under the new rules, Amoseas would formally operate the steam field and the power plant itself.

In committing to the expansion, Amoseas was responding to the eagerness of Indonesians to produce more geothermal power. Its willingness to help Pertamina's early development seems to have been enough to exempt the company from the need for a powerful Suharto relative or crony. To be sure, Amoseas did seek out a partner, a firm owned by Julius Tahija and his two sons Sjakon G. Tahija (an eye surgeon) and George Tahija (a businessman with an MBA from the Darden School, University of Virginia). Appointed to head Caltex in Indonesia, the father, Julius, had become the first Indonesian to head a major foreign petroleum venture in the country. In this position, he had developed a remarkable reputation for remaining "clean." One article describes him as "well known for his conservatism and firm stance on business ethics."[26] After refusing to approve loans from the (at the time) Tahija-controlled Bank Niaga to Tommy Suharto for a car manufacturing venture, the older son, George, said, "My father taught me that you never do things for which you owe people favors."[27] Others we questioned confirmed that Julius and his sons were not at all like the partners we have encountered in the power projects described thus far.[28] One advisor told us "they were as solid as a rock." Sure, the Tahijas had influence, but not through First Family ties, cronyism, or politics. It is probably no surprise that the Tahija group put up the money themselves for their shares—no carried-interest loans or free shares like we have seen in other projects. In fact, the two investors, Amoseas and the Tahija group, provided the entire funds for Darajat without any project finance.

Maybe another company, without previous ties to a project and without extensive experience in Indonesia, could not have pulled off an investment in power without a political partner. But Amoseas proved it was possible under certain conditions.

The Amoseas project stands out from some others in still another way. After the economic crisis hit and the company was faced with demands to lower its electricity prices, it rather quickly renegotiated the terms, from more than 6.9 cents in the original contracts to 4.2 cents/kwh.

There is a simple and plausible explanation why renegotiations for this project moved rather quickly and smoothly. For Amoseas's foreign owners—two giant oil companies—the geothermal power project was small potatoes. Indonesia's oil was what counted. In this, Amoseas was more like ITT than some other investors in Indonesian power. Neither would engage in a bitter fight that might threaten its other interests in the country. Presumably Amoseas's cooperation paid off even in the power sector. In 1997, the company obtained an additional contract, to develop the North Duri Co-generation Project, a power plant dedicated to supply its affiliate PT Caltex Pacific Indonesia. With the two projects, the company has grown to some importance in Indonesia's power industry, in addition to satisfying the more important goal of surviving as a major oil producer there.

Oil as a Lubricant for Renegotiations

More oil and gas companies owned power projects in Indonesia. Although they were less pure in their choice of partners, they all followed the Amoseas path when problems arose.

Sengkang, a gas-fed project in South Sulawesi, belonged to El Paso Energy (a subsidiary of the American El Paso Corporation, primarily a gas company) and Energy Equity Corporation (an Australian oil and gas company). Like CalEnergy, the project carried political risk insurance with OPIC. When the crisis hit, rather than rush to arbitration to claim insurance, however, it became one of the first projects to begin discussions about new payment terms and, as far as we can determine, was the first to reach some kind of accord. This was even though advisors to the Indonesians describe its negotiators as being very difficult.[29] One result was that the project grew. In 2001, the company announced that it would build an additional 50-megawatt unit. OPIC even provided additional coverage in spite of its dispute with Indonesia over CalEnergy.[30]

Unocal, another oil and gas company, led power projects at Gunung Salak[31] and Sarulla. Unocal built a reputation with Indonesians for spending money lavishly, and not only on what an advisor called a "gold plated project." The advisor held this out as a contrast to Amoseas, which had tried to economize. He told us that Unocal managers took the minister of mines and energy, Ginandjar, for a golf tournament in Bali and came back with a signed deal for a project. When it came to renegotiations, Indonesians reported finding Unocal much more difficult to deal with than Amoseas, but like the other oil companies Unocal did not go to arbitration. In the end, it settled for a lower price at Gunung Salak,[32] and sold its Sarulla[33] interests to Pertamina.[34]

Unocal later became involved in still another power project in Indonesia, Wayang Windu. The lead foreign partner in Wayang Windu had originally been Asia Power, a subsidiary of Brierley Investment, a diversified New Zealand–based investment firm with strong Singapore and Malaysian Chinese interests as well as holdings by a Singapore government company. According to one source, Asia Power had invested around $190 million in Wayang Windu, with an additional $250 million in loans, to build half the planned capacity.[35] Mired in financial difficulties, Asia Power surrendered the project to its bank lenders, who in turn brought in Unocal in 2001 as the operator (and part owner).[36] Eventually, the project seems to have ended up in the hands of a newly formed British company, Star Energy, another firm interested in Indonesian oil. Sometime during the shifts, the price of electricity was successfully renegotiated sharply downward. We do not know, however, what role, if any, Unocal had in the price drop. (See Table 16.2.)

None of the petroleum companies that led power projects claimed insurance or turned to arbitration. Some seem to have distanced themselves a bit from U.S. government pressure as well. Their managers knew where their companies' interests lay: in Indonesia's oil and gas sector.

Absences

A reader who is familiar with independent providers of electric power around the world might have noticed the absence in Indonesia of one of the largest American players in international power production: the AES Corporation.[37] In 2003, the company reported investments in 28 countries on five continents with 158 generating facilities and more than 55 gigawatts of capacity. Yet it was not present in the world's fourth most populous country, Indonesia.

AES claims a set of "shared principles": fairness, integrity, social responsibility, and fun. Those values supposedly kept AES from business in Indonesia (and from investments in nuclear energy). With respect to Indonesia, the relevant principle was presumably integrity: the fear that the level of corruption would be too much for the company. This was so even though AES did manage to invest in Nigeria, a country where corruption is arguably more rampant than in Indonesia; AES claims that it was nevertheless able to stick to its values.[38]

Another large U.S. player that had expanded abroad was also notably absent from Indonesia: Southern Company.[39] We have described this company's rejection of Tanjung Jati B. In interviews, Southern's managers were quite frank with us about their reasons for avoiding Indonesia: The corruption required to succeed might be beyond what the U.S. Foreign Corrupt Practices Act would tolerate.

We suspect that AES's and Southern's care was warranted. Unlike Amoseas, new arrivals such as AES or Southern would likely have been pushed into deals like those others accepted. This requirement and other likely invitations for unofficial payments would bring an investor at least dangerously close to the edges of the U.S. Foreign Corrupt Practices Act. Whether technically illegal or not, some of the steps that would be required would not help the image of the companies if they were reported on the front page of the *New York Times* or the *Wall Street Journal.*[40]

Wrapping Up the Restructuring

In June 2003, the chair of the ministerial team for restructuring power agreements announced that renegotiations had been completed. Of 27 projects, seven had been terminated,[41] and the government was considering

Table 16.2 Initial Price and New Terms for 27 Power Projects

Project	Original Price, (U.S. cents per kilowatt hour)	Renegotiated Price	Date of Commercial Operation	Notes
Tanjung Jati B	5.73	Maximum 5.6, with fixed at 3.85–4.6	2006	
Amurang	6.7	4.65	2006	
Sibolga	6.55	4.6	2006	
Palembang Timur	6.48	4.41	2004	
Pare-Pare	6.21	5.71 plus $12.9 million arrears	1998	
Asahan	Levelized = 6.44	Levelized = 4.4	2007	Prices divided into firm energy and secondary energy supplies.
Bedugul	7.15	70% of power price in Bali	2006	
Sibayak	7.1	4.7	2006	
Cikarang	5.99	4.47 plus $41 million arrears	1998	
Paiton I	8.5/8.2/5.5 according to period (see text)	4.93 plus $4 million/month arrears	2000	
Paiton II	6.6	4.68 plus $0.9 million/month arrears	2000	
Salak	Steam 4.3 Electricity 6.95	Steam 3.7 Electricity 4.45 Plus $144.6 million arrears	1997	
Darajat	Steam 4.3 Electricity 6.95	Steam 3.15 Electricity 4.2 Plus $25 million arrears	2000	
Sengkang	6.7	4.42 plus $30 million arrears	135-mw 1997 65-mw 2005	
Sarula	6.47	Acquired by PLN	2007	
Dieng	7.66/5.97/5.13 according to period (see text)	Acquired by Ministry of Finance, transferred to PT Geodipa: 4.45	Unit 1: 2002 Unit 2: 2006 Unit 3: 2007	Geodipa was owned 67% by Pertamina and 37% by PLN.
Patuha	7.26/5.63/4.82 according to period (see text)	Acquired by Ministry of Finance, transferred to PT Geodipa: 4.45	Unit 1: 2006 Unit 2: 2007 Unit 3: 2008	Geodipa was owned 67% by Pertamina and 37% by PLN.

(continued)

Table 16.2 (continued)

Project	Original Price, (U.S. cents per kilowatt hour)	Renegotiated Price	Date of Commercial Operation	Notes
Wayang Windu	8.4/6.52/5.58 according to period	Acquired by Pertamina then Star Energy: 4.5–4.8 (depending on how calculated)	Unit 1: 2000 Unit 2: 2006	
Cibuni	6.9	Acquired by PLN	2006	
Kamojang	6.95	Closed out		
Cilacap	6.34	Closed out		
Tanjung Jati A	5.74	Closed out		In 2005, Bakrie was seeking a partner to proceed with this project.
Serang	6.04	Closed out		
Cilegon	6.06	Closed out		
Pasuruan	5.76	Closed out		

Source: "Restructurization [sic] of 26 Independent Power Producers," industry translation of a document prepared by PLN for a speech delivered by Megawati in July 2003 (provided by an official in the World Bank office in Jakarta).

offering them to new investors as electricity demand recovered. Fourteen had been renegotiated.[42] PLN had acquired two,[43] and Pertamina, one.[44] The government had acquired Dieng and Patuha upon agreeing to reimburse OPIC. The twenty-seventh project, Karaha Bodas, remained mired in conflict. With the announcement, the minister added that "an out of court settlement [with Karaha Bodas] is being pursued by a facilitation team." Hope had not been tempered by experience. Prospects for a negotiated settlement with this company looked as gloomy as ever. In fact, these efforts would be no more successful than earlier attempts to reach a negotiated settlement with the owners of Karaha Bodas.

In summing up the new arrangements, PLN president Eddie Widiono reported that "most of the 14 IPPs [independent power producers] have agreed to sell their power at an average of 4.6 U.S. cents per kilowatt per hour except for the diesel fired Pare-Pare power plant in Makassar at 5.7 U.S. cents and Paiton at 4.9 U.S. cents." He added that the renegotiations should save Indonesia $5.5 billion.[45] The reported results of restructuring are summarized in Table 16.2.

At the time of the announcement, PLN reported that the average price for electricity it sold was Rp488, or 5.42 cents, per kwh.[46] The renegotiated power purchase agreements left little margin for PLN's distribution costs and "leakages" unless delivered prices could rise still more. The stated government goal was to increase the PLN price to 7 cents; the rupiah was appreciating, helping in reaching the goal.

Strategy and Dispute Settlement

The overall patterns for the 27 power projects support the conclusions of our in-depth case studies: Corporate strategy and ownership play a major role in how investment disputes are handled. Table 16.3 shows the approaches of all the private power projects. Three basic conclusions stand out:

1. If the lead investor has other significant interests in the country or is remaining in the power business in the developing world, it is likely to renegotiate.
2. If the lead investor is exiting the business involved or the developing world, it is likely to turn heavily to the new international system of property rights—in particular, to insurance or arbitration, or both.
3. If the lead investor is local, it has no access to the new property rights and renegotiates.
4. If the lead investor is Japanese, it is likely to turn away from the confrontational approaches of the new property rights.

Defending Business

In 14 power projects the lead investors were remaining in the business in Indonesia and in other developing countries or had other substantial interests in Indonesia. All renegotiated their agreements or consented to closing the project. Not one of these investors went to arbitration or filed political risk insurance claims. Safeguards were available to them: We believe that all the contractual arrangements with foreign firms allowed the investor to appeal to arbitration, and we know that some of these investors carried political risk insurance.[47]

Half of the projects in this category belonged to oil companies. Owners' interests in oil and gas fields likely explain their choice. They did not want to endanger their relations in Indonesia by taking the contentious steps of arbitration or collecting on official political risk insurance.

The other investors had similar reasons to avoid contentious approaches. Like ITT earlier, Sumitomo (Tanjung Jati B), Mitsubishi (Cilacap), Tomen (Tanjung Jati A and, perhaps, Pare-Pare[48]), and Siemens (a partner in Paiton II) had a wide range of activities in Indonesia, all of which could have been at risk if they had relied on the new property rights.

Mission (Paiton I), PowerGen[49] (also a partner in Paiton II), Duke Power (equal partner in Cilacap), and National Power[50] (partner in Tanjung Jati A) were all firms that intended, at the time, to remain in the international power business. Their Indonesian projects mattered to them.

Table 16.3 Power and Corporate Strategy

Project	Principal Foreign Owner(s)	Settlement	Notes
A. Lead Foreign Investor: Diversified in Indonesia, Staying in Power Business, or Japanese			
Paiton I[a]	Mission Energy (US)	Renegotiated	Mission later exited developing-country power.
Tanjung Jati B[a]	CEPA (HK) ⇒Sumitomo (J)	Renegotiated	
Paiton II	Siemens (Germany)/ PowerGen (UK)	Renegotiated	
Pare-Pare	?	Renegotiated	The lead foreign investor for this project is unclear. It is variously listed as Tomen, Wärtsilä (a Finnish company, which denies being the lead investor), and Flarck Investment B.V.; perhaps a subsidiary of one of these two parties.
Sengkang[a]	El Paso (US)	Renegotiated	Oil company.
Palembang Timur	Coastal (US)	Renegotiated	Oil company.
Salak	Unocal (US)	Renegotiated	Oil company.
Darajat[a]	Amoseas (US)	Renegotiated	Oil company.
Sarulla	Unocal (US)	Sold to PLN	Oil company.
Wayang Windu	Asia Power (NZ/ Singapore/ Malaysia) ⇒Unocal (US)	Sold to Pertamina then Star Energy	Oil company; entered as operator and part owner after creditors took over from troubled Asia Power.
Sibayak	Enserch (US)	Renegotiated	Oil company.
Cilacap	Mitsubishi (J)/ Duke Power (US)	Agreed to close out	
Tanjung Jati A	Tomen (J)/National Power (UK)	Agreed to close out	
Tanjung Jati C	A Gordon Wu company (HK)	Agreed to close out	
B. Lead Foreign Investor: Departing Developing Country Markets or Power Business			
Dieng[a]	CalEnergy (US)	Arbitration/official insurance claim	Project transferred to Ministry of Finance.
Patuha[a]	CalEnergy (US)	Arbitration/official insurance claim	Project transferred to Ministry of Finance.

Project	Principal Foreign Owner(s)	Settlement	Notes
Bedugul[a]	CalEnergy (US)	Sold to another investor	No significant investment made before suspension.
Karaha Bodas[a]	Florida Power & Light/Caithness (US)	Arbitration/private insurance claim	Unsettled at time of writing.
Pasuruan[a]	Enron (US)	Official insurance claim	Small investment made before suspension. Closed out.

C. Domestic Lead Investor

Project	Principal Foreign Owner(s)	Settlement	Notes
Amurang	—	Renegotiated	
Sibolga	—	Renegotiated	
Cikarang	—	Renegotiated	
Cibuni	—	Renegotiated	
Asahan	—	Renegotiated	
Serang	—	Agreed to close out	

D. Unclear Classification

Project	Principal Foreign Owner(s)	Settlement	Notes
Cilegon	Ansaldo Energia SpA (Italy), Sachsen Holding B.V. (Germany/Netherlands)	Agreed to close out	Unsure whether local firm, Daya Listrik Pratama, was the lead investor. Ansaldo is equipment supplier. We have not located information about Sachsen Holding.
Kamojang	Asia Power (NZ)	Agreed to close out	Asia Power had strong Singaporean and Malaysian Chinese interests (see text) and was in financial distress during the renegotiations.

[a]Indicates project discussed in text.

Perhaps even more importantly, they might have hesitated to damage their reputation elsewhere by engaging in a public battle in Indonesia. For sure, Enron's disputes in other countries were beginning to make potential host countries hesitant to do business with it. Moreover, insurers were raising questions about the wisdom of providing coverage to this company with so many disputes.

On the other hand, one could have hypothesized an offsetting consideration for firms with similar projects elsewhere: that showing willingness to renegotiate in Indonesia might have emboldened other countries to demand renegotiation. The fear of worsening relations seems to have trumped over this concern.

The one remaining foreign project where investors renegotiated or consented to cancellation was Tanjung Jati C. This project remained with one of the Hong Kong holding companies of Gordon Wu. Having invested little or nothing in the project, Wu had little reason or basis to fight cancellation. But he had not lost interest in developing infrastructure in other countries, and in this his behavior differed little from that of Mission, Duke, PowerGen, and National Power.

To return to our hypothetical art collector with insurance: These investors were like the collector who, on discovering his art is fake, might be tempted to burn down his house for the insurance. But he will feel constrained if the house contains other assets he values or if he is very concerned about maintaining his reputation.

Although these firms chose renegotiation rather than more contentious arbitration and official political risk insurance, the new property rights were relevant to them. Even if they did not draw explicitly on their rights, the fact that they could turn to arbitration or insurance must have affected their views of what a reasonable outcome would be. Confronted with an extremely obstinate host government, the investors might grit their teeth and turn away from negotiation. In a few cases outside Indonesia, that seems to be exactly what happened. The list of claims pending before ICSID contains several companies that continue to have substantial interests in Third World infrastructure. The fact that so many are taking on one country, Argentina, suggests that investors there were making very pessimistic forecasts about the prospects of renegotiations. Expected ill feelings from arbitration might be worth the cost when investors decide that negotiation is unlikely to produce something even marginally acceptable.

The new property rights affected the negotiations for this group of firms in still another way: They did seek home government support. Mission's appeal to the U.S. government is an example. Presumably when several investors are involved in disputes, as was the case in Indonesian power, home government pressure is considered sufficiently general that an investor might not expect the host government to blame any one firm. Moreover, much of the pressure is expected to remain secret, not affecting the firm's reputation in other countries. Still, the greatest pressure from the U.S. government seems to have come in defense of investors who turned to insurance. Remember the statement of Kuntoro that, when he faced pressure from the U.S. ambassador, it was always about OPIC.

Exiting the Business

There is rather compelling evidence that when foreign investors want to exit a business and have no other significant interests in the host country they readily turn to the most contentious of the new assurances, arbitration and official insurance. All five Indonesian power projects that were led by foreign firms that were exiting the Third World power business ended in arbitration or insurance claims. The promise of compensation—perhaps even large amounts, as in the Karaha Bodas case—surely discourages negotiated settlement.

We view the CalEnergy, Karaha Bodas, and Enron cases as providing at least circumstantial evidence of this kind of moral hazard associated with the new property rights.[51]

One might speculate about likely events if Paiton I had gone to the first contender, the family-firm Intercontinental, instead of to Mission. Soon after the collapse of their negotiations in Indonesia, Intercontinental's owners, the Roys, lost interest in the Third World and even in electric power. By 1997, Stephen Roy and his sister Ellen were pursuing the next fashion in investment: They founded I-Group Hotbank, a dot-com incubator in Boston. To house it, Stephen bought the huge Ames House, a mansion on Commonwealth Avenue, in Boston's Victorian-era Back Bay neighborhood.[52] But, like the power boom, the dot-com euphoria crashed, and this venture more or less ended. In 2005, the mansion's restoration was unfinished.[53] If the Roys had controlled Paiton I when the economic crisis struck, it is unlikely that they would have been enthusiastic about renegotiating a business they were leaving behind them. Paiton I could have turned into another Karaha Bodas.

In fact, the Roys' declining interest in power had resulted in the sale of most of the Intercontinental shares in 1998 to Florida Power & Light (FP&L), the same utility company that owned a substantial share of Karaha Bodas.[54] One can easily imagine that in FP&L's hands Paiton I would have gone to arbitration like FP&L's KBC project.

Our observations about investor behavior offer a counterintuitive lesson for host countries to consider: A foreign investor with other activities in the country and with a deep and likely abiding commitment to the business at hand may be the better choice when it comes to awarding large projects. Typically and understandably, developing countries often fear the influence of large multinationals that have substantial and diverse interests in their economies. But when problems arise, a government may find that the broad interests of these investors make them more agreeable and flexible as negotiating partners. The greatly feared huge and diversified ITT turned out to be a cooperative—and perhaps even meek—negotiator when Indonesia wanted to restructure its telecommunications facility. In the case of Paiton I, the Indonesians probably made the better choice when they selected Mission over Intercontinental. Although hardly meek, Mission nevertheless reached an accommodation with new conditions rather than remaining hostile.

Domestic Owners

A few of the private power projects in Indonesia were owned by domestic investors. They had no access to the new international system of property rights: no Multilateral Investment Guarantee Agency (MIGA), OPIC, or similar insurance from European or Japanese governments. It is unlikely that contracts with domestic investors in Indonesian power included rights to international arbitration similar to those obtained by foreign investors. Certainly, bilateral investment treaties and regional economic agreements do not give such rights to domestic firms. But, even if Indonesian investors had access to arbitration or insurance, they would surely have shied away from appealing to them. All the local firms had significant other interests in the country and would have to live with the government after a legal battle. Realistically, they had little choice: When problems arose, they renegotiated or, in one case, agreed to close out the project.

The fact that the new international system of property rights offers foreign investors more protection than domestic investors adds to the instability of the system. We will expand on this threat, along with other challenges to the system in the concluding chapter.

The Future of Private Power in Indonesia

By early 2003, as electricity consumption was rising with economic recovery, blackouts and brownouts were returning to Jakarta. The Indonesian president claimed that the country would need an additional $31 billion investment in the sector by 2010.[55] One estimate was that Java would need the equivalent of a new Paiton I every nine months. The new director general responsible for electric power had launched an investment tour to seek foreign firms. To encourage investment, the Indonesians passed a new electricity law in 2002 that would end PLN's monopoly, phase in competition on a regional basis, and establish a regulatory body to govern areas where competition had begun. In 2004, the Constitutional Court annulled the new law as unconstitutional, using exactly the same legal arguments that the Indonesians had used to oppose the Indosat agreement almost 25 years earlier.[56]

For several years before the Asian Currency Crisis, the World Bank had assisted the Indonesians to develop a regulation that would preclude unsolicited proposals for power projects. Facing resistance in the government, the authorizing decree was not issued until January 1998, when the

International Monetary Fund (IMF) arrived.[57] This was too late for the projects we examined. For the next round of power projects, the government has been drafting amendments to the decree. But as of 2005 no new version had been forthcoming. In February 2005, we received an e-mail from a former official in the World Bank's Indonesia office urging us to complete this book quickly. He said that the old officials were largely gone from office and lessons from the experiences of the 1990s were not being learned by their replacements. Just as officials had not mastered the ITT experience for the power negotiations, the country was again set to repeat its mistakes, he feared.

Only unconstrained optimism could lead one to believe that the projected investment needs for Indonesian infrastructure would come from the kinds of private power companies that had arrived in the mid-1990s. Those companies had invested in boom years when money was cheap and rapid corporate growth hugely rewarded; the utility markets of the industrialized countries had been stagnant and, in many cases, bound up by regulations. Many of the investors had arrived in Indonesia and other difficult markets with almost no experience in the Third World. As the investors of the 1990s discovered that their visions of gold were no more than dreams, many had retreated quickly. Moreover, some of the companies that continued in the emerging markets were themselves in serious financial trouble, unable to commit large sums to new projects. The decade of euphoria passed, and most of the early investors would not return.

To be sure, some European firms remained enthusiastic about infrastructure in the developing world, as did a number of small, very specialized American firms. New candidates were also emerging. Chinese investors, for example, were making noises about offering power to Indonesia at much lower prices than the previous investors had demanded.[58] But the capital markets were also no longer so enthusiastic about lending to infrastructure projects.

Investors' worries were justified. Experiences in Indonesia and, indeed, in many other developing countries forced multinational firms to ask themselves whether any arrangement with a host government or a state-owned enterprise was likely to be stable, especially if they came without the bargaining power that special know-how had given ITT. The risks seemed even higher with the arrival of democracy in Indonesia. Those who criticized deals with foreign investors, whether they did so for political reasons or out of genuine concern with the economics, could no longer be easily suppressed.

Moreover, new investors in Indonesia would likely find more, not less corruption. A weaker presidency meant the absence of a powerful figure to ensure that corruption did not pile up to asphyxiate the golden goose of profitable business. In addition, new policies of government decentralization gave local officials opportunities to extract money from investors. Moreover, experiences in other countries have suggested that local governments, with their own agendas, break agreements or insist on renegotiations with less concern than central governments over the consequences for the national investment climate.[59]

Neither renegotiated nor new agreements are likely to go unchallenged for 30 years in the new democratic Indonesia. Investor safety seems assured only to the foreign company that lands in a sector that is not politically sensitive or that brings some special technology or other asset that makes its presence essential. Unless, of course, the new property rights work to secure investments. The examples we have discussed show that they are more useful to some investors than to others. We also believe that the system will be increasingly challenged unless its abuses and other problems are tackled. The next chapter will review those problems and suggest some directions for change that might make the system better able to accomplish its purpose: securing commitments that are profitable for the investor and simultaneously encouraging development.

Part IV

Revisiting Privatization and the New International Property Rights System

17

Reforming for Development and Profits

The hole and the patch should be commensurate.
—Thomas Jefferson[1]

O ur Indonesian cases shed some light on the important question of who should build and own infrastructure in emerging markets. Moreover, the stories raise serious doubts about whether the international system of property rights, in its current form, can accomplish its goal of encouraging foreign investment that is helpful to development.

Has Privatization of Infrastructure Been Successful?

Investors in Indonesia's infrastructure were far from alone in facing bitter conflict. With slightly different twists, similar events occurred in many other developing countries as a striking number of infrastructure investments turned sour in the 1990s and early 2000s. Widely covered in the international business press were disputes over electric power in Pakistan, Brazil, Turkey, Nigeria, Peru, Bolivia, Argentina, and the Dominican Republic. News media reported battles with foreign investors over gas lines, waterworks, and ports in Argentina. Enron's struggle over its Dabhol power project in India even made American television's popular *60 Minutes*.[2] And these represent no more than a small sample of similar disputes.[3] Some of the conflicts were much like ITT's, following the obsolescing bargain model, but a significant number were triggered by economic crises, similar to what happened to the Indonesian electric power investments. Especially vulnerable were arrangements that were structured like debt, with fixed dollar obligations. The press covered mainly conflicts resulting from state action, but many disputes were initiated by the investors themselves, as anticipated profits looked unlikely to materialize.[4]

Wide press coverage of disputes caused investors to hesitate, but it also generated skepticism on the part of governments of emerging markets and a few officials in multilateral organizations about the revived role of private foreign investment in infrastructure development. The concern was not entirely misplaced. Although one of the foreign investments we examined was surely beneficial to Indonesia, benefits from others were quite doubtful. Three projects might well be termed disastrous.

Success

Although Indonesia in 1967 could hardly make credible commitments to ITT, given the country's recent history of expropriations, this investor thrived for 13 years by providing technology that Indonesia lacked and knew it needed. When ITT failed to honor an implicit social contract—declining to invest in a politically desirable cable—Indonesians noticed that the investor was no longer essential, and ITT's favorable investment agreement become an "obsolete bargain."

Over the 13 years, Indonesians themselves had mastered technology for international telecommunications and even for the country's domestic satellite system. Moreover, they gained some rather impressive management skills, the worth of which they had probably underestimated at the outset. As it turned out, the new skills enabled Indonesians to manage quite effectively what became state-owned Indosat. On top of all that, the decision in 1967 of a name-brand investor to commit to Indonesia came at a critical time and signaled to others that the country had become a reasonable place to invest. To be sure, Indonesia also acquired some capital, but in the total scheme of things, this was a very minor part of ITT's contribution to the country's development.

Even though ITT's Indosat was quietly nationalized in 1980, ITT gained as well in the form of fine financial returns. The conglomerate could not have regretted its decision to invest. When it came time to give up the project, management knew from its extensive experience elsewhere where it stood, its strengths, weaknesses, and long-term goals. The company's graceful exit safeguarded its strategic interests in the country, where it continued to operate in other lines of business.

Power Failure?

Electric Power

Indonesia's experience with foreign investment in electric power was far less successful.

When the government decided to pursue private investment in power, it was facing serious problems: Electricity tariffs were too low and technical and collection losses too high for the state-owned power company to finance needed capacity. The distribution system was underdeveloped, and planning and management within PLN were unimpressive.

Rather than introducing foreign investors into areas where deep problems lay, Indonesians brought them only to generation. But Indonesians already knew how to build and operate such facilities. Maybe foreigners could manage the plants a bit better than the state. Indeed, several studies confirm this.[5] On the other hand, efficiency matters little if the gains are small and especially if foreign investors capture the benefits for themselves. In contrast to ITT, foreign firms in power contributed mainly money, something Indonesians needed largely because of internal problems and the fact that multilateral financial institutions had cut off lending for state-owned infrastructure.

Lack of information about contractual terms elsewhere, internal disorganization and lack of skills, corruption, and diplomatic pressure from investors' home countries all contributed to deals that were juicy for investors but questionable for development. In the end, the contracts did not even grant Indonesia one of the most important advantages that foreign direct investment typically brings: allocation of business risks to the private sector. Worse, Indonesia agreed to pay costs for foreign money that were like those of foreign direct investment, even though risks were allocated like those of lower cost debt.

Maybe Indonesia and PLN had already borrowed too much, and could therefore ill afford more debt. But power purchase agreements that are, as a practical matter, structured as debt are no less burdensome in economic terms than if they had been accurately named. Re-labeling provides no free ride in privatization. Unless the funds are grant money, capital must be paid for and risks allocated. In an economic sense, the power purchase agreements amounted to high cost "off-balance-sheet" borrowing. Without government guarantees, they were obligations of PLN; once arbitrators interpreted comfort letters as guarantees, they were turned into off-balance-sheet borrowing by the government. Such borrowing poses the same dangers to state-owned companies and to governments that it poses to private parties who turn to this type of financing when they fear they are already up to their necks in debt.[6]

When the value of the rupiah and growth in electricity demand collapsed, PLN, like other Indonesian companies that had borrowed dollars, could not honor its commitments. Obligations under power purchase agreements fell into a no-man's land—they could not be restructured under the Paris Club or the London Club like sovereign debt, nor did bankruptcy appear to provide a solution. The resulting disputes diverted skills and attention of Indonesian officials from dealing with the economic crisis to tackling problems of private investment. And the tensions generated gigantic legal bills, created very large awards for a few investors, frightened off others, and damaged U.S.–Indonesian relations.

Unfortunately, in 2005, the Indonesian power sector was still plagued by the same problems that it had faced 10 years earlier.

What Went Wrong?

The ideological commitment of the industrialized countries and the multilaterals to privatization rested on a deep belief that governments are not competent to build and operate infrastructure well. One proponent of privatization labeled this the "grabbing hand" theory of government.[7] Privatization was supposed to push incompetent government out of the infrastructure business.

The fundamental assumption made by enthusiasts for privatization was, of course, dead wrong. As should have been obvious from the outset, privatization of infrastructure cannot get government out of the picture. Unlike the manufacture of, say, clothing, light bulbs, or steel, most infrastructure sectors can hardly be opened to all comers and regulated by the invisible hand of competition. Only government can arrange access for power and telephone lines, hydro resources, underground water pipes, communication channels, and rights-of-way for roads. At a minimum, access has to be granted investors under complicated contracts—concessions, as they are often called in Latin America. But the fact that most infrastructure involves some degree of natural monopoly or monopsony requires a deep and continuing role for government. Whether government manages infrastructure by negotiating contracts that are supposed to cover all contingencies for 30 years—like power purchase agreements in Indonesia and elsewhere—or builds a regulatory system, the task is formidable.

In the contractual approach, everything is supposed to be "right" the first time. But we have seen how hard it is to get everything right, even with contracts that exceeded 300 pages. The Indonesian stories have also shown how inordinately difficult it is to make proper adjustments later, whether problems arise from errors in judgment or lack of skills, from corruption, asymmetric information, home government intervention, or failure to address unforeseen catastrophic events. Arbitration awards, when investors resisted change, can only be viewed as punitive in their impacts.

Managing by regulation, as an alternative, seems to allow for adjustments as government learns and as events strike. But regulation that is viewed by all parties as protecting both the national interest and investors' concerns places huge demands on government—too much for countries where corruption is rampant, antitrust administration almost nonexistent, and skills scarce. One could wish otherwise, just as one wishes that poor countries were not poor, but wishing does not change the facts.

It should be no surprise that developing countries have found privatizing infrastructure to be complicated. Even California and New Zealand encountered horrendous problems in building a merchant system for electricity that functioned in the public interest. Sure, they did not do it quite right, as die-hard supporters of privatization and merchant systems still respond. But the fact that these governments with their sophisticated skills failed to get it right only underscores how difficult it is for emerging markets to succeed in the task.

The core assumption of privatization enthusiasts—that the scarcity of government skills means that privatizing is easier than improving infrastructure in state hands—has been proved too simple. Our stories tell us that even more government skill may be required to privatize and to govern privatized infrastructure than is needed for the difficult task of running state-owned enterprises well. Nevertheless, in their eagerness to encourage privatization in the 1980s, the multilaterals and aid agencies paid little attention to building skills that were necessary to manage infrastructure in state hands. At the same time, they failed to develop the skills required to privatize and to supervise privately owned infrastructure. In fact, by focusing on privatization they probably took on the more difficult job. The Indonesian stories argue that dispersed decision making, frequent turnover of personnel, difficulties in capturing lessons from experience, and corruption mean that developing lasting skills for privatization is a formidable task.

One might even conclude with regard to Indonesia's experiment, as did the World Bank's iconoclastic chief economist Joseph Stiglitz with respect to Russia's broader privatization, that privatization without regulatory safeguards "has only succeeded in putting the 'grabbing hand' [of government] into the 'velvet glove' of privatization. The 'grabbing hand' keeps on grabbing with even less hope of public restraint."[8]

Official Doubts

The World Bank estimated that private-sector investment in Third World infrastructure fell from a peak of $128 billion in 1997 to $58 billion in 2001.[9] Although Stiglitz had earlier expressed doubts about the organization's ideological stance,[10] concerns spread as data made officials wonder where funds might come from to meet future demands for infrastructure. By 2003 a newspaper report suggested that the early doubters had influenced others:

> The World Bank, the apostle of privatization, is having a crisis of faith. What seemed like a no-brainer idea in the 1990s—that developing nations should sell off money-losing state infrastructure to efficient private investors—no longer seems so obvious, especially when it comes to power and water utilities.[11]

Other multilateral institutions were also backing off from their rigid views.[12] In 2004, the Asian Development Bank (ADB), for example, was supposedly considering lending to Indonesia to build 10 small-scale hydro and geothermal power projects.[13]

Although the multilaterals were learning from experience, U.S. policy remained firmly on the side of privatization. The United States regularly insisted that privatization of infrastructure be covered in its regional trade agreements, even though the relation to trade was at best tenuous.[14] The multitude of problems similar to those we have related had not shaken the commitment of the Bush II administration to privatization as an end in itself.

Reaching a Balance

Of course, many experiments with privatization in the 1990s succeeded. Where competition can serve as a regulator, privatization is almost certainly better than state ownership. There is little doubt that steel and textile manufacture work better in private hands. Even for some infrastructure, the market might serve as an adequate regulator of private owners. The *Wall Street Journal* report cited previously concludes that private ownership is much more likely to succeed in telecommunications than in water and power.[15] But even there the case is still undecided. Many developing countries have too little administrative capacity and too much corruption for effective enforcement of competition policy, so firms that should compete may soon discover the attractions of rigged bids, price collusion, and other forms of cooperation. Markets may fail.

Still, when the preconditions are right, well-managed privatization offers a way of dealing with intractable labor issues, failures to collect bills, or other common problems of state-owned operations. One should remember Krugman's criteria for private electric power: a robust transmission system, a watchdog agency with adequate powers to prevent and punish price manipulation that can resist becoming an agent of the companies it is supposed to police.[16] Even imperfect governments may, on occasion, find that privatization is the only way to solve some of these problems. We suspect, however, that such occasions will not be as frequent as has generally been assumed.

Although state ownership has gained, and often earned, a bad reputation, it can succeed, as Indosat showed in its early years under public control and as Singapore Airlines and other state-owned Singaporean companies have long demonstrated.[17] Management seems to explain more than ownership. Development institutions would do well to devote attention to learning how to make state-ownership more efficient when private ownership is not likely to work, rather than blindly supporting privatization. The cost of ignoring this task is clear: As one reporter put it, "Today as privatization is rejected, foreign investment is plummeting across [Latin America] and the challenge is being returned to states perhaps less equipped than a decade ago."[18]

There is a risk that the pendulum may swing too far back to state ownership as disenchantment sets in. Not only is private better than state investment in certain cases, but intermediate approaches for infrastructure may capture some of the advantages and avoid some of the problems associated with private, and particularly foreign, ownership. When management is the state's weakness, an answer sometimes lies in management contracts and technical assistance arrangements. Yet structuring and negotiating these hybrid arrangements also require a great deal of forethought and skill by government. Simply substituting a new ideology that promotes vague "public–private partnerships" will not solve real problems. Moreover, the private sector will be accepted as a participant only if it shows more understanding of the environments in which it invests and is willing to accept a more appropriate balance of profits and risks than we saw in some of our stories.

It is unlikely that state investment, local private investment, foreign investment, or hybrid arrangements will alone satisfy the desperate needs for infrastructure in the developing world. Although the economic returns from roads, power plants, and other infrastructure are often very high, private returns are sometimes insufficient to offset investors' perceptions of risk. And not all governments can afford the levels of debt service required for state development. Plugging the gap between need and financial capacity will almost surely require foreign aid. In the past, aid money was rather widely available for roads and other infrastructure. In the drive toward privatization, and perhaps in response to the fact that some of the infrastructure provided by aid had not been well maintained and well managed, these funds largely dried up. The maintenance problem can be dealt with by establishing externally controlled endowments devoted to the task. Management weaknesses can be alleviated, in some cases, through reforms or management contracts. Whatever approach is taken, we believe that aid agencies again ought to be making exactly these kinds of investments that have a high return for development.

Alleviating the problems of infrastructure requires a careful examination of the causes of problems in each case. It also demands analysis of the constraints imposed by the administrative, political, and economic realities of the particular country. Meeting the huge infrastructure needs for development will surely require a mix of private investment, state investment, multilateral lending, hybrid arrangements, and very substantial aid money.

Challenges to the New International System of Property Rights

Foreign investment remains very important to development, especially when investors bring technology, management skills, and access to export markets. Control over those assets will provide sufficient protection for some investors, as it did for ITT, but many useful investments may require additional security. As should be clear, developing countries alone cannot provide the necessary credible commitments.

The current international system of protection is, however, unlikely to serve the needs. When disputes arose, those power investors in Indonesia who drew extensively on the new rights faced long battles, huge legal fees, and spoiled relations. Most investors shied away from the new property rights, fearing especially those bitter results. As a result, firms that cared about long-term relationships found promised protections to be largely illusory.[19]

Host countries have also been poorly served by the new system. For Indonesia, the outcomes of arbitration differed markedly from what would have emerged from the London Club, the Paris Club, or bankruptcy, which governed other debt-like obligations of a country or company in financial distress. Arbitrators seemed to take little account of the Asian Currency Crisis, the high economic cost of unneeded generating capacity, suggestions of corruption, and likely moral hazards. Indonesians were ordered to reimburse investors a multiple of the amount they had put into unneeded and still-unfinished projects. It was no wonder Indonesians challenged arbitrations, fought collection efforts, and questioned insurance claims. More aggressively, in 2005 Argentina, with the largest number of threatened investment arbitrations, issued public threats that it would not honor awards made under the International Centre for the Settlement of Investment Disputes (ICSID) if they failed to take into account its economic crisis and the fact that the government had treated all investors—foreign and domestic—equally.[20] Allegedly the government sponsored campaigns against lawyers, witnesses, and experts in Argentina who participated in arbitrations on the company side.[21] Disappointed with events, other Latin American countries were joining the search for new rules. Responding to emerging attitudes, the International Law Section of the District of Columbia Bar sponsored a meeting in 2005 with the title "The Resurgence of the Calvo Doctrine?" Not surprisingly, some poor countries were beginning to question whether bilateral investment treaties and the investment provisions of regional economic agreements are in their interests at all.[22] Official political risk insurance could appear next on the target list.

Even rich countries have reacted to the new external assurances. One writer described the U.S. attitude: "Arbitration is good when it corrects misbehavior by foreign host states, but not so desirable when claims are filed for alleged wrongdoing by the United States."[23] The issue of sovereignty was not lost on John Kerry, the 2004 Democratic presidential candidate. In spite of his commitment to international institutions and international law, Kerry questioned the rights that trade agreements give foreign investors in the United States to draw on external protections.[24] In plain English, he feared that arbitrators would make awards to Canadian and Mexican investors if a U.S. state or the federal government imposed new environmental standards or took other actions to meet public policy goals. The possibility of a negative reaction by the United States—perhaps challenges to NAFTA itself—may already have made arbitrators hesitant to find against Mississippi courts in a case brought by a Canadian company under the NAFTA accord.[25] In the end, U.S. reactions have not been all that different from those of emerging market countries that found the system to be insensitive to national concerns.

Collapse of the system would be unfortunate for those who believe, as we do, that a large fraction of foreign investment does indeed help with development.[26] But repairing the system requires a clear understanding of its flaws.

Rigidity

In practice, arbitrators, official insurers, and home governments—especially the U.S. government—have taken a rigid view of contract and other property rights in international investment disputes.[27] When Indonesians postponed or canceled contracts that would have required payment for electricity they did not need, arbitrators considered the contracts to have been breached, canceled them, and made awards to investors far in excess of the funds that had been spent. In determining awards, the arbitrators took little account of likely changes in demand for electricity because of the economic crisis,[28] hints of corruption, claims that the contracts were contrary to Indonesian law, and what might be considered unreasonable terms. The head of the Overseas Private Investment Corporation (OPIC) warned Indonesians that contracts have to be honored—he offered no qualifications.

In fact, contracts and other aspects of property rights are not rigidly enforced inside the industrialized countries. In spite of deep ideological commitments to the inviolability of property rights, the rich countries do not in fact hold contracts to be sacred. Paraphrasing Oliver Wendell Holmes, Posner has argued,

> it is not the policy of the law to compel adherence to contracts but only to require each party to choose between performing in accordance with the contract and compensating the other party for any injury resulting from a failure to do so.[29]

The "magic" of property rights in the industrialized countries comes not from their being absolute, but rather from a balance between individual or corporate rights and fairness, and, especially, overall economic benefits. That balance is regularly fought over in the United States, but the battles are engaged in forums that enjoy broad public acceptance. The result is a number of conditions under which contracts or other aspects of property rights may not be held sacred.[30] Let us consider a few.

Changed Circumstances

When circumstances change after a contract is formed and make it impossible or impractical, or uneconomic or inefficient, to comply with contractual obligations, courts may relieve a party of its commitments.[31] Following Posner's argument,[32] one could conclude that construction of power plants in Indonesia for unneeded power would be inefficient or uneconomic and thus grounds for not enforcing the contract. Losses might be allocated in various ways between the contracting parties,[33] but to hold only one party liable for the losses when the principal cause of nonperformance is attributable to factors that neither party could completely prevent or delay is not just.[34] The aggrieved party should not recover compensation for losses that could have been avoided by appropriate steps to mitigate the magnitude of the loss. Thus, the investor would be expected to put the proceeds of an award to work in another income-producing activity. An award would unlikely include any significant projected profits.

International law recognizes similar exceptions to contract enforcement. The U.N. Convention on Contracts for the International Sale of Goods (CISG)[35] excuses a party that fails to perform due to an "impediment" beyond its control, if the parties could not reasonably be expected to have taken the impediment into account when the contract was concluded or to have avoided its consequences.[36] The nonbinding Principles of International Commercial Contracts,[37] which parties can elect to have govern their transactions, goes further to provide relief in cases of "hardship." The Principles of European Contract Law, the governing supranational law in the European Union, gives courts authority "to distribute between the parties in a just and equitable manner the losses and gains resulting from [a] change of circumstances" that has made performance of the contract "excessively onerous."[38] If renegotiation fails, parties may go to court, which, if it determines hardship, may terminate the contract or adapt it to restore equilibrium.

Similarly, a nation may be excused from honoring a treaty if (1) the existence of the circumstances that changed constituted an essential basis of the consent of the parties to be bound by the treaty; and (2) the effect of the change radically transforms the obligations that are to be performed under the treaty.[39] Surely, both these conditions are met for a dollar-denominated take-or-pay contract when a country's currency and electricity demand collapse.

Unconscionable Terms

For many, an English literature class raises the first exposure to questions about contracts. In Shakespeare's *The Merchant of Venice*, the court went through complex machinations to avoid allowing Shylock to extract a pound of flesh from Antonio when he failed to fulfill his contractual obligations. Fiction and law differ. By Shakespeare's time, European courts regularly rejected unconscionable provisions in contracts.[40] Even Roman law could relieve a party from contractual payment obligations if the price charged for a good was more than twice a fair price.[41]

Modern courts no longer send debtors to prison, much less allow the extraction of flesh. They may instead ask whether the terms of a contract are conscionable or "just and reasonable" and refuse to enforce oppressive contracts or contracts that allocate risks of the bargain in an objectively unreasonable or unexpected manner.[42] Bankruptcy courts regularly depart from rigid adherence to debt commitments by discharging or revising overburdensome obligations without imprisoning the individual or killing the business.[43] Similar practices have emerged for sovereign borrowers under the Paris Club or the London Club, where sovereign debts of Third World countries are handled much like bankruptcy. While arbitrators and OPIC's head were taking a rigid view of debt-like electric power contracts in Indonesia, the country's very similar sovereign debt was quietly being restructured in Paris.

Public Policy

In industrialized countries, contracts with terms that are contrary to law or public policy will not be enforced. The U.S. Service Members Civil Relief Act may prohibit a lender from repossessing pledged property and overrides lease obligations if the borrower or renter has gone on active military duty after signing the obligation. The public interest in maintaining a military overrides contractual obligations.

Similarly, in the United States energy contracts are explicitly subject to a "just and reasonable" test, and terms may be measured against the public interest.[44]

In industrialized countries, private property may be taken for a public purpose under rights of eminent domain.[45] Reasonable compensation to the owner is in order, but the right of the state to take property trumps title. A taking may be accepted even if it results from public policy changes made after an owner acquired the property or contract rights.[46] Even though new environmental, safety, or zoning regulations designed for the public good may reduce the value of property by restricting its use, often no compensation is provided to the property owner.[47]

In contrast, international investment arbitrators and official insurers have been extremely cautious in public policy cases. Although the North American Free Trade Agreement (NAFTA), the 2004 U.S. model bilateral investment treaty, and more recent U.S. free trade agreements allow nondiscriminatory acts for public welfare, many issues remain unresolved: in particular, which kinds of regulatory changes on the part of the host country amount to takings and should lead to compensation.[48] In an editorial referring to investment disputes, the *New York Times* captured the problem well:

> The rules of the game are such that when companies seek to recover damages, arbitration panels tend to focus narrowly on the issue of whether a company's profits were affected by a government action. They need not consider whether the action or law in question was necessary to protect the environment or public health, or even to stop a corporation's harmful behavior.[49]

Some recent NAFTA Chapter 11 decisions have denied awards to investors who were treated equally with other firms when public policy issues were involved.[50] But tribunals under other regimes have continued to take more rigid views, regardless of whether actions were broadly applicable. [51]

Compulsion or Corruption

Courts in the industrialized countries may excuse parties from fulfilling contracts if they were entered under compulsion (duress) or corruption or if one party is not competent.[52]

In these cases, courts do not always require a high standard of proof to relieve a party from obligations. A judge may assume compulsion, for example, if a premarital contract was signed hours before the wedding, especially if the terms are out of line with expectations. In contrast, arbitration and official insurers have required very strong evidence when viewing possible compulsion or corruption. They might do well to assume that something is amiss when there are at least substantial hints of compulsion or corruption and terms of investment arrangements seem imbalanced. In many such cases, they should then order that the contract be restructured to more just and reasonable terms.[53]

Inconsistency

Awards from investor–state arbitrations have been notably unpredictable. Standards—national treatment, most favored nation treatment, fair and equitable, full protection and security, fair value, investment plus future profits, and so on—vary, and each is subject to a wide variance in interpretation and methodology. Even on a single panel, arbitrators have been far apart in their conclusions. In the oft-cited *CME v Czech Republic* case, the panel awarded the investor several hundred million dollars, while one arbitrator, in a minority opinion, said that the award should be about half as much.[54] And CME lost an almost identical claim for the same project arbitrated under another investment treaty.[55] Differences in outcome across arbitrations are so common that they led to the article *"Trois arbitrages, un même problème, trois solutions"* [Three Arbitrations, the Same Problem, Three Solutions].[56]

Consistent determination of awards depends first on standards. Current ones are very general, in some cases conflicting, and not elaborated through case law. Further, calculating awards, when they are appropriate, requires a deep understanding of methodologies.[57] There is a substantial literature in the field of finance on valuing companies or projects, but only a small amount of the analysis seems to have made its way into the legal literature. In some articles, legal writers appear to mix standards with methodologies, and to apply specific methodologies inappropriately. Legal treatments regularly fail to distinguish between cases of long-term investment and trade, unfinished and completed projects, projects where risks and uncertainties have been resolved and those where they remain, returns that are "normal" and those that reflect closely held corporate assets or questionable grants of monopoly, and cases where the disputes arise from economic crises or other "external" events and those where the host government is acting opportunistically. And this is only a partial list of issues that ought to enter calculations. We suspect that a comprehensive treatment of the complex issues will emerge only from collaboration between legal scholars and business/economics analysts.

Inconsistent standards and poorly applied methodologies undermine the credibility of dispute settlement. Unpredictability of awards also leads to more arbitrations as well as litigation challenging awards. After all, parties are much more likely to settle outside the legal process if they can rather accurately predict the outcome of the legal route.

Finally, inappropriately large awards may discourage governments from canceling contracts that ought to be revisited for good economic reasons. As Posner wrote, "Notice how careful the law must be not to exceed compensatory damages if it doesn't want to deter efficient breaches."[58]

Legislated standards cannot resolve all issues because no mechanism is in place to create comprehensive international legislation. Consistency is likely to result only from an appeals process that can lead to common law.

Asymmetry

When arbitration clauses are contained within an investment agreement, as they were in the power cases we discussed, they usually grant access for either party to the contract. On the other hand, bilateral investment treaties and regional economic agreements, which account for the bulk of current investment arbitrations, generally allow investors, but not host governments, to take their complaints to arbitration.[59]

The lack of government access is hardly a moot issue. Host governments often have serious grievances with investors. Although media coverage has concentrated on claims initiated by investors in response to government actions, in Latin America, as we have pointed out, more than half of the renegotiations involving infrastructure have been initiated by investors themselves. Investors may bid low in tenders to obtain a project, counting on improving their terms later through renegotiations,[60] but investors can also face problems of changed circumstances and other legitimate grounds for seeking contract revision. One could argue that local courts provide remedies for governments when companies fail to honor their agreements, but their decisions are unlikely to be enforced in investors' home countries, where investors' assets lie. Asymmetric access to arbitration has meant that host governments have typically acquiesced when investors have sought renegotiations, whether yielding was appropriate or not.[61] This imbalance is not likely to be tolerated forever.

We can see no reason why host governments should be denied access to the same redress under the new property rights as investors are granted.

In fact, U.S. courts have invalidated as unconscionable contracts that require employees but not employers to arbitrate employment claims. In the case of international investments, parallel rights for governments would create symmetry, something of political import. Even more significant, if investors can also be challenged for breach of contract, they are more likely to support the development of reasonable standards with respect to contract rigidity.

A second kind of asymmetry is more difficult to correct. Bilateral investment treaties, regional economic agreements, and political risk insurance generally grant protections to foreigners that are not available to domestic firms.[62] Even the United States has become sensitive to the issue, including in the Bipartisan Trade Act of 2002 the following:

> the principal negotiating objectives of the United States regarding foreign investment are to reduce or eliminate artificial or trade-distorting barriers to foreign investment, while ensuring that foreign investors in the United States are not accorded greater substantive rights with respect to investment protections than United States investors in the United States.[63]

When national rules such as tax incentives favor foreigners, political pressures have usually eventually led to equalization. The approach may be either to withdraw advantages from foreign firms or to extend similar privileges to domestic firms. The U.S. Congress has attempted to restrict foreigners' privileges. It is difficult to imagine that countries will yield the sovereignty necessary to extend today's new rights to domestic investors.[64] In the developing world, domestic firms may insist that their governments withdraw from a system that continues to advantage foreign investors.

Moral Hazard

We have already pointed to possible moral hazards in the new property rights. Insurance coverage and prospects of collecting large arbitration awards surely discourage some firms and lenders from carefully analyzing at the outset whether their contracts are likely to be stable; this is classic moral hazard. Further, our cases suggest that protections may discourage investors from renegotiating contractual arrangements when there are reasonable grounds for change.[65] Also, strictly construed rights may reduce investors' care in avoiding behavior that could trigger government reactions. Additionally, we have argued that official insurers themselves face moral hazards: It may be easier simply to pay investors' claims than to debate them if insurers can force host governments to reimburse them. At least in the CalEnergy case, OPIC appears to have been accountable to no one with respect to the legitimacy of the claim it paid.

The extent to which these kinds of moral hazard influence behavior is an unanswered empirical question. Yet perceptions may matter more than facts. We believe that perceptions of moral hazard are sufficient to justify the reforms suggested in Chapter 14.

Damages Orientation

Arbitration panels for investment disputes generally conclude with a cal-culation of damages—a monetary award—if they decide that they have jurisdiction and that the case has merit. In contrast, other judicial processes often take steps to encourage settlement, direct a party to take remedial action, or even impose new contract terms on disputants. Judges in the United States, for example, often give guidance at some early stage to disputing parties and instruct them to try again to settle their differences. Judges may also require mediation. Bankruptcy courts can revise terms of debt contracts.[66] In trade cases, World Trade Organization (WTO) panels order changes in national policies, turning to penalties (retaliation up to a designated amount) only if one party refuses to comply by a certain date.

If payment of damages can be avoided, business relationships are more likely to survive. Even supervised settlements are likely to be fairer than what judges might determine, and therefore may be self-enforcing.[67] Moreover, negotiated settlements save on legal expenses and arbitrators' time.

To capture some of the gains, an investment panel might tell a com-plaining investor that it will not award what the investor is requesting, but that the host government, for example, cannot simply walk away from the deal. In appropriate circumstances, it could add that it is inclined to tell the host government to reimburse at least the investment made thus far, call for a delay in implementation of the project, order new prices that reflect terms common elsewhere, or conduct further investigations of questionable invoices. Such guidelines can lead parties to return to the negotiating table and result in an ongoing business.[68] Moreover, pressing for negotiation can give the arbitration panel an opportunity to identify moral hazard, evidenced by the refusal of one party to negotiate in good faith. If it comes to awards, the panel's eventual allocation of losses should take into account this revelation.[69]

Alternatively, a panel might tell a host government (or the company, if it is the defendant) to reverse or modify an action. In this, it would be similar to the panels of the WTO. Or it could decide that the contract is out of line with terms negotiated elsewhere through, say, a tendering process or that external events under the control of neither party caused the dispute. In any of these cases, it might impose new terms on the parties.[70]

We are not sure why arbitration panels so consistently look to damages rather than to revised policies, new contract terms, or negotiated settle-ment. An economist might argue that the behavior of arbitrators results from the fact that they are paid by the hour or day; judges, on the other hand, are paid fixed salaries and thus have an incentive to clear their crowded court calendars. Many arbitrators vigorously deny that the pay-ment system influences their behavior,[71] but they offer no alternative explanation.

Whatever the reason for current practice, we believe that it is misdirected. Financial awards—with resulting moral hazards, bitter relationships, and wasted business opportunities—should be the last resort. We are not sure whether the solution lies in revising the financial incentives to arbitrators or another method. But change is likely to increase the stability of the system.

Foreign Relations

Intervention abroad by governments on behalf of their investors comes at a cost. In fact, it was exactly those costs that made the United States hesitant for so many years to mount strong defenses of investors in trouble.

From the end of World War II until about 1990, the United States limited support largely to pressing countries for general policies that would open doors for U.S. firms. To be sure, the U.S. government occasionally helped particular U.S. investors, but that was mainly when corporate interests corresponded closely to U.S. national interests. Collaboration with U.S. oil corporations abroad, for example, has a long, well-documented but unique history.[72]

Reluctance to support individual investors was not the result of a shortage of powerful economic weapons. Congress had long authorized penalties against countries that took U.S. property: in the Sugar Act of 1948 (withdrawal of sugar quotas), the Hickenlooper and Gonazalez amendments (withholding of aid and voting against loans from multilateral financial institutions), and the Generalized System of Preferences (withholding of tariff preferences). In practice, however, the executive branch almost always exercised its authority not to impose sanctions if it considered them to be contrary to U.S. foreign policy interests. Thus, the Hickenlooper Amendment was used only twice before 1990. Although the existence of the tools probably restrained host governments, a simple count of expropriations of U.S. property suggests that the tools were often not sufficient to deter host government actions.

Decisions on intervention were usually the result of a predictable lineup.[73] The U.S. Department of Commerce, the Treasury, and senators or representatives from the investor's home state would argue for U.S. support. The Department of State and particularly embassy personnel in the host country would stand firmly against intervention, arguing that keeping the country pro-American was the overriding concern.[74] As long as communism was perceived as a major threat, the state department usually won.

But the influence of the state department declined with the collapse of the communist threat around 1990. At the same time, Congress—especially the Jesse Helms–led Senate Foreign Relations Committee—began to challenge the foreign relations budget. Maintaining a good budget required proving the department's usefulness in ways that Congress would grasp. One young foreign-service officer told us that he had been taught, in his mid-90s training program, that the state department must support U.S. business abroad to hold onto its budget.[75] The results of the shift were clear enough in our cases.

Of course, the United States is not the only country that intervenes abroad when investment disputes arise. Interviewees mentioned support from the French and even the Danish governments, for example.[76] And the Japanese government stepped into the Tanjung Jati B case, albeit in way quite different from the American approach. Although the French may have a great deal of influence in Francophone Africa, the United States can bring much more pressure on most developing countries simply because of the size of its home market, the total amount of aid it can withhold, and the voting power of its directors in multilateral organizations. Thus, its policies remain especially influential.

The interventionism of the U.S. government of the 1990s may well turn out to be an aberration. Already by 2001, aggressive support of U.S. investors was showing signs of damaging newly emerging goals of U.S. foreign policy. Although the U.S. ambassador to Indonesia tried to push antiterrorism issues at the same time that he pressed the interests of U.S. power companies, [77] there is not much evidence that he succeeded on the antiterrorism front. The *Wall Street Journal* described the results:

> A nation [Indonesia] once robustly pro-American has become a bastion of anti-U.S. hostility. . . . This shift has multiple causes, including the war in Iraq. But among them is a widely held view here [Indonesia] that in the aftermath of the Suharto dictatorship—a time of crisis but also of promise— the U.S. threw its weight behind its business interests to the detriment of Indonesians.[78]

In the end, the United States will have to assign priorities to its goals. Commercial interests are likely to yield ground to winning the war on religious fundamentalist terror.[79]

Building a Lasting System

If external protection of investors' property rights is to survive, reforms must address most or all the following goals:

1. Institute a less rigid and more economic view of property rights and contract.
2. Develop standards that take into account national goals and encourage consistent decisions.
3. Encourage renegotiation or impose new terms where a business relationship can be kept alive.
4. Where renegotiations and new arrangements are not appropriate, assess damages at levels that do not create perverse incentives.
5. Increase the perception of symmetry in the rights granted to foreign investors and those provided to host countries and domestic firms.

6. Decrease problems of moral hazard.
7. Restrain home governments from aggressive intervention on behalf of individual investors.

Listing problems to be tackled is easier than making proposals for alleviating them. A full and detailed treatment of alternative approaches would itself fill a volume, and it would inevitably become quite technical, in terms of economics and law. The following, however, provides basic outlines of some possible approaches.

Routes to Reform

Amiable Composition

One can, at least in theory, imagine an approach to property rights (including contract rights) that would depart from the current emphasis on law.[80] Arbitrators could make decisions based only on what is "fair and just." Using this standard, they would turn to whether the terms of contracts and enforcement are appropriate, sometimes with less emphasis than under a legalistic approach on the reasons for breach (as long as they are not purely opportunistic). Arbitrators could deal with sharply changed circumstances, corruption, unreasonable terms, incompetence, or compulsion simply by noting that terms are out of line with norms elsewhere.[81] In response, arbitrators might decide to impose new contract terms on the parties. Under such a system, legal fees would be smaller. Although consistency might remain illusive, the approach might diminish moral hazard problems and encourage parties to reach their own settlement.

Models for this kind of flexible arbitration can be found in civil law jurisdictions and perhaps in some Asian economies. One arrangement, known as *amiable composition* (sometimes called *ex aequo et bono*),[82] frees arbitrators of technical legal constraints in order to reach conclusions that are fair and just. But use of this approach in international arbitrations now requires prior consent of the disputants. Somewhat similar guidelines, but with an Asian flavor, have been offered by the president of the Indian Bar Association and the vice chairman of the International Court of Arbitration of the International Chamber of Commerce (ICC):

1. Examine the truthfulness of the facts presented.
2. Ascertain whether they fall within jurisdiction.
3. Enter the mind of the parties so the judgment to be rendered is just.
4. Pronounce the verdict with kindness.
5. Judge with sympathy.[83]

As appealing as such an approach is to a nonlawyer, the chances of convincing the U.S. government or U.S. companies to adopt it are close to zero. And without U.S. participation, an international system cannot work.

Legal Approaches

A lasting and widely acceptable international system of property rights will likely remain embodied in some kind of more elaborate legal framework. As such, it will have to comprise three parts: (1) a body of "legislation" setting out standards that balance the interests of investors and the public, (2) a dispute settlement mechanism, and (3) a means of enforcing decisions. The current system is especially weak in terms of standards. The principles in place are very general, and they differ in various investment contracts, bilateral investment treaties, and regional economic agreements. Further, today there is no adequate mechanism to develop broad principles into practical common law.

Trade Law as a Model

For international trade, the WTO accord appears superficially similar to the new property rights for investors. It provides a dispute settlement mechanism comprising individual panels similar to the arbitration panels that handle investment disputes.[84] The panel members—three, or sometimes five—are appointed in consultation with the disputing parties. But there are three very important differences between the mechanisms for trade and investment.

First, multilateral negotiations for trade have led to a rather substantial body of "legislation," initially under the General Agreement on Tariffs and Trade (GATT) and later under the WTO, which provides more explicit standards than exist for investment disputes.

Second, the WTO settlement mechanism turns initially to efforts to reach settlement among the disputants, including the option of mediation. Only after these have been exhausted do disputants turn to panels for resolution. Even then, the first focus is not on compensation.

Third and very important, unlike investment arbitration, the WTO has an appeals body. The body comprises seven experts appointed for four-year terms. Membership is to reflect, broadly, the makeup of WTO membership. The appeals body resolves conflicting panel decisions and provides interpretation and clarification of the underlying "legislation." In addition, the body has served somewhat like the U.S. Supreme Court in allowing interpretations to evolve to reflect new concerns of member countries. Environmental issues illustrate this point. Following a 1991 complaint by Mexico, the trade organization ruled against the United States in a case involving tuna caught in ways that trapped dolphin.[85] The issue, of course, was environmental (or, more precisely, protection of animals). Yet by 2001, and after a lengthy appeals process, the WTO ruled in favor of the United States in a case involving a similar issue with shrimp and sea turtles.[86] Both rulings referred to Article XX of the GATT, a provision that had been in place since 1947.[87] But by 2001, the appeals unit responded to new views of environmental issues by rendering new interpretations of old legislation.[88]

An ideal solution to the problem of investment disputes would follow a model similar to that of the WTO. Multilateral negotiations would result in "legislation," which would draw on broad concepts such as national and most favored nation treatment. But any mutually acceptable outcome would also include provisions that parallel Article XX and the escape clauses of the GATT. In the case of investment, "legislation" might allow special treatment of disputes that arise out of events beyond the control of either party (such as economic crises), corruption or compulsion, and legitimate national policy concerns (environmental, health, safety, or defense, for example).[89]

A multilateral agreement would offer another important advantage. The current system for investment emerged largely from bilateral negotiations for bilateral investment treaties and trade agreements among small numbers of countries. When a rich country meets a poor country in such negotiations, the results are likely to favor the rich country, whether the issue is trade or investment. Multilateralism has offered fairer deals for trade. Most likely it would for investment as well.

Yet efforts to conclude a global agreement on investment have failed, from the investment provisions of the immediate post–World War II International Trade Organization through more recent attempts of the United Nations and the Organisation for Economic Co-operation and Development (OECD).[90] Negotiations have not bridged the gap that separates views taken by countries that perceive themselves as homes to investors from those that are primarily hosts. Further, multinational enterprises themselves have never supported an accord, and do not yet favor renewed efforts to negotiate a "WTO for Investment."

Building Common Law

An alternative to a global agreement is to build on the existing pieces of the current system to develop a common law for investment disputes.

The first step in such a process is to provide more transparency in arbitration than is common today.[91] Currently, international investment arbitration decisions are published only if the parties agree (or the decision is leaked). The confidentiality that is currently applied to some processes and awards creates fodder for political opposition and is surely considered by many to be inappropriate when governments or state-owned enterprises and public funds are involved. More importantly, unpublished and cryptic awards serve poorly as precedents. Arbitrators should be required to render written decisions explaining the basis for their awards.

The second, and equally important, step is the creation of a broadly available appeals process, and one not limited to procedural questions.[92] As one arbitration expert concluded from the conflicting decisions in the CME Czech Republic B.V. cases,

> An appeal mechanism is critical for the long-term survival of the investment arbitration system. Any system where diametrically opposed decisions can legally coexist cannot last long. It shocks the sense of rule of law or fairness.[93]

Common law relies on precedents, but this in turn requires a mechanism to resolve conflicting decisions and standards from different panels.[94] Moreover, an appeals process offers the possibility of creative response to changing views of appropriate outcomes of disputes.[95]

Our stories suggest additional concerns that could be mitigated with an appeals system. In particular, we saw arbitration procedures that were believed by one side (and perhaps both) to be faulty, and awards that were based on what we find to be standards that were, in the end, shockingly inappropriate to the facts of the cases.

An appeals body would have little legislation to which it could turn, in the absence of a comprehensive multinational agreement similar to the WTO. If, however, the panel membership were broadly representative of countries, both home and host to multinationals, it could generate accepted law out of the decisions of individual arbitration panels. A satisfactory outcome is especially likely if investment arbitration is made symmetrical, with governments having rights to bring cases. This would increase the interests of companies in building a reasonable body of law.

The most attractive place to locate an appeals body is probably within the ICSID framework.[96] First, no new organization would have to be created. Further, ICSID already serves as the arbitration forum for many *ad hoc* arbitration provisions, bilateral investment treaties, and regional agreements. Access to it is not limited to a small set of countries, as would be the case for a body operated under a regional trade agreement.[97] Finally, and perhaps most importantly in providing legitimacy and evolving law, within the World Bank Group it ought to be possible to create an appointment process that would yield broad representation. The danger, of course, is that the rich countries dominate—or will be perceived to dominate—the selection of panelists, which will thus undermine the perception that the panel can balance protection of investment with legitimate interests of host countries.[98]

To ensure that an evolving system hears the concerns of a broader constituency, more parties will need to have a voice in the process. Proposals for reform of ICSID already include the possibility that third parties be allowed to present views. This revision would serve to defuse political criticism and encourage responsiveness to legitimate social concerns, an editorial in the *New York Times* concluded.

The trade agreements that set the rules [for investment disputes] should direct arbitration panels to take a much broader view—to consider not just corporate interests but the needs of governments and their citizens.[99]

Resistance

We do not underestimate the resistance to any serious reform. The small group of lawyers who now dominate investment arbitration constitutes a formidable obstacle. Many will feel uncomfortable in introducing more economic analysis into their decision making. Many will also feel equally uncomfortable making decisions based on criteria beyond the language of a contract. Subjecting decisions to review by an appeals panel will reduce arbitrators' autonomy and increase their workload because awards will have to be crafted so that they survive challenge. Further, more predictability of outcome is likely to reduce the number of cases that go to arbitration. This, and the likely smaller awards for any lawyers who take cases on a contingency basis, will pose a threat to their income.

In the end, the best hope for reform lies in recognition by all parties that the current system is unlikely to survive without change. Moreover, reform should not be entirely in the hands of lawyers. Left on their own, they easily focus on "lawyerly" issues such as jurisdiction, admissibility, standards of proof, good faith, or severability. The underlying issues are deeply economic and political.

Concluding Comments

The wisest and most committed foreign investors cannot rely entirely on external guarantees of property rights, whether they are reformed or not. Turning to an improved system of dispute resolution is still likely to strain business relationships. Ultimately, security for most investors lies in how a particular project is perceived by its hosts—by government officials, but also in a democratic Third World by the press, labor, and nongovernmental organizations. Perceptions change. Although ITT managers in Indonesia could have reasonably predicted that their technology would provide them with some staying power, they could have also seen that the unrestrained monopoly that they had negotiated would surely someday raise eyebrows, and probably more. They might have considered that turning down a politically desirable investment would focus attention on their deal. For the power investors in Indonesia, the lack of any unique skills combined with projected returns inconsistent with the allocation of risk should have been enough to warn investors, lenders, and insurers of future problems, with or without a currency crisis.

But a stable international system that takes a balanced approach to property rights in risky countries can add significantly to investors' security. In fact, when managers make investments where they do not have a dominant and closely held technology or control over important export markets, their profits may ultimately depend on external protections.

Yet the current system is, we have argued, not viewed by various parties as fair and reasonable, or as responsive to legitimate national goals.[100] Thus, it is unlikely to survive intact. To quote one lawyer,

> As the [Karaha Bodas] case perhaps illustrates, emerging nations sometimes find themselves in impossible and unfair situations. It should hardly be surprising that they chafe under their obligations. "This is the fallout of globalization," says Nigel Blackaby of Freshfields in Paris. "Parts of the world feel that they have been failed by the absolute form of capitalism."[101]

Absolute forms of capitalism are, in fact, unlikely to survive, regardless of the wishes of proponents. Although we reiterate our conviction that the flow of productive investments to the developing world can help those nations break out of poverty, our stories from two recent episodes in the history of foreign investment remind us that inflows can sometimes result in bitterness and even greater poverty. If capitalism is to continue to contribute to the development process, it must show a softer face than that presented today by the new international system of property rights. One cannot help being reminded of those who credit President Franklin D. Roosevelt's New Deal with saving capitalism.[102] The rules that govern foreign investment—especially what we have referred to as the new international property rights—and the institutions that act as guardians and executors of those rules have to win renewed confidence of both multinational investors and sovereign host nations. Failure to reform the system to redress the imbalance between its attention to the legitimate economic and social concerns of host countries and those of investors will surely mean a retreat by those nations from the system. This will impose costs on both multinational corporations and the poor countries.

Notes

Introduction

1. According to one report, private infrastructure investment made up more than 8% of all foreign direct investment from 1984 to 2001. See Withold J. Henisz and Bennet A. Zelner, "Nine Principles for Political Risk Identification and Management," undated draft paper (2004).

2. From a sample of 33 projects, as reported in E. J. Woodhouse, "A Political Economy of International Infrastructure Contracting: Lessons from the IPP Experience," Program on Energy and Sustainable Development Working Paper Series (Stanford, Calif.: Stanford University, 2005). A World Bank study reports that 30% of a sample of 1,000 infrastructure "concessions" in Latin America (entered between 1985 and 2000) were renegotiated. If one excludes telecommunications, the figure rises to more than 41%. See J. Luis Guasch, *Granting and Renegotiating Infrastructure Concessions: Doing It Right* (Washington, D.C.: The World Bank, 2004), pp. 12–13.

3. For examples of non-government organizations, see the Web sites of UNICORN (http://www.againstcorruption.org) and ECA Watch (http://www.eca-watch.org).

4. Lawyers distinguish between property rights law, which stems from rights to physical property, and contract law. For most economists and political scientists, however, property rights comprise rights to the (exclusive) use of an asset, rights to income from the asset, and rights to alienate or sell the asset. Many of these rights are established by contracts. See, for example, Stephen Haber, Armando Razo, and Noel Maurer, *The Politics of Property Rights* (Cambridge: Cambridge University Press, 2003). In practice, an investor's concerns are similar. In our cases, contracts governed access, use, income, and disposal of assets. We will use "property rights" to include associated contracts.

5. The intensity of intervention varied from administration to administration. For an account of intervention and changing policies with respect to the Dominican Republic, see Cyrus Veeser, "In Pursuit of Capital: Concessions as a Modernizing

Strategy in the Dominican Republic," forthcoming. For a general history of U.S. intervention, see Louis T. Wells, "Protecting Foreign Investors in the Developing World: A Shift in U.S. Policy in the 1990s?" in Robert Grosse (ed.), *International Business-Government Relations in the 21st Century: In Honor of Jack Behrman* (Cambridge: Cambridge University Press, 2005).

6. Hernando de Soto, *The Mystery of Capital: Why Capitalism Triumphs in the West and Fails Everywhere Else* (London: Bantam Books, 2000).

7. There is now a vast literature on property rights. See especially work by Nobel Laureates Ronald Coase, Douglass C. North, and Vernon L. Smith.

8. The conflict between traditional property rights and the needs of a modern economy is illustrated in the tensions in nineteenth century America as construction of water-powered mills flooded lands belonging to others. Rather absolute concepts of property rights were revised to take into account development needs. For the nineteenth century story, see "Review of Joseph K. Angell, 'A Treatise on the Common Law in Relation to Water Courses,'" *American Jurist*, 1829, 25(2), pp. 30–34. Similar issues led to the U.S. Supreme Court's decision of June 23, 2005 (*Kelo v. New London*) to allow local governments to take property for economic development purposes.

9. NGOs often ask for "free and informed consent," but in no country are all property owners, even with adequate compensation, likely to give such consent to the taking of their property for the national interest. Resistance to takings under eminent domain are common even in the industrialized countries.

10. José A. Gómez-Ibáñez, "The Future of Private Infrastructure: Lessons from the Nationalization of Electric Utilities in Latin America, 1943–1979," discussion paper, Taubman Center for State and Local Government (Cambridge, Mass.: John F. Kennedy School of Government, Harvard University, January 1999, revised December 20, 2000), p. 3.

11. Figures for U.S. aid are from *USAID Strategic Plan for Indonesia: 2004–2008* (Washington, D.C.: USAID, July 28, 2004), available at http://pdf.dec.org/pdf_docs/pdaca366.pdf (accessed March 2005), and "CGI's New Commitment of 4.73 Billion U.S. Dollars for 2001," *Kompas*, February 3, 2000, available at http: www.kompas.com/kompas-cetak/0002/03/english/cgi.htm (accessed March 2005).

12. HIID's predecessor organization was called the Development Advisory Service. We will use the HIID designation throughout this book, and occasionally refer to the Indonesian project as the Harvard Group, as did many Indonesians.

13. Information about ministers with corrections is based on Embassy of the Republic of Indonesia in London, United Kingdom, "Indonesian Cabinet 1945–2001," available at http://www.indonesianembassy.org.uk/indonesia_cabinet_1945-2001.html, and "Profile of the Cabinet," available at http://www.indonesian embassy.org.uk/indonesia_cabinetprofile.html (accessed February 2005).

Chapter 1

1. James B. Simpson, Comp., *Simpson's Contemporary Quotations* (Boston: Houghton Mifflin, 1988), number 2145.

2. With the break-up of the Soviet Union in 1991, Indonesia moved from the fifth largest country to the fourth, behind China, India, and the United States.

3. See, for example, Bert Hofman, Ella Rodrick-Jones, and Kian Wie Thee, "Indonesia: Rapid Growth, Weak Institutions," paper delivered at Scaling Up Poverty Reduction: A Global Learning Process and Conference, Shanghai, May 25–27, 2004.

4. *Financial Times*, October 2, 1968, p. 7.

5. Benjamin Higgins, *Economic Development: Problems, Principles and Policies*, rev. ed. (New York: W. W. Norton, 1968), p. 676.

6. *Wall Street Journal*, July 7, 1966, p. 1.

7. Widjojo Nitisastro, "Basic Aims of Economic Planning," *Financial Times,* Survey of Indonesian Economy, October 24, 1968, p. 26.

8. Higgins, *Economic Development,* pp. 678–679; *Wall Street Journal,* May 25, 1964, p. 18; July 7, 1966, p. 1. See also Ingrid Palmer, *The Indonesian Economy since 1965: A Case Study of Political Economy* (London: Frank Cass, 1978), pp. 6–12; and H. W. Arndt, *The Indonesian Economy: Collected Papers* (Singapore: Chopmen, 1984), Chapter 1.

9. The house that one of the authors rented in Jakarta from 1994 to 1995 had been taken by Sukarno from its colonial Dutch owners and given to his protocol officer.

10. See John Hughes, *Indonesian Upheaval* (New York: D. McKay, 1967), for a contemporary account. A number of subsequent accounts have appeared, such as that of Theodore Friend, *Indonesian Destinies* (Cambridge, Mass.: Belknap Press for Harvard University Press, 2003).

11. Widjojo, "Basic Aims of Economic Planning," p. 26.

12. M. Sadli, "New Policy to Attract Foreign Investment," *Financial Times,* October 24, 1968, p. 27.

13. Law No. 1 of 1967.

14. Article 6 of Law No. 1 of 1967.

15. Some $2 billion in 2005 dollars. *New York Times,* August 17, 1968, p. 31.

16. According to Derrick Samuelson, there was only one company ahead of ITT, Freeport Sulphur, later known as Freeport-McMoRan.

17. *History of Posts and Telecommunications in Indonesia* (Jakarta: Department of Transport, Communications and Tourism, Government of Indonesia, n.d.), p. 32.

18. *History of Posts and Telecommunications in Indonesia,* p. 151.

19. The early history of ITT reported here draws largely from Anthony Sampson, *The Sovereign State of ITT* (New York: Stein and Day, 1973).

20. For examples in Latin America, see José A. Gómez-Ibáñez, "The Future of Private Infrastructure: Lessons from the Nationalization of Electric Utilities in Latin America, 1943–1979," discussion paper, Taubman Center for State and Local Government (Cambridge, Mass.: John F. Kennedy School of Government, Harvard University, January 1999, revised December 20, 2000), pp. 26–32.

21. Originally known as International Telephone and Telegraph Corporation, the company changed its name first to IT&T, and then to ITT. We will use the ITT designation, without regard to time.

22. Sampson, *Sovereign State of ITT,* pp. 49–60.

23. See "The International Telephone and Telegraph Company and Chile, 1970–71," Report to the Committee on Foreign Relations, United States Senate, by the Subcommittee on Multinational Corporations, June 21, 1973.

24. *New York Times,* March 14, 1968, p. 63.

25. Robert J. Schoenberg, *Geneen* (New York: Warner Books, 1986), Chapter 16. There had already been 40 acquisitions over the period of 1965 to 1967.

26. Sampson, *Sovereign State of ITT,* pp. 142–43; *New York Times,* March 14, 1968, p. 63.

27. See *Business Week,* November 3, 1973, p. 43.

28. Sampson, *Sovereign State of ITT,* p. 36.

29. For a comprehensive account of the Chile episode, see Sampson, *Sovereign State of ITT,* Chapter 11.

30. David Stout, "Edward Korry, 81, Is Dead; Falsely Tied to Chile Coup," *New York Times,* January 30, 2003, obituary, p. A23.

31. The growth in corruption caused widespread comment both at home and abroad. See *Wall Street Journal,* May 2, 1967, p. 1; *New York Times,* August 17, 1968, p. 31. Although not alone in being hospitable to corrupt practices, Indonesia continued to rank among the more problematic countries in this regard. See "Big Profits in Big Bribery," *Time,* March 16, 1981, p. 58.

32. For the story of a recent middleman in Africa, see David Ivanovich, "Tiny Player Strikes Gold in Huge Oil Deal," *Houston Chronicle*, March 13, 2005, p. 1.

33. See, for example, George C. Graenias and Duane Windsor, *The Foreign Corrupt Practices Act* (Lexington, Mass.: Lexington Books, 1982), pp. 20–25, for a list of U.S. firms that admitted to or were suspected of questionable payments.

34. From a retired ITT executive, Edward Masters, who had been chief of the political section in the U.S. embassy at the time and later (during the Carter administration) U.S. ambassador to Indonesia, said, in an interview on December 20, 1989, that Kim Adhyatman was "Adam Malik's bagman." The interview was about the passing of names of alleged communists from the U.S. embassy to Suharto. See "Kathy Kadane's Research: Interview with Edward Masters 3," available at http://www.antenna.nl/wvi/eng/ic/pki/kadane/int3.html (accessed April 2006).

35. Friend, *Indonesian Destinies*, pp. 118–119. Friend also reports on recent (1997 and 2000) interviews with Jack Christy, the "head of Asia for ITT," saying that ITT did not pay bribes. Christy is reported to have pointed out to the middleman that payments were illegal in the United States. But they were not illegal at the time, and ITT admitted bribery elsewhere; the idea that it would not pay in Indonesia is hardly credible. Perhaps memories had faded a bit over the intervening 30 years. Also see Friend, *Indonesian Destinies*, p. 138.

36. Personal communication to us from a retired ITT executive.

37. By the time our source confirmed the story in 2002, he had forgotten the exact sum. He agreed that it was something like $1 million to $2 million.

38. We requested, under the Freedom of Information Act (FOIA), all records from the CIA with respect to these events. The request was turned down with the statement that the agency neither confirms nor denies the existence of such documents.

39. Christy had come from ITT's corporate finance office to the communications group.

40. Galbraith was appointed ambassador on May 27, 1969. He had been counselor of the embassy and consul general at the embassy until January 1966 and is accused of at least tacit support for the military killings following the fall of Sukarno. See, for example, George McT. Kahin and Audrey R. Kahin, *Subversion as Foreign Policy: The Secret Eisenhower and Dulles Debacle in Indonesia* (New York: The New Press, 1995), pp. 226, 229–230.

41. Friend, *Indonesian Destinies*, p. 138.

42. Unless otherwise indicated, the material on Soehardjono is based on interviews with William Bell, Bernard Bell, George H. Hunter, and Mochtaruddin Siregar, deputy to the minister of state for national planning.

43. The World Bank's reputation was to be damaged in 1998 when the *Wall Street Journal* disclosed a memo leaked from the Bank's Jakarta office claiming that 20% to 30% of assistance to Indonesia had gone to corruption, strongly suggesting that World Bank management knew about this all along. See Glenn R. Simpson, "World Bank Memo Depicts Diverted Funds, Corruption in Jakarta," *Wall Street Journal*, August 19, 1998, p. 14.

44. Letter from President Suharto to the minister of communications, dated June 9, 1967.

45. Around $35 million in 2005 dollars. The investment would increase with cost overruns and later expansions.

46. Christy obtained permission to use these funds for imported equipment. Subsequent investors found this source of cheap rupiah cut off, but the new government soon abolished the foreign exchange controls of the Sukarno days.

47. In response to our FOIA request for copies of the insurance contracts, OPIC reported that they identified four contracts issued to ACR, all having terminated no later than January 29, 1981. "All four files were subsequently destroyed." Wells no longer has copies of insurance contracts that he obtained in 1980.

Chapter 2

1. Paragraph 23 assured free "extension service" from the satellite station to Telekom in Jakarta and Bandung and radio backup to the satellite facilities.

2. Paragraph 41.

3. Paragraph 47.

4. Paragraph 49.

5. Paragraph 12.

6. Paragraph 48.

7. Paragraph 50.

8. A more acceptable version might require that a company invoking a "most favored company" provision accept all the terms of the more favorably treated investors, eliminating cherry picking. But even then such provisions appeared rather dangerous to the host country. A country should be able to impose tougher terms on early investors who have the choice of mining projects, for example, while granting later investors more favorable terms to attract them to less appealing ore bodies. By the 1990s, such provisions had largely disappeared, but were not completely abandoned. They somehow showed up in the draft mining law for the Democratic Republic of the Congo (2002) and in a new foreign investment law of Montenegro (2003), for example. They could only be considered as inappropriately resurrected relics.

9. Article 57.

10. Paragraph 51.

11. Law No. 1 of 1967, Article 13.

12. Article 11.

13. Law No. 1 of 1967, Article 6.

14. Law No. 6 of 1963, and Law No. 5 of 1964.

15. Article 33.

16. This echoed Indonesia's production sharing agreements for petroleum under which title to all assets of the "investor" pass to the state-owned Pertamina when they enter the country. As a result, many assets are "leased" by the investor, to avoid their becoming state property.

17. Paragraphs 1 and 4.

18. Hence, according to paragraph 5, "all funds" invested in the project were to be covered by the Investment Guarantee Agreement signed in January 1967 between Indonesia and the United States. This made the project eligible for USAID (later, OPIC) insurance.

19. Paragraph 14.

20. Years later, arbitration tribunals would regularly classify such arrangements as constructive foreign direct investments subject to the protections connected with foreign-owned projects.

21. Quoted by Ingrid Palmer, *The Indonesian Economy since 1965: A Case Study of Political Economy* (London: Frank Cass, 1978), p. 100.

Chapter 3

1. Registered under Indonesian law on November 11, 1967.

2. On January 30, 1968.

3. The total of $8.26 million is roughly $48 million in 2005 dollars.

4. Indosat annual reports.

5. Indonesia's state-owned telephone company had gone through various reorganizations. Perusahaan Negara Telekomunikasi (Telekom) had been created in 1965 as the former postal and telephone company was divided. Telekom was converted to Perusahaan Umum Telekomunikasi (Perumtel) in 1974. Perumtel was, in turn, made into PT Telekomunikasi Indonesia (Telkom) in 1991.

6. *History of Posts and Telecommunications in Indonesia* (Jakarta: Department of Transport, Communications and Tourism, Government of Indonesia, n.d.), p. 153.

7. The riots are generally referred to as the *Malari* Incident, an Indonesian acronym for "January 15 Disaster" (*Malapetaka Limabelas Januari*). For an account of the events, possible political plotting, and the general climate of the times, see Goenawan Mohamad et al., *Celebrating Indonesia: Fifty Years with the Ford Foundation 1953–2003* (New York: The Ford Foundation, 2003), pp. 103–116.

8. According to company annual reports.

9. *History of Posts and Telecommunications in Indonesia,* p. 237.

10. From Indosat's managing director, August 7, 1979.

11. "Telecommunications Project Costs during *Repelita III* and *IV*, Revision of the Indosat–Perumtel Contract, and the Submarine Cable," September 3, 1979.

12. From Allen, Allen, and Hamsley.

13. Although USAID had issued the insurance, OPIC had taken over USAID's insurance activities.

14. Paragraph 2, article 33. The minister said this was also confirmed by Decision No. IV/MPR/1978 of the Peoples Consultative Assembly, prohibiting economic monopolies.

15. ITT headquarters personnel were not alarmed by the information that a consultant to the Indonesian government was requesting the insurance contract. In a monthly report under the caption "Government Activities on Indosat," Parapak mentioned that "The enquiry on OPIC insurance for Indosat's investment was apparently initiated by Prof. Louis Wells, a GOI consultant. His original question was 'whether OPIC in any cases alters the definition of expropriatory actions contained in the standard form contract'. No definite activities are known by the U.S. Embassy. Will follow up."

16. Included in minutes of the meeting.

17. Presidential Decree No. 52, August 30, 1980. Jonathan Parapak was probably not aware of this decree, when, two days later, he submitted his monthly Indosat review to the company's headquarters and reported "no new progress" on the Medan–Penang cable.

18. See Robert Sobel, *ITT: The Management of Opportunity* (New York: Times Books, 1982), pp. 386–391.

19. The following is taken partly from Hunter's informal minutes for the ITT team.

20. Personal communication, Oskar Surjaatmadja.

21. Personal communication, M. Sadli, referring more generally to the foreign investment agreements concluded in this early period.

22. The U.S. Weyerhaeuser Company soon decided to leave Indonesia because of problems it experienced in having to transfer 51% of the shareholding of its local business to Indonesian partners as required under the country's foreign investment regulations. See *Business Week,* November 2, 1981, p. 49.

23. The $1,384,000 difference represented the gap between a preliminary revaluation of assets carried out by Indosat in 1979 (following the November 1978 devaluation of Indonesian rupiah) and the final figure.

24. Oskar Surjaatmadja, in a final flashback, observed to us: "Before we shook hands over the price settlement, the ITT negotiators privately suggested the following three things, (a) keep Jonathan Parapak as managing director, (b) salaries of company employees should not be reduced, and (c) Indosat should not be merged with PERUMTEL. I salute ITT for making these suggestions before parting."

Chapter 4

1. Although various Web sites attribute this quote to Sir Alan Patrick Herbert, we have not been able to locate the original source.

2. Perhaps the earliest statements of the model can be traced to Raymond Vernon, "Long-Run Trends in Concession Contracts," *Proceedings of the American Society for International Law*, April 1967; Louis T. Wells, Jr., "The Evolution of Concession Agreements in Underdeveloped Countries," paper presented at the Development Advisory Service (DAS) Conference, Sorrento, September 5–12, 1968 (also released as a working paper by DAS); and Raymond Vernon, "Foreign Enterprises and Developing Nations in the Raw Materials Industries," The American Economic Review, 1970, 60(2), pp. 122–126. The most frequently cited source is Raymond Vernon's *Sovereignty at Bay* (New York: Basic Books, 1971). The concepts were originally applied to raw materials but later adapted to other industries and incorporated into the bargaining literature of international business.

3. See Louis T. Wells and David N. Smith, *Negotiating Third World Mineral Agreements: Promises as Prologue* (Boston, Mass.: Ballinger, 1976); and Louis T. Wells, "Minerals: Eroding Oligopolies," in D. B. Yoffie (ed.), *Beyond Free Trade: Firms, Governments, and Global Competition* (Cambridge, Mass.: Harvard Business School Press, 1993), pp. 335–384.

4. For a brief history of change in petroleum that draws on this paradigm, see Vernon, *Sovereignty at Bay*, Chapter 2.

5. Even in New York City, the reluctance of the original private subway companies to expand lines or to allow others to do so was an important factor in the city's eventual acquisition of the system from its private owners. For the history of ownership change, see Clifton Hood, *722 Miles: The Building of the Subways and How They Transformed New York* (New York: Simon & Schuster, 1994).

6. See Colin Lewis, "British Railway Companies and the Argentine Government," in D. C. M. Platt (ed.), *Business Imperialism, 1840–1930* (Oxford: Oxford University Press, 1977).

7. Indonesia's total foreign debt stood at $27 billion in 1983.

8. For an excellent description of the events, see José A. Gómez-Ibáñez, "Bangkok's Second Stage Expressway," Kennedy School of Government Case Program (Cambridge, Mass.: Harvard University, 1997), C15-97-1401.0.

9. Authorization to withdraw privileges under the Generalized System of Preferences was later to follow similar rules.

10. Charles Lipson, *Standing Guard: Protecting Foreign Capital in the Nineteenth and Twentieth Centuries* (Berkeley: University of California Press, 1985), p. 209.

11. *History of Posts and Telecommunications in Indonesia* (Jakarta: Department of Transport, Communications and Tourism, Government of Indonesia, n.d.), p. 189.

12. See George McT. Kahin and Audrey R. Kahin, *Subversion as Foreign Policy: The Secret Eisenhower and Dulles Debacle in Indonesia* (New York: The New Press, 1995), and Dole Scott, "Exporting Military-Economic Development: America and the Overthrow of Sukarno, 1965–67," in Malcolm Caldwell, *Ten Years' Military Terror in Indonesia* (Nottingham, England: Spokesman Books, 1975).

13. A case about hotel construction and operation was filed against Indonesia the next year in 1981, but final settlement did not occur until 11 years later.

Chapter 5

1. For alternative forms for government-owned enterprises, see Wagiono Ismangil, "Development and Control of Public Enterprises in Indonesia: Issues and Implications," paper presented at the Indonesian Congress on Efficient Management of State Enterprises, organized by the Institute for International Research at Jakarta Hilton on May 25–26, 1983, p. 4.

2. The new arrangement lasted until 1985 when a percentage fee was reintroduced—at 25% of all collected bills.

3. The amounts given in the business plan totaled roughly $5.8 million. Those amounts have been converted into Indonesian rupiah at applicable exchange rates.

4. First, to build TDMA/TRMS (Time Division Multiple Access and, Time Reference Monitoring Station) facilities for Intelsat. The next year, to construct a TTC&M (Tracking, Telemetry, Command, and Monitoring) antenna facility at the Jatiluhur location.

5. "Corruption perceptions indices" rankings are available on the Transparency International Web site at http://www.transparency.org/cpi/1995/cpi1995 .pdf (accessed December 2004). By 2004, Indonesia was followed by nine other countries in the rankings. None of the nine was included in the 1995 survey.

6. Letter dated August 20, 1982, from Jonathan Parapak.

7. Robert J. Sanders, Jeremy J. Warford, and Bjorn Wellenius, *Telecommunications and Economic Development* (Baltimore: The World Bank/Johns Hopkins University Press, 1983), p. 252.

8. See "Telecommunications Survey," *Economist,* November 23, 1985, p. 5.

9. "Telecommunications Survey," p. 28.

10. In 1991, Perumtel became Telkom (PT Telekomunikasi Indonesia). In 1995, Telkom entered "KSO" agreements with consortia (including foreign partners such as AT&T, Cable and Wireless, and Nippon T&T) to develop and operate regional systems. These collapsed with the rupiah. Although their stories parallel those of the electric power projects, we do not cover them.

11. Wayne Arnold, "An Owner of Global Crossing Surprises with Its Latest Bid," *New York Times,* December 17, 2002, p. W1.

12. In 2005, ITT Industries' products included water and wastewater treatment equipment, defense electronics and services, electronic components, and other industrial products.

Chapter 6

1. "Because of this, the future of the American system of government is dependent on the electric business continuing in the hands of investor-owned, tax-paying companies. . . . Our problem is not only to save our industry, but to save the American system of government." At the 1959 Edison Electric Institute convention, quoted in Richard Rudolph and Scott Ridley, *Power Struggle: The Hundred-Year War over Electricity* (New York: Harper & Row, 1986), p. 121.

2. Even in the United States, change was more frequent than often believed. Water systems and railroads, for example, moved from private to public hands. Ideology always has seemed to be present in U.S. debates. See Sharon Beder, *Power Play: The Fight to Control the World's Electricity* (New York: The New Press, 2003).

3. An official told us that Indonesia had received its first World Bank loan for power generation and transmission in 1962.

4. For a history of the term, see John Williamson, "From Reform Agenda to Damaged Brand Name," *Finance & Development,* September 2003, pp. 10–13.

5. The "Electric Power Utility Efficiency Study" was started in 1988.

6. The World Bank Industry and Energy Department, "Private Sector Participation in Power through BOOT Schemes," Industry and Energy Department Working Paper, Energy Series Paper No. 33, December 1990.

7. "Suharto Inc. Special Report: Children of Fortune," *Time Asia,* May 24, 1999, available at: http://www.time.com/time/asia/asia/magazine/1999/990524/cover4 .html (accessed July 2004).

8. John McBeth, "System Overload: Indonesia's Private Power Plans May Be Too Ambitious," *Far Eastern Economic Review,* October 28, 1993, pp. 57–58.

9. Other members of Team 35 included the state minister for development planning and chair of the national planning agency, BAPPENAS; the ministers of mines and energy, minister of communications, minister of trade, and the chair of the investment coordinating board, BKPM.

10. "PLN's Winning Performance," *Indonesia Business Weekly*, 2(42), September 30, 1994, p. 6.

11. Figure presumably for 1993. See McBeth, "System Overload."

12. For example, Freeport's huge copper and gold mining operation on Irian Jaya obtained power for a number of years from its own generators. Under new policies, in 1998 P.T. Puncakjaya Power, a 195-megawatt plant, was built with its power contracted to Freeport until 2017. Duke Power International was the foreign partner in the project; the principal local partner represented interests of the notably uncorrupt Tahija family. Duke sold its 85.7% interest to Freeport-McMoRan in 2003. See Duke Energy, "Duke Energy Sells Ownership Interest in Indonesian Facility," press release, July 24, 2003.

13. Caminus Energy Limited, "Electricity Sales from Privately Owned Power Stations: Issues and Principles," Cambridge, England: n.d. [1990 or earlier]. Some reports gave much higher figures. See, for example, John McBeth, "System Overload," and Zuhal, *Ketenagalistrikan Indonesia* (Jakarta: PT Ganeca Prima, 1995), p. 5, which reports more than 60% of industrial power as coming from captive sources in the period 1981 to 1990. See also Lorenzo Kristov, "The Price of Electricity in Indonesia," *Bulletin of Indonesian Economic Studies*, December 1995, 31(3), p. 77.

14. Sjahrir, "Transformasi Struktur Ekonomi, Kebijaksanaan Ekonomi dan Prospek Perkembangan Ketenagalistrikan di Indonesia," in Zuhal, *Ketenagalistrikan Indonesia*, p. 223. Still, household electrification was considered low. See Kristov, "The Price of Electricity in Indonesia," p. 79.

15. Zuhal, *Ketenagalistrikan Indonesia*, p. 3. PLN's exact capacity figures differ somewhat by source.

16. Hydro accounted for about 23% of total PLN capacity in 1989, according to Zuhal, *Ketenagalistrikan Indonesia*, p. 3.

17. For the growth in industrial demand, see Zuhal, *Ketenagalistrikan Indonesia*, p. 5. PLN's own data indicated waiting lists of 48 percent of its installed capacity. See Diana Yuliyanti, "Project Finance for Independent Power Producers in Developing Countries: The Paiton I Power Generation Project in Indonesia," dissertation submitted for Masters of Science in Civil and Environmental Engineering, Massachusetts Institute of Technology, February 1, 2001, p. 59.

18. Particularly, low and middle income customers. See Caminus Energy Limited, "Electricity Sales from Privately Owned Power Stations."

19. PLN's rates in 1994 were listed by one publication as follows: residential: 144.84 rupiah per kilowatt hour (rp/kwh); business: 154.29 rp/kwh; industrial: 134.93 rp/kwh. These were lower than rates in Singapore, the Philippines, Thailand, Malaysia, Hong Kong, and Taiwan, according to the table provided in *Business News*, October 26, 1994, p. 7.

20. Figures for1992. Perhaps not surprisingly this reported figure matches the requirements imposed by the World Bank on its loans to PLN.

21. PLN's complex tariff schedule is described in detail in Kristov, "The Price of Electricity in Indonesia," pp. 86–88. Rates made fine distinctions among customers: Small, medium, and large hotels, for example, paid different electricity rates, with the lowest capacity and energy charges to small hotels and the highest to medium ones.

22. McBeth, "System Overload."

23. Similar figures appear in Table 2 of Asian Development Bank, "Impact Evaluation Study of Asian Development Bank Assistance to the Power Sector in Indonesia," IES: INO 2003-13, July 2003.

24. Although silent on implementation, Law No. 15/1985 seemed to allow for private generation of electricity. PLN's own plan for new power to be commissioned from 1994 to 1999 specified more than 20% as coming from power purchase agreements, according to Kristov, "The Price of Electricity in Indonesia," p. 84.

25. On January 9, 1993, this organization was renamed the Directorate General of Electricity and Energy Development, and a Directorate of Private Power was established in the directorate general.

26. Under a contract to International Development and Energy Associates, Inc.

27. Some authors insist on reserving the word "privatization" for transfers of state-owned assets to private hands. Others, including us, use it also to include private development of new projects that would in the past have been done by the state. For a substantial period, Indonesians "privatized" largely new capacity, maintaining state ownership of existing capacity. For a record of privatization in Indonesia, see Tanri Abeng, *Indonesia, Inc.: Privatising State-Owned Enterprises* (Singapore: Times Academic Press, 2001).

28. The proposal for the oil-fired Hub Power Project in Pakistan had been submitted in 1987, the implementation agreement and power purchase agreement initialed in 1989, and construction started in 1991. The "levelized" tariff was 6.5 cents/kwh, but it was later renegotiated to 5.6 cents.

29. Private Sector Power Project, "Quarterly Report," June 1995. This was the report submitted quarterly to USAID by the advisors it supported. It was written primarily by Peter Jezek.

30. Hollinger was by this time associated with the Price Waterhouse Financial Sector Development Project in Indonesia, which conducted studies for the government. The report was prepared under Price Waterhouse's name and financed by USAID.

31. The best analysis of the alternatives that we have seen is in José A. Gómez-Ibáñez, *Regulating Infrastructure: Monopoly, Contracts, and Discretion* (Cambridge, Mass.: Harvard University Press, 2003), Chapter 1. A slightly different classification system appears in Christian von Hirschhausen, *Modernizing Infrastructure in Transformation Economies* (Cheltenham, UK: Edward Elgar, 2002), pp. 172–173. For an unusually clear comparison of the advantages and complexities of a system that uses contractual relations for independent power providers and a market, or "merchant" system, see Robert Thomas Crow, "Foreign Direct Investment in New Electricity Generating Capacity in Developing Asia: Stakeholders, Risks, and the Search for a New Paradigm," working paper of the Asia/Pacific Research Center, January 2001.

32. These independent power producers were authorized under the Public Utility Regulatory Policy Act of 1978 (PURPA), which exempted them from the Public Utility Holding Company Act of 1935. The options for private generators expanded with the Energy Policy Act of 1992.

33. Charles R. Frank, Jr., "Power Sector Reform: Lessons from Experience," unpublished paper, October 28, 2002.

34. Paul Krugman, "Another Friday Outrage," *New York Times*, September 2, 2003, p. A23. Similar criteria appear in connection with various approaches to structuring an electricity system in von Hirschhausen, *Modernizing Infrastructure*, pp. 25–26, 176–177.

35. Geothermal thermal contracts differed slightly, but the substance was similar.

36. See APEC Energy Working Group, "Final Report," Annex 3: Indonesia, 2001, 140; and "Indonesia: Combating Corruption In Indonesia, Enhancing Accountability for Development," The World Bank, Report No. 27246-IND November 12, 2003. Available at: http://www-wds.worldbank.org/servlet/WDSContentServer/WDSP/IB/2003/11/25/000012009_20031125111638/Rendered/INDEX/272460 IND.txt (accessed May 2005). Many documents refer to 26 rather than 27 generating facilities, omitting the Cikarang project, which was in operation by the time the Asian financial crisis struck. Supplying an industrial estate, it entered no power purchase agreement with PLN. Its early problems are reported in Kristov, "The Price of Electricity in Indonesia," p. 82. Bosshard reports obligations of 11,000

megawatts. Nick Lord, "Power Problems," *Finance Asia*, August 1999, puts the figures at 11,260 megawatts and $16.5 billion.

Chapter 7

1. Paiton is often referred to as the first and largest of the private projects. Cikarang, at Jababeka Industrial Park, was the first. Tanjung Jati B was planned to be larger.

2. For a sense of scale, consider the controversial Enron project at Dabhol, near Bombay (Mumbai), in India. Phase I of that project, for the contract signed the same year as Paiton I's, was for 625 megawatts, at a cost of about $922 million. A second phase would add 1,320 megawatts of capacity. See "Enron Development Corporation: The Dabhol Power Project in Maharashtra, India (A)" (Boston, Mass.: Harvard Business School, 1997), case N9-797-087.

3. "Construction of $2.6b Power Plant Begins," *Jakarta Post*, September 14, 1994, p. 1.

4. P. A. Jezek, "Private Power in Indonesia," Memorandum to A. Arismunandar, June 4, 1991.

5. Decree of the Minister of Mining and Energy, No. 1649K/702/M.PE/1990, November 26, 1990, as it appeared in translation in "Private Power Update Indonesia," February 1991. This was the first issue of the news circular prepared by Peter Jezek and produced by the Office of Private Power Advisor, Directorate General for Electricity and New Energy, Ministry of Mines and Energy.

6. Interviews with Paiton managers, February 2003.

7. PLN executives were understandably miffed, for it was PLN that would be paying for the electricity and the expenses of the two teams.

8. Jezek reported that his first draft of a power purchase agreement caused similar problems. It raised issues of risk allocation, bankability, and so on that had not been addressed. It was distributed anyway.

9. Now located in the Ministry of Finance, the Harvard Group commissioned a report from Peter Borre of Boston Energy Associates in 1990. From late 1990, the Harvard Group itself prepared a series of memos on the subject of private power, including "Terms of Reference for Establishing Private Electricity Generating Units at Paiton, East Java," memo to Dr. Fuad Bawazier, Direktur Pembinaan BUMN, December 21, 1990 (254/90/466); and "Private Generation of Electric Power: Pricing and Other Issues," memo to Minister J. B. Sumarlin, February 7, 1991 (254.1/91/042).

10. On the other hand, the group often brought in specialized consultants when needed. Still, short-term advisors were probably not what was required.

11. Reported to us by Jezek.

12. Private Sector Power Project, "Quarterly Report," January 1991. By April 1991, a prequalification document had been drafted. See Private Sector Power Project, "Quarterly Report," April 1991.

13. Private Sector Power Project, "Quarterly Report," January 1991. We are not sure if "office of energy" referred to the U.S. Department of Energy.

14. Reported to us by an advisor. Most foreign assistance had to be approved by BAPPENAS, the national planning agency. As one of the authors of this book discovered in 1994, the agency's professionals were wont to take off a portion for themselves and their friends. While negotiating a World Bank–funded consulting contract, he was summoned to an official's office at BAPPENAS for an 8 AM Saturday meeting with no one else present but the principal American negotiator. The official presented a list of Indonesians who were to be "hired" on contract, with no suggestion that they would do any work. The minister in charge of BAPPENAS at the time of this event was Ginandjar.

15. Interview with Peter Jezek.

16. For a list of some of the documents, see Lahmeyer International, "Final Report: Lessons Learned from Paiton One," Jakarta, November 1993, vol. 2, p. 32.

17. Lahmeyer International, "Final Report," vols. 1 and 2. This report was written before the negotiations had been completed.

18. The law firm's partner George Crozer, according to the firm's Web site, eventually represented the Indonesian government for Paiton I. Another partner in White & Case would also represent lenders to the Paiton I power project. Further, White & Case is also listed as representing PT Jawa Power in Paiton II. One of the firm's partners represented Edison Mission in the financing of its CBK Power Project elsewhere. In other words, this law firm worked for both government and investors in the power sector in Indonesia; if its Web site is to be believed, the firm also worked for both the government and the lenders for the same project, Paiton I. (Information derived from http://www.whitecase.com/cgi-bin/Public/ice-search, accessed May 2003; this information had been removed by August 2004.)

19. The Troika had become general consultants to the Indonesian government, especially to the influential Ministry of Finance and the central bank. Rachmat Saleh, governor of the central bank at the time, had originally sought out their predecessor firms, Lazard Fréres, Kuhn Loeb, and Warburg, when Pertamina's debt problems threatened to bring down the national oil firm in 1975. William Hollinger, the same actor in the ITT story and consultant on privatization, had helped in making the arrangements.

20. Private Sector Power Project, "Quarterly Report," October 1992.

21. Despite government infighting over the process and the lack of consensus among ministries on terms, some draft documents had been provided to two possible private contenders for Paiton I on September 13, 1990, inviting their comments by the end of October. More complete documents then went out on December 29. Lahmeyer International, "Final Report," vol. 1, p. 3. See Ministry of Mines and Energy, Directorate General for Electricity and New Energy, "Terms of Reference for Paiton Private Power Project," Jakarta, December 29, 1990.

22. Also known as Intercontinental Energy Corporation (or Group), the company was founded by John R. Roy to produce industrial chimneys. It claimed that one of its generating facilities for a while supplied about 10% of Boston's power. Intercontinental was eventually run by two of John Roy's children, Stephen and Ellen.

23. Bambang Trihatmodjo. For a description of some of his business interests, see *Far Eastern Economic Review*'s cover story of May 13, 1999, on Bimantara. Bambang was to break the state monopoly on telecommunications in 1993, when a company he controlled, Satelindo, was awarded licenses for international direct-dial and mobile phone services. See "Sejarah Indonesia: An Online Timeline of Indonesian History. Orde Baru—The Suharto Years: 1965–1998," available at http://www.gimonca.com/sejarah/sejarah10.shtml (accessed December 2005).

24. It seems that the PLN Pension Fund was also to be a partner. See Private Sector Power Project, "Quarterly Report," October 1991.

25. Its Bellingham, Massachusetts, co-generation plant reportedly had 430-megawatt capacity in 1991. See the Youthpowershift.org Web site, "Grandfathered Power Plants," available at http://www.seac.org/energy/powermap.php?id=190 (accessed December 2004).

26. Information from a company consultant. Our September 2003 letter to Stephen Roy requesting an interview went unanswered. We could not confirm information provided by others.

27. Efforts to reach Hagler Bailly failed. E-mails and a letter were returned as not deliverable.

28. Jeff Gerth, "In Post–Cold-War Washington, Development Is a Hot Business," *New York Times*, May 25, 1996, p. 1.

29. A former vice president of Intercontinental, Junaid Yasin "was a developer for power and industrial projects in the USA, China, India, Indonesia, UK etc." for Intercontinental. See the EnergyPulse Web site, "Junaid Yasin, President, Procure-Zone," available at http://www.energypulse.net/centers/author.cfm?at_id=160 (accessed July 2004). In Yasin's response to an e-mail, however, he indicated that none of the efforts undertaken with ABB to create projects in Nanjing, Jiangsu Province, China; Malaysia; India; or Bangladesh succeeded.

30. Lahmeyer International, "Final Report," vol. 2, p. 10.

31. Letter from Stephen B. Roy, Vice President, Intercontinental Power Corporation, to Prof. Dr. Ing. B. J. Habibie, minister of state for research and technology, April 17, 1990. The letter adds that the company's design engineer was Sargent & Lundy and that the firm was currently designing Paiton Units 1 and 2 and had performed site selection work for another project in Java. The letter was copied to the U.S. ambassador to Indonesia, John C. Monjo, and the Indonesian ambassador to the United States, A. R. Ramly.

32. Diana Yuliyanti, "Project Finance for Independent Power Producers in Developing Countries: The Paiton I Power Generation Project in Indonesia," dissertation submitted for Masters of Science in Civil and Environmental Engineering, Massachusetts Institute of Technology, February 1, 2001, p. 62.

33. One advisor believes that this employee was offered a fee of $10,000 by Roy to make introductions that would lead to an agreement, even though he was under contract to USAID at the time. We have no confirmation of this allegation.

34. In 1999, Ginandjar had the only stretch limousine that the authors had seen in Jakarta.

35. Chandra Asri. The report, probably misinterpreted, was used to argue for increased protection for the plant; the Harvard Group had opposed increased protection. The result was described in Indonesia as "Harvard vs. Harvard."

36. Perhaps Intercontinental's contributions had helped it a bit. We know only those made in New Jersey; according to the OpenSecrets.org Web site (http://www.opensecrets.org), they amounted to $10,200 from 1993 to 1997 for the Republicans, with $1,000 for Democrats.

37. He inaccurately added that this was the only U.S. firm interested. A second U.S.-led consortium had already submitted its proposal.

38. If one can believe the report of one advisor to the Indonesian government, Roy's confidence must have been somewhat less than this suggests. The advisor told us that Roy took him aside and said, "Help me get this project, and I'll make you a rich man." The advisor told us that he responded, "I work with the Indonesian government. If you have a good proposal, I will support you." In the end, the advisor did not support the project.

39. Lahmeyer International, "Final Report," vol. 1, p. 3.

40. Private Sector Power Project, "Quarterly Report," January 1992.

41. There was also a legal issue: Law Number 1/1967 explicitly prohibited full control by foreign investors of electric power production.

42. Private Sector Power Project, "Quarterly Report," January 1992.

43. Private Sector Power Project, "Quarterly Report," July 1992.

44. In 2003, Paiton managers told us that there were six bidders, in addition to the Mission-led consortium, for the project. Jezek says seven companies were invited to submit proposals. A paper by one of Paiton's employees names six groups, including Mission's partner, who were invited to bid, but the paper and those involved clearly state that only two, the Intercontinental-led and Mission-led groups actually "bid." See James Booker, "IPP Development: An Investor's Perspective," paper presented at the 4th APEC Coal Trade and Investment Liberalization and Facilitation Workshop, March 6–8, 2002, Kuala Lumpur, Malaysia. The lists of the firms differ slightly from source to source, but the groups involved seem to be agreed: GEC Alstom (Alsthom) International, PT Intan Prima Kartika

Indonesia, Sumitomo Corporation, PT Abdi Bangun Buana with Asea Brown Boveri (ABB), Intercontinental Energy Corporation, and BT Batu Hitam Perkasa. Batu Hitam Perkasa joint ventured with Mission. The Paiton interviewee's list included Cipta Cakra Murdaya, an affiliate of Asea Brown Boveri (ABB) and owner of Abdi Bangun Buana. Later, in 1999, ABB and Alstrom merged their power generation businesses.

45. Private Sector Power Project, "Quarterly Report," July 1992.

46. Gordon Wu would also end up with another power project, Tandjung Jati B.

47. The belief that the consortium "did not have and was unlikely to have the required equity financing" was stated in Private Sector Power Project, "Quarterly Report," April 1992. This report also commented that the proposal was incomplete and that the coal handling layout and arrangements were "not acceptable."

48. Lahmeyer International, "Final Report." Other consultants also describe Intercontinental's submissions this way.

Chapter 8

1. The consolidated balance sheet of the holding company reported more than $11 billion in assets in 2002. Mission Energy Holding Co, SEC 10-K, filed March 28, 2003.

2. Mission eventually branched out a bit, into housing, for example.

3. Interviews with Paiton managers, February 2003.

4. Robert Edgell, correspondence March 28, 2005. Mitsui would not grant interviews. Calls to Japanese managers in Jakarta were met with "No one is here who knows about the project" or, repeatedly, "Call back, he's out for lunch [meeting, or whatever]; no, I cannot take a message." Attempts to reach managers by e-mail in Japan went unanswered.

5. Stuart Dean, "From Lightbulbs to Locomotives: Manufacturing in Indonesia," a report from the United States-Indonesia Society, Public Affairs Programs, January 8, 2002, Washington, available at http://www.usindo.org/Briefs/Stu%20Dean.htm (accessed August 2004).

6. Dean, "From Lightbulbs to Locomotives."

7. Office of the Press Secretary, The White House, "Clinton Administration Secures Contracts for U.S. Exporters Totaling over $40 Billion, Supporting Tens of Thousands of Jobs," November 17, 1994, available at http://clinton6.nara.gov/1994/11/1994-11-17-administration-secures-contracts-for-exporters.html (accessed August 2004).

8. See "RI, U.S. Sign Agreements on $40b Projects," *Jakarta Post*, November 17, 1994.

9. The equity was to be held by General Electric Financing C.V., a Connecticut subsidiary.

10. William J. Hausman and John L. Neufeld, "U.S. Investment in Electric Utilities in the 1920s," in Mira Wilkins and Harm Schroeter (eds.), *The Free Standing Company in the World Economy, 1830–1996* (Oxford: Oxford University Press, 1996), pp. 361–390.

11. Francis Blake had been general counsel for the Environmental Protection Agency under President Ronald Reagan. With the election of George W. Bush, Blake returned to Washington to become deputy secretary in the Department of Energy, where he played a major role in developing Bush's National Energy Plan. For one version of the controversy surrounding his tenure in the Department of Energy, see Darren Samuelsohn and Suzanne Struglinski, "Key Figure in White House Energy Policy, NSR Review Resigns," *Greenwire*, National Tribal Environmental Council Web site, available at http://web.archive.org/web/

20031230234110/http://www.ntec.org/air/air/resign.html (accessed April 2006). In March 2002, he resigned to return to the private sector with Home Depot's corporate headquarters in Atlanta. Our letter requesting an interview went unanswered.

12. *Batu hitam,* literally "black rock," means coal. *Perkasa* signifies brave or strong. The confusion with Broken Hill Proprietary (BHP) of Australia was intentional, according to one of the founders, a response to a dispute with the Australian company.

13. Robert Edgell, correspondence March 28, 2005.

14. See letter of May 6, 1999, to Ralph A. Matheus, Acting Vice President for Finance, OPIC, from Robert E. Driscoll, Senior Vice President, Asia Pacific Region, Edison Mission Energy, available at http://www.softwar.net/paiton2.html (viewed August 2004). Edgell told us that Mission received background information on Hashim from the embassy.

15. A brave man, Sumitro had mounted some oblique attacks on Suharto's economic policies, especially in the 1980s.

16. Her full name is Siti Hediati Haryadi, but she is widely known as Titiek Prabowo.

17. George J. Aditjondro, "Chopping the Global Tentacles of the Suharto Oligarchy: Can Aotearoa (New Zealand) Lead The Way?" available at http://www.hamline.edu/apakabar/basisdata/2000/03/30/0037.html (accessed August 2004). See also Theodore Friend, *Indonesian Destinies* (Cambridge, Mass.: Belknap Press for Harvard University Press, 2003), p. 325.

18. John Colmey and David Liebhold, "Suharto Inc.: Special Report," *Time Asia,* May 24, 1999, available at http://www.time.com/time/asia/asia/magazine/1999/990524/cover1.html (viewed December 2004).

19. Colmey and Liebhold, "Suharto Inc."

20. See "Selected Information on P.T. Batu Hitam Perkasa," in official documents released by OPIC under the Freedom of Information Act, available at http://www.softwar.net/paiton2.html (viewed August 2004).

21. Paiton management reports investigating four sources of coal: PT Berau, PT Kaltim Prima, PT Multi-Haripan, and Adaro. (See James Booker, "IPP Development: An Investor's Perspective," paper presented at the 4th APEC Coal Trade and Investment Liberalization and Facilitation Workshop, March 6–8, 2002, Kuala Lumpur, Malaysia, p. 6.) Three of these would have offered connections to Suharto cronies. Berau was tied to PT United Tractors, which was associated with Astra. Multi-Harapan started with a concession obtained by Graeme Robertson, who then took in the Napan Group (Risyad, Pribadi) and Liem. Robertson's participation linked it to Adaro. Kaltim Prima was also linked to Adaro, according to interviews. Adaro's more direct linkages to powerful figures were especially attractive, however. Given its ties, it is not clear whether Paiton had any real choice of suppliers.

22. She held 0.75% equity interest through having 15% interest in Tirtamas Majutama. She also held interests in the coal mine that was to supply Paiton.

23. Although not clear in the ownership tables, the original concession holder also appears to have retained interests in Adaro. See "Construction of $2.6b Power Plant Begins," *Jakarta Post,* September 12, 1994, p. 1. The Spanish role was confirmed in interviews.

24. At least in 2002, New Hope was controlled by Washington H. Soul Pattinson (WHSP), a large Australian investment group.

25. For a description of the arrangement, see letter of May 6, 1999, to Ralph A. Matheus, acting vice president for finance, OPIC, from Robert E. Driscoll, senior vice president, Asia Pacific Region, Edison Mission Energy, available at http://www.softwar.net/paiton2.html (accessed August 2004). The letter points out that OPIC received a copy of the loan arrangement before it committed to the venture.

26. Loans for share purchases might be appropriate in some cases. Some tests might include: (1) Is the partner an official or close to an official? (2) Is the loan an obligation of the borrower regardless of how the enterprise performs? If not, does the interest rate reflect the allocation of risk to the lender? (3) Does the borrower have other reasonable sources of funds? (4) Does the borrower bring business assets (other than access to officials) to the enterprise commensurate with the value of the implied transfer? Such assets might include distribution, brand name, or technology.

27. Many projects came with a "designated" partner, according to people we interviewed. For a similar finding, see the report of an interview in Witold J. Henisz and Bennet A. Zelner, "Political Risk Management: A Strategic Perspective" (unpublished paper, Wharton School, University of Pennsylvania, n.d. [probably 2004]).

28. According to one electric power investor, he was asked for 10% free equity.

29. One classification of projects listed nine as having partners from the First Family and 17 as having crony partners. Hardiv H. Situmeang, "Challenges Facing PP Model in Asia: The Experience of PLN in Indonesia," presentation at 10th World Economic Development Congress, Kuala Lumpur, June 27–29, 2001.

30. Edgell told us that 15% local ownership was required by law at the time Paiton I was being negotiated, and that the number was lowered to 5% later. However, the letter of May 6, 1999, to Ralph A. Matheus, acting vice president for finance, OPIC, from Robert E. Driscoll, senior vice president, Asia Pacific Region, Edison Mission Energy, available at http://www.softwar.net/paiton2.html (accessed August 2004) says that the requirement was 5% at the time of negotiations. Confusing matters more, the decree authorizing foreign-owned power seemed to allow full foreign ownership. Laws and decrees, however, mattered less than one might suppose.

31. E-mail dated August 6, 2002, from Philip Urofsky, special counsel for international litigation, Fraud Section, U.S. Department of Justice.

32. Peter Waldman, "Heavy Hand: Washington's Tilt to Business Stirs a Backlash in Indonesia," *Wall Street Journal*, February 11, 2004.

33. Two letters to Vickers at Mission (sent in October and November 2003) went unanswered. The Indonesians we spoke with remembered no attempt by him to obtain a waiver of conflict of interest.

34. Zuhal, who was president director of PLN from April 1992 until December 1995.

35. Similar tensions over the role of advisors were eventually to develop within the Harvard Institute for International Development. When Jeff Sachs was appointed as the HIID director in 1995, old-line professionals were annoyed to no end when he began to speak out publicly on policies of countries where HIID worked. In the case of Indonesia, at least twice his public statements contradicted recommendations from HIID advisors on the ground (with respect to bank closings during the Asian Currency Crisis and tax incentives).

36. Jezek wrote a paper on electric power in Indonesia: "New Paradigms for Supplying Electricity in Indonesia: Institutional and Regulatory Restructuring of Electricity Supply to Achieve Efficiency," Centre for Strategic and International Studies, Jakarta, 1994.

37. A conversation that Ginandjar says he does not recall.

38. Monjo served 1989 to 1992, following Paul Wolfowitz's tenure.

39. Jezek reported that when he pointed out to USAID officials problems with the proposals, he was told that U.S. investment was coming in. There seemed to be little concern whether the terms were good or bad for Indonesia. For confirmation of his instructions not to "provide any support associated with evaluation of Paiton proposals," see Private Sector Power Project, "Quarterly Report," October 1991.

40. See, for example, the Private Sector Power Project, "Quarterly Report," January 1992 and April 1992.

41. "Memorandum re Paiton Private Power," from White & Case and The Advisory Group, February 24, 1992.

42. PLN head Zuhal complained in interviews that PLN had to pay a $3 million bill for White & Case's legal fees, even though the law firm was working for the government, not for PLN.

43. "Paiton Private Power," Memorandum 254/92/149, May 1, 1992.

44. Peter Bosshard, "Publicly Guaranteed Corruption, Corrupt Power Projects and the Responsibility of Export Credit Agencies in Indonesia," *ECA Watch*, available at http://www.eca-watch.org/problems/corruption/bosshard_indon_nov2000.html (accessed April 2006). The quotation is a translation from *Der Spiegel*; the original source was perhaps the November 30, 1993, Aide Memoire from the World Bank, signed by Peter Scherer and widely circulated in the Indonesian government, which said that the transmission system was not balanced for what was being negotiated with independent power producers.

45. Richard Borsuk, "Plugging In," *Asian Wall Street Journal*, Supplement, April 28–29, 1995.

46. Cikarang Listrindo, part of the powerful Lippo Group under the Riady family, which had also been charged with funneling illegal money to the Clinton campaign through John Huang.

47. Lahmeyer International, "Final Report: Lessons Learned from Paiton One," Jakarta, November 1993, vol. 1, p. 3. Although original proposals called for an implementation agreement, setting out obligations of the investor and the various ministries, this document was eventually dropped. The draft power purchase agreement had been prepared by a subcommittee of PUKS, chaired by a representative of the Ministry of Finance, whose voice now had to be heard. See also Lahmeyer International, "Final Report," vol. 2, p. 15.

48. See Private Sector Power Project, "Quarterly Report," for January 1992 and July 1992.

49. Keppres 37. (Keppres is an acronym for presidential decree.)

50. Implementing regulations for this decree were not issued until February 1993.

51. We have not been able to determine exactly how these leaks worked. One report is that local partners paid off secretaries in the government units involved in exchange for copies of all documents. Another is that the Japanese obtained information, particularly through networks developed by their trading companies. Others claim that the CIA monitored fax and telephone communications. The fact that reducing the size of the group involved in planning sessions reduced leaks suggests that the source was not simply secretaries.

52. PLN dates the start of negotiations to September 1992 and the conclusion of the agreement to February 1994.

53. Born in 1947, Edgell held a B.S. in electrical engineering from California State College and an M.S. in power engineering from the University of Southern California. See Contact Energy Web site, "New Directors for Contact Energy Ltd," available at http://www.mycontact.co.nz/view?page=/forinvestment/newscentre/pressreleases&opt=19990511 (accessed July 2004).

54. Quoted in Paul Blustein, "In Asia, an Eldorado of Infrastructure," *Washington Post*, June 4, 1995, p. O1.

55. Private Sector Power Project, "Quarterly Report and Final Report," January 1993. Jezek's contract was expiring and he thus viewed this as his final report. The contract was, however, eventually extended.

56. Lahmeyer International, "Final Report," vol. 2, p. 8.

57. For details of the links, see George J. Aditjondro, "Business Links of the Suharto & Habibie Oligarchy of Indonesia (III): A report prepared for the Berne

Declaration," n,d., available at http://www.munindo.brd.de/george/sh3.html (viewed May 2003). The general gist of the documents is clearly correct, but not every detail is easily confirmed.

58. Lahmeyer International, "Final Report," vol. 1, p. 10. Note that Combustion Engineering is a U.S. subsidiary of ABB. Alstom was to become the successor to ABB/Combustion Engineering.

59. Private Sector Power Project, "Quarterly Report," April 1993.

60. One advisor contradicted company managers by telling us that there never was such an offer. We do not know who was right.

61. Private Sector Power Project, "Quarterly Report," August 1993.

62. PLN's director Zuhal attributed these questions from above to calls made by the companies to the president.

63. Letter from Hashim S. Djojohadikusumo to President Suharto, "Subject: Proyek Listrik Swasta Paiton Phase I," July 9, 1993. In the letter, he attributes 0.57 cents of the tariff in the first years to new environmental demands and 0.62 to higher interest rates. The base for rate-of-return calculations would be complicated further by subordinated debt held by the equity investors.

64. Private Sector Power Project, "Quarterly Report," November 1993.

65. Interviews in February 2003.

66. The price in the original contract has been reported as 8.5, 8.6, 7.9, 8.53, and 6.0 cents in various sources. The numbers vary for several reasons. The contract called for reductions in price over time, but the actual delivered price also depended on fuel and other costs. The most careful report indicates that the capacity charge was to be 6.12 for years 3 to 6, 5.97 for years 7 to 12, and 3.1 for years 13 to 20. See "Paiton Energy Company—Fact Sheet (Paiton Swasta I)," available at http://www.softwar.net/paiton2.html (accessed August 2004). To these figures one would have to add a charge for fixed operations and maintenance, fuel, and variable operations and maintenance charges. The figures in the text come from "Deal Concluded for First Major Private Power Plant," *Jakarta Post*, February 14, 1994.

67. Although the decree is not crystal clear on indexing, some lawyers have argued that it required that pricing be in rupiah only.

68. John McBeth, "System Overload: Indonesia's Private Power Plans May Be Too Ambitious," *Far Eastern Economic Review*, October 28, 1993, pp. 74–76.

69. Private Sector Power Project, "Quarterly Report," November 1993.

70. See Borsuk, "Plugging In."

71. Warren Christopher had been director from August 1971 to January 1977, at which time he became U.S. deputy secretary of state, and then director (at Southern California Edison) again from June 1981 to January 1993. In January, he resigned, this time to become the U.S. secretary of state. Christopher was a partner in the law firm O'Melveny & Myers, which represented Southern California Edison at times, according to its Web site.

72. We know only that Kissinger sent a fax to Habibie and Ginandjar asking for support for the project. From handwritten notes of a Mission manager, dated March 20, with no year indicated.

73. Documents released under FOIA, "Paiton September 1994 Notes," available at http://www.softwar.net/paiton2.html (accessed August 2004). These indicate that the lobbyist attended meetings between Mission managers and Department of Commerce officials. At the time, they appear to have been working for the Jefferson Consulting Group, a Washington-based lobbying firm. Later, one of the lobbyists was president of Jefferson Waterman, a lobbying firm she helped found. It put out the *Myanmar Monitor*, an Internet newsletter "to provide a broad and balanced view" of Burma. That, of course, meant to portray the military government in a favorable light and to champion dismantlement of U.S. sanctions. She took similar contracts to build up the images of other unsavory clients,

including Croatian Franjo Tudjman and Charles Taylor of Liberia. See Ken Silverstein, "Their Master's Voice: The Burma Lobby," *Multinational Monitor,* 1998, 19(6), available at http://multinationalmonitor.org/mm1998/98june/master.html (accessed August 2004), and Silverstein, "Despots R Us: Meet Washington's Favorite Lobby Shop for Foreign Thugs," *The American Prospect,* 2002, 13(12), available at http://www.prospect.org/print-friendly/print/V13/12/silverstein-k .html (accessed June 2003). Another lobbyist was appointed by George W. Bush as deputy assistant secretary in the Department of Commerce in October 2001, where he would oversee export development for companies in the aerospace, automotive, and machinery industries.

74. One group was led by Secretary of Treasury Lloyd Bentsen. See Karen Mills, "Corruption and Other Illegality in the Formation and Performance of Contracts and in the Conduct of Arbitration Relating Thereto," *International Arbitration Law Review,* 2002, 5(4), p. 128.

75. In Article 18 of the power purchase agreement. "Power Purchase Agreement between P.T. Paiton Energy Company as Seller and Perusahaan Umum Listrik Negara as Buyer," February 12, 1994.

76. Article 15 of the power purchase agreement.

77. "Power Purchase Agreement between P.T. Paiton Energy Company as Seller and Perusahaan Umum Listrik Negara as Buyer." The power purchase agreement itself is 69 pages. The entire document contains, in addition, 19 appendices (which contain, among other things, the formulas for determining tariffs), and five schedules.

78. By Ernest J. Gerloff (Paiton), Hashim Djojohadikusumo (BHP), Robert M. Edgell (Mission), Takuji Sakuraba (Mitsui's attorney), and William D. Sheahan (GE) on behalf of the investors; and Zuhal of PLN and Sudjana, minister of mines.

79. See Borsuk, "Plugging In."

Chapter 9

1. Warren Christopher, "Expanding Opportunities for U.S. Business Abroad" (from a transcript of a speech delivered at APEC Meetings, November 7–18, 1994), *U.S. Department of State Dispatch* 5(SUPP-9), 1994, 9(2).

2. "Construction of $2.6b Power Plant Begins," *Jakarta Post,* September 12, 1994.

3. The contract (to Mitsui, Toyo Engineering, and Duke Fluor Daniel) was awarded in February 1995. See James Booker, "IPP Development: an Investor's Perspective," a paper presented at the 4th APEC Coal Trade and Investment Liberalization and Facilitation Workshop, March 6–8, 2002, Kuala Lumpur, Malaysia, p. 7.

4. From documents released under the FOIA available at http://www. softwar.net/kkn2001.html (accessed December 2005).

5. Value given in John Howard, "Deceit and Deception—US Dealings in Indonesia," Peace Movement Aotearoa Web site, September 24, 1999, available at http://www.converge.org.nz/pma/etdeal.htm (accessed August 2004). Peter Ballinger, OPIC's counsel, wrote in October 1994 that the interests of Siti and Hashim combined amounted to 2.5% through their investment in PT Batu Hitam Perkasa. This was, he said, in addition to minor interests in the coal supply chain.

6. From FOIA documents available at http://www.softwar.net/paiton2.html (accessed August 2004). Some interpret the released documents as reporting a $50 million bribe divided among Prabowo (Suharto daughter Titiek's husband) and other Suharto relatives and cronies. The reference is likely to the loan extended by the foreign owners of Paiton I to the local partner for the purchase of its shares. See, for example, Howard, "Deceit and Deception."

7. Memo of this meeting is in the FOIA documents available at http://www.softwar.net/paiton2.html (accessed August 2004).

8. As did CalEnergy, an investor to appear in a later chapter. See Howard, "Deceit and Deception."

9. Grateful Mission company executives reported that they were "largely happy with U.S. government efforts, especially Department of Commerce, Embassy, [and] OPIC. . . ."

10. International Trade Administration, U.S. Department of Commerce home page [archival copy], available at http://web.archive.org/web/20001217144600/ http://www.ita.doc.gov/td/advocacy/ (accessed April 2006). Amusingly, in late 2001 the Advocacy Center's site proudly listed its interventions on behalf of Enron in India, Nicaragua, and Turkey among its success stories. By September 2002, these "successes" had been dropped.

11. Warren Christopher, ""Remarks by Secretary of State Warren Christopher to the American Chamber of Commerce, Jakarta, Indonesia, July 25, 1996," transcript, available at http://dosfan.lib.uic.edu/ERC/briefing/dossec/1996/9607/ 960725dossec.html#top (accessed August 2004).

12. Edmund McWilliams, quoted by Peter Waldman, in "Heavy Hand: Washington's Tilt to Business Stirs a Backlash in Indonesia: Defense of Suharto-Era Deals Shows How Interest Groups Can Sway Foreign Policy," *Wall Street Journal,* February 11, 2004, p. 1.

13. Letter from W. James McNerney, Jr., senior vice president and president, Asia Pacific, to Kenneth Brody, Chairman, U.S. Export Import Bank, March 1, 1995.

14. The letter actually refers to compromise language on "the most critical issues in the areas of war, civil insurrection, expropriation and discharge of PLN's obligations."

15. Bryson, on March 13, 1995.

16. Quoted in Peter Bosshard, "Publicly Guaranteed Corruption, Corrupt Power Projects and the Responsibility of Export Credit Agencies in Indonesia," *ECA Watch,* available at http://www.eca-watch.org/problems/corruption/bosshard_indon_ nov2000.html (accessed April 2006).

17. Some reports on the Internet say that the U.S. secretary of the treasury (by this time, Robert Rubin) also pushed Mission's case, based on the list of material that the Department of Commerce refused to release in response to a FOIA request, in particular "Memo dated 4/11/95 to Jay Brandes from Orit Frenkel and Ann Wrobleski, subject Paiton Briefing for Secretary Rubin." We received no response to our letter inviting Rubin to clarify matters.

18. Handwritten notes made by Mission manager, dated March 20, 1995, "Ambassador Barry Report."

19. We do not know whether the government's counsel, White & Case, was already working for lenders to the project when it was advising Indonesia on these letters.

20. The support letter for Paiton I is included in the *Confidential Offering Circular,* March 21, 1996. For a description of the "support letters" in another case, see OPIC's FOIA Electronic Reading Room Web site, "OPIC Claim Determinations, Memorandum of Determinations, Expropriation Claim of MidAmerican Energy Holdings Company (formerly CalEnergy Company, Inc.), Contracts of Insurance Nos. E374, E453, E527, and E759," available at http://www.opic.gov/foia/ ClaimsDeterminations/1999%20Determinations/MidAmerican%20Energy.htm (accessed August 2004).

21. Letter from John F. Welch, Chairman of the Board, General Electric Company, to Prof. Dr.-Ing. B.J. Habibie, Senior Minister for Research & Technology, March 20, 1995.

22. Ibid.

23. "Indonesia Advocacy Projects," released under the FOIA, available at http://www.softwar.net/paiton2.html (accessed August 2004).

24. Bosshard, "Publicly Guaranteed Corruption."

25. Office of the Press Secretary, The White House, "Clinton Administration Secures Contracts for U.S. Exporters Totaling over $40 Billion, Supporting Tens of Thousands of Jobs," November 17, 1994, available at http://clinton6.nara.gov/1994/11/1994-11-17-administration-secures-contracts-for-exporters.html (accessed June 2000).

26. Excerpts from the cable from Jakarta to Tokyo are in Charles R. Smith, "The Mondale Mistake," *NewsMax.com*, October 30, 2002, available at http://www.newsmax.com/archives/articles/2002/10/30/153928.shtml (accessed August 2004).

27. Office of the Press Secretary, The White House, "Clinton Administration Secures Contracts." This White House press release is not clear on whether Christopher was present at the signings, although he was certainly in the country at the time; the U.S. Department of State Web site, "Warren M. Christopher, January 20, 1993–January 17, 1997," available at http://www.state.gov/r/pa/ho/trvl/ls/13043.htm (accessed August 2004. Edgell thought he was not present, according to communication to us of March 28, 2005. Our requests to Warren Christopher for information went unanswered.

28. Christopher, "Expanding Opportunities for U.S. Business Abroad."

29. Changed to PT Paiton Energy in 1999.

30. Edison Mission Energy owned MEC Indonesia B.V., a Dutch company, which held Edison's interest in the Indonesian company.

31. Mitsui & Company held its shares through Paiton Power Investment Company. Ownership information comes from *Confidential Offering Circular*, March 21, 1996.

32. General Electric's interest was held by Capital Indonesia Power I C.V., a Dutch limited partnership, which in turn was held by General Electric Financing C.V., a Netherlands limited partnership, and Global Power Investments, L.P., a Cayman Islands limited partnership. These were under the management of General Electric Capital Corporation.

33. "Operation and Maintenance Agreement," April 21, 1995.

34. The figure of $30 million was suggested, but the interviewee confessed that he did not remember the exact number.

35. "Lenders Face US$2 Billion Deals," *Project Finance International*, May 11, 1995, cited in Karin Astrid Siegmann, *Deutsche Grossbanken Entwicklungspolitisch in der Kreide?* (Siegburg, Germany: Südwind, 2000), p. 75.

36. Personal communication from Edgell, March 28, 2005. Another manager reported that Mission could not obtain political risk coverage because it could not pledge shares twice; they were already pledged to ECA lenders.

37. MIGA *Annual Report* for fiscal year 1996.

38. Adnan Ganto was "rumored" to be the shadow minister. See "Wawancara Umar Said: 'Baru Dua Bulan Saya Sudah Digoyang,'" *Tempo*, May 24, 1997.

39. This paragraph relies on interviews with an advisor to the Indonesians.

40. There is some question whether all of this was actually equity. In a little noted provision, it seems that the private side received permission to put up half of its "equity in the form of subordinated loans." Mission's chief operating officer, Robert M. Edgell, explained that this "helps us manage our total tax burden." Presumably, he was saying no more than that the firm would like to deduct some interest charges in calculating its tax bill. See Richard Borsuk, "Jakarta to Join with Companies for Power Pact," *Asian Wall Street Journal*, February 9, 1994, pp. 1, 4. PLN's case study on Paiton reports that $820 million came from the investors' own funds, and reports this is 20% of the total; it attributes $1,720 million to loans, which it labels as 80% of the funds. These percentages do not match the numbers

that the case associates with them. See Eksibit 2, Christine Taufik, and Hadi Satyagraha, "Pencabutan Gugatan Perkara Listrik Swasta PLTU Paiton Swasta I," case by PLN Jasa Pendidikan dan Pelatihan, n.d. [ca. 2000].

41. Marketable only to certain qualified institutional buyers, generally defined as a purchaser owning at least $100 million of marketable securities. See "General Rules and Regulations" promulgated under the Securities Act of 1933. The $180 million debt (Paiton Energy Funding B.V.), March 21, 1996, carried a 9.34% coupon and was due in 2014. The new issue pricing was U.S. 10-year Treasury plus 275 basis points. Source: Credit Suisse First Boston.

42. The "tombstone" published July 13, 1995, reports $1,913,750,000 of project financing.

43. Cited in Bosshard, "Publicly Guaranteed Corruption."

44. From a Mitsui manager, who read about the awards but was not involved in the project. He told us Japanese firms do not give bonuses for such negotiations.

45. One manager told us that GE did not award its managers on a project by project basis, but rather on a year by year basis.

46. "TransCanada Taps into Growing Indonesian Demand for Power," *Wall Street Journal,* Interactive Edition, January 8, 1997.

47. Quoted in Richard Borsuk, "Plugging In," *Asian Wall Street Journal,* Supplement, April 28–29, 1995. Jezek told us that the quote came from him.

48. From Private Sector Power Project, "Quarterly and Final Report," June 1995.

49. Jezek told us that he left out of frustration. In any event, interviewees told us that Jezek still feared for his family, even in Thailand, and sent them back to the United States while he remained in Southeast Asia. He moved on to Vietnam in 1997.

Chapter 10

1. Paiton owners explained that cash flow had to be high in the early years so that they could service the project's large debt. One can think of other reasons for the declining tariff—in particular, to manage political risk. The company might hope that serious attention would turn to the deal only after the price had declined to a level that would make the arrangement look less lopsided than at the outset.

2. Eddie Widiono S. (PLN head), "Laporan Perkembangan Renegosiasi PLTU Paiton I," addressed to the economic coordinating minister, document No. 834/180/DIRUT/2001-R, Jakarta, September 18, 2001.

3. R. David Gray and John Schuster, "The East Asian Financial Crisis: Fallout for Private Power Projects," *Public Policy for the Private Sector,* Note No. 146, August 1998, available at http://rru.worldbank.org/Documents/PublicPolicyJournal/146gray.pdf (accessed August 2004).

4. It cited a World Bank report, dated June 13, 1996, as source. See Suwarjono, "Meneropong Masa Lalu Ginandjar (2), Keganjilan Miliaran Dolar di Paiton," available at http://web.archive.org/web/20040615131839/http://www.detik.com/lapsus/200007/ginanjar-lalu2.shtml (accessed April 2006).

5. T. Soentoro and S. Fried, "Export Credit Agency Finance in Indonesia," in Berne Declaration et al., *A Race to the Bottom Creating Risk* (Washington, D.C.: Environmental Defense Fund, March 1999), p. 27.

6. Still another way of evaluating Paiton's prices was to compare them with prices in an industrialized country. In 2002, seven years after the Paiton agreement, the electricity tariff for residences in Boston, Massachusetts, for nonheating use was 7.334 cents/kwh (plus delivery charges). This retail price is lower than the wholesale price at the outset for Paiton's electricity. (Source: Monthly bill from NSTAR Electric to one of the authors, January 22, 2002.)

7. T. Soentoro and S. Fried, "Export Credit Agency Finance in Indonesia."

8. For a comparison of the terms of the two projects, see Larry H. P. Lang, *Project Finance in Asia* (Amsterdam: Elsevier, 1998), p. 233.

9. "PLN Criticized over Pricing of Private Electricity," *Jakarta Post*, November 29, 1994.

10. Interview with Nengah Sudja, a former PLN employee who conducted the study. He concluded that a private producer would have to charge 6.02 cents/kwh to cover its higher costs of capital.

11. These calculations are all reported in Lorenzo Kristov, "The Price of Electricity in Indonesia," *Bulletin of Indonesian Economic Studies*, 1995, 31(3), pp. 73–101.

12. Our calculation is in the appendix to this chapter. A similar figure is $598 million per year, in APEC Energy Working Group, "Final Report," Annex 3: Indonesia, 2001, and Adnan Buyung Nasution & Partners, "PLN Filed a Lawsuit against Paiton Energy" [press release], Jakarta, October 7, 1999, cited in Diana Yuliyanti, "Project Finance for Independent Power Producers in Developing Countries: The Paiton I Power Generation Project in Indonesia," dissertation submitted for Masters of Science in Civil and Environmental Engineering, Massachusetts Institute of Technology, February 1, 2001, p. 129. Our calculations summed to $581 million per year. A considerably larger figure would be due, according to PLN head Adhi Satriya, as quoted in Michael Billington, "Looting Indonesia: The Energy Brokers 'Warm-up' for California," March 28, 2001, available at http://www.odiousdebts.org/odiousdebts/index.cfm?DSP=content& ContentID=2746 (accessed August 2004).

13. These calculations assume that excess payments to Indonesians (for coal, for example) are not economic costs to the country. One could, however, count a portion of them as costs, especially as the coal company had some foreign shareholdings.

14. Assuming loan terms specified in the *Confidential Offering Circular*, March 21, 1996, and equal annual payments on principal.

15. A 15% reduction overstates the cost because foreign shareholders retain 65% of the dividends until the loan is paid off.

16. See Yuliyanti, "Project Finance," p. 182.

17. In April 2005, we asked Edgell for responses to our estimates. He would only say that the company's estimates were confidential.

18. Calculated from cash flow forecasts in Robert E. Kennedy, "InterGen and the Quezon Power Project: Building Infrastructure in Emerging Markets," Harvard Business School case 9-799-057 (rev. August 20, 2000). The Pakistan Hub project was supposed to yield 18% on equity before renegotiations, according to World Bank documents. An analysis of another power project in a developing country showed a real rate of return of 32% on equity. See Glenn P. Jenkins and Henry B. F. Lim, "Case 5. An Integrated Analysis of a Power Purchase Agreement," May 19, 2003, unpublished, but apparently written for the World Bank. The case disguises the name of the companies and the Indian state, but the numbers are actual, the author assured us.

19. Yuliyanti, "Project Finance," p. 181. Yuliyanti cites Hossein Razavi, *Financing Energy Projects in Emerging Economies* (Tulsa, Okla.: PennWell Books, 1996) and Larry H. P. Lang, *Project Finance in Asia* (Amsterdam: North-Holland, 1998).

20. The Indonesian government borrowing rate for dollars was about 1% above the 10-year U.S. Treasury bond rate. In September 1996, the Treasury rate was just under 8%. See "Federal Reserve Statistical Release: Selected Interest Rates," September 9, 1996, available at http://www.federalreserve.gov/releases/h15/19960909/ (accessed August 2004) for Treasury rates, and "Indonesia Bets Growth Will Lure Wary Bond Investors," *Investments Magazine*, February 18, 2004, available at http://investmentsmagazine.com/managearticle.asp?C=163&A=6311 (accessed August 2004) for the Indonesian borrowing rate. Rates may have been as

high as 11% a couple of years earlier. The high cost of Paiton's funds remains striking, even if 11% is taken as the base.

21. Details of the tariff structure are provided in the chapter appendix.

22. Estimates provided by Hardiv Situmeang.

23. For rough calculations, we assumed that an Indonesian manager costs $25,000/year and an Indonesian operator, $6,000; in contrast, an expatriate manager was assumed to cost $250,000 (with all costs such as housing and education) and an expatriate operator, $150,000. The results are not sensitive to large variations in these estimates.

24. Say that a PLN-run plant employs 18 managers and 63 workers at relatively high wages of $30,000 and $10,000 per year, respectively. The total cost is about $1.4 million per year compared with an annual payment for fixed costs of at least $600 million for Paiton I.

25. Lang, *Project Finance in Asia*, p. 233.

26. Tanri Abeng, *Indonesia, Inc.: Privatising State-owned Enterprises* (Singapore: Times Academic Press, 2001), p. 79. As mentioned earlier, Tanri Abeng had been the minister in charge of state-owned enterprises. The original cost of $1.77 billion for Tanjung Jati B was renegotiated down to $1.2 billion later, according to the same source.

27. James Booker, "IPP Development: An Investor's Perspective," paper presented at the 4th APEC Coal Trade and Investment Liberalization and Facilitation Workshop, March 6–8, 2002, Kuala Lumpur, Malaysia, p. 6.

28. That is, 0.12×2.5 billion. In a March 28, 2005, communication, Edgell reported to us that the additional costs were $300–500 million.

29. Details are in Lahmeyer International, "Final Report: Lessons Learned from Paiton One," Jakarta, November 1993, vol. 2, pp. 44–45.

30. Hashim S. Djojohadikusumo to President Suharto, "Subject: Proyek Listrik Swasta Paiton Phase I," July 9, 1993.

31. The profits did not initially go to Paiton's owners, although Paiton did later buy an interest in the coal mine and thus a share in those profits.

32. Peter Waldman and Jay Solomon, "Wasted Energy: How U.S. Companies and Suharto's Circle Electrified Indonesia," *Wall Street Journal*, December 23, 1998, p. 1; also published as "U.S. Power Deals in Indonesia Draw Flak," *Asian Wall Street Journal*, December 24, 1998.

33. Interviews in Jakarta, March 2001. See also Karin Astrid Siegmann, *Deutsche Grossbanken Entwicklungspolitisch in der Kreide?* (Siegburg, Germany: Südwind, 2000), p. 75.

34. The calculation is $0.036 \times 24 \times 365 \times 0.83 \times 1220 \times 1000$.

35. The frequency of renegotiation in Latin America was much higher for tendered projects than for negotiated ones. See J. Luis Guasch, *Granting and Renegotiating Infrastructure Concessions: Doing It Right* (Washington: World Bank Institute, 2004).

36. The corruption we reported for Indosat was in the original negotiations, not the renegotiations.

37. Izaguirre Ada Karina, "Private Participation in the Electricity Sector—Recent Trends," in *Public Policy for the Private Sector* (Washington: The World Bank, September 1998), cited in Yuliyanti, "Project Finance," p. 46.

38. The amounts for each component come from Taufik and Hadi Satyagraha, "Pencabutan Gugatan Perkara Listrik Swasta PLTU Paiton Swasta I," Eksibit 3.

Chapter 11

1. Quoted in Peter Waldman and Jay Solomon, "Wasted Energy: How U.S. Companies and Suharto's Circle Electrified Indonesia," *Wall Street Journal*, December 26, 1998, p. 1.

2. Exporters with dollar earnings could, of course, be exceptions. Yet palm oil producers found their exports first banned and then subject to a tax, as the government tried to hold down the sensitive cooking oil price.

3. For daily rates for this period, see "Daily Indonesian Rupiah Rate against US Dollar: 1995/01–2000/08," available at http://www.jeico.com/cnc57idn.html (accessed August 2004). Some reports say that it reached a low of Rp 17,000 per dollar in January of 1998. "Sejarah Indonesia: An Online Timeline of Indonesian History. Orde Baru—The Suharto Years: 1965–1998," available at http://www.gimonca.com/sejarah/sejarah10.shtml (accessed August 2004).

4. Hardiv Situmeang, "The Role of PLN in Electric Power Sector Development," Workshop on the Study on Power Sector Development in Indonesia, Jakarta, February 2, 2001, p. 3.

5. Because a common tariff schedule applied to all of Indonesia, higher production costs in many outer islands had left little incentive to expand in those locations.

6. R. David Gray and John Schuster, *The East Asian Financial Crisis—Fallout for Private Power Projects*, Public Policy for the Private Sector, no. 146 (Washington, D.C.: World Bank Group, August 1998), p. 4.

7. Sander Thoenes, "Excessive Confidence Casts a Pall over Indonesian State Electricity Utility," *Financial Times*. September 16, 1999, p. 6. The journalist author of this article was killed later in the month in East Timor.

8. PLN's obligations had increased as it had embarked on a "Super Crash Program" to build more generating capacity of its own.

9. Salil Tripathi and John McBeth, "Act of Desperation," *Far Eastern Economic Review*, March 19, 1998, p. 42. For the year, the average was 2.8 cents according to PLN calculations.

10. Pressure from the IMF is documented in a briefing memo prepared for Secretary of Commerce Daley by Jay L. Smith for a meeting with Mission's Edward R. Muller, August 6, 1998.

11. The conditions the IMF included in the "letter of intent" became controversial. Some viewed them as designed to topple Suharto's rule, and they blamed the U.S. government. Others saw them as the remaining reform agenda of the Berkeley Mafia and the local office of the World Bank. There could be some truth in each of these explanations. When the government closed several insolvent banks, including one controlled by a Suharto son, this was read by crony businessmen as an indication that the First Family could no longer protect those under its umbrella. The ensuing panic probably increased capital flight and thus more downward pressure on the rupiah.

12. Keppres number 39/1997.

13. Witold J. Henisz and Bennet A. Zelner, "The Political Economy of Private Electricity Provision in Southeast Asia" (working paper, Reginald H. Jones Center, The Wharton School, University of Pennsylvania, Philadelphia, 2001), WP2001-02, available at http://jonescenter.wharton.upenn.edu/papers/2001/wp01-02.pdf (accessed August 2004). Numbers conflict in published sources, as projects were subtracted from or added to various lists. See, for example, "Petroleum Report Indonesia 2001, Natural Gas." American Embassy Jakarta, 2001, available at http://www.usembassyjakarta.org/petroleum/bab-4.pdf (accessed August 2004).

14. Keppres number 5/1998, the third in a somewhat confused set of three decrees. Number 39/1997 suspended certain projects. Number 47/1997 substantially reversed 39/1997. With IMF pressure, number 5/1998 in January largely reinstated 39/1997.

15. The list of projects in various categories was something of a moving target. But the U.S. Energy Information Administration in March 1998 listed 14 projects as being "on hold": plants in East Palembang, Cilegon, Cilacap, Serang, Salak, Karaha, Cibuni, Darajat, Sibayak, Patuha 2,3,4, Dieng unit 4, and Bedugul units 3 and

4. Under review were a plant in South Sulawesi, the Asahan hydropower plant in North Sumatra, the geothermal Patuha Unit 1 plant, geothermal Dieng 1, 2, and 3, and Bedugul in Bali. United States Energy Information Administration,"Country Analysis Brief, Indonesia," March 1998, available at http://www.converger.com/eiacab/indonesa.htm (accessed August 2004).

16. Quoted in Tripathi and McBeth, "Act of Desperation," p. 42.

17. Peter Bosshard, "Conclusion: 'Risk Insurance like Candy?'" in "Publicly Guaranteed Corruption, Corrupt Power Projects and the Responsibility of Export Credit Agencies in Indonesia," available at http://www.eca-watch.org/prob lems/corruption/bosshard8_indon_nov2000.html (accessed April 2006).

18. Edison International, 1997 *Annual Report*, p. 27.

19. In September 2000, *Tempo* concluded: "Sooner or later, PLN will definitely go bankrupt." Quoted in Bosshard, "Publicly Guaranteed Corruption, Corrupt Power Projects and the Responsibility of Export Credit Agencies in Indonesia," ECA Watch, available at http://www.eca-watch.org/problems/corruption/bosshard_indon_nov2000.html (accessed April 2006). *Tempo* was banned in 1994, but it soon became active in a Web edition; by 1999, after the fall of Suharto, it had returned in full.

20. Michael Billington, "Looting Indonesia: The Energy Brokers 'Warm-up' for California," March 28, 2001, available at http://www.odiousdebts.org/odiousdebts/index.cfm?DSP=content&ContentID=2746 (accessed August 2004).

21. Although Indonesia had no functioning bankruptcy procedures, the IMF would soon insist that the country pass a new bankruptcy law. But it is difficult to find cases of state-owned utilities going through a bankruptcy process.

22. Theodore Friend, *Indonesian Destinies* (Cambridge, Mass.: Belknap Press for Harvard University Press, 2003), p. 325.

23. Friend, *Indonesian Destinies*, p. 329.

24. Friend, *Indonesian Destinies*, p. 331.

25. Friend, *Indonesian Destinies*, pp. 342, 343.

26. Mar'ie Muhammad until March 1998; then Fuad Baazier, followed by Bambang Subianto.

27. "Power Sector Restructuring Policy: The Government's Policy Program for Power Sector Recovery, Restructuring, Regulatory Reform and Private Participation," Jakarta: Ministry of Mines and Energy, August 1998. The document appears to have been prepared by a native English speaker. It was likely written by Hagler Bailly, which was providing advice to the ministry, but we are not sure. Several attempts to reach the company failed, so we assume that the company has closed.

28. PLN would be broken up, with a separate company handling outer islands. PLN would distribute on Java and Bali, but its assets would be divided into separate generation, transmission, and distribution companies.

29. Suharto's closing of *Tempo* for criticizing Habibie for the purchase of East German ships and reporting the resulting conflicts within the government illustrates the sensitivity of the previous president to public reporting of internal disputes.

30. William Liddle, "Megawati's Presidency: A Contrarian Perspective," *Jakarta Post*, October 6, 2003.

31. The minister, Tanri Abeng, came from private sector business, most immediately from the Bakrie group, and brought along several business people, including Markus Parmadi (from Lippo, who became chair of the PLN restructuring team) and Darwin Silalahi (from Bakrie). See his account of his role in this position, in Tanri Abeng, *Indonesia, Inc.: Privatising State-Owned Enterprises* (Singapore: Times Academic Press, 2001).

32. Tanri Abeng, *Indonesia, Inc.*, p. 80.

33. Keppres 139/1988 (September 11).

34. Trained as a chemical engineer in Australia, Hartarto had held cabinet positions since the early 1980s and had long been a strong promoter of large,

protected industries. His own and his family's business interests are summarized in George J. Aditjondro, "Bisnis Keluarga Para Menko, Ginanjar & Hartarto," Kabar dari *PIJAR*, March 20, 1998, available at http://web.archive.org/web/20001011195342/http://www.geocities.com/CapitolHill/Senate/1627/bisnis_keluarga_para_menko.htm (accessed April 2006) and http://www.hamline.edu/apakabar/basisdata/1998/03/20/0038.html (accessed August 2004). For another source on business ties of his children, see Dudi Rahman, "Bisnis Anak Menko Hartarto," available at http://www.hamline.edu/apakabar/basisdata/1999/02/17/0071.html (accessed August 2004).

35. Abeng, *Indonesia, Inc.*, p. 80. Other reports include the minister for foreign affairs and the coordinating minister for the economy. These may have been added later, of course.

36. At the same time, two additional teams were created: for corporate and financial restructuring of PLN.

37. He classified advisors into five categories: corporate advisor, legal advisor, financial advisor, IPP specialist, public relations, and technical/cost auditor.

38. From Hunton & Williams.

39. In March 1998, Bradley and Robert G. Fitzgibbons, Jr., an associated advisor, submitted an overview of the issues, with the projects grouped into classifications, a "summary of legal strategy," and a preliminary analysis of various options for PLN.

40. According to a World Bank official, it was pressure from CalEnergy that led USAID to discontinue support for Bradley. Soon, according to Indonesians, Bradley was pressured to give up any role for PLN. According to Hardiv, Bradley made "a great contribution."

41. A long-term advisor close to Kuntoro, Steve Simpson, may have also played some role, although he was mentioned by none of the principals we interviewed. Lazard Frères was a financial advisor; Fortune PR, public relations advisor; and, as we shall see, Lavalin, a technical/cost advisor.

42. Wells was an advisor to the Ministry of Finance at the time and visited the embassy. The power agreements were part of the discussions. Some U.S. officials were quite willing to say that the deals were bad ones for Indonesia and had to be renegotiated.

43. According to Lax, the rates were heavily discounted from their usual charges to business customers. Still, they were much higher than what Indonesians were accustomed to paying advisors.

44. Although Wells had heard earlier that companies had his memo, it was confirmed when he called for an appointment to interview managers in connection with this book. When he started to explain who he was, one of the managers said he already knew because he had the memo addressed to Ginandjar.

45. "Power Purchase Agreements," memo to Widjojo Nitisastro, Ali Wardhana, and Ginandjar, August 25, 1998 (254.1/98/603).

46. The Harvard Group, especially Timothy Buehrer, trained as a lawyer and economist, provided some help to the legal group in the Ministry of Finance with respect to later OPIC claims.

47. Interviews with members of the negotiating team.

48. Interview with Mission managers. Summers confirmed to us that this is an accurate representation of his position, although he did not remember the exact words.

49. Bosshard, "Publicly Guaranteed Corruption."

50. If he was, he might well have been skating very close to the edges of government rules that restrict lobbying by former government officials for five years (rules, however, suspended by Clinton upon his leaving office).

51. In September 2003, Christopher visited Harvard to give a talk but declined the request of one of the authors for an interview. Although Christopher's

assistant committed to asking him to review the following paragraphs for accuracy, Christopher never responded.

52. FOIA document, memo within U.S. Department of Commerce, "Subject: Secretary's meeting with Edison Mission Energy," available at http://www.softwar.net/paiton3.html (accessed August 2004).

53. Charles R. Smith, "The Corruption of Warren Christopher," Newsmax.com, available at http://web.archive.org/web/20030511114632/http://zohshow.com/News/Newsbytes/01/quarter1/0215727.htm (accessed April 2006).

54. Harmon had come to the Exim Bank from investment banking, where he had been chairman of Schroder Wertheim & Co.

55. Eduardo Lachica, "Hero and Bully: U.S. Ex-Im Bank's Clout Helps Speed Restructuring," *Asian Wall Street Journal*, May 19, 1999, p. 1.

56. Lachica, "Hero and Bully."

57. Other Exim Bank officials visiting Indonesia from October 14 to 17 were a bit more conciliatory, trying to "reinforce the message that a speedy and transparent handling of these issues is in both countries' interest," stopping short of claiming that the contracts were ironclad and had to be honored. A state department memo reporting from the meetings is reproduced at "Enrongate: A Democrat Scandal," available at http://talking_points.tripod.com/enron/id4.html (accessed August 2004).

58. Julie A. Martin, "OPIC Modified Expropriation Coverage Case Study: MidAmerican's Projects in Indonesia—Dieng and Patuha," in Theodore H. Moran (ed.), *International Political Risk Management: Exploring New Frontiers* (Washington: The World Bank, 2001), p. 66.

59. Waldman and Solomon, "Wasted Energy." The statement may have been made when Munoz visited Indonesia September 11–13, 1998, to advocate on behalf of projects in which OPIC had an interest.

60. Given the strong feelings we encountered in Indonesia when OPIC came up, we were eager to get another side for the stories we were told. But, on May 6, 2003, Munoz turned down our requests for an interview, e-mailing: "Thank you for your inquiry, [sic] unfortunately I will not be able to meet."

61. "PLN to Start Second Phase of IPP Contracts Rationalization," *Indonesian Observer*, February 16, 1999.

62. Peter Waldman and Jay Solomon, "U.S. Power Deals in Indonesia Draw Flak: Critics Accuse Companies of Using Links with Soeharto to Win Contracts," *Asian Wall Street Journal*, December 24, 1998, p. 1.

63. Castle Asia, "Syndicated Reports, Chapter 3: Energy and Power Generation," March 29, 2001, available at http://www.castleasia.com/reports/political/reviewsample.shtml (accessed August 2004).

64. The rupiah tariff was eventually raised, as follows: 29% in April 2000, 17% in two steps from July 1 and October 1, 2001, and by 6% in each quarter of 2001. See Asian Development Bank, "Impact Evaluation Study of Asian Development Bank Assistance to the Power Sector in Indonesia," IES: INO 2003-13, July 2003, paragraph 74.

65. Satriya announced that letters had been sent to all the power suppliers to invite them to renegotiate. See Abeng, *Indonesia, Inc.*, p. 81.

66. Samuelson was the exception, present for the initial negotiations and the renegotiations.

67. Diana Yuliyanti, "Project Finance for Independent Power Producers in Developing Countries: The Paiton I Power Generation Project in Indonesia," thesis for Master of Science in Civil and Environmental Engineering at the Massachusetts Institute of Technology, February 2001, p. 87.

68. Edison *2001 Annual Report*.

69. According to Paiton managers, Unit 7 was commissioned on May 21, 1999; Unit 8, on July 10.

70. Quoted in "U.S. Power Firm May Sue PLN for US $4 B if It Breaches Deal," *Business Times* (Singapore), May 13, 1999.

71. Even though family members appeared safe from prosecution, Hashim must have realized that the participation of Suharto's daughter in his businesses was no longer an asset. It is also possible that the daughter needed cash. Whatever the reason, sometime in the middle of 1998 Hashim had bought Titiek's shares in all three Paiton-related companies where she had participation.

72. Referred to in Castle Asia, "Syndicated Reports, Chapter 3." Original source from an unspecified Jakarta business publication.

73. Edison *1997 Annual Report*. Only later, by 2003, did Mission face financial difficulties, partly as a result of the California energy fiasco. Its enthusiasm for international ventures eventually declined with its cash flow situation.

74. Sander Thoenes, "Indonesian Power Project Disputes May Hit Loans," *Financial Times,* June 30, 1999, p. 6.

75. From "Export Credit Agency, Visit to Indonesia, July 11–15, 1999," document released to Marcus Chadwick, under the FOIA. Other than the schedule, other documents related to the visit were denied.

76. See the response in the Harvard Group's memo "Comments on PPA Proposal from the Export Import Bank of Japan," memo to Bambang Subianto and Budiono, August 26, 1999 (254.1/99/393).

77. Dan Murphy, "Energy: Trouble on the Grid," *Far Eastern Economic Review,* October 21, 1999, p. 63.

78. Bosshard. "Publicly Guaranteed Corruption."

79. Hardiv H. Situmeang, "Deregulasi Kelistrikan California: Pelajaran dari Sebuah Kegagalan," *Kompas,* February 9, 2001. For background of the Asian Development Bank's support for a market system, see its "Impact Evaluation Study of Asian Development Bank Assistance to the Power Sector in Indonesia," IES: INO 2003-13, July 2003.

80. Interviews, February 2003.

81. From reports in Thoenes., "Excessive Confidence Casts a Pall."

82. The memo also proposed a smaller negotiating team, to get things moving. See "Further Comments on the Paiton Situation," memo to Bambang Subianto and Boediono, September 1, 1999 (254.1/99/404).

83. Murphy, "Trouble on the Grid."

84. Interviews conducted in Jakarta, March 2001.

85. Kuntoro seems to have gotten along better with Gelbard than did most other Indonesians. He attributed this to his origins in a part of Java with an atypical culture. Equally important may have been his experience studying in the United States.

86. Bosshard, "Publicly Guaranteed Corruption."

87. This was a later and stricter version of the original and similar Gonzalez and Hickenlooper Amendments from the 1970s.

88. Before 1990, the Hickenlooper Amendment had been applied only twice— against Ceylon in 1963 and against Ethiopia in 1979. Andrew T. Gusman, "Explaining the Popularity of Bilateral Investment Treaties: Why LDCs Sign Treaties That Hurt Them," August 26, 1997, available at http://www.jeanmonnetprogram .org/papers/97/97-12.html (accessed November 2003).

89. From "Schedule of the ECA Meeting" and a memo "Appointment Confirmations-Amoseas Indonesia, Inc.," with the names of the author and recipients blacked out. The visit to Amoseas, however, was "orchestrated" by Cecil Chopin. These were documents released to Marcus Chadwick, under the FOIA. All substantive documents were denied, and names of officials in the U.S. embassy were generally blacked out.

90. Amoseas Indonesia, belonging to Chevron and Texaco.

91. On December 9, 1999. See "Lembaga Kredit Paiton Surati Lima Menteri," *Suara Pembaruan,* December 22, 1999.

92. Thoenes, "Excessive Confidence Casts a Pall."

93. Ibid.

94. Indonesians say that they paid at the rate of 2,450 rupiah/dollar, the rate used for other power suppliers.

95. Bosshard. "Publicly Guaranteed Corruption."

96. Indonesians say that eleven companies signed such agreements.

97. "Indonesia Court Decision Alarms Paiton Group," *Financial Times Energy*, December 14, 1999.

98. Billington, "Looting Indonesia."

99. Whether a decision by the Jakarta court that the contract was null and void would have invalidated the arbitration clause is not certain. The legal systems of different countries approach this issue differently, and the question had not been clarified in Indonesia. For a discussion of the issue, see: Richard H. Kreindler, "Aspects of Illegality in the Formation and Performance of Contracts," *International Commercial Arbitrations: Important Contemporary Questions* (New York: Aspen, 2003), pp. 209–284, especially 226.

100. Interviews conducted in Jakarta, March 2001.

101. "Paiton I Independent Power Plant Report on Benchmark EPC Cost Estimate," Project No. 013767 of SNC-Lavalin, Power Division, Vancouver, December 1999. For an Indonesian press report, see: Taufiqurohman, Dewi Rina Cahyadi, I.G.G. Maha Adi, "Two Steps Forward, Three Steps Back," *Tempo*, September 18–24, 2000, cover story, cited in Yuliyanti, "Project Finance," p. 28.

102. Bosshard, "Publicly Guaranteed Corruption," and "Paiton I Independent Power Plant Report on Benchmark EPC Cost Estimate," Project No. 013767 of SNC-Lavalin, Power Division, Vancouver, December 1999.

103. Jay Solomon, "Costs of Indonesian Power Plants Were Inflated," *Wall Street Journal*, December 26, 2000, p. A7.

104. The SNC-Lavalin report itemized costs for each piece of equipment. To the best of our knowledge, Paiton's managers have not raised specific challenges.

105. See Solomon, "Costs of Indonesian Power."

106. Given the high percentage of costs that were incurred in U.S. dollars, the justification for a 7% inflation rate is not obvious. Indeed, Enron argued in India that the cost of generating equipment fell over the period.

107. Badan Pengawasan Keuangan dan Pembangunan.

108. For a report of various corruption charges against Ginandjar, see "Drama in the Round House" and "Marshal 'Jonie' in Exile," *Tempo*, March 13–19, 2001, pp. 17–19. A summons had been issued for Ginandjar, but he had left for Harvard (see later). For a claim that Sudjana was involved in the illegal transfer of aircraft from Pertamina to Manunggal Air Service, an airline owned by a military foundation, see "The Tentacles of the Octopus: The Business Interests of the TNI and Police," *Van Zorge Report*, July 16, 2003. For other suggestions of corruption on the part of these officials, see Peter Waldman, "Hand in Glove: How Suharto's Circle, Mining Firm Did So Well Together," *Wall Street Journal*, September 29, 1998, p. 1.

109. Hidayat Gunadi, "Stung by Electricity from Paiton," *Banner Irklan*, December 11, 1999, available at http://web.archive.org/web/20030524210646/http://www.gatranews.net/_english/VI/4/EKO1-4.html (accessed April 2006).

110. Hidayat Tantan, "Mau Terang Tetaplah Gelap," *Gatra*, January 1, 2000, 28–29. (The English version appeared as "Light Comes but Darkness Stays.")

Chapter 12

1. Molly Ivins, *You Got to Dance with Them That Brung You: Politics in the Clinton Years* (New York: Random House, 1998).

2. Megawati was the daughter of Fatmawati, Sukarno's third of several wives.

3. In a brunch meeting, in June 2003, attended by one of the authors, he stated his enthusiasm for barter trade among the developing countries, which he thought reproduced the Western European model in the immediate post-war years. Presumably he was referring to the European Payments Union, which was actually designed to avoid the need for barter trade.

4. Theodore Friend, *Indonesian Destinies* (Cambridge, Mass.: Belknap Press for Harvard University Press, 2003), pp. 387, 388.

5. Another interpretation of the Suharto support for a monetary board was not mystical at all; the board would allow members of the First Family to convert their rupiah holdings to dollars that they could park offshore.

6. This and some of the following description of Gus Dur are drawn from an article by a prominent economist at Indonesia's CSIS, Hadi Soesastro, "Gus Dur, Economics, and the Economy," *Pacific Link*, May 5, 2000, available at http://www.pacific.net.id/pakar/hadisusastro/000501.html (accessed August 2004).

7. Economist Emil Salim and Gus Dur are quoted in Andreas Harsono, "Indonesia Must Face Nation's Gruesome Past," *Albion Monitor*, November 1, 1999, available at http://www.monitor.net/monitor/9910b/indoelect-gruesome.html (accessed August 2004).

8. Friend, in naming advisors, does not mention Soros. Perhaps he never participated.

9. Friend, *Indonesian Destinies*, p. 465.

10. Lt. Gen. Susilo Bambang Yudhoyono would be chosen by direct election as president in 2004.

11. Interviews with a lawyer advising the Indonesian side.

12. Interviews with a lawyer advising the Indonesian side.

13. An American reported Paiton and Unocal executives as celebrating Adhi Satrya's fall by singing together "the wicked witch is dead" at a meeting of the American Chamber of Commerce in Jakarta.

14. Interview with Kuntoro, February 2003.

15. At the Moran Eye Center in Salt Lake City, Utah.

16. Kwik is reported as saying that Gus Dur put greater priority on "friendship" than on dispute. See "Government to Take Action over Alleged KKN in Paiton Deal," *Jakarta Post*, December 24, 1999.

17. The complaint was to Inge Altemeier, a freelance researcher, cited in Peter Bosshard, "Publicly Guaranteed Corruption, Corrupt Power Projects and the Responsibility of Export Credit Agencies in Indonesia," *ECA Watch*, available at http://www.eca-watch.org/problems/corruption/bosshard_indon_nov2000.html (accessed April 2006). See also "Government to Take Action over Alleged KKN in Paiton Deal," *Jakarta Post*, December 24, 1999," for threat of action against Paiton I.

18. Parliament's Komisi VIII did summon a number of officials to testify about corruption. For reports emphasizing the testimony of Ginandjar, who was thought to know the most about events connected with Paiton I, see Suwarjono, "Meneropong Masa Lalu Ginandjar (2), Keganjilan Miliaran Dolar di Paiton," available at http://web.archive.org/web/20040615131839/http://www.detik.com/lapsus/200007/ginanjar-lalu2.shtml (accessed May 2003).

19. ANZ Panin Bank, Indonesia Newsletter,, December 1999, available at http://www.anz.com/Indonesia/newsletters/Dec99.pdf (accessed August 2004). For a report on parliament's concerns, see "Government's Move over Paiton Regretted," *Jakarta Post*, December 22, 1999.

20. A report supposedly from an NGO and allegedly issued by disgruntled PLN employees accused the law firm of having worked for Paiton I in the development phase and of being on Paiton's debt rating counsel consortium. We have no cover sheet for this document and no evidence to support or refute the contention.

21. K & M Engineering and Consulting Corporation and Electroconsult (of Italy).

22. His eventual departure from the United States, in March 2004, for Afghanistan might well be viewed as confirmation by the very suspicious.

23. Indonesian companies have two boards, modeled after Dutch corporate governance. The board of directors governs and represents the company. It is answerable to the board of commissioners, which is not deeply involved with the affairs of the company, except possibly to oversee major financial issues.

24. See, for example, "Wahid's Cabinet Coup," *Business Week Online* (International Edition), September 11, 2000, available at http://www.businessweek.com/2000/00_37/b3698215.htm (accessed August 2004).

25. For more on project finance, see Benjamin C. Esty, *Modern Project Finance: A Casebook* (New York: John Wiley, 2004).

26. Edison Mission Energy, Form 10-K, For the fiscal year ended December 31, 1999, Item 9, Note 12, i

27. Reflecting the tension among advisors, Kuntoro told us he called on Hollinger to assemble the group, but Jezek claimed that he proposed the meeting and contacted the foreign investors.

28. In interviews, Paiton managers were vague on the terms of Hashim's exit. They did say that he had sued the company for $240 million, but that they had settled, under the condition that he was "gone." In 2003, his shares were said to belong to Edwin Soeryadjaya (son of Astra's founder, William) and some "Australian interests." Edgell told us the partner's interest was reduced to 5%.

29. Securities and Exchange Commission, Edison International, Form 10-K, for the fiscal year ended December 31, 2000.

30. "Paiton: Between Tariff Negotiation and KKN Accusation." *IBonWEB.com*, November 24, 2000, available at http://articles.ibonweb.com/webarticle.asp?num=516 (accessed August 2004). There is some disagreement in published reports of this agreement. Christine Taufik and Hadi Satyagraha, "Pencabutan Gugatan Perkara Listrik Swasta PLTU Paiton Swasta I," case by PLN Jasa Pendidikan dan Pelatihan (n.d., ca. 2000), report that the variable charge was 1.1 cents/kwh. It is possible that the 2.6-cent figure that is often quoted includes an allocation of the fixed payments over the electricity to be delivered.

31. James Booker, "IPP Development: an Investor's Perspective," a paper presented at the 4th APEC Coal Trade and Investment Liberalization and Facilitation Workshop, March 6–8, 2002, Kuala Lumpur, Malaysia, p. 9.

32. Castle Asia, "Syndicated Reports, Chapter 3: Energy and Power Generation: January 1999," March 29, 2001, available at http://www.castleasia.com/reports/political/reviewsample.shtml (accessed August 2004). Some interviewees reported that the request was for 40 years, rather than 60.

33. Bosshard, "Publicly Guaranteed Corruption."

34. Bosshard, "Publicly Guaranteed Corruption." We do not know exactly what pressures they placed on Indonesia, but their visits alone would imply threats to future credit and insurance.

35. "US Envoy Frustrated over Freeport," *Indonesian Observer*, March 14, 2000.

36. Previous U.S. Ambassador Stapleton Roy seems at least to have considered a different view of American involvement when he cabled the following from a meeting with Indonesian Director General of Electricity Endro Utomo Notodisoerjo: "Commenting on corrupt, collusion and nepotism (KKN), Endro said that in the past there was no separation between 'power (not electric but former first family power) and business.' All the IPPs [independent power producers] have a relation with power, and it is still going on...." Quoted from documents released under the FOIA, available at http://www.newsmax.com/archives/articles/2001/1/26/192056.shtml (accessed August 2004).

37. Although there is no reason to suspect that former Ambassador Roy was improperly involved in the Paiton renegotiations, he joined Kissinger's firm and

replaced Kissinger on the board of Freeport McMoRan Copper and Gold, in March 2001.

38. By December 31, 2000, the accumulated sums amounted to $814 million, but Paiton had agreed to recoup no more than $590 million. See Edison International, *2000 Annual Report*, p. 82.

39. A letter to Jensen seeking confirmation or corrections to this section went unanswered.

40. Reported to us by a member of Gus Dur's family.

41. We do not know whether he represented ABB before the president's eye treatment or was sought out by ABB afterward.

42. For Jensen's uncomplimentary views of Kuntoro from a meeting in Cancun, see Jeremy Wagstaff, "Indonesia's Wahid Is Encircled by Scandal," *Wall Street Journal*, June 19, 2000, p. 26.

43. Kuntoro told us that before he became head of PLN he had reported to Gus Dur that the transmission-line contract was being awarded based on corruption, with the proceeds going to Habibie. Near the end of Habibie's presidency, the contract was to go to Bukaka Teknik Utama, owned by the Kalla family, connected to Jusuf Kalla (who became vice president in 2004), whom Gus Dur appointed as minister of trade and industry. It had not been signed, however, when Gus Dur took office. It was later signed, but challenged by ABB spokesmen, including by Jensen in Cancun. Eventually, Jusuf Kalla and Laksamana Sukardi were dismissed from their ministerial posts, under (unproved) accusations of corruption, and the project was retendered. ABB lowered its original bid. ABB won, and PLN had to pay $2.5 million to get out of the original deal. See Iwan Qodar Himawan and Andi Zulfikar Anwar, "Electricity in Three Spots," *Gatra*, November 4, 2000, available at http://web.archive.org/web/20031016072658/ http://www.gatranews.com/VI/51/EKO3-51.html (accessed April 2006). Documents filed with the Corruption Eradication Commission (KPK) reported Kalla's net worth at $19 million. For more details of the story, see Wagstaff, "Indonesia's Wahid."

44. Dianne Feinstein (D-California), Chuck Hagel (R-Nebraska), Paul Coverdell (R-Georgia), Chuck Robb (D-Virginia), Daniel Inouye (D-Hawaii), and John Breaux (D-Louisiana).

45. *Tekak*, number 10, year 11, January 3–9, 2000, cited in presentation by Hardiv H. Situmeang, "Challenges Facing IPP Model in Asia: The Experience of PLN in Indonesia," 10th World Economic Development Congress, Kuala Lumpur, June 27–29, 2001. As indicated, we received no response to our request to Robert Rubin for clarification.

46. In this, the paper was wrong: At least two other investors were setting an entirely new standard for lack of cooperation. Paiton and its owners would, with hindsight, be viewed much more kindly, but tempers were high at the time. Jezek was right when he had called Paiton I the "tallest lightning rod" when the original agreement was being concluded; it remained the most prominent at the time of renegotiation and the most tempting target for the press.

47. "Gus Dur Derides Paiton Deal, but Vows to Honor It," *Jakarta Post*, December 23, 1999.

48. "Paiton Power Politics," *Jakarta Post*, December 22, 1999.

49. *Suara Pembaruan*, May 12, 2001, cited in presentation by Hardiv H. Situmeang, "Challenges Facing IPP Model in Asia: The Experience of PLN in Indonesia."

50. For the complicated story of Ginandjar's claims that health problems should preclude his detention, see Eriko Uchida, "Indonesia Detains Former Economic Czar Ginandjar for Corruption," March 20, 2001, available at http://www.geocities.com/aroki.geo/0105/INA-ginandjar.html (accessed August 2003).

51. For other business interests of Ginandjar and his family, see George J. Aditjondro, "Bisnis Keluarga Para Menko, Ginanjar & Hartarto," *Kabar dari PIJAR*, March 20, 1998, available at http://web.archive.org/web/20001011195342/http://www.geocities.com/CapitolHill/Senate/1627/bisnis_keluarga_para_menko.htm (accessed April 2006).

52. Teaching note for Christine Taufik and Hadi Satyagraha, "Pencabutan Gugatan Perkara Listrik Swasta PLTU Paiton Swasta I," case by PLN Jasa Pendidikan dan Pelatihan [ca. 2000].

53. Law No. 15/1985. In this it was strikingly similar to U.S. energy legislation.

54. Fabby Tumiwa, "Briefing Paper: The Indonesian Power Sector Restructuring Is a Potential Fiasco: Critiques to ADB's Lending on the Power Sector Restructuring Program," Working Group on Power Sector Restructuring, [ca. 2000]. The document describes the group as a network of NGOs "doing advocacy on the Indonesian power sector," and "initiated by the International NGO Forum on Indonesia Development, Friend of the Earth Indonesia, Jakarta Legal Aid Institute, Indonesian Corruption Watch Bank Information Center, and Yayasan Gemi Nastiti."

55. In democratic India they would eventually force the publication of power contracts, which had heretofore been secret.

56. See Liam Salter,"From Free Market to 'Our Power,'" *Jakarta Post*, December 13, 2004.

57. For one analysis of the reasons for Gus Dur's downfall, see "Issue Brief: Indonesia's New Leadership—Megawati Sukarnoputri and Hamzah Haz (July 2001)," IRI, August 1, 2001, available at http://www.iri.org/pub.asp?id=76767677 59 (accessed January 2005).

58. The name Megawati has nothing to do with units of electricity, but rather it is a feminized version of "cloud." Sometimes it is translated as "lady of the cloud"; sometimes as "female cloud." Sukarno was wont to name his children after sky images. Sukarnoputri means "daughter of Sukarno."

59. Friend, *Indonesian Destinies*, p. 391. On the other hand, her husband, Taufik Kiemas, was in various businesses. For controversy about his activities, see Simon Elegant, "Looming Large: Taufik Kiemas, Husband of Indonesian President Megawati, Might Be the Country's Most Powerful Man," *Time Asia*, July 8, 2002.

60. Dorodjatun Kuntjoro-Jakti, a Ph.D. from University of California–Berkeley in economics and former ambassador to the United States, and Budiono, a Ph.D. from Wharton School of the University of Pennsylvania in economics, with an excellent record in the central bank and political skills from the planning ministry. See "Boediono: Finance Minister, Indonesia," *Business Week Online*, June 9, 2003, available at http://www.businessweek.com/magazine/content/03_23/b3836622.htm (accessed August 2004).

61. Brett M. Decker, "Corrupt Contracts: A Millstone for Megawati," *Wall Street Journal*, August 20, 2001, p. A14.

62. Gelbard was himself soon to be replaced. The new ambassador, Ralph C. Boyce, was confirmed in September 2001.

63. The story is reported by Friend, *Indonesian Destinies*, p. 505.

64. Ibid.

65. For delegation to these two economics officials, see William Liddle, "Megawati's Presidency: A Contrarian Perspective," *Jakarta Post*, October 6, 2003.

66. "Pulling the Plug on PLN," Laksamana.net, November 29, 2001, available at http://web.archive.org/web/20030927134301/http://www.laksamana.net/vnews.cfm?ncat=36&news_id=1564 (accessed April 2006).

67. This would continue. For various commitments under IMF Letters of Intent, see Agus Sari, "Power Sector Restructuring in Indonesia: A Brief Summary," Pelangi Indonesia (an NGO), August 2001.

68. Our request to Paiton managers for the calculations that led to the monthly payments was turned down.

69. PLN, "Laporan Perkembangan Renegosiasi PLTU Paiton I," addressed to the economic coordinating minister, Document No. 834/180/DIRUT/2001-R, September 18, 2001.

70. Dorodjatun Kuntjoro-Jakti (Menteri Koordinator Bidang Perekonomian Republik Indonesia), "Laporan Renegosiasi PLTU Paiton I," Document No. S-23 / M.EKON/09/2001, October 8, 2001.

71. Of course, any reported price is based on various assumptions about the parameters that affect price in the formulas. The 4.93 cents comprised: component A cost of 3.53, fixed O&M of 0.3 cents, variable O&M of 0.1 cents, and fuel costs of 1.0. This breakdown is from Nengah Sudja, *Menggugat Harga Jual Listrik Paiton I* (Jakarta: WG-PSR, Lembaga Studi Kapasitas Nasional, INFID, 2002).

72. Booker, "IPP Development," p. 9.

73. Farallon Capital and Nancy Zimmerman's Fixed Income Associates partnered to form Farallon Fixed Income Associates. Zimmerman was married to Harvard Professor Andrei Shleifer. Her fund was involved in Shleifer's alleged misuse of his position as an advisor to the Russian government.

74. An outline of the restructuring is provided in "Asia Pacific Refinancing Deal of the Year 2002," *Project Finance, Guide 2003.*

75. Mission, by this time, had an equity interest in Adaro, having purchased 8.17% in 1995 from Hashim. A substantial chunk of equity had gone to PT Dianlia Setiamukti as well, a firm controlled by Edwin Surajaya of Astra. In this case, Paiton also provided financing, but according to management the new share owner was to receive no dividends until the loan had been repaid. The Indonesian Bulk Terminal was owned 28.6% by New Hope in 2001. By September 2001, New Hope had acquired almost 41% of Adaro, but in 2004 New Hope was said to be selling its interest to a group of Indonesians. See U.S. Embassy, "Coal Report Indonesia 2004," Jakarta. Available at http://www.usembassyjakarta.org/econ/coal/coal-2004.html (accessed June 2006).

76. In 2003, Graeme Robertson, the Australian entrepreneur, was still president director of both Adaro, the coal supplier, and the International Bulk Terminal (IBT).

77. Booker, "IPP Development: an Investor's Perspective." The NGO report referred to the 1998 price for Adaro coal under the Paiton contract as $39.72/ton while the price of spot coal at Banjarmasin in December of the same year was $22/ton.

78. Indonesia's 1991 coal production was reportedly only 14 MMt from six producers; in 1994, it was 30 MMt from 10 producers. By 1999, production had risen to 74 MMt. Still, whether Paiton and its financiers should have been concerned about security of supply with six producers and 14 MMt is debatable. Paiton I required only 4.3 MMt to feed its boilers. Figures from Booker, "IPP Development: An Investor's Perspective."

79. Edison International, *2002 Annual Report*, p. 64.

80. Again, Paiton would provide us with no breakdown of the restructuring charges.

81. "Paiton Energy Achieves Successful Debt Restructuring," *IbonWeb.com*, February 27, 2003, available at http://articles.ibonweb.com/webarticle.asp?num= 1369 (accessed August 2004).

82. Eddie Widiono S. (PLN head), "Laporan Perkembangan Renegosiasi PLTU Paiton I," addressed to the economic coordinating minister, Document No. 834/180/DIRUT/2001-R, September 18, 2001.

83. Nengah Sudja, *Menggugat Harga Jual Listrik Paiton I*. The same figure appeared in a report in parliament and in the report from the alleged NGO, supposedly issued by disgruntled PLN employees. Our copy has no title page.

84. This same figure appeared in the report from the alleged NGO (see previous note). The report says that the actual off-take from Paiton I was only 40% of capacity in the first quarter of 2002 because of PLN's limited transmission capacity. This was expected to improve soon.

85. Nengah Sudja, "Questioning the Electricity Price of Paiton I," *WGPSR,* 2003, p. 3.

86. Quoted in Nick Lord, "Power Problems," *Finance Asia,* September 1999, p. 19.

87. When one of the authors of this book published an article in 1995 that recounted a bit of the past, a manager in GE explicitly rejected the message. Another investor in the industry tried to commission a counter to the paper from a colleague at the Kennedy School of Government, offering a substantial fee.

88. Edison International, *2000 Annual Report.*

89. Perhaps luckily for her, Rebecca Mark, who had led the Enron team for the Dabhol (India) power project, had been let go by the time Enron collapsed.

90. Information from Reuters Industry Overview site. See http://cnnfn.investor. reuters.com/IndustryCenter.aspx?industrypscode=ELECTU&target=/industries/ indhighlights/industrycenter (accessed August 2004) and http://www.investor. reuters.com/IndustryCenter.aspx?industrypscode=ELECTU&target=industrycenter (accessed August 2004).

91. Christine Hill, "Power Failure," *Institutional Investor,* November 1999.

92. International Power, "International Power Completes the Acquisition of Edison Mission Energy's International Generation Portfolio," news release, December 17, 2004.

Chapter 13

1. Stewart Macaulay, "Contracts Symposium: Almost Everything That I Did Want to Know about Contract Litigation, a Comment on Galanter," *Wisconsin Law Review,* 2001, pp. 269, 630–631.

2. Indonesian counsel claims that the arbitration was procedurally flawed. Charges include inappropriate consolidation, inadequate opportunity for Indonesians to participate in selecting arbitrators, a "false" claim by investors that a letter of comfort had been issued, the use of another case (CalEnergy) as a precedent, and the refusal of the Swiss courts to review the award. Of course, the other side disputes these charges.

3. Testimony of Ross D. Ain, Senior Vice President, Caithness Energy LLC, before the Resources Committee of the United States House of Representatives Subcommittee on Energy and Mineral Resources, Thursday, May 3, 2001.

4. This contrasts with Florida Power & Light's capacity of 21,000 megawatts at the end of 2002, as reported in the company's annual report.

5. His son, James D. Bishop, Jr., and his daughter, Barbara Bishop Gollan, also held positions in Caithness Energy and its affiliates.

6. The misspellings, poor grammar, and finally foul language in e-mails from this lawyer make one wonder about his professionalism.

7. Our June 4, 2004, request for interviews was answered on June 24 by the company's investment relations coordinator: "I did look into your request on speaking to someone about Karaha Bodas. I do apologize but we are not interested in having an interview at this time."

8. *Karaha Bodas Company, L.L.C. v Pertamina and PLN,* Hearing, Paris, France, June 20, 2000, vol. 2 of the transcript of hearings of the arbitration tribunal, testimony of Leslie Gelber. FP&L's SEC Form U-3A-2, filed February 28, 2001, also lists FPL Energy Caithness Funding, incorporated in Delaware and located in Juno Beach, Florida. It is described as participating in a solar electric generating system.

9. Dan Morain, "Generators Add to Davis Coffers," *Los Angeles Times*, November 16, 2001, available at http://www.powertothepeople.org/newswire/daviscampaign.shtml (accessed August 2004).

10. For example, Leslie J. Gelber, who became president and COO of Caithness at the beginning of 1999, had come from positions in FP&L and its subsidiaries. He was, with others from FP&L affiliates, on the board of the troubled Adelphia Communications Corporation. See Adelphia Communications Corp. 10-K/A, filed April 30, 2001; and Susan Pulliam and Robert Frank, "Inside Adelphia: A Long Battle over Disclosing Stock Options," *Wall Street Journal*, January 26, 2004. Kenneth P. Hoffman and Larry K. Carpenter, also at Caithness Energy and affiliates, had been, respectively, vice president of FP&L Energy, Inc., and vice president of development at ESI Energy, Inc., a power company owned by FP&L. Source: 10-K filings of FP&L and Caithness affiliates.

11. In the interest of readability, we do not always distinguish between Karaha Bodas Company and its owners in the events that follow.

12. Toyo Menka. One person in KBC's public relations firm in Jakarta told us that he thought that the project had originated with Tomen. Requests for interviews with Tomen in Jakarta were met with the response that the company had no one there to see. E-mails to the company in Japan went unanswered.

13. More formally known as Surakarta, a royal seat in Central Java.

14. I.G.G. Maha Adi, "The Great & Powerful Sumarah," *Tempo*, August 6–12, 2002, available at http://www.tempointeraktif.com/majalah/arsip/2nd/edition48/eco-4.html (accessed February 2003).

15. Ownership, but not a percentage, is mentioned in "Karaha-Pertamina: The Saga Continued," in *Indonesia Corruption Watch*, July 28, 2005, available at http://antikorupsi.org/eng/mod.php?mod=publisher&op=viewarticle&artid=75 (accessed December 2005). See also I. G. G. Maha Adi, "The Great & Powerful Sumarah."

16. His business activities were the subject of a later article: "Anti-corruption Movement: Sudharmono's Empire on the Spot," *Laksamana.net*, April 11, 2002, available at http://web.archive.org/web/20040113184743/http://laksamana.net/vnews.cfm?ncat=25&news_id=2458 (accessed April 2006).

17. See *Karaha Bodas Company, L.L.C. v Pertamina and PLN*, vol. 2 of the transcript of hearings, testimony of Christopher McCallion.

18. Riyadi Suparno, "Government's Battle with KBC, a Year Late and $300m Short," *Jakarta Post*, November 26, 2004.

19. *Karaha Bodas Company, L.L.C. v Pertamina and PLN*, vol. 2 of the transcript of hearings, testimony of Christopher McCallion. Executives' testimony at the same hearing suggested that Sumarah was to receive more substantial fees, although managers seemed not fully to understand them. Questions eventually arose about Loedito's authority to sign the agreement.

20. *Karaha Bodas Company, L.L.C. v Pertamina and PLN*, vol. 2 of the transcript of hearings, testimony of FP&L and Caithness managers.

21. I.G.G. Maha "The Great and Powerful Sumarah," and *Karaha Bodas Company, L.L.C. v Pertamina and PLN*, vol. 2 of the transcript of hearings, testimony of Christopher McCallion.

22. *Karaha Bodas Company, L.L.C. v Pertamina and PLN*, vol. 2 of the transcript of hearings, testimony of Christopher McCallion. For further allegations of influence, see Thomas Hadiwinata, M. Syakur Usman, and Bambang Harymurti, "When Purnomo Was Stung by Karaha," *Tempo*, December 7–13, 2004, and Purnomo's response, "'Energetic' Explanation" [letter], *Tempo*, December 14–20, 2004.

23. Keppres number 49/1991, the decree authorizing geothermal projects, also capped total taxes at 34%.

24. Descriptions of various ways of making illegal payments are described in Karen Mills, "Enforcement of Arbitral Awards in Indonesia." She includes not

only free shares and shares against loans, but buy-backs of shares and consulting fees.

25. Private Sector Power Project, "Quarterly Report," December 1994.

26. Article 1.2 of the ESC.

27. Keppres number 39/1997 (September 20). The various decrees are described in Rudy Victor Sinaga, "Pertamina Tidak Wajar Bayar Denda ke KBC," *Sinar Harapan*, January 21, 2004, available at http://www.sinarharapan.co.id/ekonomi/industri/2004/0121/ind2.html (accessed February 2005).

28. Keppres number 47/1997.

29. Keppres number 5/1998.

30. *Karaha Bodas Company, L.L.C. v Pertamina and PLN*, vol. 2 of the transcript of hearings, testimony of Christopher McCallion.

31. *Karaha Bodas Company, L.L.C. v Pertamina and PLN*, vol. 2 of the transcript of hearings, testimony of Christopher McCallion.

32. Christopher T. McCallion, in testimony reported in *Karaha Bodas Company, L.L.C. v Pertamina and PLN*, vol. 2 of the transcript of hearings, p. 238.

33. *Karaha Bodas Company, L.L.C. v Pertamina and PLN*, vol. 2 of the transcript of hearings, testimony of Christopher McCallion. Caithness gave $3,500 to the Kerry campaign in 1996. See "John Kerry (D-MA), Detailed Contributor Breakdown, 1996 Election Cycle," at OpenSecrets.org, available at http://www.opensecrets.org/1996os/detail/S4MA00069.htm (accessed March 2005). An April 25, 2005 e-mail to Senator Kerry requesting a copy of the letter went unanswered.

34. The public relations firm told us it was only 5% complete when canceled.

35. This was in March, according to "Final Award in an Arbitration Procedure under the UNCITRAL Arbitation Rules between Karaha Bodas Company, L.L.C. and Perusahaan Pertambangan Minyak dan Gas Bumi Negara," December 18, 2000, Geneva; but in April, according to "Position Paper," July 14, 2002, provided by KBC's public relations firm.

36. In February 1999, Caithness bought the California Coso geothermal project from CalEnergy, the subject of our next chapter. See CalEnergy News Release, February 26, 1999, "CalEnergy Closes Sale to Caithness of Coso Power Projects." press release, available at http://www.prnewswire.co.uk/cgi/news/release?id=38525 (access March 2005). By 2006, Caithness reported a contract in Jamaica.

37. See Ted Jackson, "High Court Decision Favors FPL," *Palm Beach Post*, June 6, 2003, which reports that an electronic search could find no evidence that FPL had ever mentioned this project in its filings with the SEC.

38. "The Case of *Karaha Bodas Company, KBC, vs Pertamina:* Questions and Answers," Paragraph 15, Exhibit B of package entitled "The Case of *Pertamina and PLN vs Karaha Bodas Company: Position Paper and Supporting Documentation,*" provided by KBC's public relations firm, APCO (n.d.). The document does not say what legal obligations Pertamina had allegedly avoided.

39. A manager from Mitsui told us that Toyota had acquired a large number of Tomen's shares.

40. A lawyer for Caithness denies that the insurance contract provided that payment would be made only after the company obtained a legal decision. Another lawyer involved with insurance contracts told us that a typical Lloyd's political risk insurance policy does not technically require a legal decision before a claim could be honored, but an insured investor likely faces two possible scenarios. In the first, the government makes a public statement that it has indeed illegally expropriated assets without compensation, and Lloyd's would pay the claim. In the second scenario, the government denies expropriation; in that event, Lloyd's might bring in an assessor who could conclude that payment should be withheld until the dispute has been adjudicated by, say, arbitration. Then, the insurer will pay if the tribunal rules that the government has expropriated the assets and the government does not honor the award. Because the Indonesian

government would certainly not admit expropriation, the likely arrangements, according to this account, would lead to arbitration as the first step toward collecting the insurance. Still, some observers believe that the insurance was paid before an arbitral award was actually made.

41. Professor of arbitration law at the Libèra Università Internazionale degli Studi Sociali, in Rome, Italy.

42. Professor of international economic law; president of the International University for African Development (Alexandria, Egypt); and partner in Kosheri, Rashed & Riad law firm.

43. Partner in Derains Associés law firm.

44. Neil Trevor Kaplan Q.C. His role was rather limited as soon as it became clear that KBC could not produce a letter of comfort from the government.

45. We were told that Mason's (see the next chapter) played a role at the early stages as well.

46. Profile on Reed Smith Web site, available at http://www.reedsmith.com/ourattorneys/viewAttorney.cfm?itemid=1461 (viewed August 2004). Jones, Day, Reavis & Pogue (later renamed Jones Day) represented the plaintiff in the Loewen arbitration case, for which we are told part of the legal fees were on a contingency basis. We do not know whether the KBC case was brought under a similar arrangement. Adnan Buyung Nasution and Partners, assisted by Neil Kaplan, Q.C., and Mason's, represented the government in the first hearing, while Buyung and Cleary, Gottlieb, Steen & Hamilton represented PLN and Pertamina in the rest of the arbitration.

47. Bill Guerin, "Under the Volcano: Indonesia's Electricity Woes," *Asia Times Online*, June 22, 2002, available at http://www.atimes.com/se-asia/DF22Ae02.html (accessed August 2004). Indonesians were later to claim that KBC had reported four different amounts for its investment, in separate reports submitted to Pertamina ($77.13 million), the Indonesian tax department ($84.895 million), the arbitration panel ($93.1 million), and the firm's auditors ($40.183 million). See "Oil & Gas: Karaha Accused of Fiddling the Books," *Laksamana.net*, July 28, 2002, previously available at http://www.laksamana.net/print.cfm?id=3318 (accessed August 2004). Also see Sinaga, "Pertamina Tidak Wajar Bayar Denda ke KBC."

48. For the award and summaries of arguments and findings, see "Final Award in an Arbitration Procedure under the UNCITRAL Arbitration Rules between Karaha Bodas Company L.L.C. and Perusahaan Pertambangan Minyak dan Gas Bumi Negara and PT. PLN (Persero)," Geneva, December 18, 2000.

49. In later public statements, Florida Power & Light estimated its investment in the project as being in the "range of $45 million." This is roughly consistent with the figures claimed by KBC, as cited here, as FPL held 40.5% of the equity. See Jackson, "High Court Decision Favors FPL."

50. The arbitrators referred to the supposedly confidential CalEnergy awards (see Chapter 14).

51. White & Case Web site, "Arbitral Terrorism," available at http://web.archive.org/web/20040622054513/http://www.whitecase.com/in_the_news_arbitral_terrorism_summer_2003.html. The rest of the article is reproduced from Michael D. Goldhaber, "Arbitral Terrorism," *American Lawyer/Focus Europe*, Summer 2003, available at http://www.americanlawyer.com/focuseurope/aterror.html.

52. Article V of the New York Convention. Not all experts agree on the interpretation of this article. For references to views on whether there can be two possible primary jurisdictions, see *Karaha Bodas Co., L.L.C., Plaintiff-Appellee, v. Perusahaan Pertambangan Miyak Dan Gas Bumi Negara; Et Al, Defendants, Perusahaan Pertambangan Minyak Dan Gas Bumi Negara, Defendant-Appellant*, Nos. 02-20042 & 03-20602, United States Court of Appeals for the Fifth Circuit, 2004 U.S. App. LEXIS 5445, March 23, 2004, Filed.

53. See Wayne Forrest, "A Case to Watch," *Membership Alert!* number 8, April 17, 2002, American Indonesian Chamber of Commerce.

54. The funds supposedly were less than 24 hours late. See "Arrêt du Tribunal Fédéral Suisse, 1e Cour Civile, 4P.36/2001," April 24, 2001. A lawyer for Caithness denies some part of this story, but did not make it clear which part.

55. According to the U.S. Court of Appeals, March 23, 2004, when an FP&L officer was asked whether FP&L had political risk insurance, he said he could not remember. Indonesian counsel failed to follow up with further questions. It turned out that the Lloyd's insurance was held by an affiliate of FP&L.

56. See the client testimonial videos on the company's Web site, available at http://www.harvest-international.com/video.htm (accessed February 2005).

57. For a story suggesting that Goldstein and his firm were involved in bribery of Indonesian officials by Monsanto, see Bill Guerin, "The Seeds of a Bribery Scandal in Indonesia," *Asia Times*, January 20, 2005, available at http://www.atimes.com/atimes/Southeast_Asia/GA20Ae04.html (accessed February 2005). For Goldstein's denial, see Muninggar Sri Saraswati, "Harvest Denies Role in Monsanto Scandal," *Jakarta Post*, January 14, 2005.

58. For a version of the story, see I. G. G. Maha Adi, "An Intermediary for Karaha," *Tempo*, August 13–19, 2002.

59. Our request for confirmation from P.T. Harvest International (by e-mail on February 9, 2005) went unanswered.

60. Bill Guerin, "Under the Volcano."

61. Quoted in "US Court of Appeals for the Fifth Circuit lifts Injunction and Contempt Finding Against Pertamina for Pursuing Legal Action in the Indonesian Courts," Pertamina press release, New York, June 19, 2003.

62. Interview with an official from the U.S. embassy in Jakarta, February 2003.

63. A'an Suryana, "U.S. Rejects RI Request over Karaha Bodas Case," *Jakarta Post*, February 18, 2003.

64. In a letter dated April 2, 2002. I. G. G. Maha Adi, "An Intermediary for Karaha." Interestingly, in 2004 Loedito faced a suit by colleagues for taking all of some $10 million "in fees" from Caithness, accompanied by the allegation that he did not actually own the Sumarah shares he claimed. See "Karaha-Pertamina: The Saga Continued," *Indonesia Corruption Watch*, July 28, 2004.

65. For cases of refusals to enforce, see R. Doak Bishop and Elaine Martin, *Enforcement of Foreign Arbitral Awards*, King & Spaulding, Houston, Texas (n.d.), available at http://www.kslaw.com/library/pdf/bishop6.pdf (accessed July 2005).

66. C. Bryson Hull, "US Court Says Pertamina Can Fight $261 mln Award," *Dow Jones Business News*, June 20, 2003.

67. *Perushahaan Pertambangan Minyak Dan Gas Bumi Negara of Indonesia [Pertamina] v Karaha Bodas Co. LLC*, No. 86/PdtG/2002/PN JktPst., Central Jakarta Dist.

68. *Karaha Bodas Co. L.C.C. v. Pertamina*, Nos. 02-20042, 03-20602, 5th Circuit, December 2003.

69. In a further effort to protect Pertamina's assets, the Indonesian government and Pertamina appealed to the U.S. Supreme Court, claiming that decisions of the New York and New Orleans appeals courts had violated the Foreign Sovereign Immunities Act. The Supreme Court declined to hear the case, on June 2, 2003 (Certiorari Denied 02-1509).

70. Position Paper, June 24, 2002, unsigned but provided by the company's public relations firm.

71. Indonesian counsel told us that the withdrawal of Keppres 37/1997 was, in fact, an effort to avoid IMF demands, but IMF pressure led to the renewed suspensions.

72. Guerin, "Under the Volcano." A similar issue arose in Turkey, when the World Bank pressed that government not to proceed on some alleged commitments on electric power projects. The companies involved claimed payment from

the Turkish government, enlisting help from the Advocacy Center in the U.S. Department of Commerce. The Turkish side argued that the halt was not their fault, but rather that of the multilateral institution.

73. See *Karaha Bodas Company, L.L.C. v Perusahaan Pertambangan Minyak dan Gas Bumi Negara,* United States Court of Appeals for the Second Circuit, August Term, 2001.

74. "Pertamina Ordered to Post 275 mln USD Bond to Resolve Dispute with Karaha," *AFX,* July 3, 2002, available at http://web.lexis-nexis.com/universe/ document?_m=afce17d6bfc9883f1548c0d917e5f9aa&_docnum=43&wchp=dGLb Vzz-zSkVb&_md5=549e2ffad641544aaf6ba5d82a8b41fc (accessed August 2004). "Indo Minister Praises United States Court Decision on KBC," *Global News Wire— Asia Africa Intelligence Wire,* July 21, 2002, available at http://web.lexis-nexis.com/ universe/doclist?_m=2d921771e0218a639da818d6033a8f60&_startdoc=26&wchp =dGLbVzz-zSkVb&_md5=6893d94b82eb766dba55046ecc76b028 (accessed August 2004).

75. Although in the meantime he had received (in 2002) an honorary Doctor of Laws from his undergraduate (1964) alma mater, Colby, presumably it was not for his honorary law degree that he was contracted by White & Case. To a reporter, he said, "This [the KBC case] is where I feel the Indonesian government is in the right. . . . They deserve help in getting the decision adjudicated in their favour." "Intelligence," *Far Eastern Economic Review,* March 27, 2003, p. 9.

76. Through the law firm Alston & Bird. The appointment letter of December 18, 2003, available at http://www.public-i.org/docs/oil/OpecIndo.pdf (accessed August 2005).

77. Kevin Bogardus, "Bob Dole: Indonesia's Man in Washington," Center for Public Integrity, September 22, 2004, available at http://www.public-i.org/oil/ report.aspx?aid=381 (accessed February 2005). The article documents some of the contacts made by Dole and his associates.

78. KBC had just lost a battle in Singapore as we were completing this book. See Jean Chua, "Karaha Bodas Loses Petral Appeal," *The Business Times* (Singapore), August 25, 2005.

79. According to one party, the existence of the insurance was revealed in hearings in Canada.

80. It rejected the applicability of Indonesian law, based on Indonesians' earlier contentions in the Swiss arbitration and the lack of a clear statement of its applicability in the contracts themselves. The default position was the law of the country where the arbitration was held. Thus, the annulment of the award by Indonesian courts was, the U.S. court concluded, not consistent with the New York Convention and the award was upheld. See *Karaha Bodas Co. L.L.C. v Perusahaan Pertambangan Minyak dan Gas Bumi,* No. 0220042cv, March 23, 2004, for a rather complete history of the case.

81. Peter Waldman, "Heavy Hand: Washington's Tilt to Business Stirs a Backlash in Indonesia," *Wall Street Journal,* February 11, 2004, p. 1.

82. As we were completing this book, lawyers were seeking a review of this decision.

83. Rendi A. Witular and Fitri Wulandari, "Pertamina Doesn't Have Funds to Pay KBC Claim," *Jakarta Post,* August 13, 2004.

84. Abdul Khalk, "Police Complete Case Files on Corruption at KBC," *Jakarta Post,* August 4, 2004. The article reports that the police named Priyant, the former head of Pertamina's geothermal division; one of his staff, Syafei Sulaiman; and Robert McKichan (presumably, Robert D. McCutchen). Not surprisingly, McCutchen was "abroad" and "had refused to comply with the police summons." See also "Power: The Way out on Karaha Bodas," in "News on Trade and Investment in Indonesia," August 23, 2004, issued by the Coordinating Ministry for Economic Affairs, Republic of Indonesia.

85. Shawn Donnan and Taufan Hidayat, "Jakarta Escalates Dispute Against US Power Investors," *Financial Express*, December 2, 2004.

86. "LSP Released from Prison," *Jakarta Post*, August 22, 2005. Loedito's payment of 10% could be interpreted as recognition of the obligation. In 2006, Indonesia was introducing to the Singapore court recently found documents that, Indonesians claimed, showed that the KBC had not discovered energy sources at the time of the arbitration that would support anything close to the electricity production that it was projecting. If the contention that the energy could not support a commercial project were to be proved accurate, then the case could take on aspects of "moral hazard" similar to that of the insured who burns his house down upon discovering that his art collection comprises fakes. At the time of this writing, the issue remained unresolved.

87. Translated from SH Rudy Victor Sinaga, "Pertamina Tidak Wajar Bayar Denda ke KBC," *Sinar Harapan,* January 20, 2004, available at http://www.sinarha rapan.co.id/ekonomi/industri/2004/0121/ind2.html (accessed February 2005).

88. Shawn Donnan, "Pertamina Still Hopes to Settle Case out of Court," *Financial Express*, July 28, 2004.

89. Oskar, head of the Indonesian team for the ITT/Indosat negotiations, had died. Sumarlin was not involved in government after 1998.

90. Translated from Sinaga, "Pertamina Tidak Wajar Bayar Denda ke KBC."

91. 1958 United Nations Convention on the Recognition and Enforcement of Foreign Arbitral Awards.

92. For a description of ICSID, see Hew R. Dundas, "Dispute Resolution under Investment Treaties," unpublished paper from the Centre for Energy, Petroleum and Mineral Law and Policy, Edinburgh, 2002. Members of ICSID also pledged to enforce decisions of arbitrations held under its auspices.

93. For an account of the largely unsuccessful efforts to use earlier Treaties of Friendship, Commerce, and Navigation to protect foreign investment, see Charles Lipson, *Standing Guard: Protecting Foreign Capital in the Nineteenth and Twentieth Centuries* (Berkeley: University of California Press, 1985), pp. 96, 97.

94. For history of the development of BITs, see Jeswald W. Salacuse and Nicholas P. Sullivan, "Do BITs Really Work? An Evaluation of Bilateral Investment Treaties and Their Grand Bargain," *Harvard International Law Review*, Winter 2005, 46(1), pp. 67–130.

95. See the ICSID Web site: http://www.worldbank.org/icsid/cases/con clude.htm (accessed August 2004); and http://www.worldbank.org/icsid/cases/ pending.htm (accessed August 2004).

96. If one counts some of the cases labeled only as "construction" as infrastructure, the number grows.

97. Of them, 92 were filed within the immediately preceding three years. See "International Investment Disputes on the Rise," Occasional Note, UNCTAC/ WEB/ITE/2004/2, November 29, 2004 Arbitration was increasingly popular for handling various kinds of international business disputes as well. The International Chamber of Commerce reported the following: 1923–1978: 63 cases/year; 1979–1990: 291 cases/year; 1992–2001: 450 cases/year; 2001: 566 cases. Source: Charles N. Brower, Charles H. Brower, II, and Jeremy K. Sharpe, "The Coming Crisis in the Global Adjudication System," 2003, 19, *Arbitration International*, pp. 415, 437–438. Goldhaber reports 18 arbitrations with claims of $1 billion or more. Also see Michael D. Goldhaber, "Arbitration Scorecard: Treaty Disputes," *American Lawyer/Focus Europe*, Summer 2005, available at http://www.americanlawyer. com/focuseurope/treaty0605.html.

98. See "Award, *CMS Gas Transmission Company v The Argentine Republic*," ICSID Case NO. ARB/01/9, distributed to the parties on May 12, 2005.

99. Goldhaber, "Arbitration Scorecard."

100. Term from Patti Waldmeir, "How America Is Privatising Justice by the Back Door," *Financial Times*, June 30, 2003, p. 8.

Chapter 14

1. In the Philippines, Mananagdong, negotiated in July 1994; the same year it contracted for a hydropower and irrigation facility at Casecnan; it subcontracted to Ormat for Upper Mahiao; and the company acquired a third geothermal facility, Malitbog, when it bought Magma.

2. A. Kukuh Karsadi and Carry Nadeak, "Beaten in Three Court Sessions," *Gatra*, May 15, 1999, available at http://www.odiousdebts.org/odiousdebts/index.cfm?DSP=content&ContentID=2484 (accessed August 2004).

3. There seems to have been an American developer involved in either the Dieng or the Patuha projects. Through P.T. Royal Perintis Abadi, he may have owned some of the rights before CalEnergy entered. One source identified him as Dan Dahlo-Johnson. We have no independent confirmation of his role.

4. O'Shei was president and chief operating officer of CalEnergy Asia and president of CalEnergy Development at various points in the 1990s.

5. A letter and an e-mail to David A. Baldwin of CalEnergy requesting information about the Indonesian projects went unanswered. A former employee of CalEnergy, however, provided us with some information in interviews.

6. We will generally refer to the parent and its holding companies as CalEnergy, even though the parent's name changed to MidAmerican before the story ends.

7. According to Karen Mills, PLN was not yet ready to agree to the terms but was forced to sign. The signing included contracts for Dieng, Kamojang, Karaha Bodas, Patuha, and Wayang Windu. See Karen Mills, "Corruption and Other Illegality in the Formation and Performance of Contracts and in the Conduct of Arbitration Relating Thereto," *International Arbitration Law Review*, October 2002, 5(4), pp. 126–132.

8. Private Sector Power Project, "Quarterly Report," August 1993. Some drilling had been done at the site by Pertamina or PLN and a small plant may have already been operating.

9. MidAmerican Holdings Company Ltd. 10-K report for the fiscal year ending December 31, 1999, reported different commitments: The first four units in this account would total 220 megawatts and would cost $450 million; a second stage would expand the capacity to 400 megawatts and run total cost to $1 billion. The company notified the Indonesians on June 27, 1995, that the schedule was changing, to combine Unit 1 and Unit 2 and produce 60 megawatts. This change was never accepted by the Indonesians, they claim.

10. CalEnergy shared ownership (47% each) with Peter Kiewet & Sons, a construction company, which itself held 34% of CalEnergy's shares. It seems that Kiewit never took down all the equity it was entitled to take. In October 1997, Kiewit's interests were all bought by CalEnergy.

11. See U.S. Embassy, "Indonesia's Geothermal Development," Jakarta, [2002], available at http://www.usembassyjakarta.org/download/geo2002.pdf (accessed August 2005). Other reports give different percentages.

12. From Savitri Setiawan and Alex Mirza Hukom, "The Enterprising Military," *Indonesia Business Weekly*, July 6, 1992, p. 5, cited in Adam Schwartz, *A Nation in Waiting* (St. Leonards, Australia: Allen & Unwin, 1994), p. 133.

13. Oddly, we have been told both stories, and also that it made fertilizer. Maybe there were two or three plants.

14. See, for example, Ramadhan K. H., *H. Priyatna Abdurrasyid, Dari Cilampeni ke New York: Mengikuti Hati Nurani* (Jakarta: Pustaka Sinar Harapan, 2001), Chapter 20.

15. MidAmerican Holdings Company Ltd. 10-K report for fiscal year ending December 31, 1999.

16. CalEnergy also revised the project schedule for Patuha, in a letter on June 28, 1996.

17. Mohamad is spelled differently in various sources. At some point, Achmad Kalla acquired shares in this company.

18. By a lawyer working on the Indonesian side.

19. CalEnergy, 10-K report for fiscal year ending December 1997.

20. The potential environmental impact of this project quickly became controversial. See "Eksplorasi Geothermal Energi, Bedugul," Lembaga Bantuan Hukum Bali, June 24, 1997, available at http://www.hamline.edu/apakabar/basisdata/1997/06/24/0009.html (accessed August 2004).

21. Statement from Don O'Shei, Jr., president and chief operating officer of CalEnergy Asia, in "CalEnergy Confirms Status of Geothermal Projects in Indonesia and Existing Construction Schedule Unchanged," *PRNewswire,* September 24, 1997, available at http://web.archive.org/web/20020919095600/http://www.cleanenergy.de/News_archive/07_12_97/240997_1.html (accessed June 2002).

22. "CalEnergy Reports a 229% Increase in Revenues," news release, distributed by *PRNewswire* on behalf of Northern Electric, January 29, 1998.

23. According to the decree, if construction or development had begun, a project belonged in the "continued" category. CalEnergy said that the first unit at Dieng was close to completion and that suspending any part of Dieng was inappropriate since all four parts were under the same contracts.

24. The full letter is online, available at http://www.hamline.edu/apakabar/basisdata/1998/01/31/0010.html (accessed August 2004).

25. "International Arbitration Panel Announces Favorable Rulings for Himpurna California Energy and Patuha Power," press release, May 4, 1999.

26. For the requirement, see Julie A. Martin, "OPIC Modified Expropriation Coverage Case Study: MidAmerican's Projects in Indonesia—Dieng and Patuha," in Theodore H. Moran (ed.), *International Political Risk Management: Exploring New Frontiers* (Washington, D.C.: The World Bank, 2001), p. 59. The usual OPIC requirement was that the investor seek recourse through whatever dispute resolution mechanism covered the allegedly breached agreement. For a decision indicating that an arbitration award is not always necessary, see *Bechtel Enterprises International (Bermuda) Ltd; Ben Dabhol Holdings, Ltd; and Capital India Power Mauritius I v OPIC,* AAA Case No. 50 T195 00509 02, September 25, 2003, available at http://www.opic.gov/FOIA/Awards/2294171_1.pdf. Our FOIA request for a copy of the insurance contracts for CalEnergy was denied.

27. Indonesians argued that the invoice was inappropriate because the secondhand Italian plant had failed its commissioning test (at least partly based on poor extraction of sulfur); capacity was greater than called for in the contract and PLN lines could carry; and the company had withdrawn its personnel and therefore could not deliver power. The parties disagreed on whether PLN had to authorize departures from original capacities. After repairs, the plant passed the commissioning test, probably in December 1998.

28. CalEnergy, 10-K report for fiscal year ending December 2000.

29. Quoted in Witold J. Henisz and Bennet A. Zelner, "The Political Economy of Private Electricity Provision in Southeast Asia" (working paper, Reginald H. Jones Center, The Wharton School, University of Pennsylvania, Philadelphia, 2001), WP 2001-02; original source cited as *Dow Jones On-line News,* September 4, 1998.

30. Some indication of this appears in Huw Thomas, "Project Restructuring/ Rehabilitation Restructurings and Work-outs, Arbitration and Alternative Dispute Resolution for Distressed Projects in Asia," presented at the Asia Development Forum Workshop, Private Investment in Infrastructure: Financial and Regulatory

Risks, Manila, June 7–8, 2000, p. 6. The exclusion of developing countries in the company's new strategy had become even more obvious by 2003. Although it had interests in gas fields and pipelines in Australia, Poland, and the United Kingdom, it had not continued developments in the Third World. It still had the four holdings in the Philippines, which had been negotiated along with the Indonesian projects; however, rumor had it that these were also for sale.

31. Sometime during the process, a foreign consultant discovered what he believed to be an additional explanation for CalEnergy's hurry to get out of its Indonesian projects. When a private investment group led by Warren E. Buffett's Berkshire Hathaway showed interest in acquiring the company, the deal was conditional on settlement of CalEnergy's claim against Indonesia. He thought that Buffett's interest was based partly on the pot of money that the company could eventually receive from OPIC.

32. From interview with former CalEnergy lawyer.

33. It seems that Himpurna, CalEnergy's partner at Dieng, protested the arbitration, at least according to the report of a lawyer working for Indonesians. The tribunal did not pursue the lawyers' claim that the CalEnergy side might not have authority to bring arbitration without the consent of Himpurna.

34. According to a former CalEnergy lawyer.

35. Later called Karim Syah. One of its founding members was an American, Karen Mills, who was to become deeply involved in the CalEnergy case. She had long been in Indonesia and had recently passed the exams of the Chartered Institute of Arbitrators (in 1993 to 1995). She would gain practical arbitration experience quickly with this and other cases.

36. It was rather unusual that de Fina was not a lawyer. Nevertheless, he had served on several arbitrations, was listed at the Hong Kong Arbitration Centre, and was a member of other prestigious bodies of arbitrators. In his guarded response to questions, de Fina requested that we include the following statement, if we drew on any of his comments: "I request that you make it clear that I have provided a very limited response in the particular circumstances of this matter as already being in the public domain and to that extent absolute confidentiality in respect of the questions posed was deemed not to apply." Two lawyers were eager to point out to us that he was one of three arbitrators who were later removed for misconduct with respect to fees in an Australian case: *ICT Pty Ltd v Sea Containers Ltd* (2002), NSWSC77, New South Wales Supreme Court, February 2002.

37. His distinguished academic and professional record is available on the Apa & Siapa Web site at http://www.pdat.co.id/hg/apasiapa/html/P/ads,20030625-44,P.html (accessed February 2004).

38. The stories that were told to us by a lawyer for the Indonesians, Priyatna, de Fina, and an alternative chair appeared contradictory. A follow-up question to de Fina to resolve apparent differences was answered: "I will not enter into any further correspondence with you."

39. For the allegations of conflict of interest, see *Patuha Power Ltd. v Republic of Indonesia,* Interim Award," September 26, 1999, p. 60.The award has been reproduced in Mealy's *International Arbitration Report,* January 2000, 15(4), pp. 292–429.

40. "Jan Paulsson, Public International Law Sector Profile," Freshfields Bruckhaus Deringer Web site, available at http://www.freshfields.com/practice/pil/people/enprofiles/jasp_profile1.asp (accessed August 2004).

41. PLN first named Harjono Tjitrosoebono, but he declined. One report was that he thought that his previous position as a legal advisor to PLN generated a conflict of interest. Another was that his wife objected, on health grounds; he died soon after these events.

42. Keppres number 37/1992.

43. Essentially the same story was reported to us by Indonesian counsel and by a former lawyer for CalEnergy. Our offer to Coudert to let them review our

account of events was rejected based on "client confidentiality." Our response that it was the client who had complained was met with silence.

44. According to the firm's Web site, it specialized in construction and engineering, energy, infrastructure, and users and suppliers of information and technology. See "Mason's, About Us," [archival copy], available at http://web.archive.org/web/20041009160129/http://www.masons.com/php/page.php?page_id=aboutus (accessed April 2006).

45. Priyatna, Indonesian arbitrator for the later round of arbitration, claims that the arbitrators were harassed in this first round, but he was not involved at the time. See H. Priyatna Abdurrasyid, "They Said I Was Going to Be Kidnapped," Commentary in *Mealey's International Arbitration Report*, June 2003.

46. That firm told us that they would not undertake such a task, but that there were plenty of "two-fers" who would do it, referring to small security firms.

47. According to Karim Sani lawyer Karen Mills, the story became public in 2004 when Buyung told it at a conference in Bali that she attended. See also Priyatna's memoirs, Ramadhan K. H., *H. Priyatna Abdurrasyid*, Chapter 20.

48. This was before the abortive attempt to bring the IMF into the KBC case.

49. He published a book on Indonesian law in 1974. He had worked earlier at Coudert (according to legal advisors to Indonesians, with Paulsson). Remember, Coudert had withdrawn from this case for reasons of conflict of interest. Hornick's testimony was countered by Indonesian legal authority Fred Tumbuan, of Tumbuan Pane.

50. Actually, they claimed the 30 years started from the completion of the last unit. Thus, profits might accrue for as long as 42 years. Harvard Business School professor Richard Ruback presented calculations in this as well as in the KBC case.

51. "International Arbitration Panel Announces Favorable Rulings for Himpurna California Energy and Patuha Power," press release, May 4, 1999.

52. USAID, "Tsunami Reconstruction, Update—December 2, 2005," available at http://www.usaid.gov/locations/asia_near_east/tsunami/pdf/tsunami_update_120205.pdf. (accessed December 2005). We believe that this figure excludes substantial in-kind contributions.

53. He referred to Indonesians as "bozos" several times during the interview.

54. District Court of South Jakarta, No. 271/PDT.G/1999/PN.JKT.PST and 272/PDT.G/1999/PN.JKT.PST, September 17, 1999. See also the report of the second arbitration, in Albert Jan van den Berg (ed.), *ICCA Yearbook Commercial Arbitration*, vol. 25 (Dordrecht, the Netherlands: Kluwer Law International, 2000).

55. Robert Silberman, president and COO, quoted in Nick Lord, "Power Problems," *Finance Asia*, September 1999, p. 1.

56. For an interpretation that the penalty applied only to the companies, see Mark Kantor, "The Limitations of Arbitration," *Journal of Structured and Project Finance*, Fall 2002, p. 4. Indonesian counsel we interviewed said that the penalty explicitly applied to the parties and the arbitrators, and that it applied to counsel for the parties as well.

57. Mark Kantor recognizes a "moral hazard" at this point. CalEnergy was willing to proceed with the arbitration and incur the risk of losing its investment because it had insurance coverage. See Mark Kantor, "International Project Finance and Arbitration in Public Sector Entities: When Is Arbitrability a Fiction?" *Fordham International Law Journal*, 2001, 24, pp. 1122–1183.

58. His side of the story appears in H. Priyatna Abdurrasyid, "They Said I Was Going to Be Kidnapped." He also reports a slightly different version in his memoirs, Ramadhan K. H., *H. Priyatna Abdurrasyid*. See also van den Berg (ed.), *ICCA Yearbook Commercial Arbitration*, pp. 188–193.

59. Communicated by letter No. S-350/MK.01/1999, September 17, 1999, signed by the Minister of Finance.

60. Ramadhan K. H., *H. Priyatna Abdurrasyid*. In correspondence with us, Priyatna says he was discussing "a total amount of US$1,000,000, countering the fine rendered by the District Court." Why he would be fined if he did not attend is unclear. In this account, he did not mention the income he would forgo by not participating.

61. In another account, this statement was made in Amsterdam rather than Washington. And Priyatna claims that his wife received "threatening phone calls from unknown people" that were "brute and rough."

62. "Four or five Indonesian officials" in some accounts.

63. "Kalau Pak Priyatna tidak bersedia secara suka rela, terpaksa kami akan melakukan *kidnap*." Priyatna did not reveal to us the names of officials from the Ministry of Finance.

64. See *"Patuha Power, Ltd. v. Republic of Indonesia,* Interim Award," September 26, 1999, for statements by the three parties.

65. Law No. 30 of 1999. See Karen Mills, "Enforcement of Arbitral Awards in Indonesia: Issues Relating to Arbitration and the Judiciary," *Transnational Dispute Management* (TDM), April 2006, 3(2). On-line journal available at http://www.transnational-dispute-management.com/

66. United Nations Commission on International Trade Law (UNCITRAL), *UNCITRAL Arbitration Rules,* U.N. General Assembly Resolution 31/98, Section 2.

67. See Jacques Werner, "When Arbitration Becomes War: Some Reflections on the Frailty of the Arbitral Process in Cases Involving Authoritarian States," *Journal of International Arbitration,* August 2000, 19(4), pp. 7–103, and the arguments in the arbitral award.

68. According to *The American Heritage Dictionary of the English Language,* 3rd ed. (Boston: Houghton Mifflin, 1992).

69. From an OPIC official who was not present.

70. We have been unable to locate any such accounts, and the parties involved could identify none to us.

71. The mention of secret police was in a letter to me from de Fina, March 10, 2005.

72. The 1930 case of *Lena Goldfields Ltd. v Russia* was decided by two arbitrators in the absence of the Russian-appointed arbitrator. But the contract had explicitly stated that the majority could reach a decision in the absence of one arbitrator.

73. Priyatna, "They Said I Was Going to Be Kidnapped," p. 31.

74. Ramadhan K. H., *H. Priyatna Abdurrasyid,* Chapter 20.

75. De Fina told us that he and Paulsson are still subject to the Indonesian court fines for participating in the arbitration. On the other hand, Paulsson reported visiting Indonesia several times afterward with no mention of fines.

76. Priyatna, "They Said I Was Going to Be Kidnapped," p. 32; and Ramadhan K. H., *H. Priyatna Abdurrasyid,* Chapter 20.

77. In particular, Priyatna reports on harassment in the first arbitration, where he was not a participant and was denied copies of submissions at the insistence of the company side.

78. The claims were filed in May 1999. Three amendments to the claim were subsequently filed. See OPIC, "Memorandum of Determinations: Expropriation Claim of MidAmerican Energy Holdings Company (formerly CalEnergy Company, Inc.), Contracts of Insurance Nos. E374, E453, E527, and E759," available at http://www.opic.gov/foia/ClaimsDeterminations/1999%20Determinations/MidAmerican%20Energy.htm (accessed February 2005).

79. Julie Martin, an official of OPIC at the time of the claim and author of a paper on the events, did not respond to e-mails. George Munoz, head of OPIC at the time, explicitly declined to be interviewed. We did hold an interview with an OPIC lawyer involved in the settlement.

80. On October 1, 1999, apparently before the final ruling had been formally issued.

81. OPIC says it had carried out what it calls a "forensic audit" to determine whether CalEnergy had actually invested as much as it claimed. The conclusion was that they had invested much more. On the other hand, we have been told by two sources that lenders received nothing, having failed to have insurance proceeds assigned to them. We do not know how much of CalEnergy's recovery was accounted for by borrowing.

82. According to Martin, "OPIC Modified Expropriation Coverage," p. 63, the private insurers were a Lloyd's of London syndicate, Unistrat Corporation of America, Ace Global Markets Limited, and Sovereign Risk Insurance Ltd. The authors obtained a draft "settlement agreement, assignment and release" between OPIC and the Indonesian government that lists two of these names and a number of syndicates, including R. S. Childs and Others and M. E. Brockbank and Others. In any event, OPIC would collect claims for them.

83. On May 18, 2004, we filed a FOIA request for a copy of these documents. On June 10, we were denied copies, based on FOIA subparagraph (b)(5), saying that "the document at issue—a draft legal memorandum—reflects an intra-agency communication that is deliberative in nature and antecedent to OPIC's decision with respect to the final resolution of this matter, the disclosure of which would harm OPIC's deliberative process. In addition, this document is protected by the attorney work-product privilege." What we know of its arguments comes from interviews.

84. Endnote 23. Unfortunately, in the publicly available (Internet) version, locations for endnotes after number 17 are not indicated in the text. See OPIC, "Memorandum of Determinations."

85. The source of the alleged police report may have been a news release from MidAmerican, September 29, 1999, reported by Sustainable Energy & Economy Network, available at www.seen.org/db/Dispatch?action-OrgWidget:196-detail=1 (accessed August 2005).

86. "Desperately Searching for Priyatna," Review and Outlook, *Asian Wall Street Journal*, October 1, 1999, p. 8. The newspaper report probably relied on the September 29, 1999, company press release, cited above, which said "required or forced the departure [of Priyatna]." Presumably the account of the alleged police notification relied on the same source. The *AWSJ* reports that a PLN spokesman reported hearing allegations of "kidnapping," but he denied them.

87. OPIC, "Memorandum of Determinations."

88. Interviews with OPIC official.

89. Interviews with OPIC official.

90. As of September 2003, OPIC had denied 25 claims and paid 267. See Robert C. O'Sullivan, "Learning from OPIC's Experience with Claims and Arbitrations," in Theodore H. Moran and Gerald T. West (eds.), *International Political Risk Management: Looking to the Future*, vol. 3 (Washington, D.C.: World Bank, 2005). The paper does not provide details of denials: for example, the number that involved political risk coverage or the reasons for denial.

91. The legal term is *subrogation*. For the details, see Martin, "OPIC Modified Expropriation Coverage Case Study," p. 60.

92. It is not clear to us whether OPIC received all the shares or 90%, the percentage of equity it had insured.

93. "Asia Development Forum Workshop: Private Investment in Infrastructure," June 7, 2000, available at http://www.worldbank.org/wbi/wbiep/adf/papers/thomas.pdf (accessed June 2002).

94. See Jacques Werner, "When Arbitration Becomes War." This rather intemperate article refers to the "coerced repatriation" of Priyatna.

95. We were told that DATI had to collect from OPIC, which insisted on settling for less than the award—ironic, given OPIC's insistence on enforcement of contracts and awards.

96. Gary Nageri Munthe, "Indonesia Agrees to Pay OPIC Insurance Claim," *Indonesia Finance*, October 12, 2000. Indonesian counsel reports that invoices of these contractors were included in the sums CalEnergy claimed and for which it was reimbursed, even though they had not been paid (and were, according to the same reports, never paid by CalEnergy).

97. Letter from the American Chargé d'Affaires ad Interim to the Indonesian Minister of Foreign Affairs," January 7, 1967, signed by Jack W. Lydman, and Letter from the Indonesian Minister of Foreign Affairs to the American Chargé d'Affaires ad Interim, January 7, 1967, signed by Adam Malik. Note that this is the same Adam Malik who appeared in the ITT/Indosat story and whose personal financial interests were defended assiduously by the U.S. Central Intelligence Agency. The letters comprise the "Investment Guarantees: Agreement between the United States of America and Indonesia, Effected by Exchange of Notes, Signed at Djakarta January 7, 1967," Treaties and other International Acts Series 6330, U.S. Department of State.

98. The OPIC contention is rather clear in a report on a speech by Peter Watson, president and CEO of OPIC, September 6, 2001. He was paraphrased as saying: "OPIC then sought reimbursement from the Indonesian government, which under normal procedure would be considered responsible for the debt." Reported in: The United States–Indonesia Society, "Update on Indonesia's Settlement with OPIC," USINDO Brief.

99. In a letter from PLN on or about October 22, 1999.

100. In denying our FOIA request for the agreement, filed on May 18, 2004, OPIC responded on June 7: "The responsive claims cooperation agreement constitutes confidential business information the disclosure of which is likely to cause substantial competitive harm to the private insurers and impair OPIC's program effectiveness." How OPIC's program effectiveness or the insurers could be harmed by releasing an agreement under which they had already collected is unclear.

101. OPIC and MIGA's policies on cooperation agreements with private insurers differed. A MIGA official told us that MIGA would, at least at the time, have informed a host government of such a compact when it sought approval for insuring a project.

102. Subsequently, we have been told that the CalEnergy contract had only one departure from the model: a clause that triggered a claim if the host government refused to honor an arbitration award. This, of course, was critical to this case.

103. Our requests under the FOIA for copies of the insurance contract were also refused.

104. ANZ Panin Bank, *Indonesia Newsletter*, July 2000, available at http://www.anz.com/Indonesia/newsletters/July2000.pdf (accessed August 2004).

105. This story was told to us separately by three people who were present. As noted earlier, George Munoz refused our request for an interview, and the OPIC official we did interview said he knew nothing of this event.

106. Michael Billington, "Looting Indonesia: The Energy Brokers 'Warm-up' for California," March 28, 2001, available at http://www.odiousdebts.org/odious debts/index.cfm?DSP=content&ContentID=2746 (accessed August 2004).

107. ANZ Panin Bank, *Indonesia Newsletter*, July 2000.

108. "Platt Petrochemical Report: OPIC Faces Long Wait for $290-million Claim for Indonesian Geothermal Plants, 800 Mwe," Green Green: Financing News for the U.S. Geothermal Industry, October 18, 2000, available at http://web.archive.org/web/20040211060652/http://www.bl-a.com/ECB/Green+Green/093000.htm (accessed April 2006).

109. Analysis of political situation can be found in Idris Kyrway, "Analysis of the Political Situation in Indonesia," Kyrway Report 2000-6 (Jakarta: Support for Decentralization Measures, October 2000). More on Indonesia financial details can be found in Gary Nageri Munthe. "Indonesia Agrees to Pay OPIC Insurance Claim," *Indonesia Finance*, October 12, 2000.

110. The claims become official debts to the German state, which are then subject to restructuring under the Paris Club.

111. Dates from Watson, "Update on Indonesia's Settlement with OPIC."

112. *Down to Earth IFIs Update*, No. 19, September 2001, available at http://dte .gn.apc.org/Au19.htm (accessed August 2004).

113. According to some Balinese, it is a "holy and sacred place." See I Wayan Ananta Wijaya, "Bedugul Geothermal Project Raises Controversy," *Jakarta Post*, August 29, 2005.

114. By 2004, the project was to be developed by PLN and Pertamina.

115. The arguments were that the initial generating capacity was larger than specified in the agreement and beyond the capacity of PLN's lines and that the project had failed the first commissioning test.

116. For histories, see B. E. Clubb and V. W. Vance, "Incentives to Private U.S. Investment Abroad under the Foreign Assistance Program," *Yale Law Journal*, January 1963, 72, pp. 457–505; G. W. Ray, "Evolution, Scope, and Utilization of Guarantees of Foreign Investments," *The Business Lawyer*, July 1966, 21, pp. 1051–1068; Kenneth W. Hansen, "PRI and the Rise (and Fall?) of Private Investment in Infrastructure," in Michael B. Likosky (ed.), *Privatising Development* (Leiden, the Netherlands: Martinus Nijhoff, 2005), pp. 109–113; and Charles Lipson, *Standing Guard: Protecting Foreign Capital in the Nineteenth and Twentieth Centuries* (Berkeley: University of California Press, 1985), Chapter 7.

117. The investor had to be prevented "from exercising its fundamental rights as shareholder or as creditor," "disposing of securities," or "exercising effective control over the use of disposition of a substantial portion of its property...." The agreement went on to exclude "abrogation, impairment, repudiation or breach...of any undertaking, agreement or contract...unless it constitutes Expropriatory Action in accordance with [the previously stated criteria]." American Arbitration Association, *Anaconda Company and Chile Copper Company-Overseas Private Investment Corporation: Arbitration of Dispute Involving U.S. Investment Guarantee Program*, July 17, 1975.

118. *Anaconda Company and Chile Copper Company*, paragraph 27. The arbitrators cited Raymond Vernon's *Sovereignty at Bay* (New York: Basic Books, 1973), pp. 46–53, and "Mining the Resources of the Third World: From Concession Agreement to Service Contracts," *Proceedings of the 67th Annual Meeting of the American Society of International Law* (Washington, D.C.: ASIL, 1973), pp. 227. The parties to the arbitration were in an unusual position: The company argued that acts of the Chilean government did not amount to expropriation while OPIC took the opposite stance, claiming that expropriation had occurred before insurance was in effect.

119. Mainly, by insuring against a government's failure to honor an arbitral decision. See Hansen, "PRI and the Rise (and Fall?)," p. 121. Some European insurers offer explicit coverage for breach of contract. In the CalEnergy case, OPIC also accepted the argument that assets had been expropriated.

120. An alternative could be something like the German system, whereby claims become part of state–state debt and may be written down in Paris Club debt restructuring talks.

121. On the other hand, insured companies do appeal to arbitration if an official insurer denies a claim.

Chapter 15

1. From an interview in 2005. A *kris* is the traditional wavy Javanese dagger.
2. Private Sector Power Project, "Quarterly Report," August 1993.
3. Enron had planned two more generating facilities in Indonesia. For both, see Private Sector Power Project, "Quarterly Report," November 1993.
4. Ownership and head can, of course, be different. The links are consistent, however. See Power Highlights, "Indonesia Economic Highlights," The Economic Section, U.S. Embassy, Jakarta, January 1997, available at http://www.hamline.edu/apakabar/basisdata/1997/03/14/0047.html (accessed August 2004). Hardiv also lists Johanes Kotjo as Prince's owner, in Hardiv H. Situmeang, "Challenges Facing IPP Model in Asia: The Experience of PLN in Indonesia," at the 10th World Economic Development Congress, Kuala Lumpur, June 27–29, 2001.
5. In another letter, Brown wrote, "I would like to bring to your attention a number of projects involving American companies which seem to be stalled, including several independent power projects. These projects include the Tarahan power project, which involves Southern Electric; the gas powered projects in East Java and East Kalimantan, which involve Enron [followed by other projects]." He concluded, "Your support for prompt resolution of the remaining issues associated with each of these projects would be most appreciated." The letters are reproduced on line at Enrongate: A Democrat Scandal Web site, available at http://talking_points.tripod.com/enron/id4.html (accessed August 2004).
6. Abhay Mehta, *Power Play* (New Delhi: Orient Longman, 2000). Enron convinced the U.S. government to threaten Mozambique's aid funds and induced President Clinton to hint to the Mozambican president that he would not sign the pending Bilateral Investment Treaty if Enron did not receive a contract it wanted there. Enron's efforts to obtain U.S. government support for its disputes in India, the Dominican Republic, Nigeria, Turkey, and Argentina are evidenced in documents provided online at the Public Citizen: Critical Mass Energy Program Web site, available at http://www.citizen.org/cmep/energy_enviro_nuclear/electricity/Enron/foia/index.cfm?ID=9372&relatedpages=1&catID=108&secID=1838 (accessed August 2004).
7. MIGA, "Investment Guarantee Guide," n.d., provided to us in 2003.
8. Under certain conditions, the World Bank and other multilaterals also offer partial risk guarantees on debt. For details, the World Bank Partial Risk Guarantees page, available at http://web.worldbank.org/WBSITE/EXTERNAL/PROJECTS/EXTFININSTRUMENTS/EXTGUARANTEES/0,,contentMDK%3A20260268~menuPK%3A542563~pagePK%3A64143534~piPK%3A64143448~theSitePK%3A411474,00.html (accessed August 2005).
9. The total amount of approved coverage was $60 million.
10. It is not clear to us why MIGA required no arbitration. Its coverage for breach of contract generally pays upon a government's failure (after 365 days) to pay an award. See Kenneth W. Hansen, "PRI and the Rise (and Fall?) of Private Investment in Infrastructure," in Michael B. Likosky (ed.), *Privatising Development* (Leiden: Martinus Nijhoff Publishers, 2005), pp. 109–113.
11. Personal communication from a MIGA official.
12. Jambi-Kertapati, according to a MIGA official.
13. Quoted in Ann Moline, "Assessing Risks in Emerging Markets," *Bizsites: Plants, Sites, and Parks Magazine*, October/November 2001.
14. MIGA's clause invalidated insurance if the insured investor broke laws of the host country. For sure, Bambang did not need a loan from other equity holders to obtain his shares. (For his assets, see Box 7.2.)
15. Multilateral Investment Guarantee Agency, *2003 Annual Report*, Washington, p. 52.
16. Reported to us by a MIGA official.

Chapter 16

1. For figures, see Mari Pangestu, "Indonesia: Trade and Investment Linkages," in W. Dobson and Chia Siow Yue (eds.), *Multinationals and East Asian Integration* (Singapore: The International Development Research Centre, 1998), Chapter 9; available at http://web.idrc.ca/en/ev-9345-201-1-DO_TOPIC.html (accessed February 2005). The figures from BKPM exclude investment in petroleum and are otherwise notably unreliable.

2. Tomen may have been the lead investor in the small ($70 million) Pare-Pare project. Wärtsilä of Finland responded to an e-mail saying that it was not the lead investor. As reported earlier, Tomen did not respond to requests for interviews or to e-mails concerning their interests in Indonesia. Japanese companies had substantial holdings, we believe, in two projects that had not begun: Cilacap (where Mitsubishi and Duke Power/Energy had equal shareholdings) and Tanjung Jati A (Tomen with British National Power).

3. See Private Sector Power Project, "Quarterly Report," December 1994.

4. It was 7.39 cents/kwh according to "Akhirnya Pembangunan PLTU Tanjung Jati-B Dimulai Juga." The 5.73 figure is given in Nengah Sudja, "Questioning the Electricity Price of the IPP's: Case Study of Paiton I, a Consideration to a Win-Win Solution," paper presented to the 13th INFID (International NGO Forum on Indonesian Development) Conference on Inequality, Poverty and Impunity: The Challenge of Indonesia in the Era of Democratization and Globalization, Yogyakarta, Indonesia, September 29–October 2, 2002; and 11th International Anti-Corruption Conference, May 25–28, 2003, Seoul, Korea; PowerPoint presentation available at http://www.11iacc.org/download/add/WS5.5/WS%205.5_P1_Sud jaPPPl.ppt (accessed April 2006). It is also used in "Restructurization [sic] of 26 Independent Power Producers," an industry translation of a document prepared by PLN for a speech delivered by Megawati in July 2003 (provided by an official in the World Bank office in Jakarta).

5. Private Sector Power Project, "Quarterly Report," August 1994.

6. Siti Hardiyanti Rukmana. *Indonesia Newsletter*, ANZ Panin Bank, September 1999.

7. Southern's story was told to us by one of its executives.

8. "Pembangunan PLTU Dimulai Agustus," *Suara Merdeka*, July 29, 2002.

9. Sumitomo Corporation, "Construction Resumes on One of Indonesia's Largest Thermal Power Plants," *Business News*, July 31, 2003, available online at http://web.archive.org/web/20030908031402/http://www.sumitomocorp.co.jp/english/news_e/20030731_171404_kiden_e.htm (accessed April 2006).

10. See Hisako Motoyama and Nurina Widagdo, "Power Sector Restructuring in Indonesia: A Preliminary Study for Advocacy Purposes," Bank Information Center Report, November 1999, available at http://www.bicusa.org/bicusa/issues/powersect.pdf (accessed August 2004.)

11. Although we do not know when the Japanese first raised this possibility, it was announced in August 1999, when proposals were being made public for a competitive electricity market.

12. *Indonesia Newsletter*, ANZ Panin Bank, September 1999.

13. Sander Thoenes, "Excessive Confidence Casts a Pall over Indonesian Electricity Utility," *Financial Times*, September 16, 1999, p. 6.

14. "Platts Global Power Report," September 4, 2003, pp. 7–8. An earlier announcement appeared in "DPR: Tuntaskan KKN Kontrak Listrik Swasta," *Kompas*, June 20, 2002.

15. "Tanjung Jati Will Use Leasing Scheme," from *Tempo* and *Bisnis Indonesia*, October 9, 2001, available at http://web.archive.org/web/20020123081911/http://www.mincom.co.id/News_Update/News_2001/011012.asp (accessed April 2006).

16. This date came from a quote from the project manager in "Pembangunan PLTU Dimulai Agustus," *Suara Merdeka*, July 29, 2002.

17. For a brief description, see "House Wants Tanjung Jati B Project Restarted," *Jakarta Post*, February 20, 2003.

18. "Extension of Time in Completion of the Disposal of the Tanjung Jati B Power Project," Announcement of the Stock Exchange of Hong Kong, Limited, June 3, 2003, available at http://www.asiawind.com/pub/hksr/news/030603/09-47 (accessed July 2003).

19. Price and completion date from "Restructurization [sic] of 26 Independent Power Producers."

20. The earliest reference we have to this possible buyout is in "Sumitomo Has Already Acquired Tanjung Jati B," *Ibonweb*, February 20, 2000, available at http://articles.ibonweb.com/webarticle.asp?num=587 (accessed August 2005). Kuntoro is quoted as saying, "However, as the project stopped, the Japanese then acquired all the project from the local partner." By 2003, Sumitomo owned all the equity in the project through wholly owned Summit Power Capital Limited (50%), Summit Power Holding Limited (35%), and PT Summit Niaga (15%).

21. The case filed in 2002 by Saluka Investments, a Dutch affiliate of Nomura, with Nomura of Europe, at the European Court of Human Rights at Strasbourg, France, with the claim that the government violated the European Convention of Human Rights and Freedoms. The Czech Republic also filed a counterclaim against Nomura. None of the arbitrators is Japanese.

22. Motoyama and Widagdo, "Power Sector Restructuring in Indonesia."

23. We hesitate only because we cannot be confident that press reports of the arrangement are accurate and complete.

24. Chevron and Texaco merged in 2001.

25. See the archived version of the Amoseas site, available at http://web.archive.org/web/20041015190812/http://www.api.or.id/amoseas.htm(accessedApril2006).

26. Budi Putranto, "A Matter of Integrity," *IbonWeb.com*, June 2002, available at http://articles.ibonweb.com/magarticle.asp?num=1009 (accessed April 2006). There were those who pointed to his wealth to argue that the reputation was not thoroughly deserved, but we have seen no evidence to challenge the reputation.

27. Puranto, "A Matter of Integrity."

28. Later, one of the foreign advisors recommended that George Tahija be made head of PLN when Satriya was dismissed. Tahija told us that he did not want the job, saying that his family would "kill him" if he accepted. He wanted to stay out of politics, and could not do so at PLN.

29. Salil Tripathi and John McBeth, "Act of Desperation," *Far Eastern Economic Review*, March 19, 1998, p. 42.

30. See "IPP Sulawesi Energy to Extend its Capacity," *IbonWeb.com*, February 19, 2001, available at http://articles.ibonweb.com/webprint.asp?num=718 (accessed August 2003). Sengkang was operated by Sulawesi Energy, which was owned by Energy Equity (47.5%), El Paso Energy International (47.5%), and Triharsa Sarana Jaya Purnama (5%, affiliated with Siti Hardiyanti Rukamana, a Suharto daughter). In 2003, El Paso's long-term plan included divestment of several of its non-U.S. operations, including its Indonesian investments. See "El Paso Corporation Announces Long-Range Plan," press release, December 15, 2003, http://web.archive.org/web/20040604232559/http://www.elpaso.com/press/newsquery.asp?sID=4223 (accessed April 2006).

31. Gunung Salak started on an earlier foundation. Jezek was originally to be project manager in the 1980s, when construction was to be done for Pertamina. Contractors were changed, so he was not involved.

32. See "Unocal Reaches Agreement with PLN and Pertamina on Indonesia Geothermal Contracts," news release by Unocal, July 23, 2002. Unocal's partner in

Salak was Nusamba, a Bob Hasan company. Hasan, Suharto's closest crony businessman, was jailed for corruption.

33. In Sarulla, Unocal had the same partner as in Salak.

34. Unocal's Sarulla was transferred to PLN.

35. See Nick Stride, "Dog Gone," *IDG Communications Ltd*, June 1, 1999, available at http://unlimited.co.nz/unlimited.nsf/0/c131f99d6f9ebe27cc25693b007 e1aed?OpenDocument&Click= (accessed June 2004). Also see Murray Horton, "Seize the Suhartos' NZ Assets: Update on CAFACA's Campaign," Foreign Control Watchdog Web site (Christchurch, New Zealand), December 1999, available at http://www.converge.org.nz/watchdog/94/4seize.htm (accessed June 2004).

36. "Indonesia's Geothermal Development," U.S. Embassy, Jakarta, 2002, available at http://www.usembassyjakarta.org/download/geo2002.pdf (accessed June 2004); and "Unocal Geothermal Indonesia," July 14, 2003, available at http://www.unocal.com/geopower/ugi.htm (accessed March 2004).

37. According to the World Bank PPI Project Database, AES was the top (by number of projects and by value) sponsor of private energy projects in the developing countries during the decade of the 1990s. For its projects, see the World Bank Group, Private Participation in Infrastructure database at http://rru.worldbank.org/PPI/Reports/customQueryAggregate.asp.

38. See John McMillan and Ade Dosunmu, "AES in Nigeria" (Stanford, Calif.: Stanford Business School, February 15, 2002), case No. 1B 29.

39. On the World Bank PPI Project Database, Southern was ranked fifth, after AES, Enron, Electricité de France, and Endesa (Spain).

40. The reader will have noted that the deals were questioned in reports of the *Asian Wall Street Journal* and in at least one article in the U.S. edition.

41. Tanjung Jati A, Tanjung Jati C, Cilacap, Serang, Cilegon, Pasuruan, and Kamojang. The president's announcement (see next paragraph) says six.

42. Darajat, Paiton I, Paiton II, Pare-Pare, Sengkang, Tanjung Jati B, Salak, Amurang, Sibolga, Palembang Timur, Cikarang, Asahan, Sibayak, and Bedugul.

43. Cibuni and Sarulla.

44. Wayang Windu.

45. Fitri Wulandari, "Government Renegotiates IPP Contracts," *Jakarta Post*, July 5, 2003.

46. A'an Suryana, "Government Completes Contract Renegotiation with 19 IPPs," *Jakarta Post*, February 20, 2003.

47. El Paso carried OPIC insurance on the Sengkang project; Siemens, for Paiton II, German official insurance. See Heike Drillisch and Nicola Sekler, "Bilaterale Investitions-Abkommen und Investitionsgarantien," working paper, Weltwirtschaft, Ökologie & Enwicklung, Berlin, 2004, p. 30. GE, in Paiton I, had insurance that covered a portion of its equity, but it had sold most of its equity by the time the crisis hit.

48. As reported earlier, we are not sure of Tomen's interest in Pare-Pare.

49. PowerGen sold off some or all of its international power later.

50. National Power PLC "demerged" to create International Power PLC, which held power projects in many countries and which in 2004 bought the overseas generating projects of Edison Mission Energy.

51. In writing about the CalEnergy projects, Julie Martin (formerly of OPIC) recognizes the roles of long-term interest and possible moral hazard in the decision whether to renegotiate or to turn to arbitration or insurance. See Julie A. Martin, "OPIC Modified Expropriation Coverage Case Study: MidAmerican's Projects in Indonesia—Dieng and Patuha," in Theodore H. Moran (ed.), *International Political Risk Management: Exploring New Frontiers* (Washington, D.C.: The World Bank, 2001), p. 65.

52. The magnificent building was to be restored, with Roy living on the top two floors and the rest used for his new business interest.

53. Ellen Roy became a senior lecturer at MIT's Sloan School, in entrepreneurship. In 2003, Governor Romney named her Environmental Affairs Secretary in the Massachusetts government, over objections expressed in a letter-writing campaign by almost 80 environmental groups that favored the incumbent.

54. Ellen Roy seems to have retained some shares. The matter became controversial in 2005, when the Massachusetts tax authorities reported the company as delinquent in tax payments. See Stephanie Ebbert, "State Official Tied to Firm That Owes Taxes," *Boston Globe*, May 5, 2005, p. B1. Controversy over the tax issues soon settled down, but in July Roy resigned from her state post to "spend time with her kids."

55. Shawn Donnan, "Indonesia Revives Infrastructure Projects Delayed by Asian Crisis," *Financial Times*, July 9, 2003, p. 7.

56. Article 33 of the 1945 Constitution.

57. Keppres number 7/1998.

58. See, for example, "China Firm Joins Indon Partners to Build US510m Java Power Plant," *Business Times—On-line Edition*, June 3, 2003, available at http://web.archive.org/web/20030623142010/http://business-times.asia1.com.sg/story/0,4567,83289,00.html (accessed April 2006).

59. The conflicts over the Dabhol project in India, the Bangkok toll road in Thailand, and Azurix's water project in Argentina all began with local or subunits of government.

Chapter 17

1. Thomas Jefferson to James Madison, June 20, 1787, *Papers* 11, pp. 480–481, quoted in *The Founders' Constitution*, vol. 1, chapter 8, document 11 (Chicago: University of Chicago Press, 1987), available at http://press-pubs.uchicago.edu/founders/documents/v1ch8s11.html.

2. Broadcast on *60 Minutes*, CBS television, April 14, 2002; viewer generated, unofficial transcripts available at http://puggy.symonds.net/pipermail/india-ej/2002-April/000152.html (accessed April 2006).

3. See footnote 2 in the Introduction for various counts.

4. Perhaps more than half were investor-initiated. See J. Luis Guasch, *Granting and Renegotiating Infrastructure Concessions: Doing It Right* (Washington, D.C.: The World Bank, 2004), pp. 12–13.

5. For example, see John Nellis, *Privatization in Latin America*, Working Paper 31, (Washington, D.C.: Center for Global Development, August 2003), p. 10.

6. The World Bank counts the full value of partial risk guarantees against a country's borrowing. According to Hansen, this has limited the attraction of the approach, since off-balance sheet financing moves onto the balance sheet. Kenneth W. Hansen, "PRI and the Rise (and Fall?) of Private Investment in Infrastructure," in Michael B. Likosky (ed.), *Privatising Development* (Leiden, the Netherlands: Martinus Nijhoff, 2005), p. 124. But broader infrastructure commitments are not regularly counted as national liabilities.

7. Andrei Shleifer and Robert Vishny, *The Grabbing Hand: Government Pathologies and Their Cures* (Cambridge, Mass.: Harvard University Press, 1998). Ironically, Andrei Shleifer was later found guilty of defrauding the U.S. government as a Harvard advisor to Russia on privatization. The events hastened the closure of the Harvard Institute for International Development, the source of the Harvard Group in Indonesia. See David Warsh, "Judge Finds Against Shleifer, Hay, and Harvard," July 4, 2004, and his "A Narrow Technical Issue," December 12, 2004. On line. Available: http://www.economicprincipals.com.

8. Joseph E. Stiglitz, "Whither Reform? Ten Years in Transition," keynote address, Annual Bank Conference on Development Economics, World Bank, April 28–30, 1999.

9. Figures cited in World Bank conference on Private Sector Development, session on "Private Sector Interest in Infrastructure Investment: Is the Downturn Transitory or Enduring?" organized by Timothy C. Irwin, April 22, 2003.

10. Stiglitz was not alone. The World Bank's country office, under Dennis de Tray, had from the outset criticized the local power arrangements—including First Family participation. Ironically, the country office was later criticized by World Bank headquarters, after the crisis struck, for having tolerated Indonesian corruption.

11. Michael M. Phillips, "The World Bank as Privatization Agnostic," *Wall Street Journal*, July 21, 2003, p. 2.

12. Change can move slowly. In March 2005, the World Bank posted the following question on one of its discussion boards: "What can be done to convert infrastructure concessions into attractive business propositions?" Surely, the goal ought to be finding ways of building infrastructure that serves development purposes, not to make attractive business propositions. See: http://rru.worldbank.org/Discussions/Discussion.aspx?id=60 (accessed March 2005).

13. In fact, in spite of its enthusiasm for a merchant market for power, the ADB had provided some funds in the 1990s to PLN to build power projects.

14. It tried, for example, to make privatization of telecommunications a condition for the Central American Free Trade Area. See Richard Lapper, "Embattled Costa Rica May Derail US Free Trade Plans," *Financial Times*, October 13, 2003, p. 12.

15. Michael M. Phillips, "The World Bank as Privatization Agnostic."

16. Paul Krugman, "Another Friday Outrage," *New York Times*, September 2, 2003, p. A23. Similar criteria appear in Christian von Hirschhausen, *Modernizing Infrastructure in Transformation Economies* (Cheltenham, England: Edward Elgar, 2002), pp. 25, 26, 176, 177; and in Nellis, *Privatization in Latin America*, p. 20.

17. Singapore Airlines, under state ownership, was regularly rated among the world's best airlines.

18. Juan Forero, "Latin America Fails to Deliver on Basic Needs," *New York Times*, February 22, 2005, p. C2.

19. In 2005, Venezuelan president Chavez drove the point home: Any oil company that challenged new policies through arbitration would be excluded from bidding on future projects.

20. Michael Casey, "Argentina Opens a New Front in Financial Fight," *Wall Street Journal*, March 7, 2005, p. A16. For challenges from Pakistan, Russia, and the Seychelles, see William A. Isaacson, "Enforcement Difficulties are Increasing," *National Law Journal* [online], October 7, 2002. For legal barriers to enforcement of awards against Argentina, see Carlos E. Alfaro, "Argentina: ICSID Arbitration and BITs Challenged by Argentina Government," *Mondaq.com*, December 21, 2004, accessed at http://www.alfarolaw.com/ima/tapa/alfaro3.htm (April 2006). Other articles on the topic also can be found at Mondaq.com.

21. "El Respecto por el Abogado," *La Nación*, July 15, 2005, p. 20.

22. For papers and arguments on both sides of the issue for Pakistan, see *Transnational Dispute Management* [online], October 2004, 1(4), table of contents available at http://www.transnational-dispute-management.com/samples/toc.asp?key=5 (accessed April 2006).

23. Guillermo Aguilar Alvarez and William W. Park, "The New Face of Investment Arbitration: NAFTA Chapter 11," *Mealey's International Arbitration Report*, January 2004, pp. 39, 41.

24. "Kerry Plan on Trade Irks Firms," *International Herald Tribune*, July 20, 2004, p. 17. See also International Institute for Sustainable Development, *Private Rights,*

Public Problems: A Guide to NAFTA's Controversial Chapter on Investor Rights, (Winnepeg, Manitoba: IISD/World Wildlife Fund, 2001), available at http://www.iisd.org/pdf/trade_citizensguide.pdf (accessed August 2004); and Adam Liptak, "NAFTA Tribunals Still U.S. Worries," *New York Times*, April 18, 2004, p. 19.

25. Michael D. Goldhaber, "A 'Completely Appalling' Decision," *American Lawyer/Focus Europe*, Summer 2004, available at http://www.americanlawyer.com/focuseurope/appalling04.html (accessed April 2006). The article responds to the arbitration decision in the Loewen case brought under NAFTA against the United States to challenge the decision of a Mississippi court. See also Adam Liptak, "Nafta Tribunals Stir U.S. Worries," *New York Times*, April 18, 2004, p. 20.

26. Research on the impact of BITs on investment flows is conflicting. For negative views, see Jennifer Tobin and Susan Rose-Ackerman, "Foreign Direct Investment and the Business Environment in Developing Countries: the Impact of Bilateral Investment Treaties," draft paper, June 4, 2004; UNCTAD, *Bilateral Investment Treaties in the Mid-1990s* (New York/Geneva: United Nations, 1998), Sales No. E.02.II.D.4; and M. Hallward-Driemeier, *Do Bilateral Investment Treaties Attract FDI? Only a Bit . . . and They Could Bite*, World Bank Working Paper No. 3121 (Washington, D.C.: World Bank, August, 2003). For a somewhat more optimistic view, see Eric Neumayer and Laura Spess, "Do Bilateral Investment Treaties Increase Foreign Direct Investment to Developing Countries?" unpublished paper, November 2004. For a study purporting to show larger effects, but which we found unconvincing, see Jeswald W. Salacuse and Nicholas P. Sullivan, "Do BITs Really Work? An Evaluation of Bilateral Investment Treaties and Their Grand Bargain," *Harvard International Law Journal*, Winter 2005, 46(1), pp. 67–137. We have seen no empirical research on the effect of official political risk insurance.

27. Proposed multilateral agreements drafted by business and home governments have typically taken a similarly rigid view. See, for example, Article II of Draft Convention on Investments Abroad, in "The Proposed Convention to Protect Private Foreign Investment," *Journal of Public Law*, 1960, 9, pp. 115–124. The original draft was said to have been generated by German businessmen.

28. The panel for the CalEnergy case mentioned the external problems, but nevertheless made an award that we find extraordinarily large.

29. Richard A. Posner, *Economic Analysis of Law*, 3rd ed. (Boston: Little, Brown, 1986), p. 106.

30. We do not offer a comprehensive treatment of all exceptions to enforcement of various aspects of property rights, including contracts.

31. Civil law and common law jurisdictions have, not surprisingly, handled changed circumstances somewhat differently. The former have tended toward explicit legislation, while the latter have relied more on what one author calls "judicial fictions" to arrive at similar results. See, for example, Leon E. Trakman, "Winner Take Some: Loss Sharing and Commercial Impracticability," *Minnesota Law Review*, February 1985, 69, pp. 473–482.

32. According to Posner, awards that penalize the party that breaches a contract for efficiency reasons provide undesirable compulsion to adhere to uneconomic contracts. See Posner, *Economic Analysis of Law*, p. 108.

33. For a treatment of how losses may be allocated, see Trakman, "Winner Take Some," pp. 484–519.

34. Trakman, "Winner Take Some," p. 485.

35. U.N. Doc. A/Conf. 97/18 Annex 1, 1980.

36. CISG, article 79.

37. UNIDROIT (International Institute for the Unification of Private Law) Principles, article 6.2.

38. Dionysios P. Flambouras, "The Doctrines of Impossibility of Performance and *Clausula Rebus Sic Stantibus* in the 1980 Convention on Contracts for the Sale of

Goods and the Principles of European Contract Law: A Comparative Analysis," *Pace International Law Review*, Fall 2001, 13, pp. 261–293.

39. See Article 62 of the "Vienna Convention on the Law of Treaties," entered into force on January 27, 1980, United Nation Treaty Series, vol. 1155, p. 331.

40. Some reviewers claim that Shakespeare was not an accomplished lawyer. The classic attack seems to be William C. Devecmon, *In Re: Shakespeare's Legal Acquirements: Notes by an Unbeliever Therein* (New York: The Shakespeare Press, 1899). Later critics excuse Shakespeare because the time of the fictional trial is not clear in the play.

41. See James Gordley, "Equality in Exchange," *California Law Review*, 1981, 69, pp. 1587, 1620, 1621.

42. Constance E. Bagley and Diane Savage, *Managers and the Legal Environment: Strategies for the 21st Century*, 5th ed. (Mason, Ohio: South-Western College/West Legal Studies in Business, 2005), pp. 221–224. So-called "contracts of adhesion"— boilerplate contracts offered on a take-it-or-leave-it basis to a party—may be invalidated by courts, under the unconscionable criterion.

43. Rough rules have developed for ending contracts of firms in bankruptcy. Not only may debt be restructured or discharged, a lease may be broken, with the landlord receiving past-due rent plus the greater of one year's rent or 15% of three years' rent. See Michael Brick, "Andersen Seeks Graceful Exit to Leases," *New York Times*, March 12, 2003, p. C6.

44. If U.S. electric power agreements are not considered to be "reasonable" and "just," the Federal Energy Regulatory Commission has the authority to reorder contracts between parties under Section 206 of the Federal Power Act.

45. What is legitimate public purpose has long been a subject of debate, one that was rekindled in 2005 with a U.S. Supreme Court decision confirming that property can be taken for private development if the private development serves a public purpose. New legislation to protect the environment or the architectural integrity of a community can reduce the value of an owner's property. Although compensation is much debated, it is seldom provided in the latter cases. Foreign policy goals may also override contractual commitments. The U.S. government found public policy reasons in 1990 to suspend delivery of F-16 jets to Pakistan. It even refused to refund deposits of $140 million. See, for example, "F-16 Fighting Falcon," on GlobalSecurity.org, available at http://www.globalsecurity.org/military/world/pakistan/f-16.htm (accessed July 2004) and Rauf Klasra, "US Rejects Request for Revising F-16 Payment Accord," *Dawn: The Internet Edition*, February 2, 2001, http://web.archive.org/web/20041117060334/http://www.dawn.com/2001/02/02/top3.htm (Accessed April 2006).

46. In the U.S., the power of states to change contracts, to regulate contracts between other parties, and to bind future legislatures is the subject of a vast amount of law. One of the interesting early cases was *Stone v Mississippi,* 101 U.S. 814 (1879). The state had chartered a company to run a lottery for 25 years, but prohibited lotteries the next year. The Supreme Court upheld the state's action. Subsequent decisions have upheld (and circumscribed) related actions.

47. See, for example, *Penn Central Transportation Co. v New York City,* 438 U.S. 104 (1978), in which the U.S. Supreme Court upheld New York City's restrictions, without compensation, on the owners' construction of an office building over Grand Central Station after the Landmarks Preservation Commission designated the station as a landmark.

48. In a carefully argued case, a tribunal upheld the right of California to prohibit the use of a gasoline additive, when doing so diminished the value of a Canadian investment. See the 307(!) page "Final Award of the Tribunal on Jurisdiction and Merits, between Methanex Corporation and the United States," April 3, 2005, a NAFTA case under ICSID, available at http://www.state.gov/documents/organization/51052.pdf (accessed August 2005).

49. *New York Times,* September 27, 2004, p. A30. Note that some regional trade agreements and BITs allow specific exceptions to the general rules. The United States, for example, has excluded affirmative action from coverage.

50. In addition to the Methanex case, see Guillermo Aguilar Alvarez and William A. Park, "The New Face of Investment Arbitration: NAFTA Chapter 11," *Yale Journal of International Law,* 2003, 28, pp. 365–407.

51. For fears that BITs, with their broad definitions of takings, will interfere with sovereign rights to regulate damage to the environment, labor rights, and other matters, see "Report of the Subcommittee on Investment Regarding the Draft Model Bilateral Investment Treaty," January 30, 1994, and a letter to Wesley Scholz, U.S. Department of State, and James Mendenhall, Office of the USTR, from the AFL-CIO, Center for International Environmental Law, Earthjustice, Friends of the Earth–U.S., National Wildlife Federation, Oxfam America, and Sierra Club, dated January 16, 2004.

52. Contracts may, for example, not be enforced against minors and mentally retarded parties.

53. For an argument that the burden of proof should fall on the company if there is a suggestion of corruption, see Karen Mills, "Corruption and Other Illegality in the Formation and Performance of Contracts and in the Conduct of Arbitration Relating Thereto," *International Arbitration Law Review,* 2002, 5(4), p. 130. For a rather thorough treatment of arbitration when corruption was likely, see Richard H. Kreindler, "Aspects of Illegality in the Formation and Performance of Contracts," Albert Jan van den Berg (ed.), *International Commercial Arbitration: Important Contemporary Questions* (The Hague: International Council for Commercial Arbitration, 2002).

54. "Final Award: *CME Czech Republic B.V. v. Czech Republic,*" March 14, 2003, available at http://www.cetv-net.com/iFiles/1439-Final_Award_Quantum.pdf (accessed August 2004); and Ian Brownlie, "Separate Opinion on the Issues at the Quantum Phase of: *CME v. Czech Republic,*" March 14, 2003, available at http://www.cetv-net.com/iFiles/1439-seperate-op-pdf-1403.pdf. The dispute raised other controversies as well.

55. Michael D. Goldhaber, "Wanted: A World Investment Court," *Transnational Dispute Management* [online], 2004, 1(3), available at http://www.americanlawyer.com/focuseurope/investmentcourt04.html (accessed April 2006). He expresses worry about consistency in the outcome of the large number of similar arbitrations pending against Argentina. See also Thomas Wälde, "Introductory Comment to the *CME/Lauder v. Czech Republic Litigation,*" *International Legal Materials,* 2003, 42, pp. 915–918.

56. Brigitte Stern, *Revue de l'Arbitrage,* 1980, pp. 132–191. The reference comes from Michael Goldhaber, "Wanted: A World Investment Court."

57. Some arbitrators, for example, seem not to have understood that future cash flow should already account for "return of investment." Adding the two for, say, a 30-year power project is duplicative.

58. Posner, *Economic Analysis of Law,* p. 108.

59. Cases of host governments bringing investors before arbitration panels are extremely rare. One frequently cited case is that of state-owned *Tanesco v Independent Power Tanzania* (ICSID case ARB/98/8), brought under contractual provisions, not a BIT. Gabon seems to have brought a case against Société Serete S.A. (ICSID Case ARB/76/1), but as it was settled before judgment, little information is publicly available. Counterclaims, of course, are more common.

60. The figures for Latin America are reported in Guasch, *Granting and Renegotiating Infrastructure Concessions,* p. 16.

61. The contract for Aguas Argentinas, for example, was renegotiated twice at the investor's insistence before the investor appealed to arbitration when the government wanted to change the terms after an economic crisis had struck.

62. For a well-written argument that the terms of NAFTA's Chapter 11 favor foreign investors over domestic firms, see "NAFTA's Threat to Sovereignty and Democracy: The Record of NAFTA Chapter 11 Investor-State Cases 1994–2005," *Public Citizen*, February 2005, especially page 12.

63. Bipartisan Trade Promotion Authority, Division B, Title XXI, Section 2101 (b) (3).

64. The World Bank has considered political risk insurance for domestic investors, but nothing has come of the deliberations.

65. Some would argue that encouraging investors into what they perceive to be risky countries is the purpose of government-sponsored insurance. This may be, but it is not clear that development is served by encouraging investors to negotiate contracts that are likely to explode.

66. For a discussion of methods of "judicial adjustment," including allocation of losses in contract disputes, see Trakman, "Winner Take Some," pp. 500–518.

67. For a discussion of advantages and methods of judiciary-encouraged inter-party settlements, see Trakman, "Winner Take Some," pp. 492–500. In some jurisidictions, civil servants may face restrictions on reaching settlements before final judgments are rendered.

68. This seems to have happened in *Antoine Goetz v Burundi* (ICSID Case No. ARB/95/3), in which Burundi was told to provide compensation within four months, without a specified amount, or to issue a new free-zone certificate to the plaintiff. The parties negotiated a settlement. On the other hand, in cases where the investor is using arbitration as a way of withdrawing from the business, as appeared to be the motivation in the CalEnergy and Karaha Bodas cases, the approach is less likely to succeed. But it may help in identifying such cases and lead to adjustments of awards accordingly.

69. See Trakman, "Winner Take Some," pp. 493, 515.

70. Trakman, "Winner Take Some," p. 487, notes that modifying the terms of a contract "is far more justifiable...when interdependent parties have bound themselves for a long period of time to perform in a market that is relatively closed to alternatives." Thus, imposing new contract terms is more likely to be appropriate for investments than short-term sales contracts.

71. For an exception where an arbitrator argues a similar point about fees and incentives see Mills, "Corruption and Other Illegality," pp. 130, 131.

72. See Daniel Yergin, *The Prize: The Epic Quest for Oil, Money and Power* (New York: The Free Press, 1993).

73. For a more extensive treatment of U.S. post-War attitudes toward its foreign investors, see Louis T. Wells, "Protecting Foreign Investors in the Developing World: A Shift in U.S. Policy in the 1990s?" in Robert Grosse (ed.), *International Business-Government Relations in the 21st Century: In Honor of Jack Behrman* (Cambridge, Mass.: Cambridge University Press, 2005).

74. State Department resistance to punitive action was not always overt. One of the authors of this book, for example, played the role of go-between when Indonesia was charged, in the early 1980s, with having expropriated a U.S. company (Sea Oil General Corporation) under Sukarno and not paying compensation. Although Senator Inouye (D-Hawaii) was leading a movement to apply the Hickenlooper Amendment, officials in the U.S. embassy were quietly working with Indonesians in opposition to the threat.

75. Interview, Jakarta, 2003.

76. For claims of German government intervention in the case of Paiton II, see von Torsten Engelhardt, "Freunde auf Immer und Ewig," *Financial Times Deutschland*, November 11, 2000, available at http://www.ftd.de/pw/in/1061495.html?nv=rs (accessed April 2006).

77. Richard Clarke credits U.S. Ambassador Gelbard with pushing the Indonesians to fight against terrorism. If terrorism was high on his agenda, one

wonders why he took such strong stances on behalf of U.S. investors in battles likely to weaken his hand on terrorism. See Richard A. Clarke, *Against All Enemies: Inside America's War on Terror* (New York: Free Press, 2004), p. 233. Some interviewees told us that Gelbard lost influence in Indonesia early on because of his stances.

78. Peter Waldman, "Washington's Tilt to Business Stirs a Backlash in Indonesia," *Wall Street Journal*, February 11, 2004, p. 1.

79. That others believe this as well is evidenced by Dole's argument when he lobbied for Pertamina in the Karaha Bodas case. Kevin Bogardus, "Bob Dole: Indonesia's Man in Washington," Center for Public Integrity, September 22, 2004, available at http://www.public-i.org/oil/report.aspx?aid=381 (accessed February 2005). The article documents some of the contacts made by Dole and his associates.

80. As legalistic as U.S. arbitration is, the limits on judicial review of arbitration contained in the U.S. Federal Arbitration Act sharply limit courts' ability to vacate awards even if they are based on errors of fact or law.

81. For an article that describes an (unpublished) ICC arbitration where guidelines for presumptions of corruption in commissions appeared, see José Rosell and Harvey Prager, "Illicit Commissions and International Arbitration: The Question of Proof," *Arbitration International*, 1999, 15(4), pp. 329–348. The authors argue against strong standards of proof. For more cases and argument, see Matthias Scherer, "Circumstantial Evidence in Corruption Cases before International Arbitral Tribunals," *International Arbitration Law Review*, 2002, 5(2), pp. 29–40. See also Kreindler, "Aspects of Illegality."

82. For a list of some countries that explicitly provide for this kind of arbitration, see Li Hu, "Arbitration *ex aequo et bono* in China," *Explore and Research-Forum in Arbitration*, 2001, available at http://www.arbitration.org.cn/en/viewcontent.asp?id=29 (accessed August 2004). For French rules governing insurance disputes, where *amiable composition* is the default method, see the Web site of Centre Français d'Arbitrage de Réassurance et d'Assurance at http://www.cefarea.com. For the introduction of this form of arbitration into English law, see Nicholas Gould, "Arbitration and Litigation: Benefits in the Context of ADR," paper prepared for International Business Conferences Summer School, August 2003, available at http://www.fenwickelliott.co.uk/articles/ADR/arb_and_lit_benefits. htm (accessed August 2004).

83. Fali Nariman, quoted in Anneli Knight, "West Slowly Meeting East on International Arbitration," *Lawyers Weekly*, October 26, 2004, available at http://www.lawyersweekly.com.au/articles/31/0c01a231.asp (accessed September 2004).

84. For trade, the disputants are always states; for investments, they are a state and an investor.

85. On January 25, Mexico filed a GATT case against a U.S. embargo on shrimp caught in ways that killed dolphins. For an analysis of the ruling against the United States, see *Tuna Dolphin GATT Case (TUNA Case)*, available at http://www.american.edu/projects/mandala/TED/TUNA.HTM (accessed July 2005).

86. See "USTR on WTO Decision Supporting U.S. on Shrimp-Turtle Law," October 22, 2001, available at http://usinfo.state.gov/topical/econ/wto/01102201.htm (accessed July 2005).

87. Article XX allowed nondiscriminatory departures from core GATT principles to protect public morals and human, plant, and animal life, to conserve exhaustible resources, and to ban goods made with prison labor. For a brief history of "moral exception" provisions, see Regina Abrami, "On the High Road: Trade, International Standards, and National Competitiveness," *AccountAbility Forum*, Spring 2005, pp. 39–47.

88. In a case brought by Antigua against the United States and decided in 2005, the WTO for the first time used a clause allowing restrictions to "protect public

morals or to maintain public order" to allow the United States to restrict online gambling, if it did so evenhandedly.

89. A broadly acceptable agreement would most likely also impose constraints on investors themselves and their home countries.

90. The original OECD effort was marked by the OECD Draft Convention on the Protection of Foreign Property. For history, see Charles Lipson, *Standing Guard: Protecting Foreign Capital in the Nineteenth and Twentieth Centuries* (Berkeley: University of California Press, 1985), chapters 3, 4; Edward M. Graham, *Global Corporations and National Governments* (Washington, D.C.: Institute for International Economics, 1996), and Stephen Young and Ana Teresa Tavares, "Multilateral Rules on FDI: Do We Need Them? Will We Get Them? A Developing Country Perspective," *Transnational Corporations*, April 2004, 13(1), pp. 1–30.

91. NAFTA Chapter 11 cases are quite transparent. For presentations to the panel from environmental groups and transcripts of hearings in the Methanex case, see U.S. Department of State, "Methanex Corp. *v.* United States of America," available at http://www.state.gov/s/l/c5818.htm (accessed August 2005). Public access and release of hearings is not typical of investment arbitration.

92. For a number of papers, articles, and slides on the subject, see documents from "Appeals and Challenges to Investment Treaty Agreements: Is It Time for an International Appellate System?", 2nd Conference of the British Institute of International and Comparative Law's Investment Treaty Forum, available at http://www.biicl.org/index.asp?contentid=999 (accessed August 2005).

93. Nigel Blackby, of Freshfields, Bruckhaus, Deringer, quoted in Goldhaber, "Wanted: A World Investment Court."

94. For a similar argument supporting a "permanent tribunal for North American dispute resolution" under NAFTA, see John P. Manley, et al, *Building a North American Community* (New York: Council on Foreign Relations, 2005), Independent Task Force Report No. 53, p. 22.

95. An appeals process also offers some control over the possibility that arbitrators themselves become corrupt, either through direct payments or, more subtly, through eagerness to attract more appointments from a class of client.

96. UNCITRAL provides an alternative, but one for which broad approval might be more difficult to obtain.

97. The United States is now including consideration of appellate processes in its bilateral and regional trade agreements. The Singapore–U.S. agreement illustrates. A permanent mechanism similar to that of the WTO has been proposed for NAFTA, for reasons similar to ours; see Manley et al., *Building a North American Community*. Separate processes for bilateral and regional trade arrangements raise the possibility of a number of appellate processes with access limited to investors from or in the United States. Better would be a dominant process to generate widely accepted common law.

98. There have been proposals for reforming ICSID. See ICSID, "Possible Improvement of the Framework for ICSID Arbitration," ICSID Secretariat Discussion Paper, October 22, 2004. For a skeptical view of the proposal, see South Centre, "Developments on Discussions for the Improvement of the Framework for ICSID Arbitration and the Participation of Developing Countries," South Centre Analytical Note, February 2005. Proposals surviving in 2005 concentrated on technical issues: arbitrators' fees, access of third parties, and publication of awards. See ICSID, "Suggested Changes to the ICSID Rules and Regulations," Working Paper of the ICSID Secretariat, May 12, 2005.

99. *New York Times*, September 27, 2004, p. A30. Note that some regional trade agreements and BITs allow specific exceptions to the general rules. The United States, for example, has excluded affirmative action. The Methanex case is again instructive, as the panel heard from a variety of interest groups.

100. For a paper arguing that the current system fails to take into account the public interest of the developing countries, see "Proposed Amendments of ICSID Rules: Process Related, and Substantive Issues on ICSID Reform for Developing Countries," South Centre, Geneva, August 2005.

101. Michael D. Goldhaber, "Arbitral Terrorism," *American Lawyer/Focus Europe*, Summer 2003, available at http://www.americanlawyer.com/focus europe/aterror.html (accessed April 2006), and *Transnational Dispute Management* [online], July 2004, 1(3).

102. Seymour Martin Lipset and Gary Marks, *It Didn't Happen Here: Why Socialism Failed in the United States* (New York: W. W. Norton, 2000).

Index

Page numbers followed by "t" denote tables; those followed by "b" denote boxes; and those followed by "n" denote endnotes

365